JOANNA, GEORGE AND HENRY

A Pre-Raphaelite Tale of Art, Love and Friendship

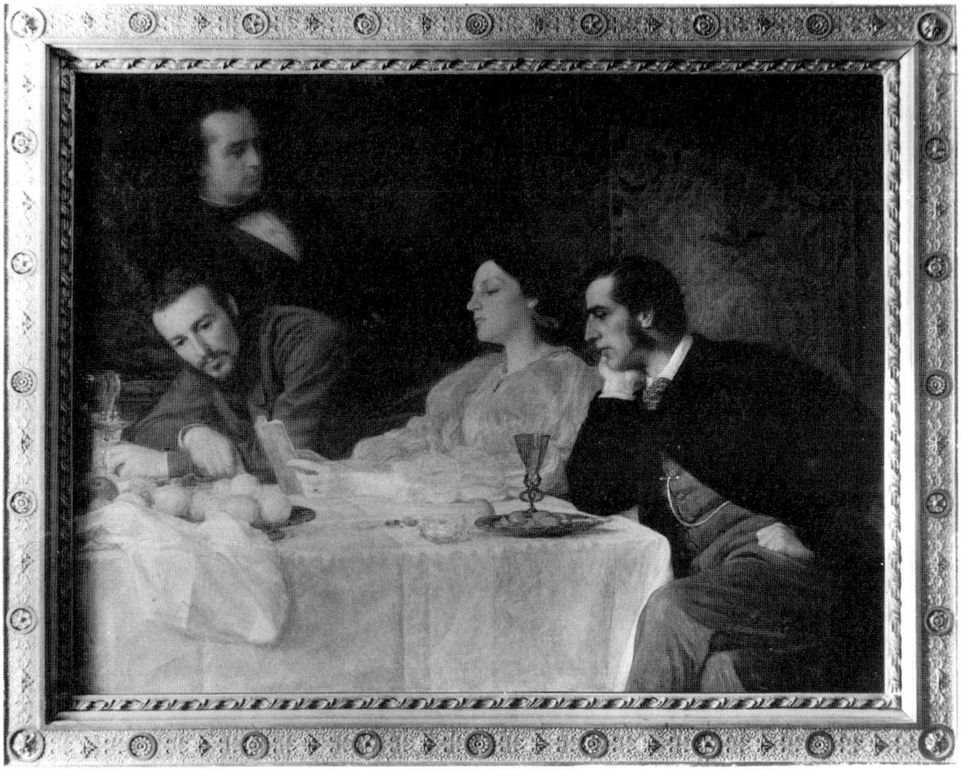

Conversation Piece *Henry Wells*

This painting shows George, Joanna and Henry sitting at a table, with their friend, John Clayton in attendance. Henry began the picture in 1860 but did not finish it until after his wife's death. It was exhibited at the Royal Academy in 1862, and praised 'most tenderly' in The Times, but was destroyed by an incendiary bomb in 1942. This photograph, by Philip Street, has survived.

JOANNA, GEORGE AND HENRY

A Pre-Raphaelite Tale of Art, Love and Friendship

Sue Bradbury

THE BOYDELL PRESS

First published 2012
The Boydell Press, Woodbridge

ISBN 978-1-84383-617-9

The Boydell Press is an imprint of Boydell & Brewer Ltd
PO Box 9, Woodbridge, Suffolk IP12 3DF, UK
and of Boydell & Brewer Inc.
668 Mt Hope Avenue, Rochester, NY 14620, USA
website: www.boydellandbrewer.com

This publication is printed on acid-free paper

Printed in Great Britain by

CPI Group (UK) Ltd, Croydon, CR0 4YY

Contents

Dedication

To Anne Christopherson, great-granddaughter of Joanna Boyce and Henry Wells, whose support for this project has made it possible, and who has kept their memory alive by the presentation of their sketchbooks to the British Museum and of two of Joanna's paintings to Tate Britain

Acknowledgements

Joanna, George and Henry opened up a new world for me and I owe a great deal to those who have been my guides and mentors in its creation. Many of the books I consulted are listed in the Select Bibliography, but my special thanks must go to those who undertook specific research on my behalf, allowed me access to their own research, and were tirelessly generous with their knowledge and expertise. They include Pamela Gerrish Nunn, a pioneer in the study of women artists of the period, who read this book at an early stage and spared time on a visit to England from New Zealand to help and advise me; Laurel O. Petersen, who helped to catalogue Joanna Boyce's sketchbooks for the British Museum and provided detailed research on the work of Thomas Couture and his Paris atelier; Katie Tyreman, who made her excellent PhD thesis, 'Victorian Women Artists', which specialises in Joanna's work, available for me to consult, and my friend Angela Thirlwell, author of *William and Lucy*, a biography of William Michael Rossetti and his wife, and *Into the Frame: the Four Loves of Ford Madox Brown*, who gave me endless encouragement and a good deal of solid background material. The text is based on a transcript checked in part by Christopher Newall whose notes provided an invaluable first stage, and the project has benefitted throughout from continual support of Joanna and Henry's descendants. Finally, my sincere thanks go to Fionnuala Jervis, whose knowledge of the Pre-Raphaelite world is encyclopaedic and whose skilled editing has saved me on many occasions from myself. Any mistakes or misinterpretations that remain are mine alone.

SUE BRADBURY

MARCH 2012

The initial preparation of the text, financial support for the project, information of all kinds about the pictures and letters, and photographic work, often in difficult circumstances has been supported by many of Joanna and Henry's descendants, and a wide range of other helpers. Special thanks go to John Roberts, for his recreation of the image central to the whole story, the double portrait on ivory which appears as plate I. Another picture has presented particular problems, 'Letters and News at the Lochside': we are grateful to Elizabeth Macdonald for her detailed analysis of the people portrayed, to Sarah Winnington-Ingram at Arisaig House, Ann Martin, editor of West Word, and Mairi Mooney, curator at the West Highland Museum. Philippa Martin provided information about the pictures by Henry Tanworth Wells in the Government Art Collection.

The predecessor to this book is Julia Ford's thesis 'Mr. and Mrs. H. T. Wells: A Critical Biography', which made an excellent starting point. For documents, photographs, and access to pictures, as well as financial support we are grateful to Charles Barber; Euan Bell-Scott; Mark Charrington; Emma Cooke; Sam Frost; Cassandra Goad; Hallam Goad; Justin Goad; Katharine Harris; Susan Hughes; Miles Hunt-Davis; James Hutchings; Lewis Hutchings; Mark Jackson; Penelope Jackson; Philip Jackson; Tim Jackson; ; Rosemary Kitchin; Peter McIlwraith; Nigel Ostrowski; Andrew Sells; Oliver Sells; the late John Street; Jonathan Street; Simon Street; Tim Street; and Joanna Wood.

If over the course of the twelve years since this project began, we have forgotten any of the names of those who have helped, we can only offer our sincere apologies. To those listed above, we are most grateful.

TIM GOAD RICHARD BARBER

March 2012

List of Plates and Illustrations

Colour plates

Between pages 80 and 81

Black and White Illustrations

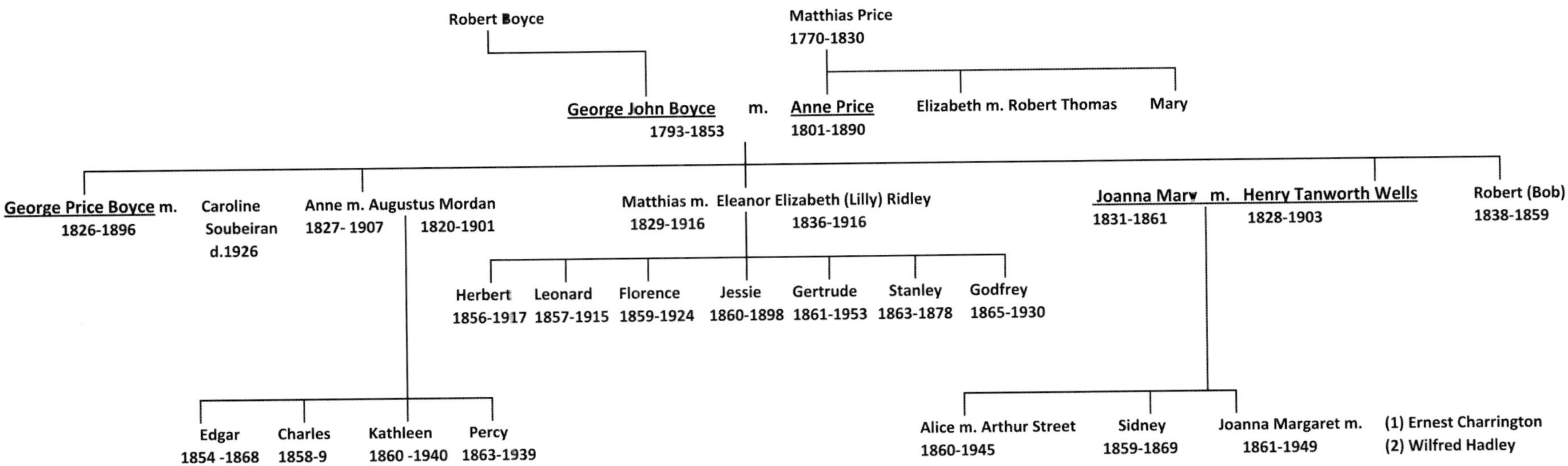

Boyce Family Tree

INTRODUCTION

This story begins during the Second World War. In 1942 Hitler ordered his infamous Baedeker raids on England, which were aimed, not at strategic industrial targets, but at cities famous for their beauty and architecture. Bath was among them and suffered terrible damage. The artist John Piper was sent to record the aftermath of the bombings, and one of his most dramatic images shows the jagged scar in an elegant Georgian terrace where a house had been comprehensively destroyed by an incendiary bomb. (*Plate II*)

The house belonged to Alice Street. She was then eighty-two years old, and widowed. The bomb had actually fallen next door, but a strong wind caught the flames and whipped them across to the untenanted attic of Alice's home. Roused by their neighbours, Alice, her daughter Marakita, their maids and their 'billettees' escaped unharmed; and afterwards Marakita, having wrapped her mother up against the cold, went back to salvage what she could. But, as Alice later wrote, there was no one to lend a hand: 'Our people had either fled or fainted, and the neighbours were naturally preoccupied in clearing their own belongings from their threatened homes.' Reaching the drawing room, Marakita snatched a Gilbert Stuart portrait that was standing loose on an easel, while from the dining room she managed to cut away four small paintings by her grandmother and a drawing by Dante Gabriel Rossetti before the heat drove her out of the house.

These were the sole survivors of an artistic legacy that had included a rare collection of Italian primitives, a Renaissance cassone (marriage chest) from Florence, some 'very delightful early works' by Edward Burne-Jones, an early Millais, a Ford Madox Brown and an important water-colour by Turner – all inherited by Alice's husband, Arthur, from his father, the architect George E. Street. (Marakita was named after George Street's first wife, Marique.) Alice's own contribution to the collection consisted of the paintings, drawings and miniatures that had come to her on her father's death in 1903.

Almost all these were by her parents. Her father, Henry Tanworth Wells, was an accomplished miniaturist and portrait painter; her mother, Joanna Boyce, an artist who, from a young age, had commanded the respect and admiration of John Everett Millais, Dante Gabriel Rossetti and John Ruskin. Immediately after Joanna's tragically early death in childbirth, Henry spent many hours trying (and in his view, failing) to build the kind of monument to her that would cement her reputation not just as an artist but also as an exemplary human being – an endeavour that became, effectively, his life's work. According to Alice, his most fervent ambition was to write a memoir of Joanna, and about fifteen years before he died, he took all the letters that had passed between them to their Surrey cottage in the hopes that they would revive his fading memories. There he spent long hours locked in his room, reliving their years of strong emotions, triumphs and tragedies until 'it nearly broke his heart'. Though he initially intended to destroy all their letters – and did indeed destroy many of his own – he could not bring himself to burn 'his loved one's words', nor could he accomplish what he had set out to do.

So Alice, the elder of his two daughters, inherited the task of carrying out her father's wishes. He entrusted the letters to her, with the instruction to put on record a brief life history of his beloved and talented wife; but it was 1930 before Alice found herself in a position to begin the task. The delay proved fortunate in one way, for in addition to her mother's diaries of her young womanhood and her father's of his early tours in Italy, the diaries of Joanna's brother George, kept from the age of sixteen almost until he died, found their way (how, we do not know) into her keeping. George was also a painter, and, reading his diaries, Alice became convinced that his involvement in his sister's life and work was, in its own way, as important as Henry's. She determined that, though Joanna would be the main focus of her memoir, it would tell the story of not one, but three, youthful talents emerging at a time of artistic revolution in England.

What Henry had failed to do in his old age the incendiary bomb very nearly accomplished. Most of the original family history was destroyed. The unedited letters and the original diaries perished, along with much of the contemporary evidence of Joanna's stature, in particular, as an artist. Though extracts from George's diaries, an invaluable resource, had been published by the Old Water-Colour Society in 1941,[1] it must have seemed to Alice that, as far as Joanna was concerned, most of the building blocks required to construct the memoir had gone – including the manuscripts, typed transcripts, and the original brief account that she had written when she first squared up to her father's legacy more than twenty-five years after his death. Days passed in the aftermath of the bombings before Alice remembered that her sister, as well as inheriting half their parents' artistic heritage, also possessed a copy of the transcribed letters, diary entries and early records. At the age of eighty-three, the indefatigable elder daughter again took up the task of raising a family memorial.

1 *The Diaries of George Price Boyce*, originally published by the Old Water-Colour Society, 1941; reprinted with an introduction and notes by Virginia Surtees (Newmarket 1980).

She died in 1945, after which, her great-great-nephew, Richard Barber, tells us:

> The transcripts were forgotten, or at least remained unknown to most of the family, until a study day was organised at his home at South Park, Blechingley, by my cousin Tim Goad. It was an intriguing occasion: pictures familiar from childhood as part of the background of my grandparents' house and those of their contemporaries suddenly took on a context and meaning, but the real discovery was the reappearance of the transcripts, produced hesitantly from a Tesco carrier bag with an enquiry as to whether we 'knew' about this. We expected to find correspondence that would throw light on the artistic achievements of all three – Henry, Joanna and George – but what we did not know was the extraordinary human drama that they also contained.

The transcripts are still in the possession of the family, and it is on them that this 'Pre-Raphaelite Tale of Art, Love and Friendship' is based.

❁

The Boyces were a powerful and close-knit family – an arresting mixture of artistic aspiration, creative imagination, religious devotion and upward mobility. The father, George John Boyce, whom Joanna portrays as a kindly, unselfish and affectionate man, was also a businessman with flair. He began his working life as a wine merchant (he still had a considerable cellar when he died), and though he is described in his will as a 'silversmith', it appears to have been as a pawnbroker that he prospered financially. Pawnbrokers – often referred to as 'Uncle' – were the banks of the poor in the Victorian era, and though their reputation, in the hands of social commentators like Dickens, was not always savoury, they provided a flourishing and necessary service. Certainly by 1842 Mr Boyce had established a very successful business at 51 Theobald's Road in London, and by 1845 he had added a second shop in Lisson Grove.

He married Anne, the 'pretty and fascinating' (according to Alice) youngest daughter of Matthias Price, in April 1825. Her father was a prosperous farmer from Orleton, in Herefordshire – described by a neighbour, Humphrey Salway of Richard's Castle, as 'a great friend, a first-rate sportsman and a thoroughly straightforward and kind man, typical of the old yeomanry'. Anne had two sisters, who both figure in the story that follows. The elder, Elizabeth, married Captain Robert Thomas, a merchant seaman many years her senior, and they settled at Ashford Bowdler, not far from Orleton and very near Ludlow. They had no children of their own and, as the letters and diaries attest, lavished a great deal of love, attention and occasionally unwanted interference on their nieces and nephews. Anne's other sister, Mary, who did not marry, was also closely involved with the family.

George and Anne Boyce began their married life in Bloomsbury in London, but within a few years had moved to 5 Park Place Villas at Maida Hill, close to Paddington Green. This handsome and comfortable residence, complete with footman, cook and housemaid, remained the family home until Anne Boyce's death in 1890, at the great age of eighty-nine. They had five children. The first, George Price, was born in September 1826 while the family was still living in Bloomsbury, and it is possible that the next two, Anne Elizabeth and Matthias, were also born there. Joanna Mary, their fourth child, however, was born at Park Place Villas on 7 December 1831, as was their last, Robert, in 1838.

George went to school at Chipping Ongar, Essex, near the home of his paternal grandfather. In 1842, when he was only sixteen, his parents took him to Paris, where, after a fortnight's sightseeing, they left him for a year in the care of M and Mme Gachotte. He was assiduously tutored in all general subjects, including drawing and German, but seems to have had little or no contact with boys of his own age. His solitary leisure was spent visiting interesting buildings and developing the love of ancient and vernacular architecture which became so central to his art. He returned to England and, in 1843, began training with the architect Thomas Little in Northumberland Street. There he met George Devey, who had become a pupil of Little's in 1837 and had already gained a reputation for exceptional draughtsmanship. Devey, too, was passionately interested in vernacular buildings and materials, and evidently became both mentor and friend to the younger man – George records visiting him in October 1849 to borrow a 'surveying book' and Devey was a guest at George's 'exhibiting party' on 23 October, which featured 'pigeon pie, fowls and ham' and some excruciating singing. A glutton for education and culture, George attended lectures at the Royal Academy, the Royal Institute of British Architects[2] and London University, and even joined his sisters at their weekly German lessons. In 1846 he joined the architectural partnership of Wyatt & Brandon as an

[2] The Institute of British Architects in London was established in 1834 by several well-known architects of the time, including Thomas Leverton Donaldson, who became the first Professor of Architecture at University College, London. It was granted a Royal Charter in 1837 and the words 'in London' were dropped from its name in 1892.

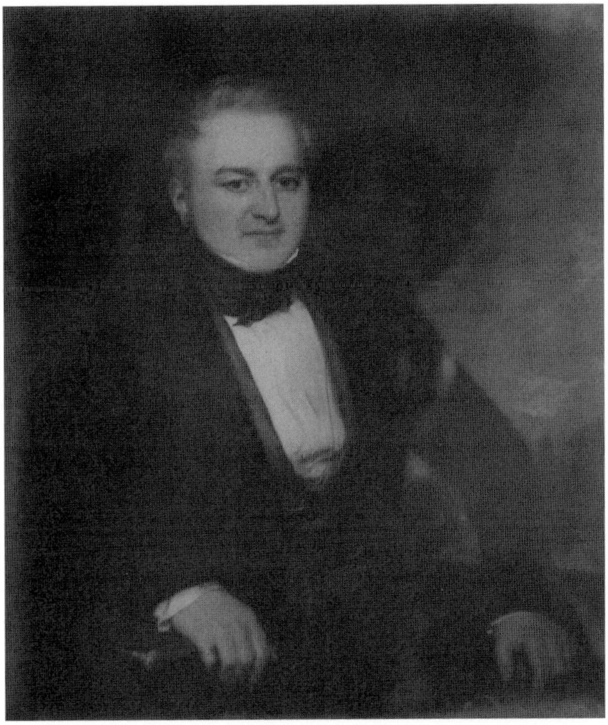

George John Boyce
Ramsay Richard Reinagle

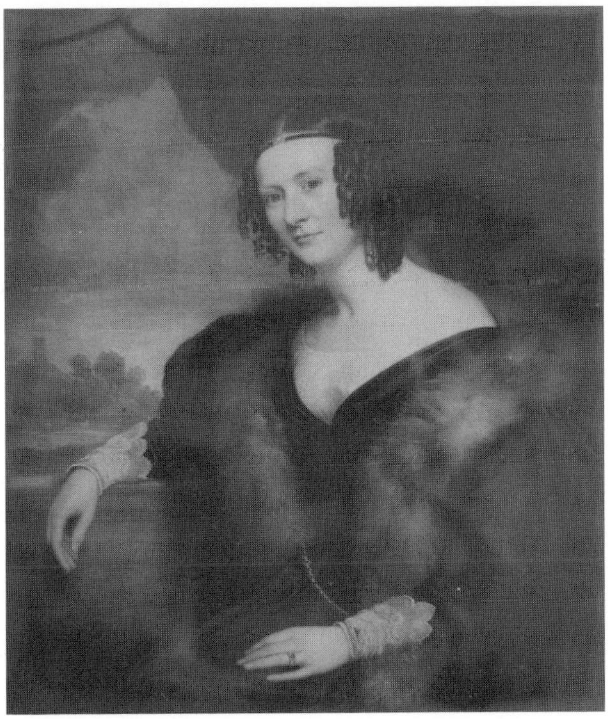

Anne Price Boyce
Ramsay Richard Reinagle

'improver',[3] but even then he was determined to become an artist and had begun to attend classes at the Royal Academy Schools. He was a restless spirit who loved travelling and drawing out of doors. It was not surprising that the ideals of the Pre-Raphaelite Brotherhood, founded in 1848, appealed so strongly to him.

That the Boyce parents were apparently happy to encourage their eldest son's artistic leanings was unusual. For Mr Boyce, it may have been a way of living out his own creative longings, for he assiduously fostered both George's and Joanna's talent, and more than once accompanied them on extended sketching trips. But Mrs Boyce also championed their artistic ambitions, though rather more capriciously and perhaps with an eye to the social circles in which she was anxious to move. It was clear, however, that both parents could look to their second son, Matthias, to take an interest in the business. He had a keen mathematical brain, chose the law as his profession, and gave his leisure hours to whist and chess, at both of which he was an expert.

Joanna, the heroine of this story, was five years younger than George, and it was not until their father's death that sister and brother became really close. Of all the children she was arguably her father's favourite, and from the beginning he ensured that she was given the encouragement and confidence to develop her gift. In the summer of 1843 (she was not yet twelve) she studied landscape and architecture under Charles John Mayle Whichelo, and her first drawing book is full of increasingly complex studies of castles, cottages and Gothic churches. Though sketching tended to be regarded primarily as a social and practical accomplishment for girls (Charles's brother, Henry Mayle Whichelo, was the author of a popular students' guide to sketching landscape, designed to help the young traveller abroad), the maturity of Joanna's style, even at that age, is impressive.

She attended school, starting at the Misses Townshend on Clapham Common as a boarder at the age of seven and a half, and moving to Mount Albion House, in Ramsgate, in April 1845. The school was large and lively and Joanna played a leading role there. She had an excellent singing voice and was already a talented pianist: a concert programme, for 30 September 1846, shows her performing two piano solos as well as some ensemble pieces. A favourite with her teachers and popular with her fellow pupils, there are hints, too, that she was a force to be reckoned with. In 1852 she received a letter from a pupil she had 'mothered' at school which said: '*Petite mère*, knowing your somewhat irate

[3] 'Improver': The Oxford English Dictionary describes an 'improver' as someone who accepts the opportunity to improve at a trade either wholly or in part instead of wages. Though 1858 is cited as the earliest usage, it was evidently common currency before then. George notes in his diary the agreement he later made with Wyatt & Brandon on 1 May 1848, by which he received a salary of £40 a year.

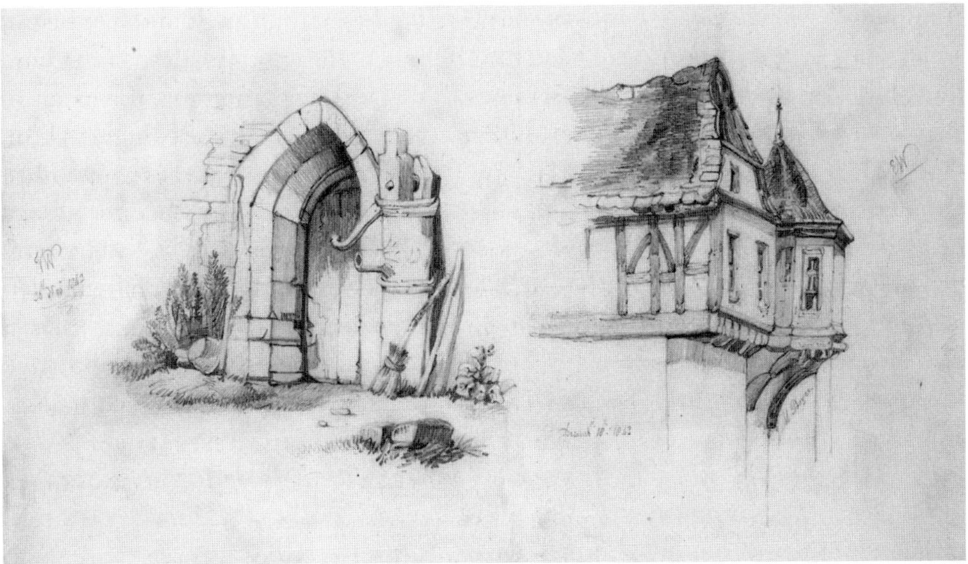

Early sketches *Joanna Boyce*

In the summer of 1843, Joanna, who was not yet twelve, studied landscape and architecture under Charles John Mayle Whichelo

nature I fear it will be vain work endeavouring to mollify your indignation when receiving this written instead of verbal *adieu*.'

There were constant interesting visitors to the Boyce household, several of whom became key figures in the lives of George and Joanna. William Boone, one of their father's closest friends, was an antiquarian bookseller, based in Bond Street, who specialised in finding rare treasures for individuals and institutions – often by combing the *quais* on the Left Bank in Paris. Among his purchases was an initial illuminated by Stefano da Verona in 1430 and cut from a church service book, which he bought from the booksellers Payne & Fosse on 24 June 1850 and sold on to the British Museum the same day. He involved himself wholeheartedly in Boyce family matters, invariably siding with Mrs Boyce whom he adored. (George noted wryly that Mr Boone took a crusty view of artists, with their wide-awake hats and long hair – 'in short, immoral and conceited'.) A frequent attender at Mrs Boyce's bridge evenings, William Boone regularly brought with him a companion to make the fourth at a rubber. This was Spencer Hall, a translator, editor and antiquarian who became particularly fond of George and Joanna, and took it upon himself to ply them with interesting and instructive reading. He had been librarian at the Athenaeum since 1833, remaining there until his death in 1875 and amassing one of the choicest collections of reference books in London. He was a kindly man: when George (with Joanna often in attendance) was confined to lodgings in Hastings and Brighton for many months in 1850 seeking treatment for a damaged hip, he made several journeys to cheer him with books and the London gossip.

The third character in the drama was Henry Tanworth Wells, whom George first met in the summer of 1849 at Betws-y-Coed in Wales. This beautiful spot, centred on a primitive little inn called The Royal Oak, had become a place of pilgrimage for art students and landscape enthusiasts, partly because of the sublime scenery and partly because of the presence each year of the much-loved and admired landscape painter, David Cox.[4] Henry, though only twenty-one at that time, had been articled to the fine art firm of Dickinson's[5] in Bond Street for nearly seven years and had already acquired a reputation as a skilled painter of miniatures and an accomplished producer of chalk portraits. George made several sketching trips with Henry, and commented in his diary that during art discussions 'Wells waxed fierce'. Indeed, 'fierceness' was one of Henry's qualities: he was a proud man with a strong sense of propriety and justice.

Like Mrs Boyce, Henry came of old yeoman stock: his family owned some eight or nine farms and smallholdings on the southern edge of the North Downs, between Guildford and Horsham, and Henry stood to inherit two properties from his father. His mother, Charlotte Henman, was the daughter of an architect, an energetic, cultivated and adventurous woman who did not intend to spend her days bringing up children in the country. She persuaded Henry's father (who was, according to Alice, 'of a comparatively weak and yielding nature') to let the farms and invest their small combined fortune in a business in London. Though he never prospered as a merchant, Wells and his wife settled at 6 Stanhope Terrace, near Hyde Park, where Charlotte brought up six 'bright and nice looking daughters in habits of thrift and frugality'. Their one son, Henry, named after his father, was born on 12 December 1828. He inherited his mother's strong character, determination and intelligence, and was soon packed off to school at Lancing where he thrived. Not only were his intellectual qualities recognised and encouraged – he won many prizes – but he realised almost straight away that

4 David Cox (1783–1859) may have begun visiting Betws-y-Coed as early as 1802. His biographer, F. Gordon Roe, agrees that he was often in Wales from 1805 onwards and was there every year from 1844 to 1856, with the possible exception of 1855. His painting of King Charles in the oak tree at Boscobel, which he produced as a sign board for the inn, still exists: it is framed and glazed and hangs above the main fireplace at The Royal Oak.

5 The firm of Dickinson's, print seller, lithographic publisher and photographic agent, was located at 114 Bond Street. Joseph Dickinson's apprentices, who included his son, Lowes Cato Dickinson, were trained primarily to produce lithographic portraits, though both Lowes and Henry graduated to portrait painting and developed close associations with the Pre-Raphaelite circle. After his father's death, Lowes Dickinson and two of his brothers, William and Gilbert, took over the firm, which was renamed Dickinson Brothers and had offices in both London and Brighton.

he was destined to become an artist. This ambition did not please his parents, his mother in particular believing that such aspirations could only end in the gutter, but Henry insisted, and with the help of a sympathetic schoolmaster an acceptable compromise was reached. He was just fourteen when, at the end of 1842, he began his apprenticeship with Dickinson's.

It proved a hugely beneficial step. Not only was he able to master the elements of draughtsmanship required for his work with the firm, his employers realised early on that he had exceptional talent. When he was not yet sixteen they granted him a course of study in Paris, and he began to attend evening life classes at Maddox Street[6] in order to gain the expertise required for producing miniatures and chalk portraits. Photography was in its infancy, so miniatures and other forms of portraiture were fashionably in demand – especially by the aristocracy.

Miniatures had been popular at court since the reign of Henry VIII, and, until the early 1700s, were mostly painted on vellum. From 1720 onwards, ivory took the place of vellum, though it was in many ways a far less forgiving material, being antipathetic to water-colour and with an oily, slippery surface. By the time Henry was serving his apprenticeship, thick polished ivory had been replaced by thinly cut sheets, with a specially ground surface to add bite, but miniature painting was still an incredibly demanding skill. Henry became very accomplished very quickly: as early as 1846 one of his portraits – probably a chalk drawing – was accepted for the Royal Academy Annual Exhibition, and in 1847 he produced a miniature of a boy and girl which, according to an anonymous reviewer, 'combined unsophisticated charm with precociously delicate workmanship'.

Henry supplemented his income, as so many artists did, by giving private lessons, and – as a smattering of drawing and music was regarded as an essential female accomplishment – his pupils tended to be young ladies. Though most of these lessons took place in London, he was often invited to attend his pupils at their country houses, where, personable and spirited, he mixed with people of position and culture who delighted in his company. (The kind of blurring of class distinctions that Henry evidently enjoyed was dramatised by Wilkie Collins in his novel, *The Woman in White,* published in 1860, in which the love of the drawing master, Walter Hartright, for his pupil, Laura, flowers in the every-day intimacies of the art lesson.)

[6] In 1845 some students who had become unhappy with the Government School of Art and Design, recently established at Somerset House, set up their own establishment at Dickinson's Drawing Gallery in Maddox Street. In 1848, as Leigh's Art School, it moved to 79 Newman Street, with James Mathews Leigh (1808–60) as Principal.

Mrs Boyce took to Henry immediately. From the moment George introduced him into the family she welcomed him, enjoying his conversation and the assurance with which he expressed himself on art and on the defining subjects of the times. He became part of the family. Then three things happened: George Boyce senior died, Henry fell in love with Joanna, and Mrs Boyce changed her mind about Henry.

At a personal level the story is fascinating enough. During the extended interregnum between their meeting and their marriage Henry and Joanna wrote to each other almost continually, making us privy to their most intimate thoughts and feelings. And from the obstacles that were put in their way, we come to know every member of the family – not least Joanna's mother, who, after the death of her husband, had no one to curb her violent snobbery and capacity for emotional blackmail. And because George was a friend and confidant to both his sister and her suitor, he plays – in spite of his tendency to slip away on solitary drawing expeditions or to the convivial studios of his Pre-Raphaelite friends – a pivotal role in the story.

Art was the tie that bound them. On 9 December 1851, Joanna, just twenty, recorded in her diary: 'Joseph Mallord Turner died. England's greatest artist. His works for truth, colour, infinite space, sublimity, imagination and repose have never been surpassed and very rarely equalled.' She went with her father on the 30th to attend Turner's funeral in St Paul's Cathedral: 'The service very impressive. The choristers chanting as they led the procession along the nave ... Nearly all the RAs and ARAs were present, a great many as mourners. After all was over we went down to the crypt and saw the coffin in the ground, lying but a few feet from Sir Joshua Reynolds.'

For the previous decade English art had been in a state of revolt, and for Joanna and her artist friends Sir Joshua Reynolds had come to symbolise a moribund establishment. He had been the first President of the Royal Academy, founded by George III at the end of 1768 to promote art and design through education and exhibition, and it was he who laid down its three main precepts for aspiring artists – first, to study the works of one's predecessors, secondly, to observe the accepted rules of art, and thirdly, to follow one's own judgment. By the middle of the nineteenth century, the first two had become set in stone, while the third had been conveniently forgotten. The great innovator in landscape painting, John Constable, had died in 1837, Sir David Wilkie, painter of much-loved genre scenes, in 1841. A faint-hearted malaise gripped an Academy in which only one giant remained. So when, in 1843, Turner, initially the darling of the establishment, exhibited his 'Sun of Venice Going to Sea', with its ghostly ship, its glassy lagoon and mysterious enveloping sky, it caused consternation. As he became even more nonconformist the consternation increased, his paintings variously described by his critics as 'confused dreams', 'frantic puzzles' and 'gorgeous monstrosities'. This was not what the Royal Academy expected from its favourite son.

There was no doubt in Joanna's mind as to Turner's genius. Though in practice she subscribed throughout her working life to the first and third of Reynolds's precepts, his was by now a dead hand on English art. A critic called John Ruskin, visited the Royal Academy Annual Exhibition in 1843 and declared that he 'was quite certain of the villainousness of the pictures' but found it difficult to prove. On 13 May he wrote in his diary: 'Nothing but ignorant unmeasured vapid abuse of Turner in the periodicals; I believe it is spite, for I cannot conceive ignorance so total in any number of men capable of writing two words of English.' As for English art in general, he pronounced contemptuously: 'Cattle-pieces and sea-pieces and fruit-pieces and family-pieces, the eternal brown cows in ditches, and white sails in squalls, and sliced lemons in saucers and foolish faces in simpers.'

The first volume of Ruskin's celebrated *Modern Painters*, published that same year (he was only twenty-four), was conceived as a defence and vindication of his beloved Turner, but it contained the seeds of a new artistic revolution – that of the Pre-Raphaelites. Articulate, passionate, and supremely confident, Ruskin told the young artists of the day, who included the precociously talented John Everett Millais, the devoutly single-minded William Holman Hunt and the charismatic man of art and letters, Dante Gabriel Rossetti, what they wanted to hear. In the second volume of *Modern Painters*, published in 1846, he gave them their rallying cry. They should go, he said, 'to Nature in all singleness of heart, and walk with her laboriously and trustingly, having no other thought but how best to penetrate her meaning; rejecting nothing, selecting nothing, and scorning nothing.'

The Pre-Raphaelite Brotherhood was founded at 83 Gower Street, London, in September 1848. Perhaps it was the Royal Academy Exhibition that year that lit the fuse: nothing had changed, and Holman Hunt remarked contemptuously that 'there was such a lack of courage and individualism in the painting of these things, and so slavish an adherence to one technical formula, that it would not have been difficult to believe that half the pictures were the work of a single competent and laborious hand'. Yet throughout Europe this was a year of revolutions that must have seemed, to a newly confident generation, to be entirely about youth and change. Bliss was it, in that dawn, to be alive when Karl Marx's 'Communist Manifesto' was published, when scientific debate was the province of Everyman, and ideas – religious, political, social and artistic – demanded to be taken seriously. Millais had entered the Royal Academy Schools in 1840, aged only eleven, the Academy's youngest ever student; Holman Hunt joined in 1844 at his third attempt. They became friends, marching – a little self-consciously perhaps – with the Chartist movement and taking a studio together in Cleveland Street. Shortly afterwards they met Rossetti and, over a volume of Carlo Lasinio's engravings of the frescoes in the Camposanto in Pisa,[7] which seemed to them to represent the perfect antidote to the vacuous sound and fury of the art establishment, the idea for the Brotherhood was born.

The original PRB was effectively a secret society. There were to be seven members – Rossetti seems to have regarded this as a mystic number – so to Millais, Rossetti and Holman Hunt were added Dante Gabriel's brother, William Michael, painters Frederic Stephens and James Collinson and the sculptor Thomas Woolner. All (except perhaps William Rossetti) were determined on artistic careers and all were bent on artistic revolution. They were not making an easy choice. Shortage of 'tin' was a constant problem and several of the PRBs were forced, sooner or later, to rethink their lives. Stephens abandoned serious painting in favour of teaching, art history and criticism; William Rossetti took on the mantle of critic and chronicler to the Brotherhood, while supporting his family as a full-time civil servant in the Excise Office; Woolner, a gifted sculptor, nevertheless despaired of making a living and left for Australia in 1852 – one of the million and a half Britons who emigrated in pursuit of gold or, at least, a better life. Woolner later returned to prosper in England, but the painting by James Collinson, 'Answering the Emigrant's Letter' , which was exhibited at the Royal Academy in 1850, was a poignant and effective illustration of the phenomenon and was among the first to draw its subject from the lower social classes. Yet on Whit Sunday that year Collinson resigned from the Brotherhood. A devout Roman Catholic convert, he had reverted to Anglicanism in order to become engaged to Rossetti's sister, the poet Christina, but in 1850 he returned to the Catholic fold. Christina released him from his engagement and he left the PRB saying that he 'could not as a Catholic assist in spreading the artistic opinions of those who are not'.

At the beginning, however, all that mattered was the revolt against 'slosh' – the PRB's term for Sir Joshua's artistic legacy – and though John Ruskin was by

7 Carlo Lasinio (1759–1838) was an Italian engraver who moved to Pisa in 1807 as *conservatore* of the Camposanto. He worked hard to protect it from the ravages of the Napoleonic wars and made his meticulous, if rather laboured, engravings of the frescoes as a record.

no means the only inspiration for the Pre-Raphaelite movement, he became, once it was launched, its most eloquent champion. The PRB philosophy was curiously mixed: it was based on the belief that artistic development had foundered on the work of Raphael and that most painting since was a pale reflection – in their own words 'dismal and overblown' – of that Renaissance genius. To find a new path it was essential both to look backwards, to a dream of the past, and forwards, to a bold contemporary realism. In this they were inspired by William Dyce[8] and Ford Madox Brown among older painters, both of whom had been influenced by the German Nazarene movement. Dyce was unashamedly enraptured by the artists of the Quattrocento, while Ford Madox Brown always claimed that it was he who gave the Pre-Raphaelites their name.

The techniques the PRBs employed were as distinctive as their subject-matter. The brilliance of colour that was their hallmark was achieved by applying paint with tiny brush-strokes onto a white, sometimes still wet, ground. It was extremely time-consuming and made much of the new chemically manufactured pigments – chrome and cadmium yellow, emerald green, crimson lake and a whole series of purples – which were derived from petroleum and did indeed reflect the kind of iridescence seen in a drop of gasoline.

Above all, the Pre-Raphaelites were story-tellers. Rossetti and Hunt drew up a 'List of Immortals' who deserved to feature in their paintings, with Christ at the top, and Homer, Dante, Chaucer, Goethe, Keats and Shelley among those accorded two stars. But whether their subjects were plucked from literature – other favourite sources were Shakespeare, Cervantes and the Arthurian legends – or arose from what the French poet and art critic, Charles Baudelaire, called 'the heroism of modern life, and the thousand existences which formed the floating life of a great city',[9] the aim was always to tell a tale.

In 1849, Millais exhibited 'Isabella' and Holman Hunt, 'Rienzi', at the Royal Academy, while Rossetti showed his 'Girlhood of Mary Virgin' at the Free Exhibition at Hyde Park Corner. As agreed, all three had signed their works 'P R B'. The curiosity they aroused turned to outrage the following year when Millais exhibited his 'Christ in the House of His Parents'. (*Plate III*) The Press had been invited to the Royal Academy opening for the first time, and much of the tumult that followed was precipitated by Angus Reach, who revealed the names of the artists behind the mysterious signature in the *Illustrated London News* on 4 May 1850.

8 William Dyce (1806–93). Scottish painter with a strong interest in design and manufacture. In 1837, he came to London where for five years he headed the newly-established Government School of Art and Design, which eventually became the Royal College of Art. He worked for Prince Albert at Buckingham Palace and Osborne House, and is best known for his Arthurian frescoes in the House of Lords.

9 From *Art in Paris 1845–1860* by Charles Baudelaire, quoted by Julian Treuherz in *The Pre-Raphaelites* (Stockholm 2009) p. 40.

The ensuing ill-tempered debate on Pre-Raphaelitism lasted well into 1851. The arch-idealist Holman Hunt contemplated returning to the City to make a living, and even Lizzie Siddal, Rossetti's model, was castigated for her ill-omened red hair.(*Plate IV*) Charles Dickens wrote in *The Times* on 7 May: 'Their faith seems to consist in an absolute contempt for perspective and the known laws of light and shade, an aversion to beauty in every shape and a singular devotion to the minute accidents of their subjects, including, or rather seeking out, every excess of sharpness and deformity.'

Given Dickens's own relish for the grotesque, this was a low blow, but in time the combined onslaught of the 'unbelievers' and the doughty defence mounted by Ruskin and his followers, had the effect of bestowing celebrity status on the Pre-Raphaelites. To their seductive banner many of their contemporaries were happy to flock, and even as the big three, Millais, Holman Hunt and Rossetti, began to go their separate artistic ways (as early as 8 November 1853, Dante Gabriel was quoting Tennyson to his sister, Christina: 'So now the whole Round Table is dissolved!'), the rebellion they had sparked embraced not only a new generation of Pre-Raphaelite followers but a wider community of artists who would never entirely fit the mould.

For Joanna, George and Henry, the Pre-Raphaelite movement was of crucial importance. Though all three were, in different ways, independent of it, they moved in its orbit and breathed its atmosphere. George became one of Dante Gabriel's closest friends (to the extent of sharing at least two mistresses with him) and was admired and liked by his fellows both as an artist and collector. He attended their gatherings, belonged to the same clubs, and recorded his life as a member of their circle in his diary.

Henry, as a successful commercial miniaturist and portrait artist, had established himself in a different artistic tradition, yet he shared with the Pre-Raphaelites their respect for colour and painstaking attention to detail, studied alongside them, and made close friends among their number. William Michael Rossetti remembered him as 'among the earliest of my artistic acquaintances: I knew him certainly before the formation of the PRB and possibly as far back as 1846.'[10] Henry himself wrote much later to Frederic Stephens, recalling his meetings with the Rossetti brothers in 1848, when he and Dante Gabriel attended the same life classes at the Maddox Street gallery. They used to walk home together:

[10] William Michael Rossetti, *Some Reminiscences* (London 1906) p. 154.

> Rossetti frequently asked me into his house to see his earliest water colour work and later I went to see his Mary Virgin painting while it was going on in Holman Hunt's studio. In the summer of 1849 Dante and Wm Rossetti, Lowes Dickinson[11] and myself had nude models in my studio at the back of Bond Street and I still have the capital beginning of a painting for a Mrs De Banks as she called herself which Rossetti let me have when he shirked finishing the life study – a shirking that was constant.

Henry was always proud of having been George's 'first painter friend' following their meeting in Wales in 1849 and was convinced that he was responsible for introducing him to Rossetti. In his letter to Stephens (dated 29 January 1897) he added: 'I tell you all this to show how much I knew of Rossetti before he knew Boyce and as Boyce knew nothing of painters when I met him in 1849 I am pretty sure the road to D.G.R. was thro' me.'[12]

Joanna, from an early age, was her own woman. She worked formidably hard and was in demand for portrait heads while still in her teens. She was lucky in that her father encouraged her to make the most of her gifts, and George, though protective of her as a woman, always treated her as an artistic equal. Henry, while he could be critical and overbearing, was to prove endearingly proud of her talent. But like other aspiring women artists at that time she faced the enormous problem of being taken seriously. Significantly, the male Pre-Raphaelites were among those who did recognise female talent but, as Pamela Gerrish Nunn and Jan Marsh have pointed out,[13] beyond the confines of that coterie it was a different matter. In particular, Ruskin, so eloquent in the Pre-Raphaelite cause and a professed admirer of Joanna's work in later years, was quoted as saying that 'women were natural imitators but poor inventors'.

Many of the women artists who did succeed were closely allied to artistic men. Rosa Brett, Emma Sandys and Rebecca Solomon were, like Joanna, the sisters of artists; Lucy and Cathy were the daughters of Ford Madox Brown; Elizabeth Siddal, Dante Gabriel's model, lover and (eventually) wife, was tutored by him and encouraged to paint. Anna Mary Howitt and Barbara Leigh Smith (later Bodichon) came from radical families with advanced educational ideas and a more feminist outlook. Both had studied in Germany; Anna Mary Howitt

11 Lowes Cato Dickinson (1819–1908): Portrait painter and Christian socialist. He believed passionately in a liberal education for the artisan, and was a founder of the Working Men's College which opened in 1854 in Red Lion Square and where, along with Ruskin and Rossetti, he also taught.

12 Oxford, Bodleian Library MS Don.e.60, ff.83r–85v.

13 Jan Marsh & Pamela Gerrish Nunn, *Pre-Raphaelite Women Artists* (London 1998).

published a book – *An Art-Student in Munich* – which certainly influenced Joanna, while Barbara Leigh Smith, who was one of five illegitimate children of an M.P., enjoyed an unusual degree of independence thanks to a generous personal allowance from her father. But the pressure on Victorian women to conform to the 'angel in the house' stereotype remained strong, and there were huge obstacles to the pursuit of a career. No women artists were included at the Exposition Universelle in Paris in 1855 and none appeared in the Manchester Art Treasures Exhibition of 1857.

Nor did they have the same opportunities to meet their fellow artists. Membership of the Cosmopolitan Club, which included Leighton, Millais, Browning and eventually Holman Hunt, was much coveted by male members of London's literary and artistic élite, though, as Anthony Trollope remarked in *Phineas Redux*, 'its attractions were not numerous, consisting chiefly of tobacco and tea'. The Hogarth Club, inaugurated in 1858 as an exhibition and social society by the very artists – including Ford Madox Brown, Rossetti and Holman Hunt – who purported to admire what women were doing, did not include them. (It did not specifically exclude them either, but none was invited to join.) The 'Society of Female Artists', which was founded in 1855 in an attempt to provide a similar network to that enjoyed by men, carried little weight with the artistic establishment and its first exhibition, in 1857, was poorly supported. Without a wider context in which to exhibit their work, it was hard for women to have faith in their achievements. They had no habit of self-promotion and tended to undersell themselves: when Marie Spartali[14] sold her first painting, her father proposed that she should give it away. Spartali herself later wrote:[15] 'I recognise as usual that I have chosen a subject too difficult for my limitations, and yet it seems impossible to attempt only what one feels sure of', and many of Joanna's letters express a similar dissatisfaction with her progress.

Yet Joanna was no amateur. For nearly seven years after leaving school she studied in every kind of artistic establishment open to her, and the range of work she produced in her short life – seventy-five art works and nine private sketch books – testify to her determination to be taken seriously. Moreover, she knew her worth: 'I have talents or a talent and with it the constant impulse to employ it – not for notoriety or fame, but for the love of it and the longing to work'. Though it is impossible to imagine that Henry, chauvinist though he could be, would ever

[14] Marie Spartali (1843–1927) was the daughter of a Greek consul living in England. She studied art alongside Ford Madox Brown's children in Fitzroy Square, and later married the American journalist and painter, William Stillman (see note 174).

[15] Letter dated 31 January 1890 (Fitzwilliam Museum, Cambridge). Quoted in *Pre-Raphaelite Women Artists* by Jan Marsh & Pamela Gerrish Nunn (London 1998) p. 46.

have tried to stop her painting, she could not rid herself of the fear that marriage would inevitably force her to choose between being an artist and being a wife and mother. Before she met him she had mortgaged months and years to the care and support of her brothers, George and Bob, during periods of illness. She did this both because it was expected of her and because she saw it – in strongly religious terms – as her duty. In this context her dedication, tenacity and early success – her portrait of a Welsh boy was exhibited at the Royal Society of British Artists in 1853; her 'Elgiva' at the Royal Academy in 1855 become all the more admirable. And though her regard and admiration for the Pre-Raphaelites is clear and her debt to them apparent, it was never slavish. She fought from the very beginning for her own voice, and she found it.

What follows is essentially a love story, but it is a love story with a difference. The characters of Joanna, Henry and George emerge vividly from the past through the exceptional quality and boundless vitality of their letters and diaries. Their families, their friends, their work, their ideals, their travels, their illnesses, their quarrels and their passions were played out against the brilliant, constantly shifting backdrop that was Victorian England in the mid-nineteenth century. Public events – among them the Great Exhibition in the Crystal Palace at Hyde Park, the funeral of the Duke of Wellington, the Crimean War and the Indian Mutiny – set their mark on private lives.

They took trains, were sea-sick crossing the Channel, attended lectures and exhibitions, patronised fashionable doctors, went to theatres and pleasure gardens, indulged in séances, played games, shared models, studied at drawing clubs and art schools and – endlessly and in detail – dissected their own and each other's work.

Most of the first-hand information we have about the artists of this period has inevitably come from men. The lack of surviving material by or about women artists has rendered them more invisible to posterity than in fact they were. In addition, as Jan Marsh[16] pointed out, the Pre-Raphaelite ethos became associated with a particular kind of woman's face, and this alone tended to cast women in the role of tragic heroine or fatal siren. Witness William Allingham's description of Lizzie Siddal: 'Her pale face, abundant red hair and long thin limbs were strange and affecting – never beautiful in my eyes.'

For this reason alone, Joanna's letters constitute a treasure trove. That she was, as Spencer Hall shrewdly observed, 'an Artist even in pen as pencil',[17] is a stroke of extraordinary luck. Life was a fragile thing. Joanna's death in childbirth,

16 Jan Marsh, *The Pre-Raphaelite Sisterhood* (London 1985).
17 Letter from Spencer Hall to Joanna, 1 January 1856.

when she was only twenty-nine would be just another of those all too common domestic tragedies were it not for the extraordinary account she gave of herself. She had a rare genius for self-expression, and though George and Henry outlived her by many years, with her death the light dims on their stories. Joanna brought out the best in them, and thanks to a discovery in a plastic carrier bag, the tale of three artists who shared so much can be conjured to life in the colours and textures of their own choosing.

1

ARTISTS IN THE FAMILY

'Ah, but a man's reach should exceed his grasp, Or what's a heaven for?'

'Andrea del Sarto'[18]

Joanna was very lucky in her brothers. The earliest surviving family letter was written to her from Brighton, where he was staying with family friends, by Matthias on 30 October 1844: 'The Ioway Indians have been exhibited at B[...]s[19] Cricket Ground and in the evenings at the Town Hall. I was much amused and particularly with their ball play, in which it was their aim to throw it on the target out of very strange sort of sticks – all others hindering them by pushing the ball out of their sticks and standing before the target and stopping it, as it came near.'

This lively description of a game of lacrosse was followed by news of the weekly meetings he and his friends had organised 'when no English is to be spoken' and 'no amusement except music, work and chess to be entered into'. He added: 'I hear you are learning the Polka. I hope you like it.'

George's earliest letter, dated almost a year later on 15th September 1845, was more pompous and elder-brotherly and began (this was to be characteristic of him) with an apology for not writing before. He was conscious of 'the desperate hugging' he had received on the day she went back to school. He and Matthias had been visiting their Aunt and Uncle Robert in Ashford Bowdler, where their mother was staying while the London house in Park Place Villas was being decorated,[20] and on their return journey he had particularly noted the industrial landscapes through which they passed: 'Our journey from Stourbridge to Birmingham was a very striking one, as the road passes among the numerous coal-pits, lime-kilns and furnaces of the district – all of which were sending up huge volumes of flame and smoke, and as it was dark at the time, we saw this curious species of illumination to a great advantage.'

18 The quotations at the beginning of each chapter are all taken from poems by Robert Browning, whose work was much admired by Joanna, George and Henry.

19 Probably Box's Cricket Ground, home of Brighton Cricket Club until 1847.

20 There were evidently a great many renovations at 5 Park Place Villas, including the 1845 decorations and a further period of refurbishment in 1848.

Unable to resist educating Joanna, he also included a potted history of the castles round Ludlow, but his great news – 'the wind up, the climax!' – concerned the Bone Well,[21] near Richard's Castle, a beauty spot much loved by the whole family. He wrote: 'I captured a bone!!! Unfortunately my conscience whispers to me to say that Mamma found four, two of which were much better than mine.'

Joanna left school at Christmas 1847, determined at that stage to develop her musical talents, especially her singing which, along with her languages, had flourished under the direction of her headmistress, Mme Charrière. Park Place Villas was again being refurbished, so she and her sister spent more than half the following year with Mr and Mrs Lahee and their twin daughters, Emma Rose and Rose Emma, who were friends of the family. There they received the following letter from their father, written on 17 July 1848:

> My dear dear girls, the whole time you have been absent your truly kind, thoughtful, anxious and sincerely affectionate mother has had continued anxiety and little or no relief. I believe your return home is now fully settled for tomorrow week, when I expect to see you looking blooming and happy. Your dear mother, (who is looking poorly and is certainly not in spirits) will require all your kindness and attention.

He clearly adored his girls. Equally clearly, their mother was, even then, of an emotionally demanding disposition. George and Matthias were already launched on their respective careers in architecture and the law – indeed George was now earning £40 a year as a trainee with Wyatt & Brandon – but Mr Boyce was responsible for, and very protective of, his remaining children, including Bob, the youngest, who had been in delicate health since birth.

There were indications, too, that though George was working hard at Wyatt & Brandon, the beauties of natural scenery increasingly absorbed him. He may also have felt the tread of his younger sister at his back. In spite of her declared intention to study music and singing, she was also, thanks to her lessons with Whichelo, an accomplished sketcher of landscapes and architecture,

[21] The area round Ludlow was famous for its 'Bone Bed' – two layers of sedimentary Silurian sands, marine shale and limestone, about 413 million years old, which ran for forty-five miles between Ludlow and Gloucester and contained the spines, teeth and scales of ganoid fish. It was discovered in 1835 by Dr J. Lloyd and the Revd T. T. Lewis, and Roderick Murchison's subsequent investigations attracted great popular interest. The actual 'Bone Well' at Richard's Castle was a spring – probably a 'holy well' – which cast up fish bones during wet weather.

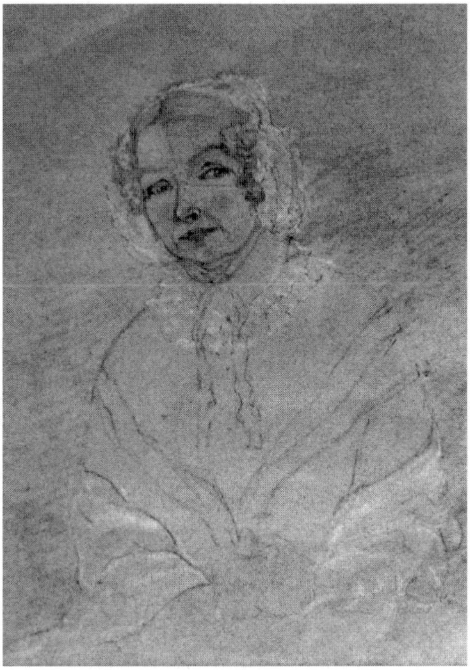

Anne Boyce

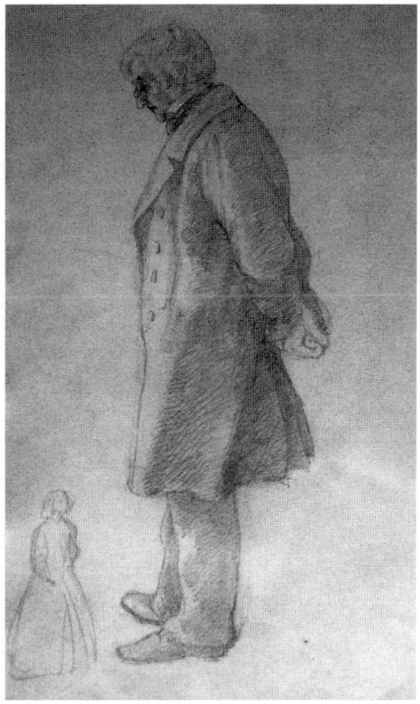

George John Boyce

Joanna sketched her parents on a number of occasions, and when she left home, one of the possessions she most craved was the 'small portrait of dear papa out of my study'. She did manage to extract a large chalk portrait of her father , and an oil painting of Anne.

and was demonstrating a particular interest in portraiture. There are far more sketches of people than landscapes in her early sketch books, and she was skilled at capturing the personalities of her friends and family. This, coupled with her admiration of the sketches George made in Wales in 1848, may have encouraged her to put music aside in favour of a course at Cary's Art School[22] in Bloomsbury in 1849; while George chose to go back to Wales – to that rallying point for art students, Betws-y-Coed – in the company of John Pollard Seddon, a fellow-pupil in the Wyatt & Brandon office.

On 31 July 1849, in a letter to his father, George described something of the magic of the place:

22 Francis Stephen Cary (1808–80) had studied under Henry Sass at Sass's School for Drawing and Painting in Charlotte Street, Bloomsbury. He took over the running of it from Sass, advertising it in 1840 as a School of Design for the Education of Artists and the Instruction of Amateurs. There was a separate establishment for ladies.

> I have just taken up your note … on return from perhaps the most beautiful valley in North Wales – that of the Lledr. A stormy, yet brilliantly illuminated sunset rendered it this evening truly sublime. The Moel Siabod, the principal feature, appearing as it received the lurid light reflected from the clouds quite incandescent … I get on very well with Seddon. His elder brother [Tom] arrived yesterday and is an amusing fellow.
>
> How gets [Joanna] on at Mr Cary's? I sadly want her to introduce some figures in my smudges. There are plenty of my favourites here – pigs – but they are never quiet a minute and consequently awkward subjects for sketching.

The presence of David Cox and the influence of other artists he befriended that year – J. B. Surgey, a landscape painter who endlessly delighted George by improvising on the piano, John Seddon's brother, Thomas, a gifted young artist who had imbibed his inspiration from Ruskin, and Henry Tanworth Wells, a miniaturist, who took over the spare bed in George's room after Tom Seddon left – were the spur George needed to give up architecture for painting. (*Plates V and VI*)

On 6 October, he called at Wyatt & Brandon's offices to tell them he would no longer be working there. Instead he spent his days 'finishing up' sketches, visiting Henry at Dickinson's to see his Welsh sketches ('All very clever, especially a moonlight and an interior') and attending a life class set up by the Seddon brothers in the Gray's Inn Road – Walter Deverell,[23] Dante Gabriel Rossetti and Ford Madox Brown were among the artists present on 5 November. At the end of the month he began studying in the Antique School at the Royal Academy. By now he was coming into constant touch with the Pre-Raphaelites and their followers, and particularly with Rossetti, whom he much admired. He later became Rossetti's first patron, buying his water-colour 'To Caper Nimbly in a Lady's Chamber' for five guineas – the first of many pictures by Rossetti that he acquired during his life.[24]

Joanna resumed her lessons at Cary's on 16 November. Having attended classes there throughout the summer, she had spent the intervening period with her aunt and uncle in Ashford Bowdler while her parents visited their youngest son, Bob, at school in Littlehampton. It is clear from a letter she wrote to her

23 Walter Howell Deverell (1827–54). Pre-Raphaelite artist, reputed to be the handsomest man in London, who shared a studio in Red Lion Square with Dante Gabriel Rossetti. He, his mother and the poet, William Allingham, were responsible for 'discovering' Elizabeth Siddal and introducing her to Rossetti.

24 The picture, which George bought in March 1852, was much altered by Rossetti during its lifetime, and was later retitled 'The Borgia'. In 1854, Rossetti gave George an earlier pen and ink drawing he had made as a preliminary study.

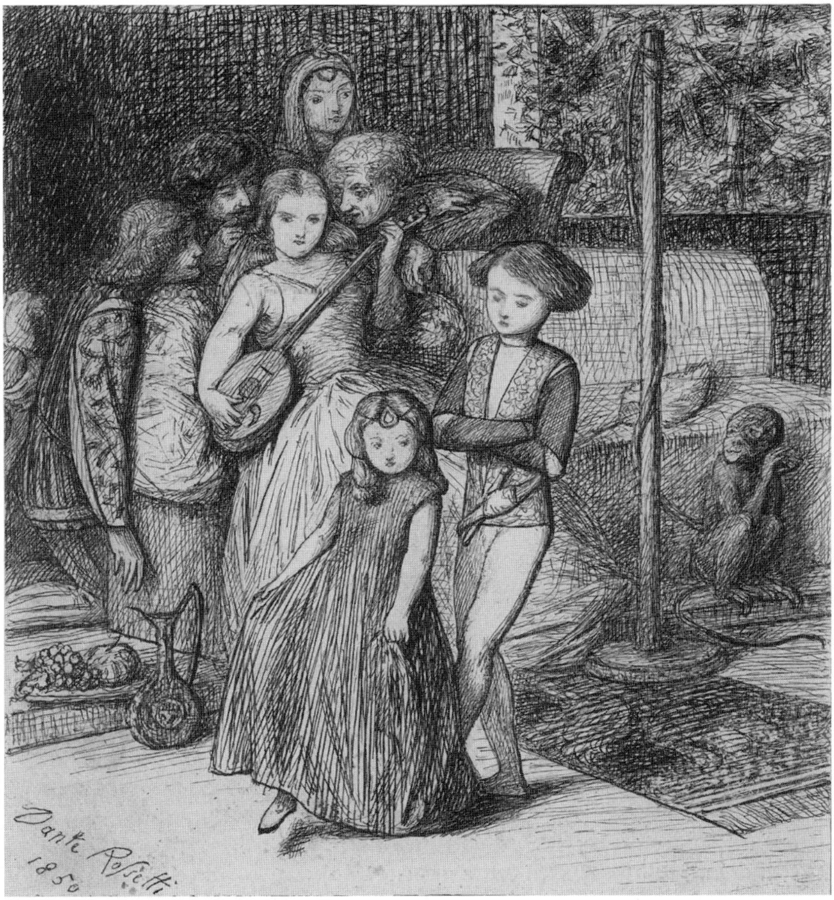

'To caper nimbly in a lady's chamber
To the lascivious pleasing of a lute'

This is the original drawing for Dante Gabriel Rossetti's much altered watercolour

mother in October that as a daughter she felt herself much loved: 'I am so very glad that you and dear Papa found darling Bob so well. I trust you are enjoying yourselves at Littlehampton and that you will have a nice trip with Mr William Boone after your return. The idea of going into Switzerland with you two next year (what can I say?) enraptures me.' She added: 'How can we help thinking of you my dear Mother, when we visit the scenes of your infancy and girlhood, and of our dear Father? For we cannot recall the one to remembrance without the other, blessed as we are with two parents of the kindest and best that ever lived.'

George was older, and more alienated and insecure. After a coming-of-age party for his friend Fred Warren on 19 December, he complained: 'Everyone's health proposed but mine. I was born to be trodden on – myself and my feelings too. It cannot long remain thus – to smile when sick at heart will wear one out at last ... Tom Hakes[25] is now my only friend.'

That winter was harsh. George, who had damaged his hip in an accident in Wales in 1848 and sprained his foot on Boxing Day 1849, nevertheless went skating in Regent's Park on 14 January 1850. What happened is unclear (he records going for a long walk with Hakes on the 20th so there wasn't an obvious accident), but by 7 February, a further dislocation of his hip had effectively disabled him. The 22nd found him lying on a sofa in the study colouring a drawing he had made in Wales of Vale Crucis Abbey, reading Henry Francis Cary's translation of Dante's *Divine Comedy*, learning Italian and relishing a 'glorious speech by Robert Peel on a matter [relating] to Protection and Free Trade and a clever but sarcastic reply of Disraeli'. Various doctors descended, even a cousin embarking on a medical career. Treatments included bed rest, the application of blisters and a splint 'for complete immobility'; but the pain became fiercer, and after four weeks of this treatment George's health had seriously deteriorated.

The advice of a distinguished consultant, Sir Benjamin Collins Brodie, was sought. Sir Benjamin was a physiologist and surgeon, attendant on the monarch since George IV, who had pioneered research into bone and joint disease. On 27 April George recorded: 'Sir B. Brodie came to see me – said something about the membrane of the joint being affected – offered no difference in treatment – wrote prescription for quinine and iron mixture – said I was to remain in chair in study for another three weeks. Said ligaments were not affected. 2 gn fee.' His woes were exacerbated by the rejection of his drawing 'Ludlow Castle' by the Royal Academy three days earlier.

Eventually, on 30 May, no better and now suffering from chronic inflammation of the joint, George and his parents travelled to Hastings where they found lodgings at 4 Breed Place, facing the sea. He was in considerable pain. His diary entry for 18 June reads: 'On live coals all day.' Distractions consisted of visits from family and friends – Mrs Boyce remained with him until 10 June, and both his sisters paid him extended visits – and short walks along the Parade to do some sketching. Joanna became his most constant companion, having temporarily given up her studies to be with him. (*Plate VII*) That all this anxious attention was not entirely welcome is evidenced by George's diary entry for 6 July: 'My father is in tears because Joanna is, and the latter because I will not be

25 We know very little about Tom Hakes except that he was one of Matthias's school-friends in Brighton, became a regular companion of George's, and later fell from grace by flirting with Joanna.

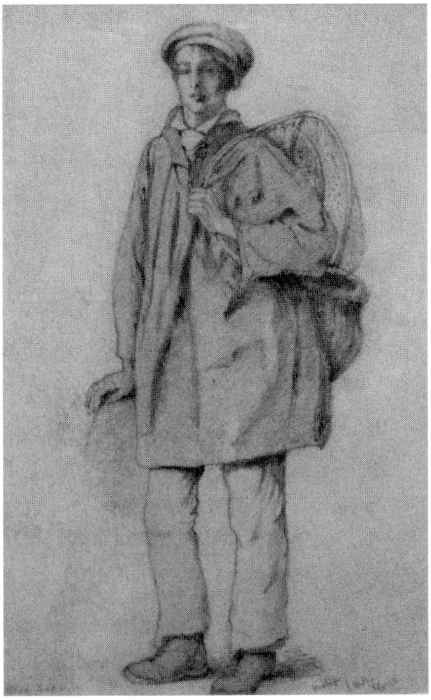

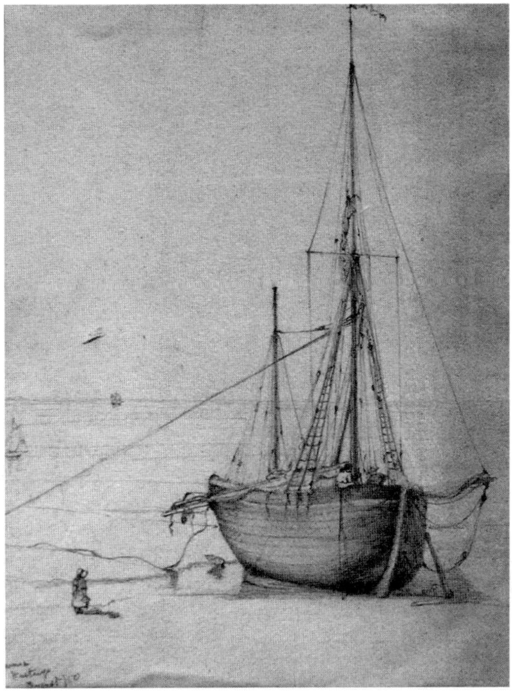

Alfred Todd *Fishing Boats at Hastings 1850*

Joanna kept George company while he was in Hastings seeking a cure for a serious injury to his hip, and though their activities were necessarily circumscribed, she produced a number of sketches, such as these.

more helpless than needs be. Oh, that I were in the wilds of N Wales with one faithful but manly attendant and a few books and drawing materials. Come what would, 'tis the happiest life I can think of.'

After three further months of useless treatment, George was moved to Brighton on 2 September. His father had heard of a bone-setter called Henry Harrap[26] who was reputed to have had some success with similar hopeless cases. Harrap's immediate view was that the doctors had weakened the joint, thus allowing the bone to shift even further from the socket, and George reconciled himself to a new routine in which he was wheeled in a bath chair to Harrap's on alternate days, rested the inflamed joint, applied soothing lotions, and submitted to a strong adhesive plaster round the thigh and extending from waist to below the knee. This was designed to encourage the thigh bone to revert to its normal position.

26 Henry Harrap was a professional 'rubber' or masseur who gained a reputation for curing joint and bone problems. He practised at 29 Grand Parade, Brighton, and in the 1860s he and a Mr Bennett set themselves up as 'orthopaedic surgeons'.

He found lodgings at Stanstead House in Marine Parade, with a Huguenot family called de Paris. Joanna, who had kept him company in Hastings while other members of the family came and went, followed him to Brighton on 4 September. He was also visited by Matthias, Bob and their mother, and by Messrs Boone and Hall, who arrived on 14 September bearing books. The de Paris children were being educated in music and the arts, and George enjoyed long and heated discussions with his namesake, George de Paris, on drawing and colour. The evenings were enlivened with much music, including choral and solo singing. George, like Joanna, had an excellent voice and, unlike his self-conscious and self-critical sister, enjoyed using it.

At last George's health began to improve. Joanna returned to London and to Cary's in November, and George began taking walks, writing letters to his sister in French, entertaining himself by playing Harrap's piano and making plans for the future. On 1 January, in spite of his diminishing interest in the profession, he achieved the Freedom of the City as an architect, and on 23 February wrote cheerfully to Joanna:

> Edouard de Paris, who has now and then of late given us some 'delicious' and soul-stirring music of Beethoven and in the second degree of Mozart and Haydn, all of which he plays with great feeling and spirit, was good enough to take me about a week ago to see several fine pictures, amongst much rubbish, belonging to a Mr Wheeler here. They were mostly of the Dutch School, of which there were two absolutely inconceivable specimens as regards imitative execution by Mieris.[27] In one the peculiar texture of material of a richly coloured drugget, with its roughness and stray threads when viewed on the edge of the folds, was positively delusive, as was also a rich velvet mantle resting on it ...
>
> You told me nothing of the gallery of Portraits I hear you are making. Be sure you do justice to the originals, which I never did.

George remained in Brighton until early April. Though his hip continued to trouble him and he returned more than once to seek Harrap's help, he gradually resumed a normal life. He was back in London to witness the procession for the Great Exhibition on 1 May: 'Never saw the streets in such densely-crowded state

27 Probably Frans van Mieris (1635–81), along with Gerrit Dou (Gerard Dow), the most important of Leiden's 'fine' painters. He was famous for the delicacy of his small-scale genre pictures and his talent for painting fabrics and materials. His grandson, also Frans van Mieris (1689–1763), followed in his footsteps, though not as famously.

before. Jacks on the green, acrobats, jugglers and performances of all descriptions going on.' On the 27th, he visited the Crystal Palace in Hyde Park for the first time: 'The aerial effect of the same enhanced by the rich and brilliant colours of the various fabrics suspended about was more bewitching than I expected,' and accompanied his sisters to the Royal Italian Opera: 'Beethoven's "Fidelio", the grandest piece of music I ever heard.'

He found himself back in a London bursting with confidence. Prince Albert had been a leading light in planning the Exhibition which, though it purported to be a showcase for the works of industry of all nations, was really intended to trumpet Great Britain's role as industrial leader. The Crystal Palace itself dominated Hyde Park. Designed by Joseph Paxton and erected under the auspices of structural engineer Charles Fox and a committee which included Isambard Kingdom Brunel, it was the world's largest single structure and was an ideal symbol of Britain's greatness. The exhibits that filled it – drawn from the arts, medicine, science, shipbuilding, railway engineering, architecture, horology and textile manufacture, and embracing such wonders as glass-blowing, photography, safety lamps and the electric telegraph – were designed to celebrate progress in every sphere. Colonial raw materials and moving machinery were particularly popular with visitors, and there were marvellous treasures to be seen, such as the Koh-i-Noor diamond, then the largest in the world, and the eighth-century Tara brooch, as well as more extravagant inventions, like Rodgers & Sons' sportsman's knife with eighty blades and a collapsible piano for gentlemen's yachts.

George visited again on 16 June, travelling by bus, and was particularly taken with the India, China, Africa, Persia and Turkey departments – 'these displaying the requisite knowledge and feeling for colour and its right application … all the others looked poor, meagre and inharmonious.' He records taking refreshment while sitting opposite 'the prettiest of all the Hebes, a very pretty fair girl with wavy hair, loving eyes and winning ways.' George was always susceptible.

The months he had spent as an invalid made him particularly alert to his youngest brother's problems. Though Bob had always been delicate, it is clear from George's diary that he thought his brother played on this to elicit extra sympathy, especially from their father and Joanna. On 23 June he noted: 'They indulge him in the habit of learning his lessons aloud in our sitting room, do not stop him from enquiring at the slightest difficulty without endeavouring first to solve it himself nor from constant repetition aloud of his by-heart lessons – a bad system this.'

By 26 June he was plunged in argument with both mother and father about the best method of educating Bob, and his description of his father's 'impatient, random and personal mode of argument' as giving rise to dispute rather than rational discussion, provides an interesting corrective to the generally saintly picture we have of George Boyce senior.

Nevertheless, when George was anxious to go back to Wales to sketch, his father, concerned that he would overstretch himself, undertook to accompany him for the first week. This time George spent nearly three months at Betws, sketching hard, defying the weather, and at last getting to know the great man – David Cox. His hero worship is apparent:

> *5 August:* While sketching, David Cox came and shook hands with me. He has put up here [the Royal Oak]. After dinner I made an evening sketch on grey wrapping-up paper. David Cox saw it and approved.
>
> *10 August:* Met Mr Cox ... who took me some way along the road down to the Llegwy to show me a subject. I stopped to listen to some simple and moving singing, in the Welsh chapel.
>
> *26 August:* Too wet to go out. Mr Cox with the greatest kindness gave Mr Beck[28] and myself a lesson in water-colour painting, explaining to us by working two drawings before us ... We cast lots for the drawings afterwards ... Mr B got the prettiest, an idea of Beeston castle, with a beautiful blue distance and white clouds near horizon. Mine is a mountain subject with flat ground in mid-distance, and a bridge and tree in foreground ...
>
> Completed drawing from Church, which Cox said looked like a pre-Raffaelite drawing.

It was on this trip that he made the acquaintance of the Naylor family (father and daughter went on to play important roles in George's and Joanna's lives), and Francis William Topham, a water-colourist who arrived in Betws on 24 September and proved a great hit, largely because of his skill at conjuring: 'I never went into such paroxysms of laughter or at any rate not for a long time. He swallowed jugs and potatoes.' George added: 'A very pretty and interesting girl sat for some time in the chimney corner.' (*Plates V and VI*)

By the time he returned to London on 11 October, the Seddon life classes had outgrown their quarters in the Gray's Inn Road, and its habitués were renting

28 Not identified.

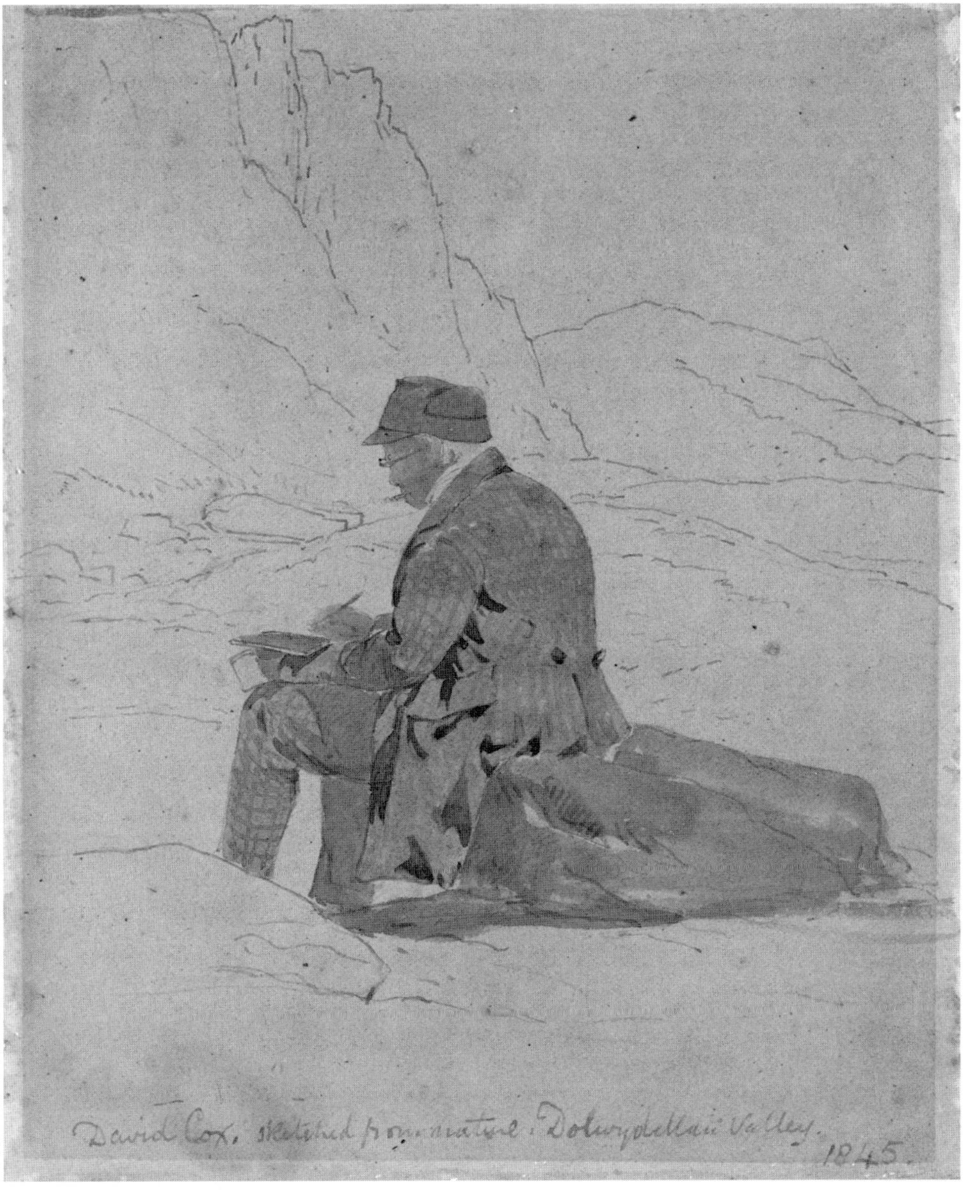

David Cox sketching — *Harry Johnson*

Young artists flocked to Betws-y-coed to sit at the feet of the distinguished landscape painter, David Cox. Harry Johnson made this charming drawing of him 'en plein air' in 1845.

larger premises in Clipstone Street. They called themselves the Artists' Society, and George had been elected to membership on 2 October, paying £1.9.6 for the first quarter, and £1.1.0 for the entrance fee. He attended classes for the first time on 23 October to draw a female nude model called Mrs May. Life classes, both nude and costumed, took place on three evenings a week at which George regularly met his artist friends – the Seddons, Surgey, Rossetti, John Clayton (a designer of ecclesiastical stained glass), the sculptor Henry Hugh Armstead[29] and of course Henry Wells. On 6 November he 'tasted some sardines for the first time. Very delicious'.[30]

❖

Joanna, meanwhile, was blossoming. She studied at Cary's, attended lectures on anatomy by John Marshall[31] at Leigh's, worked daily on her drawing and, in spite of the constant worry about Bob's health – she was a dutiful girl – had some fun. Earlier in the year, on 17 May, she wrote to her brother Matthias describing a dance she and her sister Anne had attended and giving a lively group portrait of some of the leading literary and artistic figures of the day:

> Your sisters had never anticipated the honour of meeting so many distinguished artists.[32] Leslie is a most quaint looking man; his wife a very sweet looking woman with the features and complexion often seen in his works ... Mr Frith brought his wife ... From the little I saw of her I should not have said she was pretty. Mr Ansdell danced a quadrille with me. He is a pleasant, good-natured sort of man, short and commonplace looking. I could hardly bring myself to believe he painted the fine pictures we have seen on the walls of the Academy with his name attached to them. Egg was present, but no one pointed him out to me. All I remember of him is that he is wild looking and that he trod on

29 Henry Hugh Armstead (1828–1905). Trained as a silversmith and became a sculptor. He and Henry quarrelled, but were eventually reconciled. Armstead married Henry's sister Sarah in September 1857.

30 In her edition of George's diaries, Virginia Surtees notes that the famed chef, Alexis Soyer, had observed in 1851 that sardines were to be found on the south coast. He felt their high price (two to three shillings for a box of twenty-four) would discourage their coming into fashion.

31 John Marshall (1818–1891): Anatomist and surgeon. In 1878 he published *Anatomy for Artists*.

32 It was indeed a distinguished gathering. The genre painter Charles Robert Leslie (1794–1859) had been elected to the Royal Academy in 1826. Joanna's host, Edward Matthew Ward (1816–79), a narrative painter best-known for his murals in the Palace of Westminster, became a full RA in 1855. William Powell Frith (1819–1909) and Augustus Egg (1816–63), both friends of Charles Dickens, were already Associates and became RAs in 1852 and 1860 respectively, while Richard Ansdell (1815–85), animal and sporting artist, became an RA in 1870.

> my toe. Wilkie Collins, one of the performers at Devonshire House,[33] an author, was among us. Neither his manners nor his appearance were prepossessing...
>
> Ward, our host the associate [of the RA], is a stout man. His face has a mixture of heaviness and intelligence. He appears to me to have much physical lethargy counterbalanced by strong mental energy. However, if this be true, he seemed determined to subdue his body that night, for evidently with the view of keeping us merry, he seized hold of a lady and danced with her fiercely – madly round the room. The rapid heaving of his great body had at once a ludicrous and terrific effect.

Her formidable powers of observation and vitality of expression were already apparent, her portraits were beginning to be known and admired, and the artistic circles in which she was moving were influential. It was not surprising that Henry, who must have heard much about her from George, was anxious to make her acquaintance.

He had engineered an introduction as early as February that year, on the pretext of finding out from Joanna's father what he owed Madame de Paris for his board and lodging while visiting George in Brighton. In a somewhat ingenuous letter, he told Mr Boyce that he had arranged an 'open sesame' for the family to visit Mr Baring's picture collection. As he was painting portraits of the Baring family at the time, this had the merit of establishing his credentials on two fronts.

By the end of 1851 Henry was a welcome visitor at Park Place Villas, which was more than could be said for George's friend Tom Hakes. On 7 December George wrote in his diary:

> Mother grieved me much by assuring me that Tom Hakes had behaved far more cruelly towards Joanna than I thought or can think possible. She thinks that he has gone so far as to kiss her. Hitherto I have always considered the great attention I have seen him pay to some girls to arrive from natural weakness and thoughtlessness, and I have told him as much. But this fact is without excuse and most unfeeling. I fear he lets his feelings carry him away so far as to be unable to retreat without wounding the other party.

33 The performance in question had taken place only the day before. Wilkie Collins had been introduced to Charles Dickens by Augustus Egg in March and had joined Dickens's amateur theatrical company. They performed Bulwer-Lytton's *Not so Bad as We Seem* before Queen Victoria and the Prince Consort at Devonshire House on 16 May.

He was relieved to note that there was no sign that Joanna thought about him, or 'dwell upon his conduct'.

Like Joanna, George attended Turner's funeral on 30 December, and, with his father and sister, was admitted to the vaults afterwards: 'I remained to see the stone rolled over him and to assist in adjusting the same – they first threw a basket full of human bones on and beside the coffin before rolling the stone over it. It was placed between the resting places of James Barry, the painter (next to which was that of Sir Joshua Reynolds), and Constantia, the great grand-daughter of Sir Christopher Wren, next to the tomb of Sir Christopher himself.'

Joanna's description of Turner's funeral prefaced the diary she kept during 1852. It made her thoughtful. In the small hours of 22 February, when her sister was snoring and the fire was low, she wrote: 'The little gas flame that darts so brilliantly from the coal, reminds one of a great artist or poet who flashes like a meteor on the world, and the cloud of smoke that follows instantly on its extinction, of the host of feeble copyists and imitators that invariably follow in the wake of great men, but have no light of their own and reflect none of his.'

Her diary paints a picture of a home life both cultivated and sociable. She attended lectures and exhibitions, usually with her father, and it was he who encouraged her in serious religious thought. In one sense the household was strictly Victorian – Divine Service was attended both morning and evening on Sundays – but it was also scientifically engaged: Joanna attended lectures on geometry and geology as well as anatomy.

And it was health-obsessed, with good reason. George was, at the very least, accident-prone, Bob was a chronic invalid, and Joanna herself, for all her force of character, suffered badly from asthma and was often ill. Both George, and to an extent Joanna, had inherited their father's depressive tendencies. In consequence any hint of illness was a cause for concern – the possibility that Matthias might have contracted TB raised a flurry of anxiety – and the family doctor, who was both friend and advisor, was constantly appealed to. It was a time when many diseases, barely understood, could cut even the most robust life brutally short.

Mrs Boyce, herself invariably the picture of health, entertained a wide range of friends and acquaintances, of whom the Ridleys, with their four striking daughters, and the Moores were among the most intimate. Joanna immortalised the two elder Ridley sisters, Lizzie and Charlotte, in her pictures 'Elgiva' and 'La

Veneziana', and her study of Lilly, who became Matthias's wife, was accepted for the Royal Academy exibition of 1855. Hennie Moore, the younger sister of Anne's school friend Maria, became, and remained, Joanna's staunchest and most admiring friend.

Augustus Mordan, a widower with two young daughters, also figured in the gatherings as a determined suitor to Anne. A pencil manufacturer, he was, before he moved into his own house, Corinth Villa at 17 Finchley Road, a lodger at 48 Canonbury Square, the home of Thomas Girtin. Girtin was the son of the famous water-colour painter of the same name who had been a companion of Turner. George recorded a visit there on 5 February to see 'a goodly collection' of the father's drawings – 'all of them interesting, many beautiful, some very excellent colour in two or three of them'. Girtin's wife told George that, 'far from being dissipated, the painter's character was exemplary – he had been a teetotaller from his 16th year who enjoyed refined society'.

Mordan proposed to Anne on 23 January and was accepted. He proceeded to shower both Anne and Joanna with bouquets and presents and took them to plays and operas – on 26 February Joanna recorded: 'With A.M., Anne and Ma to hear Mrs Kemble read *Midsummer Night's Dream*. The play beautifully and admirably read, especially the humorous parts … She coarse, plain, ill-tempered looking. Music, Mendelssohn's, splendid.'

Joanna enrolled at Leigh's School of Art, in Soho, in early February. Founded in 1845 as a more forward-looking rival to the Government School of Design so recently established at Somerset House, its life classes were open to both male and female students (the Government School of Design's idea of life classes for women consisted of a man wearing a suit of armour), and its teaching methods were relatively informal. Henry and Dante Gabriel Rossetti had been among its first students. Her father, at the time, was sitting to Henry for a portrait and she visited Henry's studio on 20 February to be shown his drawings and paintings. Henry was never shy of offering criticism and advice – a 'kindness' that Joanna appreciated. She was not uncritical herself – on 11 March she wrote in her diary that Henry's likeness of her father was 'not good'. She was working on her own portrait of her father by then, as well as on a portrait of Lizzie Ridley.

On 7 April she and her father went to Paris together. In the company of William Boone they commenced 'the round of the sights with great energy' – the cathedral, the Panthéon, the Hôtel de Cluny and the Luxembourg. Joanna wrote: 'Modern French paintings in merit below our third-rate artists – disgusting in colour, false in feeling, theatric in attitude, and studied and cut-dried classicalism in drawing of figure and draperies. Then into Gallery of pictures – all but a few beneath criticism – one of Ary Scheffer[34] – father weeping over son … Fine in colour, painting and feeling – perfect repose.'

Her opinions were forthright: she thought most of the pictures at the Palais Royal 'below mediocrity'. She was not well enough to see the picture galleries at the Louvre, which was frustrating, but amused herself on the way home with making a sketch (lost, alas) of the sufferers during the uncomfortable cross-channel passage: 'Ladies' cabin an amusing study.'

The Royal Academy Exhibition opened in May. Joanna pronounced 'Millais's "Huguenot and lady" exquisite'. She did not return to Leigh's at this point, but worked on portraits of children and a drawing of a cast at home. When there were no children available she began a self-portrait ('very bad') but she preferred drawing children. On 29 May she recorded: 'Tom Seddon spent the evening here. Praised my little girl (Sophie) which pleased me much. Tom Seddon, very amusing.'

At this time, however, George was less than popular with the mother of a certain Helen Field. He had evidently paid his addresses to her before, and too lightly. On 9 June he noted: 'Went with Joanna to an evening party at McArthurs. Mrs and Helen Field were there, the former, as usual, behaved very distantly and rudely to me, saying goodnight to Helen and Joanna and not noticing me who sat by them. Fortunately she left before supper appeared, and I had some very pleasant chat with Helen who is as pretty, artless and winning as ever; and with none of her mother's low-bred pride. Recommended Ruskin's *Modern Painters* to Helen's reading.'

Two days later he was writing: 'I feel as if I were much with Helen I should grow desperately in love with her again. She looked over my Welsh sketches and was much interested in some of them. How I should like to have told her that I could think of no greater pleasure than roaming about with her in these lovely lonely places.'

After Anne and Mordan's marriage on 19 August, followed by a flutter of anxiety about the state of Matthias's lungs – 'perfectly sound as yet … but over exertion would cause what we so much dread' – Joanna and her father set off for Betws to join George for long days spent sketching. There were occupational hazards to working out of doors, as she recorded in her diary:

> *3 September:* After 6 o'clock dinner went down with George to sketch, midges horrid.

[34] Ary Scheffer (1795–1858). Painter of Dutch extraction who went to France in 1811. He was associated with the romantic movement, though his style was initially classical. He later turned to the Dutch masters for inspiration. From the 1830s onwards he fell foul of the art critics while remaining the most popular artist of his generation. Joanna admired his work and later visitied his studio.

> *4 September:* With Pa to sketch. Moved to another place on the river. Began another sketch. Storm, scrambled about the rocks near the bridge and saw the mill.
>
> *6 September:* With Pa to sketch. Midges maddening.

Joanna was introduced to the legendary David Cox and described, on 13 September, going for a walk 'towards churchyard, my favourite stroll by twilight. David Cox outside his cottage. Chatted with us and showed us his pictures. Made a sketch from my mem[ory] of him when I returned home.' She was less star-struck than her elder brother.

On 14 September she recorded: 'Finished my picture' – this was almost certainly the first landscape she ever painted from nature, and after her father's death she remembered how he used to carry her things for her, sit with her while she worked, and fetch her lunch. She was well aware of her own impatience and self-absorption: 'How grateful I ought to be to God for giving me such a kind, self-denying, unselfish father, and how much more I ought to check my impatient and fretful spirit.'

On 2 October she wrote a long letter to her brother Matthias: 'The weather has been so rainy since Monday that any out of door sketching has been out of the question, so I have had recourse to a child in the village, a sturdy, solemn little chap, who stands very still, while his elder sister, of whom I have tried to make a study, is the most provoking fidget I ever came near.' The 'solemn little chap' was Elias Owen, and Joanna's picture of him (since lost) was the first she ever exhibited – at the Royal Society of British Artists in Suffolk Street in 1853.

Always dissatisfied with her work, she found praise hard to accept:

> By the bye, my dear brother, I am seriously grateful to you for the hint you gave me in George's letter about affectation and pleased you judge me guiltless of it. The fact is what I do is so far inferior to what I admire, that I cannot help showing it when I hear my drawings unduly praised, as they so often are. Yet I think I must confess that I sometimes say more than I should if I duly weighed my words; but not from affectation, I assure you, but partly from a sort of discomfort and nervousness that makes me say anything that comes uppermost. But indeed I value few things more than a gentle reproof, kindly spoken by you or anyone whom I respect and LOVE.

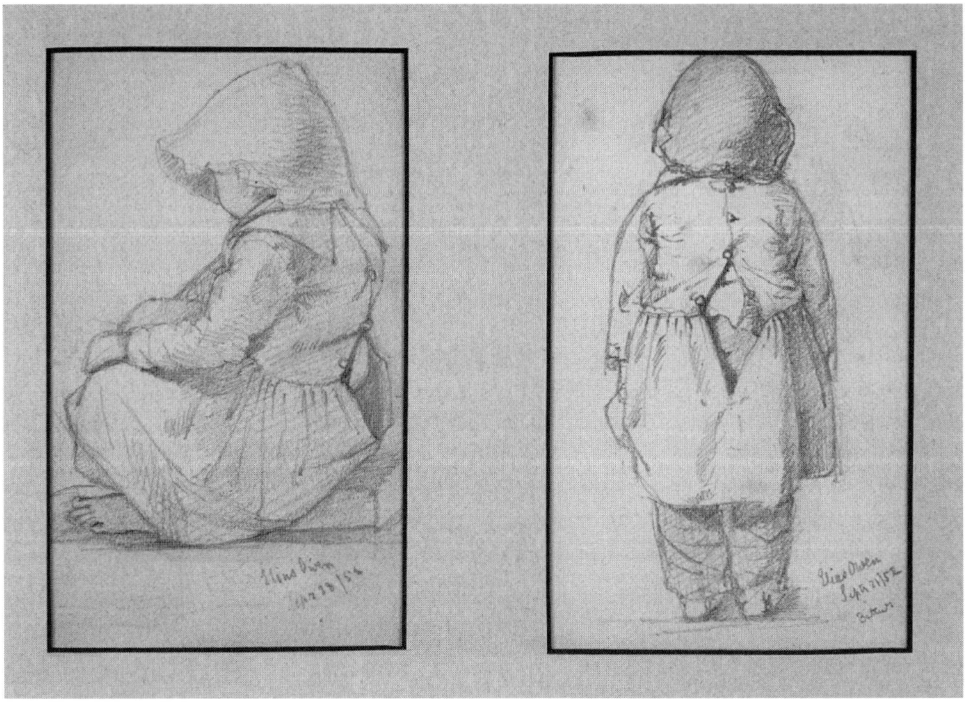

Studies of a Welsh Boy *Joanna Boyce*

Matthias had evidently also visited Betws: 'The boy Jack speaks of you and has a lively and pleasing recollection of you in some way connected with squibs and wasps and wishes you would come down again. But I am sorry to find he is a very bad boy, a thief and a storyteller to wit, though his face has to my fancy such an ingenuous and intelligent expression.' Her painting of 'The Little Red-Haired Boy' *(Plate X)* could well be Jack.

George, she told Matthias, was out sketching in the wet weather: 'He did think of trying something in oil and probably will if weather and time permit, but the smell of turpentine seems to annoy him very much.' She was convinced, however, that he was destined to succeed in his profession.

Henry, meanwhile, had been making a rapid tour of Germany – a hell-for-leather dash round every picture collection, building and church, and not omitting any famous viewpoints in the neighbourhood. He got back in time to make chalk portraits of Sir Watkin Williams Wynn[35] and other worthies and was in high good spirits.

35 Sir Henry Watkin Williams Wynn (1783–1856). Knight Diplomat who, following various postings in Europe as Envoy Extraordinary, became the British Representative in Copenhagen. He remained there for thirty years and was nominated a KCB in 1851.

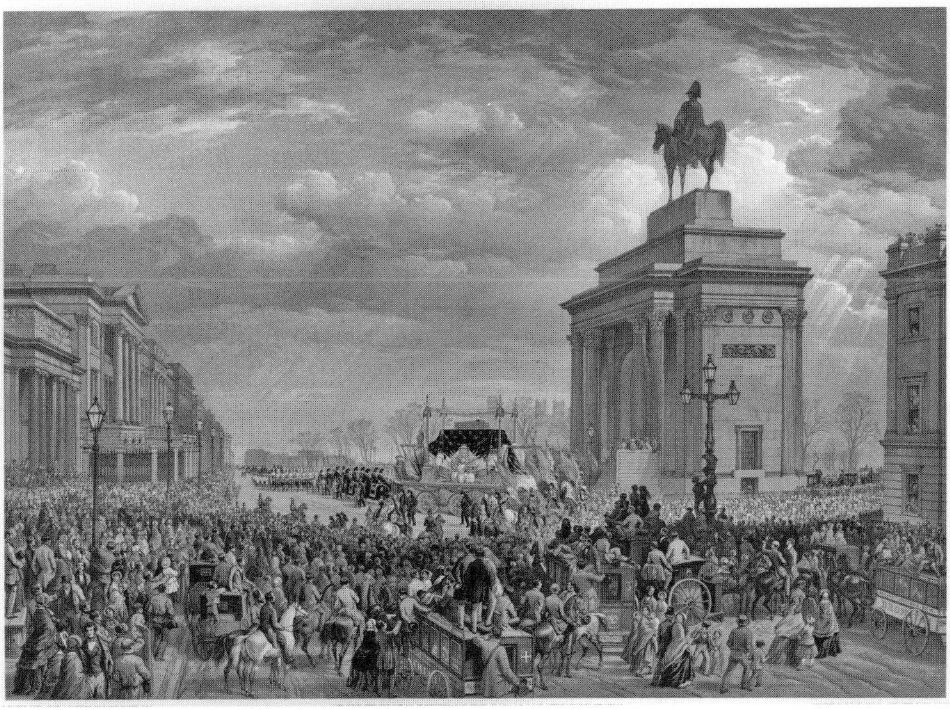

Funeral Car of The Duke of Wellington passing Apsley House *Louis Haghe*

The Duke of Wellington died on 14 September 1852 and both George and Joanna attended his lying-in-state. His funeral was held at St Paul's Cathedral on 18 November and more than a million people lined the route. The procession, wrote Joanna, 'was fine but not solemn ... We all up at 5 – to our places easily.' Thomas Picken's engraving of a painting by Louis Haghe shows the funeral car passing Apsley House, on Hyde Park Corner, the home of the Dukes of Wellington.

On 13 November, Joanna, Anne and their parents went to Chelsea for the Duke of Wellington's lying in state: the crush was too great and they had to extricate themselves, but George got in after four hours, while Joanna returned with her father on the 16th and gained entry then. 'Fine effect but not so grand as I expected' was the verdict.

On 6 December, the eve of her birthday, she wrote: 'Tomorrow I shall be 21. God will help me to carry out every good resolution to be self-denying and to curb my temper and to redeem the time and not to regret with peevish jealous discontent that my youth is passing. Time has never stayed for any man – then why for me?'

In 'The Flight of the Duchess', Robert Browning, a favourite poet of them all, wrote: 'What a thing friendship is.' George would have agreed. His relationships with his friends were, for the most part, easy and relaxed, while those with his family were often complicated and paradoxical. He chafed at their 'smothering' during his illness and shied away from emotional ties, yet was easily slighted and prone to melancholy. At the beginning of 1852 he wrote:

> My mother spoke to me touching my gloominess. I had nothing to answer. How little do my friends with whom I make effort to be cheerful and pleasing suspect that my heart and soul are adrift and lost in a sea of unaccountable and indefinite longings and regrets. Music, and now and then a line of poetry, are almost the only things that seem to agitate the deeper springs of my nature.

He told his 'dear and good father' that he would be happier if he could go into 'a beautiful part of the country and live quietly and work diligently for a time'.

Yet his artist friends saw little of this side of him. He had a reputation for being 'a good sort of fellow' – kind, capable of 'larking' and always vulnerable to a pretty face. In *Some Reminiscences*, William Michael Rossetti described him as being 'of agreeable person and address'. Although he had the advantage over many of them in having a private income, his capacity for hard work and genuine passion for drawing ensured that he was never regarded as a dilettante. He attended Clipstone Street diligently, learned the science of rainbows from a teacher at Leigh's Art School, attended Charles Leslie's fifth lecture on landscape painting, and met Millais for the first time. On 12 November, Rossetti wrote to him to ask if he might borrow his water-colour back to send to the Winter Exhibition in Pall Mall. He ended 'I am to be with Wells on Thursday evening. Shall I see you?'

On 30 December 1852 George wrote an extended entry in his diary which gives an insight into the life that was evolving for him:

> Went down to Dante G. and William Rossetti's chambers at 14 Chatham Place, Blackfriars Bridge. Met there Wells, J. P. Seddon, Clayton and Mr Munro, Mr Stephens and Mr Hughes.[36] Rossetti

[36] This entry gives a good indication of the breadth of George's (and Henry's) artistic acquaintance.

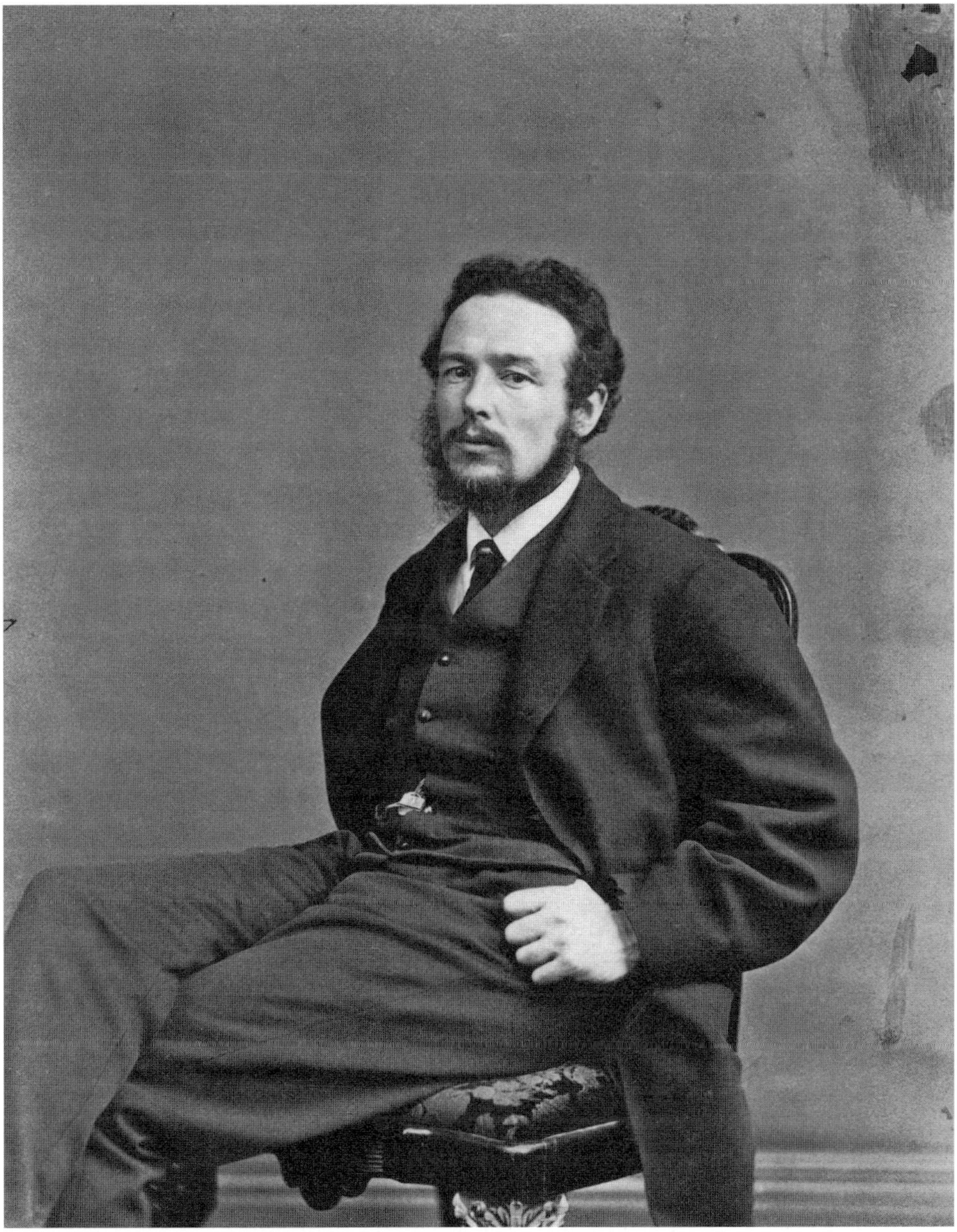

George Price Boyce

Though George had his melancholy and solitary side, among his artist friends he was generally thought to be 'a good sort of fellow'. He was kind, capable of 'larking' and vulnerable to a pretty face.

showed me his studio but none of his works (which is his way). He had for our entertainment a series of anastatic[37] drawings designed and coloured by the Hon. Mrs Boyle,[38] some of which as beautiful in feeling, natural simplicity, and colour, and in poetical treatment as almost anything I have seen. They illustrate a nursery rhyme. Also a grand and most striking mask of Dante taken from a cast of him in death; a tracing of his head in Giotto's fresco with the eye imperfect; a pen and ink sketch by Millais from Keats's 'Isabella'. In the physical way, roast chestnuts and coffee, honey and hot spirits. His room has a jolly balcony overlooking the river, the reflection of the lights on the bridge and quays, etc, were charming. Conversation throughout delightful, resulting methought from the happy and gentlemanly freedom of the company generally. There was only one of D. G. Rossetti's works to be seen in the room, and that was a sketch, study of a man, back view. Gabriel Rossetti invited me to his studio next Thursday.

On 1 January 1853, George's friend Francis Topham 'candidly' advised him against trying for membership of the Old Water-Colour Society. This august organisation had been founded in 1804 by a group of artists who felt that their talents were insufficiently appreciated by the Royal Academy. Gaining admission was formidably hard. Topham himself had first been a member of the New Society of Water-Colour Painters, but resigned in 1847 to join the Old Water-Colour Society. He was in a position to propose George as a member, but was cautious about doing so, perhaps because George had not yet produced a substantial enough body of work. In the meantime, Tom Seddon and Rossetti were increasingly anxious to move George on to painting in oils: they were convinced that he would find it easier to establish a reputation in that medium, and his resistance became something of a preoccupation among his friends.

On 28 January George visited Rossetti to see his 'Annunciation picture', (*Plate XI*) which had been exhibited at the National Institution when George

37 A method of facsimile printing that involved taking the image to be printed and brushing it with highly dilute nitric acid so that those areas of the paper with nothing on them were bitten through onto a plate. The original was usually destroyed in the process.

38 Eleanor Vere Gordon Boyle (1825–1916) became one of the most important female illustrators during the 1860s. Her first illustrated book, *Child's Play*, was published in 1852.

was laid up with his hip. Rossetti had resumed work on it: 'The Virgin one of, if not the most exquisite conception I have ever seen, her head, golden hair and blue eyes (although painted from his sister who is darkish) full of intense thought and awakened and glowing religious awe, almost my idea of a woman's head and much like Lizzie Ridley … Had a long chat with him about Turner, for whose work I was sorry and surprised to find he had not the highest possible admiration.'

Of his meeting with Millais, he wrote: 'Somewhat egotistical and little real, his attention being easily distracted. He jerked out some good remarks', while Holman Hunt 'struck me as thoroughly genuine, humorous, good-hearted, straightforward English-like fellow. Said he was bound for Syria before long'. He also found himself caught up in a fierce debate at Clipstone Street on 5 March, defending Ruskin against the charge of being 'a man of no talent and a mere stringer together of words'.

Nor were his interest and acquaintance restricted to artists. At the Ridleys on 13 May, the lawyer William Moxon[39] entertained them with insights into the 'habits and practices' of poet and essayist, Leigh Hunt,[40]

> assuring us that the character of Skimpole in *Bleak House*, his prototype, is not at all exaggerated by Dickens. Hunt, most delightful and fascinating in company, but the day after, the amused guest is pretty sure to receive a specious note from Mrs Hunt, purporting to be without the cognisance of Mr H, lamenting that some evil individual has put in execution in their house, and if Mr So and So would kindly add £10 or so to the 20 or 30 lent by Messrs So and So, it would relieve the family of much distress, etc. Mr Moxon said that Leigh Hunt regularly existed in this way, contriving to have a Sheriff's Officer in the house.

But George was always poised for some kind of flight. On 20 May he and Tom Seddon departed for the Channel Islands and France: 'Bid goodbye to dear Mother and Joanna as affectionately as my cold heart would allow.' His letter to his mother from St Helier, Jersey, is full of a painter's observations:

[39] William Moxon was the barrister brother of Edward Moxon, poetry publisher and friend of Wordsworth and Tennyson. A number of Pre-Raphaelites contributed to Edward's celebrated illustrated edition of Tennyson's Poems, published in 1857.

[40] James Leigh Hunt (1784–1859). Poet, essayist, journalist and friend of the Romantic poets, Shelley in particular. He was always short of money, and was instantly recognised in the character of Skimpole by his contemporaries. In 1847 he had been granted a Civil List pension and an annuity from Shelley's son, but the habit of borrowing persisted.

> We left Southampton by packet at about 12, and reached this nondescript place at midday to-day, feeling only a little uncomfortable. I remained on deck the whole time and watched the moon and the expanse of waters and impressive growth of the dawn, which began with long streaks of rose and violet sky, enclosed between a cold grey curtain of clouds and an horizon of purplish-green sea. Then came slowly up the large glowing disc of the sun streaked with purplish vapour and burning more and more brilliantly till we came in sight of Alderney and Sark and the quaint groups of pointed rocks between, and so on. The sea was a little broken among the islands but elsewhere very smooth ...
>
> *Sunday evening* ... After church this morning we made an excursion to Mont Orgueil Castle and St Grouville's bay and were very pleased. The bold rock-rooted castle jutting out grandly into the sea and finely lighted up by the setting sun. The greatest drawback in the scenery is the absence of old and unlopped trees – nearly all are denuded of their lower limbs, and, now that the foliage is so scanty, look very meagre and unhappy.

They docked at St Malo on 25 May:

> The Customs House officers came on board and after inspecting passports went so far as to feel the outside of our pockets, which so offended T. S. that he got very angry and indignant, which made them more suspicious. They took away from me a revolver pistol and Murray's Handbook to be '*réclamés*' at the Custom House. T.S. went to the *sous-préfet* to know if a small canister of gunpowder would be admitted – No! [41]

Joanna wrote to her brother, now in Dinan, on the 31st, with news of various family entertainments, including a séance. Table-turning had become all the rage in Europe following an outbreak of psychic phenomena in America in 1848 known as the 'Rochester Rappings'. By 1852 it was well-established both as entertainment and as a subject for scientific investigation:

[41] The right to bear arms had been enshrined in English law since 1689, and the carrying of pistols for self-defence was common in mid- to late-Victorian England. Samuel Colt's latest revolver, the Colt Navy, was a popular exhibit at the Great Exhibition. For Tom Seddon, who was travelling on to Egypt after parting from George, a gun would have been essential, and on 7 June 1861 George records taking delivery of a Deane and Harding revolver 'of newest and most approved design'.

Hat and table-moving was our occupation for an hour or two. The hat spun round capitally, but the table wouldn't budge. We all thought unconscious muscular exertion might possibly have caused it, and it appears that Sir David Brewster[42] and a number of scientific men who met last week at the Duke of Argyll's for the purpose of testing it, came to the same conclusion.

Papa and Mammy are engaged at double dummy, are incessantly bemoaning the rarity of trumps, laughing, squabbling etc; while Mat stands by and coolly informs them at intervals that they are playing very badly; then he closes his lips in a style that would have passed muster at Delphi and only reopens them to pronounce the same statement at some fresh faux pas ...

Have you commenced sketching? We earnestly hope you will continue to derive benefit from the change – take the greatest care not to overtire yourself ... We all reckon on your having a Daguerreotype or Calotype[43] of yourself taken with beard and moustache.

On 7 June she wrote to him again at Dinan. Anne was now expecting a baby, 'though she has not made you an uncle yet'. Kensington Gardens, she said, 'are just in the pride of their spring beauty'. He had evidently confessed to an ill-advised adventure because she added: 'What a fortunate escape you had from serious accidents in the mad ride with tipsy John. I trust you have no ill effects from it in your hip or otherwise. How are you progressing with your sketching?'

By 20 July George had reached his goal – the little village of Gabas, situated in a beautiful valley in the Pyrenees. Untroubled by distractions, he settled to serious work, but within days grave news reached him from home. Anne had suffered a very difficult confinement and though her son, Edgar, was born safely on 28 June, she developed puerperal fever and for a while her life hung in the balance. No sooner had she begun to recover than their father was taken ill with what was believed to be phlebitis.[44] Joanna was left to look after Anne at Corinth Villa while Mrs Boyce returned to Park Place to care for her husband. By the time the news reached George, both Anne and his father were thought to be recovering, so he decided to await more definite information. On 31 July Henry wrote to reassure him that his father was 'going on favourably',

42 Sir David Brewster (1781–1868). Physicist, astronomer, mathematician and inventor of the kaleidoscope. Joanna later consulted his work with reference to problems with her eyesight.

43 Daguerrotype and calotype were both early photographic processes. Calotype had the advantage of being able to produce multiple images, whereas daguerreotypes were largely restricted to a single image.

44 Inflammation of a vein, usually in the leg, caused by a blood clot.

adding: 'I have sought constant information of his state, for besides being your father, I feel he has honoured me with his friendship and in so fatherly a manner that I return it with affection.' Henry was planning to leave for Venice in mid-August. 'I must not be away longer than six weeks, therefore I must do it quite as a traveller, not as an artist. I wish you were going to be my companion.'

In fact, Mr Boyce rallied only briefly, but it was not until 23 August that George was alerted to the change. He wrote in his diary: 'Unfavourable news of dear Father, who had been seized with a great depression of spirits … More miserable days, just as my cheerfulness was beginning to return. Tried hard to pray, but the cold unimpressiveness of my heart is truly awful. I cannot – at least I hope not to – remain long in this dreadful state.'

On 4 September he received a telegraph message: '"*Père pire, veuillez revenir*."[45] Packed my things at once.'

❖

He arrived home on 8 September:

> Found, as I feared, no hope left of Father's recovery … Thought at first he did not recognise me, but he could not speak for deep feeling and he is unable to shed a tear … At his request showed him the drawings I had been making abroad. He was most pleased with the two at Dinan, which Mr Swan has bought. 'That's beautiful … You should have a great deal for these drawings, George. You should have 15 gns a piece.'
>
> *9 September:* Sat much with Father during the day and all night giving him his food, reading to and praying for him … I promised to love Joanna, Mother etc, and cherish them. He made me promise not to look at the bad wound at the lower extremity of his spine[46] – asked where Wells was and said he was a good fellow.

Between them, the family tended him day and night. He was soothed and comforted by anything to do with the church – the bells 'give him wonderful solace' and he spoke affectionately of George's drawing of Westminster Abbey *(Plate XII)*, hung with a selection of his children's pictures where he could see them from his bed. George wrote:

[45] 'Father worse. Please come back.'
[46] Probably an ulcer or infected bedsore.

13 September: With Father from 10 pm last night to 5.30 this morning. I slept until 1. After dinner sat with and read the Psalms to Father. The nurse, to our disgust and further distress, got dead drunk, Mat and I obliged to let her down on the floor in the servants' room.

19 September: Easier but much weaker. The doctors came in the middle of the day to dress the wound. They bore strong testimony to Joanna's praiseworthy conduct and attention to Father … Mordan came this evening. Mother and he talked together a bit, the former exaggerating dreadfully in her account of messages left by Father, and the frequency of his enquiries after Mordan.

Mr Boyce died on 20 September. Joanna's heart-rending account of his illness and death is a sustained tribute to her love for him. If George contributed the sketches, she painted the finished picture in all its emotional intensity:

From the very first day he loved me to read the Psalms to him and to say the Lord's Prayer and three times he took the Sacrament. Ma and I did not feel satisfied, notwithstanding his love for the Bible, that he was exactly in a right state, so, at dear Ma's request, I asked him if he really felt his own sinfulness and grieved at it. He assured me that he did and that his only hope was in God through Jesus. How I thanked God for this. Sometimes I doubted whether I had done right in disturbing perhaps his simple, childlike faith in God's mercy and love, but I think not. One day, I shall never forget it, as I was sitting by his side, I heard him ejaculate: 'Oh God, forgive me, I have been very wicked! God have mercy upon me, Christ have mercy upon me.' I was so delighted at the proof of his repentance that I could not forbear saying 'Oh my darling Papa, you have made me so happy, now I'm certain if you die you will go to Heaven.' He turned his dear head on his pillow looking into my eyes he said with the most exquisite smile 'You dear creature, you dear creature.' I read the Bible – the Psalms principally – and the prayers of the liturgy constantly to him. Nothing gave him so much pleasure except George and me singing hymns … Once, when we went to his bedside immediately we had finished, he said, 'My dear children, if anything could make me wish to live, it would be your singing, but even that can't do it.'

For nearly three weeks, leading up to his death, Joanna slept in her clothes in order to be ready when he needed her in the night, and she took George's place by his side from four until six. When he had gone, she grieved that 'Never, never again shall I know a father's love or have those dear arms around me that have sheltered me from infancy.' Her one comfort in her sorrow – and she recognised it immediately – was her new closeness to her brother:

> Since that day when he tried to comfort me in my grief for dear Papa and showed me his own heart and looked so affectionately into my eyes and tried to conquer himself with such strong, simple, manly earnestness, I felt as though I had found a brother that was lost to me. May that thin, sad mist of estrangement never rise insensibly between us again. He may appear cold, selfish, and even wound my feelings deeply, but never will I forget that hour of perfect love, or that I have a dear brother George, whose heart is noble at bottom, though for the time nothing but the scum may be seen.

We do not know what caused the rift between them. George may well have been a difficult patient in Brighton. He lacked his sister's moral idealism and could be thoughtless in his dealings with women (though his outrage over the behaviour of Tom Hakes towards his sister was proper enough). But they had shared a great deal and it is clear from Joanna's diary that she felt the estrangement to be her fault: 'I have always loved him and the consciousness that I have lost his affection was very, very bitter to me.' She was determined never to lose him again.

2

REFUGE IN WORK

'Works done least rapidly, Art most cherishes'

'Old Pictures in Florence'

After their father's death, Joanna took on the task of arranging a change of air for the family at Torquay. This was essential – her own health was giving cause for concern – but it was not easy. She wrote to George, already staying at the Roughwood Inn, on 18 October, asking him to reserve lodgings from 'Tuesday next':

> I should have preferred starting some days sooner, but I saw it was best to consult Mammy's fancies entirely, or I should never get her away at all. I begin to doubt whether change of scene can do much for the spirits, though I feel certain it will do everything for the health and it may perhaps relieve this wretched weariness and want of energy, but nothing but time will lighten this enduring heavy consciousness of something lost that was very, very dear and that never can return. That word, never, seems to have such far deeper and deadlier meaning now than before.

At the end of a letter dated the 24th, confirming the arrangements, she added: 'Mamma very much wishes to have a sofa in the sitting room and linen sheets on her bed. She cannot sleep with calico.'

George met them at the station and conveyed them to their cottage at Babbacombe, which was, Joanna noted in her diary, 'prettily situated and wonderfully cosy inside'. Brother and sister spent their days sketching, she missing terribly 'the dear encouraging eyes of my darling father, to whom alone I was sure of giving pleasure'. Nevertheless she completed a study of a red-haired boy, which she gave to George, and began 'a little painting of a lady' and a landscape which became her first gift to Henry. She hardly knew how to please her mother, writing on 12 November: 'Many nights I have cried myself to sleep, but never let Ma know it, till this night she discovered it by accident. She is very angry – unjustly so I think, as I have hidden every sign of grief since we came here – never sighing aloud, though Mammy constantly does – and always trying to divert her thoughts.'

In spite of the dismal emotional atmosphere, George managed to complete two outstanding water-colours – one 'Anstis Cove', the other 'Babbacombe Bay'. (*Plates XIII and XIV*) Both were exhibited at the National Institution Exhibition at the Portland Gallery the following year, and on 1 April an anonymous critic in the *Spectator* pronounced 'Anstis Cove' the best work in the show: 'everything is felt and rendered with the single-hearted reliance on nature that is the test of a true vocation.'

Henry, having returned from his travels in Venice and the Italian Lakes, was now busily occupied fulfilling commissions for various noble families. He wrote to George on 13 November from Vale Royal, Cheshire, home of the Cholmondeley family,[47] describing his adventures in portraiture:

> At Oxford I commenced a group of four children and a dog in water-colours on paper. Owing to circumstances I had to leave the drawing unfinished, but will finish it and do the Mother's portrait when I pass through the city on my road back to London. My quarters were with Mrs Granville Somerset at All Souls College. At Kirtlington Park I remained a fortnight and never passed a happier time. I did chalk portraits of Sir George, Lady Dashwood and the two Miss Dashwoods. The Miss D.'s were lovely subjects. The evenings were spent delightfully by hearing good music and kindly conversation and having a game or two of chess with the youngest Miss Dashwood, who found me an everlasting victim of defeat, but I was fast improving under her tuition and becoming dangerous when I had to leave. In leaving I had only one consolation and that was a great one, ie: an invitation from Lady Dashwood to visit them at times, when I can obtain a day or two's holiday. They liked my portraits very much, and I shall do something more for them when they come to town. The house I am staying at now is a famous old place. It was an Abbey built in Edward I's time and many of the rooms have the same walls and roofs as when they were inhabited by the Monks.

He had almost more work than he could manage, including portraits of the Egerton family and a full-length miniature of Lord Newark's wife, for which he had to travel to Holme Pierrepont, near Nottingham.

[47] Henry does not vouchsafe what he was doing at Vale Royal at this time, though he returned there in 1856 to produce some family portraits.

> Yesterday I had a letter from Jenkins to say that last Wednesday he had proposed my name to be a member of the 'Graphic',[48] and that I was elected under the most flattering circumstances, for more votes were given to me than to any painter Candidate, and there was but one opinion of my work etc, etc. This is all very delightful and I (mentally) rub my eyes, scarcely daring to look this sort of fame in the face …
>
> I am indeed one of the luckiest of men. I have so many friends personal and professional, good health and worldly affairs prosperous enough to supply every one of my modest desires. I don't write this exultingly but thankfully. You are living in a very charming place and I shall persist in expecting a good sketch or so.

As usual, he could not resist some words of artistic advice:

> One word about 'dodges'. You are of course perfectly right in not trusting to them, especially to other people's; but you must be careful not to refuse a quick way of painting because it is a quick way. I can conceive a man painting a large piece of sea or water in a few hours better than if he spent on it as many days. But he could only have attained the proper knowledge by very many elaborate and (as I should think) faulty studies …
>
> I suppose your sister is painting as carefully and as well as ever. You two are sure to back each other up well against any heretic leaning towards the doctrine of 'Slosh'.

At Torquay depression and illness ruled. Joanna squabbled continuously with her mother. On 26 November they all returned to London, Joanna noting in her diary: 'Mat looking pale and thin. I dreadfully low.' George took immediate refuge in the Artists' Club where, on 28 November, at a 'nude sitting', he heard 'a very believable rumour that Wells thro' Sir Edwin Landseer's recommendation[49] was

[48] The Graphic Society was a drawing club founded in 1832 for the purpose of hosting regular conversazione and exhibitions. By the 1850s these were being held in the library off Flaxman Hall at University College. George first attended a meeting on 5 January 1852.

[49] This proved to be true (see p. 50). A gifted painter of animals, Sir Edwin Henry Landseer (1802–73) was hugely popular, both with the middle-classes and with the aristocracy. Queen Victoria gave him regular commissions, but he is probably most famous for the lion sculptures at the base of Nelson's Column in Trafalgar Square. He was knighted in 1850.

commissioned to paint the Royal children. He is a lucky fellow,' wrote George in his diary, 'and deserves all his good fortune.'

He returned to Park Place Villas after his class: 'Back home to tea. Mother would scarcely speak a word. She had been sobbing with anger and vexation for some time when Mr Boone called. He endeavoured to comfort her – dear good man. But she would not [be comforted] and shortly after left the room. I told Mr B. how when we delivered an opinion which happened to be contrary to hers, she seemed to imagine that we did it purposely to oppose her. When Mr B. said "there are your children around you" – she rejoined "I am nothing to them".'

In the wake of her husband's death, the full forces of Mrs Boyce's caprice and fury were visited upon her children. Their focus now was Matthias and his proposed marriage to Lilly Ridley. Mrs Boyce was determined that this should not take place until Lilly was twenty-one, and she vowed that unless Matthias gave her his word she would do everything in her power to prevent it. Her tantrums were not new, but without their father to cushion the wilder blows her children were at a loss as to how to soothe her. The only consolation, George added, was that 'our dear Father is no longer the victim of those goading and exasperating and uncharitable moods. Mother went off to bed, refusing to take any supper or ought else. She seems not to repose the least confidence or trust in any of us.'

But for Henry, at least, things were going well. He wrote to George from Holme Pierrepont , also on the 28th, confirming his new commission:

> I can't resist writing to tell you of more good luck that has happened to me. The Queen has sent for me to go to Osborne and paint a miniature of the Princess Mary of Cambridge. I have had some little correspondence about it. The first notice was a letter, which Sir Edwin Landseer sent last Monday evening to Stratford Place[50] (not knowing I was absent) appointing me to call on him the following day at 2 o'clock, as he wished to speak to me about a small commission to be done at Windsor Castle etc, etc. On Wednesday I answered him from Vale Royal describing my plans, but promising to return on the shortest notice if it was advisable. Yesterday I had my answer from the Palace, written by a Miss Skerrett. Her Majesty desires me to go to Osborne as soon as my engagement here ceases and before I fulfil my Oxford engagement. So I shall return to London on Saturday evening next, and start for Osborne early on Monday morning. I

[50] Henry rooms were at 15 Stratford Place.

> expect it is to be a smallish miniature, and indeed I hope it may be, as the present commission is not so much to be considered as what it may bring afterwards, and my other engagements, which are just now rather numerous, will permit me to do better by a small than a large miniature.

Meanwhile Joanna was recording in her diary, in French, the altercation over Matthias and Lilly: '*Maman pleurant. George et moi calmes et froids.*'[51] Matthias's engagement was not the only potential flashpoint. Business and financial matters, requiring prompt attention, were made almost impossible by Mrs Boyce's refusal to relinquish control over her children's lives. On 29 November George wrote:

> Mother, having discovered that her wardrobe had been opened in her absence, began complaining to Matthias about it. Mat freely and quietly said that he had opened it, so that some silver articles therein, which it was imperative to value for the Legacy and Probate duties, might so be valued by Loft's brother, who was here with the scales for that purpose. This would not satisfy her, but she began accusing Mat of etc, etc, and that she was being treated in the most shameful and disrespectful way …
>
> I could bear it no longer, told her that I could not bear Matthias traduced without comment, and that I wished she would have some little trust and confidence in us and in our attachment and sincerity. At this she said I turned upon her, tramped her underfoot etc, and a great deal more that was not easy to bear even from Mother. Joanna came next for it – 'she had never since dear Father's death shown the slightest affection for her, had always sided against her'. Mat's goodness and calmness and tact at last brought her a bit round to him, but as I advanced and asked for a kiss as she was going to bed, she uttered some expression of loathing and rushed upstairs. I went to bed wishing myself dead, as how often have I not before.

By the following day all was sweetness and light. George attended a 'very delightful' evening at the Ridleys, where Lilly and Lizzie played part of the Pastoral Symphony and George himself rehearsed the bass part of 'Elijah'. On Boxing Day a month later, ever susceptible (he had already expressed a more than passing interest in Jeannie Naylor during his sojourn in Wales) yet wary

[51] 'Mother crying. George and I calm and cold.'

of commitment, he wrote: 'I could scarcely prevent showing some noticeable attention to Lizzie … she interests and draws me very much … but a host of conflicting feelings destroy all decided action in me, and I feel I shall be – what I am more than half already – a miserable old bachelor.'

❁

Throughout the early months of 1854 the Boyce family remained in a state of distress. Anne was married, Matthias working, and George, though he still slept at home most of the time, escaped during the day to a studio he had rented in Great Russell Street,[52] so Joanna bore the brunt of caring for her mother and her invalid brother. The children had always received generous allowances from their father, and, in accordance with the provisions of Mr Boyce's will, Matthias was able to arrange a distribution of funds which assured them a measure of financial independence. This doubtless fuelled their mother's fears, not only about her own financial security, but about losing control over her offspring.

It was another very hard winter. On 1 January Joanna wrote: 'I stayed at home because of my chilblains.' She and George joined a choral group which met at the Lunns'[53] house and included the Millais brothers, and on 3 January both she and George record attending a musical meeting where George 'joined the basses in Haydn's 3rd Mass Lachrimoso'. Joanna had a wretched evening – 'sang badly … I am so nervous, restrained and awkward' – but admitted to a 'funny and pleasant dream this morning about W'. Their cab horse fell down coming home: 'No harm done,' said George. By 4 January the snow was eight or nine inches deep. Bob swept the path round the back garden and Joanna ran round it to please him: 'Put me in a glow and did me good.' She passed the time sketching 'pencil feet' and finishing Bob's 'muffetees'.[54] Mrs Boyce celebrated the New Year by quarrelling with both her sister Mary and her daughter Anne.

George was still hopeful that he might this year merit admission to the Old Water-Colour Society, but was told by Francis Topham that his sketches, though finished in themselves, were 'without that amount of art which should constitute pictures'.

On 9 January, he invited Fred Warren and Henry to tea: 'The latter disgusted that the Queen, for whom he is painting the Princess Mary of

[52] His rooms were in the house of William Eavestaff, a pianoforte manufacturer, whom George later commissioned to make a piano for him.

[53] Possibly the home of Henry C. Lunn (1817–94), music critic and prophet of the English musical Renaissance. He advocated an English school of music and the creation of a 'grand National Opera'.

[54] 'Muffetees' – knitted woollen cuffs.

Cambridge for a Royal Collection, does not allow him a personal interview, but sends her messages second-hand by Miss Kennett.'

In fact Henry was granted an audience later that month and reported back to George that the Queen 'was gracious and complimentary, liking his miniature of the Princess much. The latter', Wells says, 'is a gleeful damsel, and retails to him with spirit and cleverness whole scenes from "Box and Cox"[55] and other farces.' (*Plate XVIII*)

Between the demands of her family and the good works expected of a Victorian woman (on 6 January she visited her model, 'poor little Sophie, took her some port wine, she looked very pale and weary. God help me to help her through Christ's sake and to his Glory'), Joanna was working industriously away on her Devon pictures: 'Painted out sky of Babbacombe landscape and touched little painting of lady, which I have given to Aunt Mary.'

But her main concern was the health of their fragile brother, Bob. The practice of mesmerism had become widespread by the 1850s and most Victorians, whatever their social status, had experienced this strange phenomenon, whether as entertainment, therapy or in the form of scientific demonstrations. Charles Dickens, George Eliot and William Gladstone had all attended such demonstrations, and dramatic experiments were performed at Prince Albert's birthday party in 1849. Also known as 'animal magnetism', it involved inducing a state of trance in the subject, usually through a combination of eye contact and sweeping movements of the hands very close to, but not touching, the surface of the skin.

At a time when the diagnosis of illness was random, the line between physical and psychological states blurred, and many of the available cures hazardous and uncertain, there were plenty who believed mesmerism to have miraculous powers. Harriet Martineau was one of them, and her experiences are a good example of contemporary attitudes. The social and political reformer had fallen seriously ill in Europe in 1839, when she was diagnosed with 'a prolapsed uterus and polypous tumours' (probably an ovarian cyst). For five years she resisted mesmerism, partly because she thought it right to 'wear out all other means first' and partly because she was surrounded by people who regarded it as 'a delusion or an imposture'. She turned to it eventually because she was increasingly nervous about 'her miserable dependence on opiates' and within months her health improved until, gradually, she was able to wean herself off all medicines.[56]

55 'Box and Cox'. A one-act farce by John Maddison Morton, based on a French original. It was first performed in England at the Lyceum Theatre in London on 1 November 1847, and became extremely popular.

56 Harriet Martineau (1802–76) described her experiences in *Life in the Sickroom* (1844) and *Letters on Mesmerism* (1845).

One of the foremost practitioners of therapeutic mesmerism was Dr John Elliotson. A charismatic man, he attracted his fair share of controversy, resigning from University College Hospital in 1838 and going on to found his own mesmeric hospital in 1849. He was something of a celebrity, featuring by name in Wilkie Collins's novel *The Moonstone* and adding scientific lustre to the fashionable passions for table-turning and spirit-rapping. It was to Dr Elliotson that Joanna now turned in search of a 'cure' for Bob, who was physically enfeebled, probably epileptic, and unable to take proper rest.

Dr Elliotson did not undertake the task himself, but taught Joanna the necessary passes. While this meant that treatment could be carried out at any hour of the day and night, it begged the question of how much skill was actually involved. It was, however, normal practice. Harriet Martineau's mesmerist didn't attempt to teach her maid how to do it – the maid simply copied the passes she saw him make.

Once again Joanna, over-dutiful, shouldered the family burden. On 12 January she wrote in her diary: 'Mesmerised Bob for the 1st time. He did not go to sleep, but felt drowsy towards the end of the half hour. We passed it in perfect stillness. He takes his iron medicine – has his back rubbed downwards for half an hour and has the wet sheet bath of a morning. God bless the means we are taking for his good.'

She kept it up throughout January. She was not expecting a quick cure, but as a treatment it proved incredibly demanding. Her diary records a litany of low spirits and exhaustion: 'Mesmerised Bob. Slight drowsiness about the middle of the half hour – no sleep'; 'Mesmerised Bob, very tired'; 'Wretched night … I mesmerised Bob – 4th time. He went off to sleep once or twice and woke again. Could not tell whether it was the mesmerism or not.' And on 18 January: 'Ma changed the time for the mesmerism to half past 10, in every way inconvenient to me, but as I have made up my mind not to consider myself, I was wrong to repine for an instant. Still, I cannot help thinking how worthlessly my time is passing – how grieved my poor father would have been. Bob dozing part of the time, but a constant itching prevented him going off.'

Even though she was sharing some of the mesmerising with Alice, their maid, she was completely worn out. It was a relief to begin painting and drawing again, though she was, as usual, dissatisfied with everything. 'Lizzie Ridley sat – large chalk sketch – unsuccessful'; 'Maria – like, but badly painted – bad in colour.'

By 11 February she and her mother had begun to quarrel about Bob's treatment: 'Ma, I find, wavering again over Bob and Dr Elliotson. She says she has <u>no faith</u> in mesmerism and will, I fear, give it up without a fair trial. I believe mesmerism to be the only chance of curing Bob's mental disease, but I cannot help thinking he ought to have a strong man and good mesmeriser instead of myself and Alice.' Convinced though she was that it was 'God in his goodness who first caused me to think of mesmerism for Bob', she was not convinced that she and Alice were the best instruments of the divine will.

George, mercifully removed from the everyday anxieties of life at Park Place Villas, concentrated once again on the Old Water-Colour Society, submitting seven drawings and studies to support his application for Associate Membership. On 8 February he went with Topham to the Graphic Society, where Millais's 'Ophelia' was exhibited, along with 'several beautiful drawings by Girtin and Turner'. He was gratified to be asked by Henry Wallis (painter of 'The Death of Chatterton') the price of his 'Westminster Abbey' (fifteen guineas) and his address: '1st nibble.' On the 9th, he attended 'a grand Soirée at Luxmoor's – a very pretty girl.' On the 13th he was not unduly put out to learn that not one of the thirteen candidates for the OWCS had been elected. Matthias had told him that his inheritance would amount to £4,200 – or 'about £200 p.a.' – thus sealing his financial independence – and he was already planning a trip to Venice.

Bob's suffering, on the other hand, seemed never-ending. He had severe neuralgic pains in his back and legs, and was getting very little sleep. Dr Elliotson called several times, and Maria Moore was co-opted to sit with him from time to time. Joanna succeeded in 'drawing the pain' from him, but as she became more fatigued her efforts became correspondingly less effective.

It seemed that everyone's health was under siege. On 17 February Joanna recorded: 'Maria Moore ill with cold – unable to come. Ma's cold bad. My head bad – had to go to bed with splitting headache. Bob not up.' On the 18th: 'George bad cold' – so even he was not wholly immune to the family problems – 'Dr Elliotson called unasked and unpaid, very kind. My head bad again – Bob in bed.'

Somehow she continued to work – now on several portraits at the same time. On 22 February 'George gave me his first sitting. Made only a sketch in charcoal on paper about ¼ of an hour – a good deal like him.' On the 24th she worked on Maria Moore's portrait and 'sketched George's head on to canvas without him'. On the 27th, 'Lizzie Ridley sat to me, made her portrait worse.' On 2 March, she attended the Government School of Design[57] for women – valuing the 'severe and thorough grounding' it offered. On the 3rd, 'Maria sat to me – improved her.'

The prospect of war with Russia had been in the air since the Russian navy had destroyed the Ottoman Turkish fleet in the Black Sea the previous November. In January 1854, the British and French fleets entered the Black Sea to prevent the Russians invading Turkey and the Crimean War began. Henry, always more politically engaged than George, 'had now got a military heat on –

[57] A separate Female School of Art had been established in 1853.

painting some people in the military department'. On 20 February the two of them witnessed 'a battalion of the Grenadier Guards fully equipped for active service inspected by Prince Albert. They start for the Russian Campaign tomorrow'.

While Joanna held the fort at Park Place Villas, George whiled away the next three months on his own work. He was in constant touch with other Pre-Raphaelites, enjoying a burgeoning friendship with Dante Gabriel Rossetti, and meeting Ruskin for the first time. On 2 March he took his drawing of Anstis Cove to the Portland Gallery, 'priced at £10'. He attended Clipstone Street regularly for the weekly drawing sessions. The gatherings were as important for the talk as for the drawing. On 3 March he wrote: 'Got so interested in a warm discussion on Pre-Raffaelitism, Ruskinism etc that I quite forgot the sketching.'

On the 5th he went 'by appointment' to visit Henry at Stanhope Terrace and was introduced to his mother and six sisters – 'Two (I think Maria and Sarah) pretty and intelligent.' They went on to visit Tom Seddon's father for news of Tom – 'last heard of in Cairo' – and eventually to Park Place Villas for tea:

> On the way home Wells told me of a sort of rupture between himself, Armstead and Smallfield,[58] about an understanding that Smallfield should help him with his miniatures 3 days a week for ½ guinea. They thought he had given him up, which was not the case. Wells tea'd with us and admired Joanna's portraits of Lizzie Ridley and Maria Moore. In the evening Mother entered upon Miss ------'s attractions and desirability as a wife for me – the desire that she and Uncle and Aunt Robert felt that it should be brought about. Told Mother that I knew that her and their wishes were entirely for my welfare but that I had no sympathy or particular partiality for Miss ------ and that I did not intend to think of marriage for 2 or 3 years at least – and that Miss ------'s large fortune was not the least allurement to me – thought her a pleasant, kind and amiable girl and nothing more.

Henry's quarrel with Smallfield and the sculptor Henry Armstead rumbled on for some time. Henry felt that his reputation had been impugned, by Armstead in particular, and was anxious that his more excessive accusations

[58] Frederick Smallfield (1829–1915). A painter of genre scenes in oil and water-colour, much influenced by the PRBs.

should be publicly withdrawn. George called on him to discuss matters further on 21 March, before going on to visit the poet William Allingham[59] and finding him 'in complete *déshabille*'. 'He showed me a very curious and interesting series of plates by the "Sublime Madman" Blake, illustrating the Book of Job.'

George had also been planning to exchange drawings with Rossetti. On 13 March he wrote:

> Found him at home but unwell; he sleeps little at nights. A young man of the name of Hughes[60] was painting a picture of Orlando inscribing his mistress's name on a tree. Parts nicely painted. Rossetti showed me an exquisite drawing of his from the Vita Nuova, Dante receiving visitors on the anniversary of Beatrice's death. He showed me too a little unfinished drawing of Dante, Beatrice, and two others, in Paradise, which he promised to finish for me, as I liked it, and would like some work in exchange. (*Plate XV*)

Later Rossetti, who was being pursued by debt collectors, told George that the 'duns' had reminded him that he could not do anything in the way of exchanging drawings, but that he could let George 'have it in the way of business, if I liked it'. George duly visited Rossetti's studio on 27 March, where he was at work on a portrait of Allingham: 'He showed me the drawing I saw a week or two ago – He had worked on it a bit – told him I should still much like to have it and he agreed – would want £15 or guineas.' The day before George had met Millais at church and as they were walking home Millais invited him to join a 'sketching club he was setting on foot … on my saying I should be too great a muff, he said "No", and mentioned with commendation my two drawings at the Portland.'

Joanna worked on her various portraits all through March. They were of George, Mrs Campbell ('painted purple drapery'), Lizzie Ridley ('painted on throat') and Byron – probably a model of that name –'dressed in a Saxon head-dress and painted it loosely in – wonderful improvement'. She was under pressure to send her portrait of Lizzie to the Royal Academy. On 26 March she wrote: 'Wells called to see my painting of Lizzie. Very kind in telling me what it wanted. Ma wishes me very kindly to send Lizzie to the Exhibition. I would give

59 William Allingham (1824–89). Irish poet and man of letters. A close friend of Dante Gabriel Rossetti and something of a literary lion-hunter. His diaries are crammed with wonderful anecdotes about Browning, Carlyle and Tennyson, all of whom he knew.

60 Arthur Hughes (1832–1915). Discovered the PRB through their magazine, the *Germ*, and became an ardent acolyte of Rossetti. Dante Gabriel's brother William described him thus: 'If I had to pick out from my once numerous acquaintances of the male sex the sweetest and most ingenuous nature of all … I should probably find myself bound to select Mr Hughes' (*Some Reminiscences*, p.147).

a great deal not to send it so soon after dear Pa's death. I cannot bear the idea, but George and Wells urge it too and I fear I must yield.'

Joanna had also been taking singing lessons, but the strain on her voice was too great, and she was obliged to give them up, at least until the summer. Hennie Moore, Maria's sister, had become a particular friend and evidently gave considerable comfort during this time. 'She sees beneath the surface and sympathises with my hidden feelings and there are few others who know I feel more than I show … how I wish dear Ma would not urge me to send Lizzie to the Academy.'

By 3 April she was struggling: 'Painted all day, but could not finish it. Ma dreadfully vexed.' And on the 4th: 'Ma very angry. I attempted to tell her I was sorry but she would not hear a word.' In the circumstances it must have been hard to accompany George and Matthias to see Henry's pictures (he was sending five miniatures to the Royal Academy – the one of Mrs Cumming,[61] according to George, 'by far the most interesting and finest thing he had yet done') and be lectured by him for failing to submit a picture herself. Perhaps it was a satisfaction to visit the Portland Gallery and find 'Miss Howitt's[62] pictures not at all marvellous – very good in feeling – portraits well chosen – painting bad in colour and surface'. On 26 April, following a fierce altercation with her mother in the presence of Spencer Hall, Joanna wrote in her diary: 'I have some thought of giving up painting altogether, my painting room and all. I have no comfort at all in it now. Nothing gave dear Papa more pleasure than for me to work at it, and nothing seems to annoy Mamma so much. I have been reading Anna Mary Howitt's *Art-Student in Munich*. I feel confident, were I placed as she has been, and blessed with sound health and God's blessing, I could do greater things in the painting way than she has, but I feel it is my plain duty to give up all hope of improvement in painting, rather than in any way neglect Mamma. I have a difficult path to steer, but God will lead me.'

Yet just when she must have given up hope, the following day brought an improvement in the family weather: 'Mamma went to Corinth Villa [Anne and Mordan's house]. When she came back, told me that Wells had spoken of my painting to Anne in a way that has revived hope in me. It seems to have made dear Ma more anxious for my improvement. She would consent even to my going to Munich or Düsseldorf with a fit companion. She is very kind – but I must not be

61 Mrs Cumming was the wife of Captain Arthur Cumming, commander of HMS Glatton, an ironclad floating battery, moored at Sheerness, which Henry later visited.

62 Anna Mary Howitt (1824–84). With Barbara Leigh Smith, one of the foremost women artists of the period. Her parents were literary radicals who went to Germany so that their daughter would benefit from a more enlightened education. Later in the year she and Joanna visited each other.

selfish and I fear there is little chance of my going, all things considered. Patient continuance in well doing is what I want – indeed patience of all kinds.'

Joanna's frustration with her progress highlights the obstacles in her path. A tough perfectionist, she was ravenous for experience, criticism and education. Had she been a man she could have moved easily from private art school to free tuition at the Royal Academy; as a woman she would have to rely on private tuition, ladies' classes and foreign study. George's experience could not have been more different.

On 8 April Millais had called on George in Great Russell Street: 'He thought I painted a good deal like old Hunt – wish I had a little of his genius! He wants to finish his picture of Ruskin (looking on falling water) from some spot nearer than the Highlands. I recommended him the neighbourhood of Capel Curig.'

Rossetti also called, spending seven hours working 'on the old drawing I have of his, in which I cut out the head of the dancing boy and inserted a fresh piece of paper at the back. He improved it much in parts – especially the heads, but left it unfinished.' This was the 'To Caper Nimbly' water-colour that George had bought from Rossetti in 1849. '[Rossetti] said he thought the most beautiful combination of colour in a picture to be green, blue, and carmine – all inclining to purple, but the general tone of the picture to incline to yellow. An opal I showed him elicited this.' They walked together back to Rossetti's studio at Blackfriars Bridge where he gave George two pen and ink sketches – 'one of his first idea of the drawing "to caper nimbly in a lady's chamber", the other a siren followed by 2 men in a boat'.

On 21 April, Ruskin and his father visited:

> They admired Rossetti's drawings much, especially the Dante and Beatrice one. They praised also the Welsh sunset study I have promised to Dante Rossetti, and the study of the twisted birch tree … On my expressing my liking for after sunset and twilight effects, [Ruskin] said I must not be led away by them, as on account of the little light requisite in them, they were more easy of realisation than sunlight effects. He was very pleasant and friendly and encouraging in manner, and showed no conceit, grandeur nor patronising mien. A most delightful feeling seemed to exist between him and his father.

Joanna did not exhibit at the Royal Academy that year. She visited it on 1 May with George: 'Frith came up – shook hands with me – said he was sorry I had not sent to the Royal Academy – "and I daresay you think there are a great many worse pictures here." "Yes," I said and we parted. Holman Hunt's pictures of 1. "Christ" and 2. "The Awakened Conscience" wonderfully fine.'

A week later, George 'heard the painful intelligence that Mrs Ruskin was about suing Mr R. for divorce or separation'. The Ruskin marriage had long been the subject of intense speculation. Having married Effie Gray in 1848, Ruskin made her so desperately unhappy that, in April 1854, she left him. Millais had, by this time, fallen deeply in love with her and his portrait of Ruskin languished incomplete.[63] The scandal was immense. Millais wrote to Hunt to say that the only topics of conversation in London society were the war in the Crimea and the Ruskin marriage, eventually annulled on the grounds of Ruskin's 'incurable impotency'. The exact reason may never be clear (Effie told her parents that he had found her 'person' repugnant) but even after her marriage to Millais the saga continued to give rise to comment, and the taking of sides, among their contemporaries.

❖

All three – Joanna, George and Henry – managed to escape abroad before the end of the year. George was the first to go. On 6 June, only too aware of the great loss the family had incurred since he last set out on his travels, George departed for Venice. When he bade his mother and Joanna goodbye, 'it seemed as if I were deserting them.' Before he started, he had written to Ruskin, his influential new acquaintance, and on 14 June Ruskin replied from Vevey, in Switzerland. It was a generous letter to an aspiring young artist.

> My dear Sir
>
> Owing to my absence from England, I most unfortunately did not receive your letter till it was too late to answer it, and I do not know if this note will reach you in Venice, but it must take its chance.
>
> I am vexed at thinking that I have perhaps been partly instrumental in leading you into the expense and trouble of a long journey, when there was quite enough material to employ you delightfully nearer home. But as you <u>are</u> at Venice, I congratulate myself, in the hope of at last seeing a piece of St Marks done as it ought to be: It cannot but be quite supererogatory to point out to you the superior interest of St Marks to all else in the city. It answers

63 In the event Millais returned to Scotland in June and the portrait was completed by the end of the year. *Pace* George's suggestion, Ruskin insisted that Millais return to Scotland to complete the picture. The rocks, he said were of 'a different strata'.

precisely to your wishes, as expressed in your note, 'near subject – good architecture – colour – & light & shade'. I think the more you study it, the more you will enjoy it. I mean especially the outside, the inside having often been tolerably drawn – but the outside never yet as it ought to be especially the eight lateral open porticos, and the beautiful northern door, on the dark side, in the piazzetta de' Leoni. I do not know exactly how far, at first sight, you may be able, for yourself, to distinguish what is really best worth your while. For my own part, it always takes me a week or two before I find out the best things, and unless you have been accustomed to the study of architecture, you may be so dazzled by the splendour of effect in Venice, as not to estimate justly the value of Verona.

But I should strongly recommend you, after you have done with St Marks, to quit the Venetian canals, and to make a most careful study of the Porch of the Duomo of Verona, which in its Gryphon sculpture, is the finest thing I know in North Italy – while of course – the little group of the Scala monuments is altogether unrivalled in the world for sweet colour & light and shade … Venice will retain some of her canal effects for twenty years yet, but the Scala monuments may be destroyed in a fortnight…

Please send me a line directed Poste Restante – Lucerne, Suisse, to say if you have got this – and if I may write still to Venice – as I want to say more.

George's answer has not survived, but his diary shows the extent to which he followed Ruskin's recommendations. The sensuous beauty of Venice intoxicated him. There was a full moon when he arrived and he would 'float in a gondola to and fro the Grand Canal in a dream of delight'. He spent his mornings labouring on one subject, his afternoons on another, conscientiously recording every stone and leaf in obedience to Ruskinian precepts, while letting off steam by producing beautiful spontaneous sketches and what he referred to as little moonlight 'blots'.

In the meantime he was not short of advice. Henry also wrote to him, on 16 July, and after congratulating himself on introducing Joanna to his friends the Miss Farwells – 'I begin to understand the relish which match-makers enjoy in their craft' – he opined:

I am rather surprised by your letter that you would not have made a painting of San Marco unless Ruskin had prompted you. For my part

I found the fascination so strong that I thought nothing would please me more than being able to paint constantly both the interior and the exterior. I certainly hope you will make at least one drawing of the interior and that you will do it on a large-sized paper ...

Do you not think some of the boatmen with their brown faces and thick glossy hair fine subjects for painting? I'm glad you appreciate the Colleoni[64] but how is it that you don't place the Bellini first amongst the pictures of Venice?

I quite understand your anxiety to do your best at Venice before you leave it, but I also think that you have much sketching time between now and the beginning of October, and besides it is not requisite to have six drawings to show the Old WC people. Make two or three large drawings, real subjects and not nooks, and those and a folio of sketches ought to get your election ... I shall grumble if you do not bring back some moonlights from Venice. (*Plate XVI*)

In a rather cross letter to Joanna, dated 24 July, George threatened Henry with a rancorous rejoinder – probably on account of his Bellini comment – before grumbling: 'I believe Byron spoke of the good looks of Venetian women. Where that's gone to is another mystery. They are for the most part tight-laced, unintellectual looking beings, and in the morning slovenly and I am told dirty, and certainly so in many of their habits. I don't believe at any rate that the Brides of Venice[65] would have ever been rescued if they had nothing more to boast of than their living representatives.'

He had changed his lodgings three times and had ended up taking, for a month, 'a small room (being in the roof, rather warm just at present) on the Riva degli Schiavoni and close to the Ducal Palace'. Venice, he said, was 'quite the noisiest place I've been in. The people are incessantly overcharging, cheating, squabbling; shrieking and bargaining, and are in fact about the most degenerate race I've come across. The bells of the hundred churches seem to be ever making as much and as early noise as they possibly can, and bad musicians haunt the place at even. Opera airs are violently performed on bad instruments in many of the churches.'

Ruskin's second letter, begun on 28 June but not posted until 20 July, had not reached him at this point. It came on the 25th while George was still in the throes of composing his complaints to his sister. He had evidently pleased

64 Henry regarded the vigour of this equestrian statue as the epitome of 'pluck'.

65 'The Brides of Venice', an opera by Julius Benedict, was first produced at Drury Lane Theatre in 1844 and inspired a melodramatic response from a number of artists and engravers.

Ruskin with his enthusiasm both for the Alps – 'no one is ever enthusiastic enough' – and for St Mark's, about which Ruskin wrote:

> I believe, on the whole, the outside is the finer study – the inside is too Rembrandtesque – too much dependent on flashing of gold out of gloom – which is always effective – but comparatively vulgar ... What do you mean by the marbles losing colour by Efflorescence? They are as far as I remember – quite smooth & perfect – except some of the red marble – which crumbles, but into a more vivid red ... Besides – there is one point, as far as I know, never drawn – & to be done quietly – if you make friends with the old porter of the ducal palace, and get into the upper loggia at the corner. St Mark's portico comes in somehow so[66] – with the top of the broken square capital of the St Jean d'Acre pillar underneath – & St Mark's place behind most beautifully.
>
> – But it would take a horrible time ...
>
> You really must allow some time for Verona in returning.

Nevertheless he warned against too much sight-seeing: 'Artists ruin themselves by confusing impressions of different characters. People never consider that there is such a thing as mental as well as physical indigestion, and everybody I see is half dead of it.' On recommending that George leave himself time to make a drawing of Rouen Cathedral (he was concerned about the parlous state of northern architecture), Ruskin said it could be digested 'as cheese after dinner'.

George agreed wholeheartedly. It is tempting to imagine him a solitary figure, but in fact Venice was full of visitors and brother artists. They included a young student from the Wyatt & Brandon office named Cutler, who arrived on 4 August and stuck to George like a leech for the next five weeks, distracting him while he worked and even reading aloud to him while he struggled with his painting. On 12 September, George made the following exasperated entry in his diary:

> Cutler declares he has no pleasure in travelling, wishes he could return to England with a good grace – but his tour is considered to be 'professional' and he must visit many of the principal towns of Italy. He has already been 6 or 7 months from England and has not made a single sketch – considers Titian, Tintoret and Raffaele etc bad painters – prides himself on being the second in London to wear ½-round handkerchiefs and the first in Russell Street to wear high collars and in

66 At this point Ruskin inserts a small sketch

> paying no attention or respect to the opinions of the greatest authors, painters or critics – has perfect faith in his own judgment and reads nothing but novels ... Bid him goodbye, recommending him to do some little sketching before returning to England.

In the meantime, as he told Joanna, he struggled to make up his mind about Venetian painting: 'The picture I fancy I should most have liked to steal of those I've yet seen was a John Bellini at the church of the Redentore. The head of St John was to be doted on to madness; such a union of tenderness, thoughtfulness and beauty I couldn't have conceived. Leonardo's head of Christ in its present state did not seem to me at all comparable to it.'

He was particularly struck by the fact that three of Venice's favourite painters – Basaiti, Vivarini[67] and Cima da Conegliano – made no use of 'bright or even subdued sunlight effect in any of their works – a curious circumstance when the beauty and striking nature of these effects impresses every Venetian traveller'.

The collector in him had been dealt a blow – 'I can't tell you how annoyed I was to find this morning that a piece of old tapestry of fine Venetian colour I had my eye upon, had just been sold' – and he was missing Wales: 'I even dare confess that here in Venice I often long for the mountain valley, its torrents, its freshness of foliage and sublime forms. Venice feels very much like a vision, which is ever endeavouring to enchant and enslave you with its beauty. Its romance is sometimes at the full, sometimes on the wane, as I believe all must find who remain long in it.'

❁

Though the subject of mesmerism no longer figured in her diaries and letters, Joanna's life was still dominated by Bob's ill health. In mid-May Mrs Boyce took him to Brighton to consult 'Dr' Harrap and try the strengthening effect of sea air, and then, back in London, to consult another orthopaedic surgeon, Mr Adams. At the end of July Joanna went alone to stay with her aunt and uncle in Shropshire, and on 5 August, 'in a most uncomfortable state of catarrh', wrote to George to bring him up to date.

After upbraiding him for denying them an address to write to, she went on: 'And now I will tell you how it is I am at Ashford without Mamma, which is I assure you a great disappointment to me.' Mr Adams, she said, had come to the

[67] There were three Vivarini – Antonio, Bartolomeo and Alvise – but George does not say which artist he is referring to.

conclusion that there was 'contraction of the muscles and tendons, and that he could improve [Bob's] running and jumping considerably by dividing the two tendons Achilles and by stretching them as they rejoined and so increase their length as much as required'. Having assured them that he performed such operations every day, Mrs Boyce, Joanna and the Mordans decided that it was worth trying:

'One leg was performed on, Mordan and I were present, it was over in a minute and was almost painless – not one drop of blood fell from the tiny incision made by the knife. The other leg will probably be done in a few days – of course he is obliged to keep his legs up and will for some weeks, but he is in good health and spirits. This explains why Mamma is still in London, as of course it was requisite for one of us to be with him, and she insisted on my coming ... but in a short time I hope she will join me bringing Bob with her.'

In the event Bob's lengthy recuperation made this impossible. The second Achilles tendon was operated on, and Joanna later reported him 'quite strong on his legs again', but there was a general feeling that it had not been a success. 'All seems so vague and uncertain,' she wrote. She was unsure whether she would be able to visit the Naylors in Wales, or whether the planned tour to Italy with the Mordans would take place. She told him a little more about her new friends, the Farwell sisters, to whom she had been introduced by Henry: 'They are very nice girls and Bertha, the one I drew, was a very congenial companion. Mrs Wade Browne, the grandmamma, is a charming old lady and Miss Belfield, an old friend, a spinster of a "certain age", one of the most cheerful, simple and intelligent women I have ever had the good fortune to meet.' She had also met their close family friend, John Douglas Cook,[68] the exuberant editor of the *Morning Chronicle*, and, later, of the influential *Saturday Review,* who had interested himself in Bertha's artistic education. She was struck by the kindness and attention Cook paid to 'Berty' or 'Piggy', as he called her, while entirely neglecting her sister, Emma. 'Their father', she wrote, 'shows even more partiality – it is a matter of surprise to me that her temper and disposition are not ruined.'

She had seen the King of Portugal and his brother, the Duke of Oporto, at the opera. 'Mordan would insist on taking a box for us twice to see [Giulia] Grisi in *Lucrezia Borgia* and in *Norma*, although the music of the latter opera is poor after Meyerbeer's and Mozart's, still I enjoyed it exceedingly. I never knew before what Grisi was.' Though her trip to Italy was uncertain, she had not entirely lost hope of 'calling to you out of a gondola some

68 John Douglas Cook (1808?–68). He became founding editor of the *Saturday Review* in November 1855, and Joanna contributed reviews to some of the early issues of the magazine.

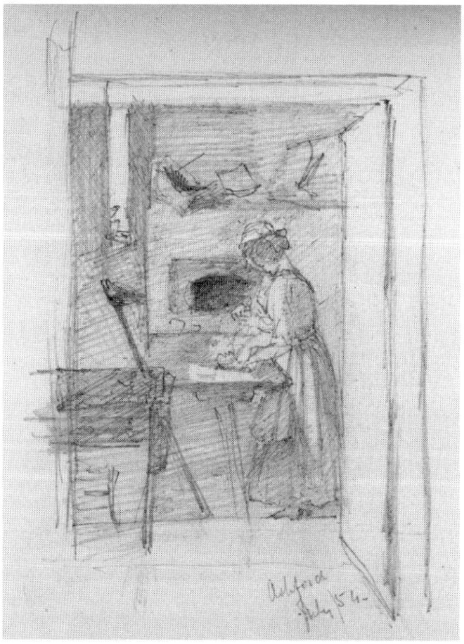

Ashford - interior

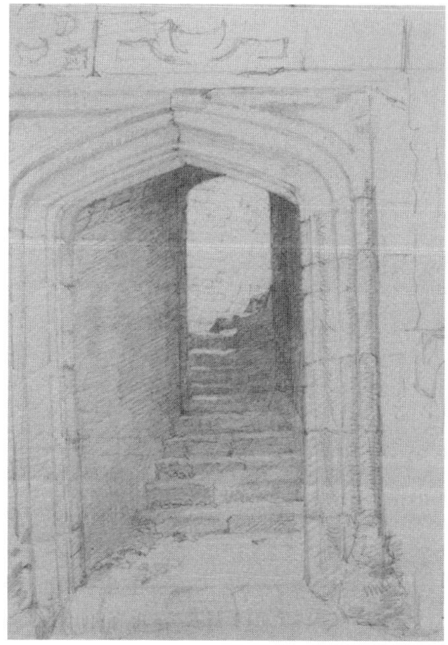

Ludlow Castle

Both the above drawings were made by Joanna during a visit to her aunt and uncle at Ashford Bowdler in the summer of 1854.

morning', and she added: 'What conflicting notions we do get of Venice – you describe it as noisy – quietness I had always imagined one of its characteristics owing to the mode of transit.'

George was still in Venice on 10 September when Henry wrote to him announcing his own travel plans. He was at Windermere at the time, completing miniatures of Francis Dukinfield Astley, his wife Constance[69] and their three children, but hoped to leave for Italy before the end of the month in the company of his friend Clement Folkard (the Folkards were relations of the Boyces). The plan was to join the Farwells, their grandmother and John Cook in Florence and Rome.

By 7 October Henry had reached Nice and was writing stoutly to George: 'Our letters crossed, but as I am *en voyage* I want another to reach you before you leave Venice ... I think you have been working yourself into a very fighting-cock state of mind, for you show fight in so many matters. You think the interior of San Marco is not to be painted without gum and body colour – and as you are not

[69] The Astleys became close friends. Their house in the Lake District, situated at the southern end of Windermere, was called Fellfoot, and they owned another in Scotland, Arisaig, which Henry visited on several occasions.

au fait in the use of those ingredients you must relinquish the subject altho' you appear to like it. In answer to this it appears to me that if gum and body colour are sometimes so indispensable, it is nearly time you chose some subject which would oblige you to practise with them.'

He and Folkard then travelled to Genoa, where on 11 October, Henry attended mass at the Church of Sta Maria de Carignano, 'given in thankfulness of the passing of the cholera ... Everything is sad at Genoa – they have lost 5,000 inhabitants and 40,000 have quitted it in fear.' They went swiftly on to Pisa – a journey that included a two-day excursion over the Apennines in a very inferior diligence. Henry's seat was on the outside and he was severely chilled. In spite of hot drinks and a hot footbath, he developed a fever and it was not until 17 October that he was fit to proceed to Florence. He was still hoping that George would join him – 'I had written a letter of persuasion from Nice' – but a reply awaited him saying that George would be unable to do so: 'He gives very good reasons for not coming. I should have liked very much to have gone over Florence with him.' In fact, *pace* George's initial views on Venetian women, his lingering in Venice had everything to do with a beautiful girl in a house in San Benedetto whom he had visited on 16 October: 'She left me suddenly on hearing a bell – rather suspicious.'

Suspicious it may have been, but on the 17th, George went to the police to get a passport for a further fortnight's stay in Venice and then returned to the house: 'Saw the pretty girl – made a sketch of her whilst at her needlework – Teresina Vani – made a couple of profiles of T, as I found her eyes too disturbing in front.'

On the 22nd he wrote: 'To Campo S. Ben. – no Teresina. A game going on. One of the party a woman – What were my intentions? etc, etc.' She was absent again on the 25th. On the 26th: 'Bought a little gold cross for Teresina – rushed to the Campo san Benedetto and left it at her house with my love. Mouthful of grub – then to lodging – took *barca* to station with Aitchison. Arrived at Verona at 9 pm.'

There he remained from 26 October until 14 November, where he produced, in obedience to Ruskin, a superb early morning painting of the 'Tomb of Mastino II della Scala'.

❁

Finally Joanna was able to go abroad, though not to Italy. This must have been a disappointment to Henry: there are several hints that he had hoped his party and that of the Mordans might coincide in Rome, where he would be able to introduce

Joanna to its artistic treasures. But Mordan could not be spared from his business for more than a month, so he, Anne and Joanna contented themselves with a month's tour of Belgium, Holland and Germany instead. It appears that Joanna was able to travel on Mordan's passport. They left on 9 September and Joanna kept a cheerfully factual diary of their doings.

The crossing from Dover was a rough one; Joanna was seasick and Anne sprained her ankle, so was unable to join Joanna and Mordan as they explored Bruges – 'into a Church in the twilight – many figures in long black cloaks kneeling in silence – on for a walk by canals and mills'. The next day they all visited the Church of Nôtre Dame to see the tombs of Charles the Bold and Mary of Burgundy, and then to the hospital of St John: 'pictures by Memling exquisite – especially the presentation in the Temple, being one wing of an altar piece – wonderfully simple and grand – drapery fine … Thence to the Academy of Painting – John van Eyck's portrait of his wife – very fine … dinner at table d'hôte.'

They travelled to Antwerp via Ghent, and so to Rotterdam and the Hague. Joanna summed up her impressions in a letter to her 'darling Mammy', dated 18 September:

> We left Rotterdam and reached here last night. Rotterdam though not exactly picturesque is curious – a network of canals, bridges and houses. We went into the Cathedral yesterday during a service, an immense congregation seemed nearly to fill it. After listening some minutes to the odd nasal tones of the emphatic Dutch preacher, we were delighted by the splendid organ breaking in with the symphony of a hymn. Then there rose steadily and in unison the voices of more than a thousand human beings, the music very simple and grand. I have never heard anything so impressive in sacred music. It seemed to me that the whole world should thus join in praise to God.
>
> *19 September:* We are here settled in the Hôtel Bellevue, a comfortable and beautifully situated house, which last qualification surprised me, Bellevues generally are the ugliest places for miles around … Yesterday this pretty town was very gay as the King, who holds his court here, went to open Parliament in state. We saw him exceedingly well in his state carriage drawn by 8 English grey horses with scarlet trappings. The whole affair was very gay thanks to the sun and the military, but some of the carriages looked like invalided [*sic*] flies with omnibus horses. The people in Rotterdam were all

pale, fishy, ugly – here they are much healthier in appearance. The ordinary costume of the peasant in Holland is neither picturesque nor striking – in Belgium it was far otherwise; every time I went out I spied something fresh and picturesque. Antwerp especially I was delighted with. It was one feast of Rubens, Vandycks, splendid Churches, picturesque streets and market places filled with groups I longed to calotype. As for sketching, except from memory, it is out of the question. Once in the market place in Bruges I and Mordan seated ourselves in chairs lent us by a fruit seller, but a crowd soon collected and I started off in a rage. At two or three hotels Mordan has very kindly tried to get the girls in costume to sit, but has found it impossible, the parents, knowing that those who sit to artists are generally bad characters, will not allow them to earn money in this way.

The following day – the anniversary of her father's death – she added this yearning and sorrowful paragraph, before sending her letter home: 'Oh dear Mammy, God grant we may meet him who we lost this day last year again in Heaven. Neither time nor place can banish him from my constant remembrance, and I know too well where your thoughts must be to fear I am bringing a painful subject to your mind … I feel more and more how great your loss is.'

The children's loss was also great. George, away from home, was sunk in gloom – 'Bitter thoughts crowd upon me … I rarely think on God. Where all this will end, I know not – certain it is that my present life is a most blighted one' – while Matthias, who was fretted constantly by their mother on the subject of the business, was quite ground down. Moreover he was anxious to marry Lilly Ridley 'in about a year's time … I know Mamma will object but I have determined to get her consent.'

Away from it all, at least for a while, Joanna and the Mordans set themselves a punishing schedule of sight-seeing and gallery visits. At the Hague they saw Rembrandt's 'Bathsheba' in the Steingratz collection, then, at the palace of the late king William II, his 'magnificent collection', including fifty Memlings and sketches by Raphael and Michelangelo. 'When he died, leaving no Will, the pictures were put up to public auction and neither the King nor the people had the spirit to buy them, so by far the great part is gone.'

They left the Hague on the 21st and travelled by rail to Amsterdam, where Joanna 'was nearly sick with the stenches from the canals'. Following an orgy of Rubenses, Van der Helsts, Rembrandts and Gerrit Dous, she visited the Palace – 'up to the top of the tower – interesting view – the chimes played while we were up there' – and after dinner 'to fair – most picturesque and interesting – women sitting baking tiny pancakes on tin pans.'

On 24 September they moved on by carriage and rail to Hanover ('two red whiskered bearded guards – had meat tea – very nice') and thence to Düsseldorf and Cologne. Their days were spent walking, visiting collections of pictures, trying out their German and recording impressions of hotels and churches: 'To St Ursula – the Church chock full of bones – the tomb of the saint a recumbent marble figure – beautiful. Saw many relics – some thorns from the Crown of the Saviour etc, etc – one, the pots containing wine at the feast at Cana and the priest professing to believe in its identity tumbled it about as if it were a saucepan. These things pain me inexpressibly. The lies and humbug of these hypocritical priests.'

On 1 October they caught the train to Aix-la-Chapelle, and on to Brussels on the 2nd, where their stay was dominated by the fate of Sebastopol. The siege of the city had only just begun and would last for a year, but at this point – as evidenced by the entries in Joanna's diary – news of its capture was expected daily. Finally, on 5 October they started home:

> At 3 o'clock we left Brussels for Calais – that is to say Anne and I did, just as the train was moving off. As Mordan had not joined us in the carriage, we were looking out very anxiously for him when he rushed frantically along the platform past us. I called loudly after him, but in vain, we were already leaving Brussels and Mordan behind us. Anne and I looked at each other in blank dismay. Then we determined to alight at Mechlin, the next station, and watch for him in every train that arrived from Brussels. The two next did not bring him; so as there was an hour and a half's interval before the next, we decided on getting a peep at Mechlin and having one franc between us we took a commissioner, who promised to show us everything for that sum. I was more pleased with the exterior of Mechlin Cathedral standing as it does in a large old square than any other cathedral. Its tower is of immense height and of lovely proportion. We both regretted Mordan was not with us. Having seen a splendid Vandyck 'Crucifixion' at another Church and Rubens' grand altar piece we returned to the station where we caught Mordan by the next train.

They arrived in Calais at 3 in the morning, and rose in time to catch the Channel steamer later the same day. 'Sketched girl,' Joanna wrote. 'Not ill, amused by watching occupants of cabin. Dover in pouring rain 5 pm.' She journeyed home alone by train on 9 October: 'Sole passenger in the carriage for the first part – then young curate – an unmitigated ass. I tried to take the conceit out of him – no go – talked a great deal about young ladies running after curates.'

England had not been spared by the cholera epidemic that had swept Europe, but in a letter to George on 2 November, Joanna was able to reassure him that no one they personally knew had died of the disease, though 'Mary Williams nearly sank under it'.

She had loved her 'delightful trip' with Anne and Mordan, and told him they were all longing to see 'dear Georgy again … with the most luxuriant and artistic growth of hair on his face he can possibly present'. In the meantime John Cook and Bertha Farwell had brought Anna Mary Howitt to see her paintings, and she had gone with them in their carriage to visit Anna Mary Howitt's studio in Highgate, according to Joanna, 'the loveliest little place in the world'.

❋

In Florence, Henry spent eight hectic days indefatigably sight-seeing: 'Ghirlandaio, Fra Angelico and Masaccio are the men to be most studied. To me the frescoes [in the Carmine Church] by Masaccio are the great revelation.' He wrote to George: 'I should select Florence as the best place for educating an artist.' He and Folkard arrived in Rome on 31 October, where they were 'guided through the city on this, our first night, by Mr Taylor and saw the Colosseum by moonlight – it was almost awful to look upon – the sweep of shadows etc'. Taylor was an American who knew Rome well and was to prove 'an excellent and very kind cicerone'. With him they explored the Appian Way, crossed the forum and ascended the Capitoline Hill. Later Henry lay on his back in the Sistine Chapel and 'with a good opera-glass' saw 'very distinctly these grand frescoes of Michael Angelo's'.

He also visited the studios of a number of painters and sculptors, including that of Frederic Leighton:[70] 'He has a large picture, 15 ft in length and nearly completed, which he intends for the RA – Cimabue's picture of the Madonna being carried in procession. Leighton appears to be a painter of great talent – not more than 23 or 24 years of age.' On 20 November, he bade farewell to the Michelangelos, and was intrigued to meet a great many bishops and priests leaving the Sistine Chapel where they had been locked in argument over 'a very important article of the Catholic faith, that is the "Immaculate Conception of the

70 Sir Frederic Leighton (1830–96). Studied mainly abroad, before settling in London in 1859. He built himself a villa with a large studio in Holland Park in 1864, to which, in 1877, he added an exotic Arab hall. He became a lynchpin of the Holland Park circle, was knighted in 1878 and, in 1896, became the first artist ever raised to the peerage.

Virgin". This point has been under discussion for centuries and they have at last by a great majority decided it.'

Henry left Rome on 22 November. Folkard, preferring a sea-crossing to Marseilles to the chill of the Mont Cenis pass, had left a few days earlier. Henry spent a day in Siena, a day at Pisa and a further four days at Florence before leaving in a diligence for Bologna on the 30th *en route* for home.

George's envoi to Italy, written on 16 November, reached Joanna from Cremona, where he had been forced to wait for the diligence to Milan. He was wishing he had given himself more time in Verona:

> It is backed by green hills and has a rapid river rushing through it turning a host of waterwheels … The bridges and banks of the river very picturesque and a quantity of the most interesting architecture imaginable – moreover a large and ancient piazza teeming in the morning with market people and their huge umbrellas. NB. I always find something very enjoyable in the sound of thousands of voices, when you don't distinguish any one in particular … You may judge how cold it was – and it's getting worse daily – when I tell you that long icicles hung from many of the mill wheels. My hands too are so covered with chilblains, one or two of which look very likely to break, that I scarcely dare even to make a five minutes' sketch …
>
> Let me find my luggage safe at Milan tomorrow morning and get across to St Gothard pretty comfortably, with a few grand effects on the road to bless one's eyes and memory withal, and the rest of the journey will be comparatively easy work … It gives me great pleasure to hear you so much enjoyed your trip and derived sanitary as well as mental benefit from it. Although you say nothing of the Memlings at Bruges (from haste I conclude) you surely must have seen and enjoyed them … How many sketches have you made of Edgar in his plumpness? … [71]
>
> You have formed, I perceive, just about as exaggerated a notion of my growth of beard as of my sketches. A few straggling hairs on the upper lip, and a lump on the chin, which affects the carrot – *et voilà tout*!

71 Edgar was the Mordans' son. Following their return from the Continent, Joanna had evidently been indulging her love of drawing children and babies.

On 9 December he was back in London and attending a lecture given by Ruskin at the Architectural Museum in Canon Row: 'After the lecture I spoke to him and he immediately asked when he might come and see my drawings. I said in about a fortnight. He said: "Not before? Pray don't go and botch them in the studio." Hoped I was a confirmed Pre-Raphaelite.'

3

A FALTERING ROMANCE

'I would that you were all to me, You that are just so much, no more.'

'Two in the Campagna'

On 9 May 1855, according to his daughter Alice, Henry begged a private interview with Joanna at which he declared his love for her. He took a calculated risk. The Boyces had prospered in a way his own family had not, and they moved in more exalted social circles. Yet, as Alice's account makes clear, Henry had become a welcome visitor in the Boyce household on his own merits. He was commercially successful and, as a sought-after miniaturist, mixed with people of 'position and culture'. His friendship with George was of long-standing, and Mrs Boyce, flattered by the esteem in which he held her daughter's work, clearly enjoyed his 'lively talk, the zest and assurance with which he expressed his opinions on all matters of art of the topics of the day'. He was also confident that Mr Boyce, had he lived, would have looked favourably upon his suit and, though Joanna had never hinted at her own feelings, he had complete faith in his capacity to inspire her love with his – by now an absorbing passion.

She refused him, firmly asserting that, though she cared for him, she 'had no desire to take up the responsibilities of married life and wished to remain free to carry on her life's work'.

A month earlier, the portrait of Lizzie Ridley that she had struggled with throughout the previous year, now transformed as 'Elgiva', had been chosen for exhibition by the Royal Academy – a phenomenal achievement for a young woman artist. (*Plate XVII*) Her study of Lizzie's sister, Lilly, who later married Matthias, was also accepted, and on the day that Henry proposed, Spencer Hall wrote to offer her his congratulations:

> I have not yet been to the Royal Academy so have not seen Miss Lilly – sitting like Puss in the Corner of the East Room. Never mind where you are now placed – resolve to struggle for your own position.

> Cultivate your talents with a strong religious feeling that you are responsible for their exercise and every good thing and every perfect thing cometh from above. This was the strength of the great Artists of Old … Generally speaking the world, though wildly idolatrous or blindly unjust at intervals, is equable in judgment. Success does attend merit. To draw an example from your own circle – look at Wells cleaving with eagle wing the air towards the Temple of Fame.
>
> Yours truly, most truly, Miss Juno

His letter is a reminder that while Henry was going from strength to strength, for Joanna the struggle had only just begun. The effort involved in completing 'Elgiva' in particular was all-consuming, not least because she began it after the death of the person she most loved. The poignant and beautiful picture, which had begun as (to her) an unsatisfactory chalk drawing of a family friend, had been changed into something altogether more ambitious – the first in a projected series of oil paintings of influential women. Queen Victoria's desire – for the sake of her beloved Albert – to re-establish the Anglo-Saxon origins of the monarchy was well known (and evidenced by the murals in the House of Lords), and it may have been this – together with the mid-Victorian penchant for early medieval themes – that prompted her choice of subject.

Elgiva, the wife of the tenth-century King Edwy, was persecuted by Archbishop Odo of Canterbury on the grounds of her kinship with the king. She was forced into divorce, branded and exiled to Ireland. When she later returned to England she was brutally murdered. While Joanna's 'Elgiva' may have been based on the novel by W. Burnett Coates, published in 1852 and popular at the time, she undoubtedly had access to other Anglo-Saxon sources (thanks to Spencer Hall) and owned a chart of the kings and queens of England.[72] The story was well-known: in 1843 Millais had produced a drawing in which he showed Elgiva being dragged away on the orders of the Archbishop. Joanna chose to depict not a scene but an emotion – stoic grief. Her Elgiva is pale and still, her style undecorated – the paint luminous and finely blended, the suggestion of a halo in the gold band around her head. For Ford Madox Brown it was 'the best Head in the room'.[73]

Given how mightily she had laboured for this success, it is understandable that she was reluctant to be subsumed by the Wellsian tidal wave. What is less

72 Two other possible sources are David Hume's *The History of England* (1754–62) and Sharon Turner's *History of the Anglo-Saxons* (1799–1805).

73 *The Diary of Ford Madox Brown*, ed. V. Surtees (New Haven CT 1981) p.138.

understandable is that – given her characteristic forthrightness – she was unable make her position clear.

For Henry was not about to take no for an answer. He asked for a further interview, which was granted, and at which Joanna took refuge in her family responsibilities, thereby giving him the impression that her refusal was for the time being only. He wrote: 'I see clearer what a prize I shall have when I obtain your hand, and believe me that when Bob has lost the care of his mother and shall require yours, I shall hope to be your helpmate in what you place before you as your love-like duty.'

This brought forth a swift rejoinder: 'Owing no doubt to some fault in my words or manner, I find that every time you see me, you go away more confident of ultimately changing my decision.' The very idea of being persuaded to engage herself to anyone made her miserable. She thought it better that they did not meet again.

Henry was 'knocked over by her decision' but, nothing daunted, pleaded not to be forbidden her presence, and she, in a perplexity which was to plague their on-off engagement, couldn't bring herself to make a complete break – 'though it has been my wish, and still is, to remain single.'

Immediately afterwards, she and her mother left for a long visit to her Aunt and Uncle Robert at Ashford Bowdler. From Bisham Abbey, where he was staying with some professional friends, the Vansittarts, Henry sent her an expansive and descriptive letter, his feelings bursting out at the end: 'I am possessed with the hope that when you are in quiet and by yourself you may sometimes wish me near you … Oh why can you not fling yourself onwards and not catechise at every timid step?'

The first extended missive from Joanna to Henry begins with the words: 'I think you have the faculty for letter-writing, for my own part it is the occupation I most dislike and have the least aptitude for, needlework perhaps excepted.' Yet letter-writing became their main method of communication, charting not only their thorny emotional path but also their artistic progress, and Joanna proved an enviably articulate and outspoken correspondent. By 6 June she was hard at work on a study of an uncooperative child model:

> On Saturday I captured the 'incipient Juryman' and began another study of him. He was dreadfully unmanageable, full of mischief. After numerous threatening and forgiving I took him downstairs on the way to his mother, he screaming. We were already within a few steps of the cottage, when he suddenly seemed to discover that I was in earnest, and awful visions of the birch wielded by this mother's arm stared

> him in the face. 'I will be a good boy now' with his arms tight round my neck was the result, so I carried him back in an unusually docile state ...
>
> I want to know how your sister is progressing. I trust the prize is hers by this time ...[74] I have received a letter from Anne which displeased Mamma, her name is not mentioned, though of course included with the rest of us in kind messages. It is a pity she did not write some kind message to Mamma only, it would have been so valuable to Mamma just now.

Joanna had yet to discover that even the most conscientious efforts to please Mamma would not avail if Mamma wished to be displeased.

Henry replied exuberantly on 7 June. He had visited the Farwells at the home of their grandmother, Mrs Wade Browne, and had met John Cook there. Cook had described Joanna as 'a first rate fellow' and told 'Piggy' that she could not compare to her. His robustly affectionate mode of address, both to Bertha and his admired 'Johnny' did not, it seems, raise eyebrows among their acquaintance.

Francis Topham had called and the two of them had discussed George's 'art, conduct and prospects', about which they were both concerned: 'I cannot disguise from myself that George is a fearful body to move – it is still to me a problem where the lever is to be placed ... He has painted in Wales, in Italy and amongst the Pyrenees, but he has not yet produced a picture. He has brought back admirable paintings of <u>things</u> and sketches of effects, which show how well he can appreciate and interpret them, but he has never united the double faculty.'

They were convinced that George's temperament was to blame: 'He dislikes taking the plunge. I wish we could find the way to trip him up unawares; he would find that he could swim and would afterwards like the water.'

Revelling in praise of his beloved, he added: 'Topham thinks you a very, v-e-r-y clever girl'. He told her his plans: 'I have an invitation from Mordan asking me to dine with him at the "Star and Garter" Richmond next Tuesday. On Thursday next I am going to give a whitebait dinner to some friends at Greenwich. On Saturday afternoon I shall go to Novelli's[75] at Dulwich and, according to custom, pass the Sunday there' and he finished by exhorting her 'to write an answer to my letters on the evening of the day you receive them'.

He did convey the news she had asked for – that 'Augusta will have the Countess of Hardwick's prize, having run a "dead heat" with another young

74 Henry's younger sister Augusta was a student at the South Kensington School of Art.

75 In April 1856 Joanna refers to Henry's painting a miniature for Novelli. This was probably Dr Augustus Novelli, a doctor who graduated from Trinity College and later lived in Hyde Park Square.

lady' – so the sternness of her rejoinder was perhaps uncalled for, but she must have begun to despair of ever persuading the blithely confident Henry that she was not 'his' to be dictated to – whether on the subject of replies to his letters or anything else.

On 10 June she wrote to her 'dear Mr Wells' once again, insisting that 'this matter between us shall be ended at once and forever'. She would not marry, she said, 'unless something most unforeseen happens to change my way of thinking … Now that my mind is made up, I tell you at once … Do not write to me. You could not, even if you would, change my decision.' She added: 'You have a strong will, use it now and think of me in friendship only. I have some claim to this, for I am doing more now towards your life-long happiness … by this one step than I could be any other.'

Henry was tenacious. He knew instinctively that Joanna was not indifferent to him, but could not grasp her profound and very real terror that, should she marry him, she would mortgage, perhaps forever, her artistic soul. He loved her and he loved her art, and he believed sincerely that the sheer strength of his feelings would, in the end, banish her reservations. Crucially at this stage he had the support of her mother, with whom he had evidently discussed Joanna's rejection. Consequently he took no notice of her instruction that he cease writing to her, and plunged into a long letter which must have taken him all night to compose:

> I directly oppose your desire and write this … If I accede to your dictates, I give myself up to such unhappiness and utter disappointment as I have not courage to look in the face. I do not think I have earned such a fate … If it were not for the useful friendship of your Mamma, your letter of this morning would have been unintelligible in everything but its decision, and I cannot thank her too much for having given me such ample comments upon your motives … From these reports I discover that the very immediate cause of your sudden determination is the belief that my love will not endure. To oppose to this my most firm belief that it will be lasting and improving is only to give one assertion for another – and yet what else can I do? …
>
> I understand that you are afraid that I regard you more as the clever companion than as the wife. You are greatly mistaken if you think my blood is seeking to marry a nurse or a preceptor. I want to marry you because I feel I want to live with you and because I feel you are the very person to complete my existence, which is unsettled, even unhappy, separated from you …

I am told that you have misgivings whether your personal charms would secure that constant love that belongs to a wife … Until the receipt of these letters I considered that the only obstacle to our engagement was your doubt whether you could love me … but now your Mamma writes me that you confess to liking me and that you think you could not help being very fond of me if much alone in my society … Why should you feel that after a time I should not care for you? I am the better judge in this matter … I too well understand my welfare to allow it to depend upon the accidents of letters – mine have already done me ill service.

I shall arrive at Ashford within two or three hours of the time when this will be given to you on Wednesday morning. I must see you … If you told me that you did and must detest me, or if I was given roundly to understand by your friends that the home I have to offer was not worthy of your acceptance, I would receive the decision as best I could and take no steps to disturb it … Whatever your decision I must see the lips move that utter the words.

Believe me to remain, dear Joanna,
Most unalterably yours
Henry T. Wells

He enclosed with this letter another, dated 12 June (although by then he was well on his way to Ashford) and addressed to Joanna's mother:

My dear Mrs Boyce

The same train as will carry this letter will take me to Birmingham. I shall sleep there tonight and start at 8.10 tomorrow morning for Shrewsbury. I shall reach Ludlow at 11.16 am two hours or so after you receive this letter – I shall hasten at once to Ashford to have an interview with Joanna. I have written a letter to her, which I enclose in this, and I beg she will read it directly … Your last letter was of the greatest possible use in prompting many of the arguments in my letter to Joanna – I hope I shall not be convicted of breach of confidence.

The real motive for Joanna's reluctance to marry – that her artistic ambitions would inevitably be compromised – had, as Alice later remarked in a note on Henry's letter, escaped both him and Mrs Boyce. He hurried to

Ashford and, in Alice's words, 'came, saw, and confidently believed that he had conquered'. He and Joanna became engaged. He caught the last train to London, arriving at Paddington at half past four on the morning of 13 June. Later that day he wrote joyously to his beloved: 'It was very broad daylight, but when I reached home I darkened my room and succeeded in having three hours sound sleep.' He had made, he said, 'a jubilee day' with his mother to celebrate his prize, and intended to follow this with a 'bachelor carousal' at Greenwich: 'You have been sadly worried of late, as your dear pale face, when I first saw you, too well told. But all that has passed now … doubtless we know each other more thoroughly than if everything had run smoothly from the first.'

It must have seemed so settled at last. Mrs Boyce had advanced his suit. Joanna had succumbed. But her misgivings returned to haunt her as soon as he had gone and on the next day she wrote to tell him so:

> My dear Henry
>
> Those three words seem to go together very strangely, but perhaps in a little while it will be different. It is but a few hours since I saw you, and yet I have something I must tell you at once to ease my mind. You have a right to know what is passing in my heart and I will not defraud you, though I fear I shall give you pain. I am a mystery to myself, how then shall you understand me? When I woke this morning I felt as though some heavy care were pressing upon me – the events or rather the one event of yesterday seemed like a strange dream, and I almost hoped that I should not find the ring, but I am looking at it now shining on my finger. What thoughts does it bring to light? Let me be truthful at least, however much I fail in other ways – wonder and pride in your unwearied love for me, and no little fondness for the giver, still I am uneasy if not unhappy, why is this? It is that I have so long taught myself to look on engagement and marriage as things to be dreaded and avoided, that I cannot suddenly reconcile myself to them? Or is it that I have deceived myself as to the nature of my feelings?
>
> Those were difficult words to write, but I am determined to be sincere with you however much it may cost me or indeed either of us. Believe me, I am not <u>capricious</u> in the slightest degree, and if once I felt that my <u>whole heart</u> was yours nothing but death should part 'us twa', and I do believe that the day will come when I shall be able to tell you so without one doubt to dim the brightness of our future … If you think me fickle or cruel in writing this tell me so. It may be

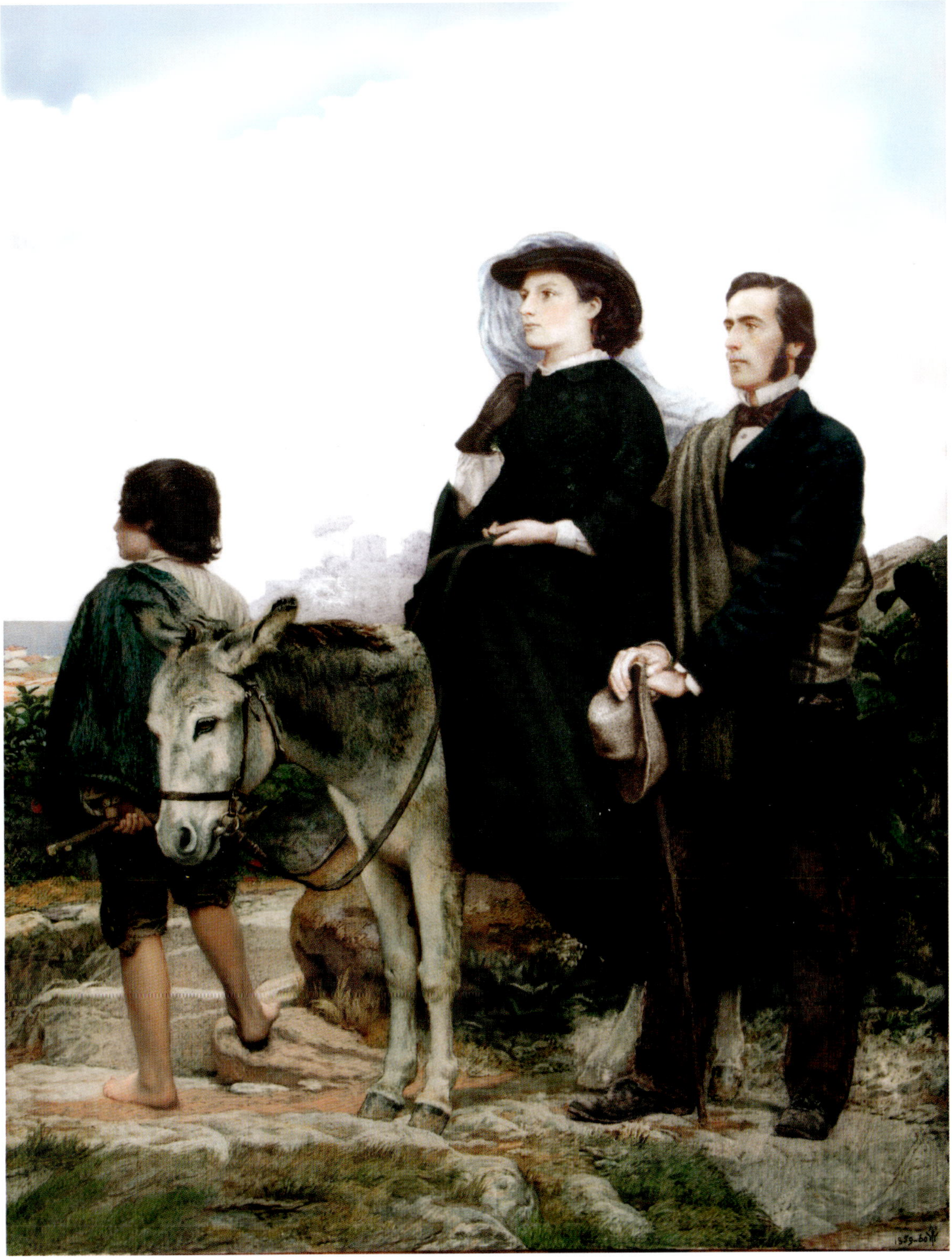

I. *Joanna and Henry on a mountain excursion in Italy* Henry Wells

On 14 September 1859, Joanna told George that Henry had acquired 'an immense ivory, on which he intends painting our two precious selves as though taken on one of our mountain excursions in Italy – I on donkey back.' The original water-colour, on an ivory on slate panel, 20" x 16", was completed in time to be exhibited at the Royal Academy in 1860. Though badly damaged since then, it has been beautifully recreated, with the help of a black and white photograph, by John Roberts.

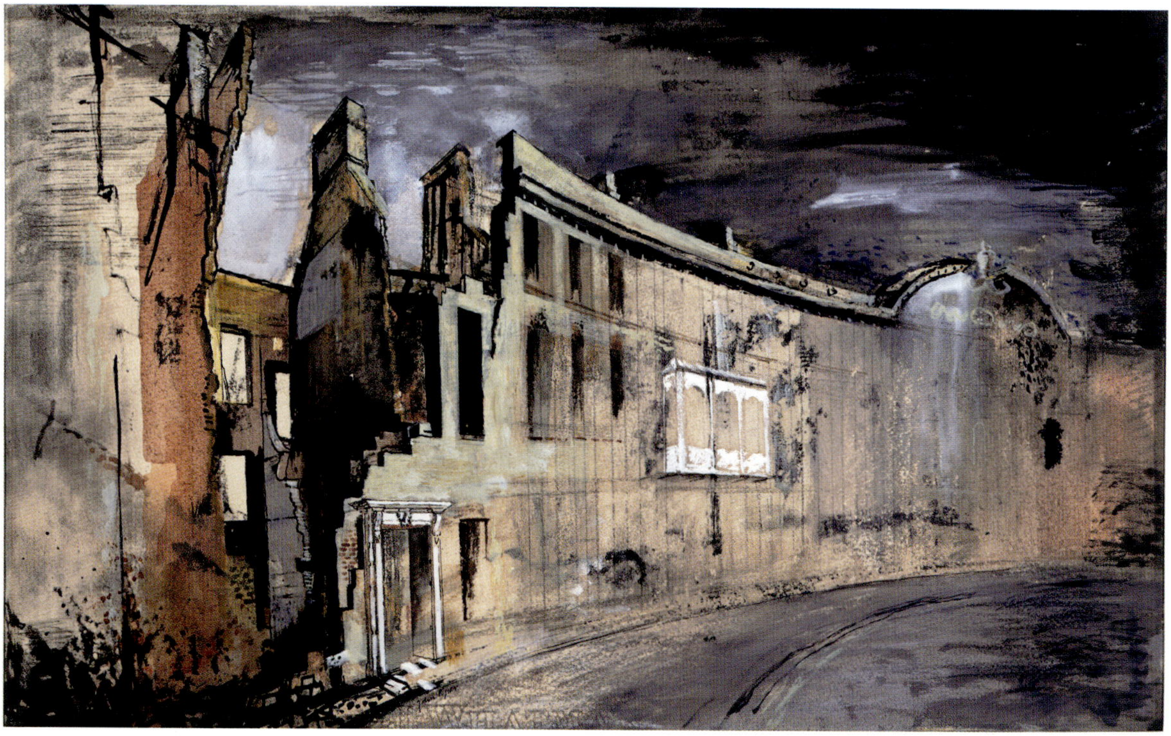

II. *42 Somerset Place, Bath* John Piper

John Piper was working as a war artist in Bath at the time of the Baedeker raids in 1942 when Alice Street's house was destroyed. With it went many of the paintings described in this book, the originals of the letters and documents upon which the book is based, and an extensive collection of Pre-Raphaelite and early Italian paintings

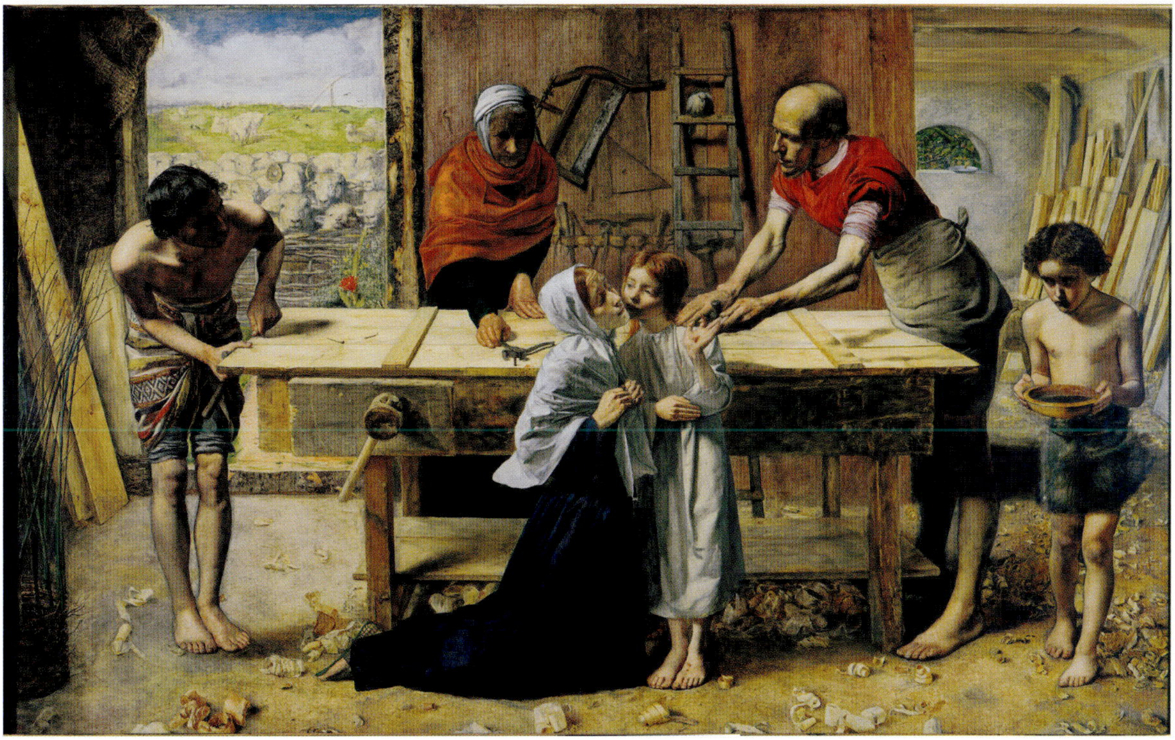

III.*Christ in the House of His Parents* John Everett Millais

Also known as 'The Carpenter's Shop', this picture was exhibited at the Royal Academy in 1850, signed, as the Pre-Raphaelite Brotherhood had agreed, 'P.R.B.'. The identities of the P.R.B. artists were soon revealed in the press and an acrimonious debate ensued, in which Millais was vigorously attacked for showing the Holy Family as 'ordinary'.

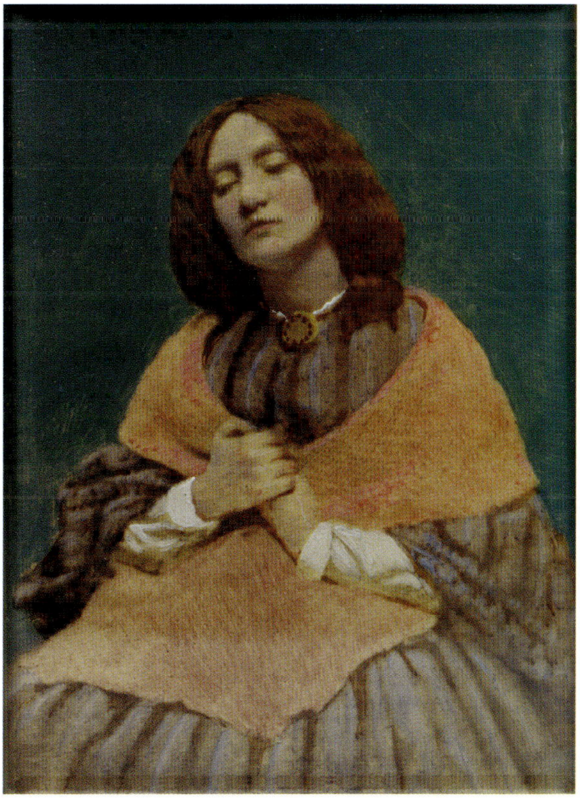

IV.*Miniature of Elizabeth Siddal*
attributed to Dante Gabriel Rossetti
Painted over a photograph

Elizabeth Siddall was discovered working in a milliner's shop by the artist Walter Deverell, his mother and the poet William Allingham. She began sitting to Rossetti towards the end of 1851 and, with her unusual looks, became an icon of Pre-Raphaelite beauty. Allingham wrote: 'Her pale face, abundant red hair and long thin limbs were strange and affecting.'

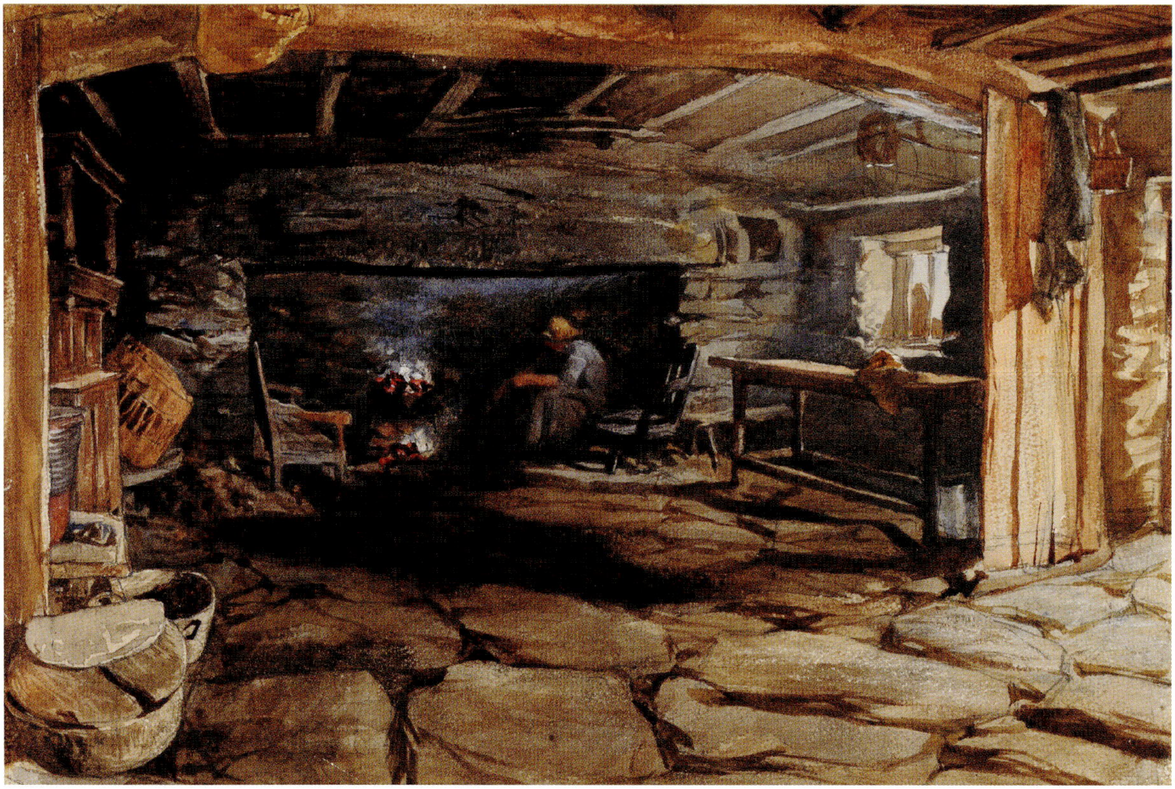

V. *A farmhouse kitchen in Betws-y-Coed, North Wales* Henry Wells

Henry painted this picture in Wales in July 1849, when he and George first met. It was an unusual choice of scene, in that most visiting artists chose to paint out of doors. George later visited Henry to see his Welsh sketches and noted in his diary on 6 October: 'All very clever, especially a moonlight and an interior.'

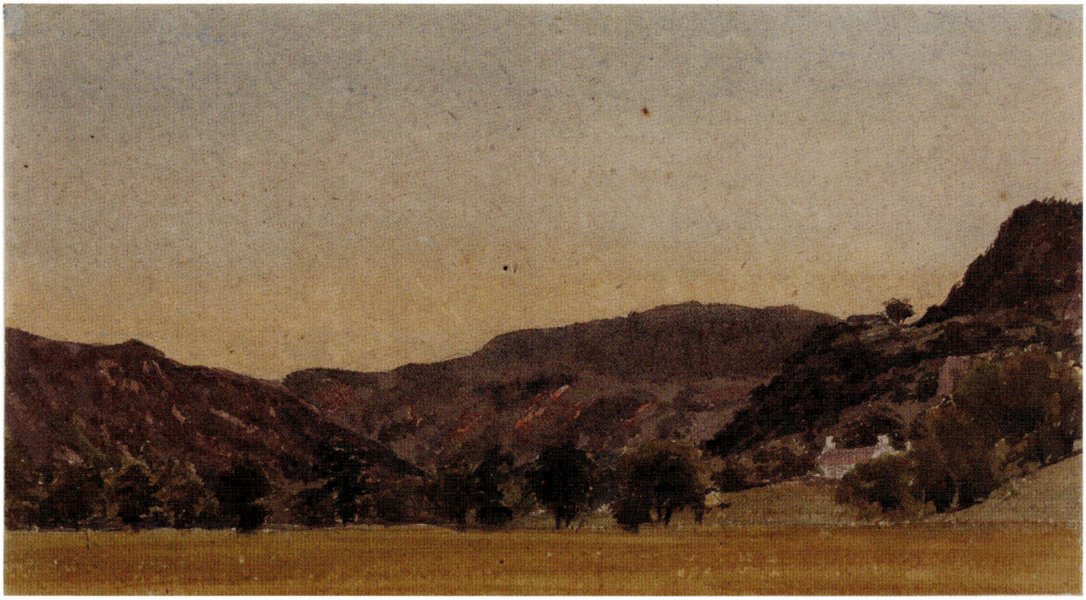

VI. *Betws-y-Coed in the evening* George Price Boyce

Evenings, sunsets and moonlights were a much more typical choice of subject for artists at Betws-y-Coed. On 31 July 1849 George noted in his diary: 'After dinner I made an evening sketch on grey wrapping-up paper. David Cox saw it and approved.'

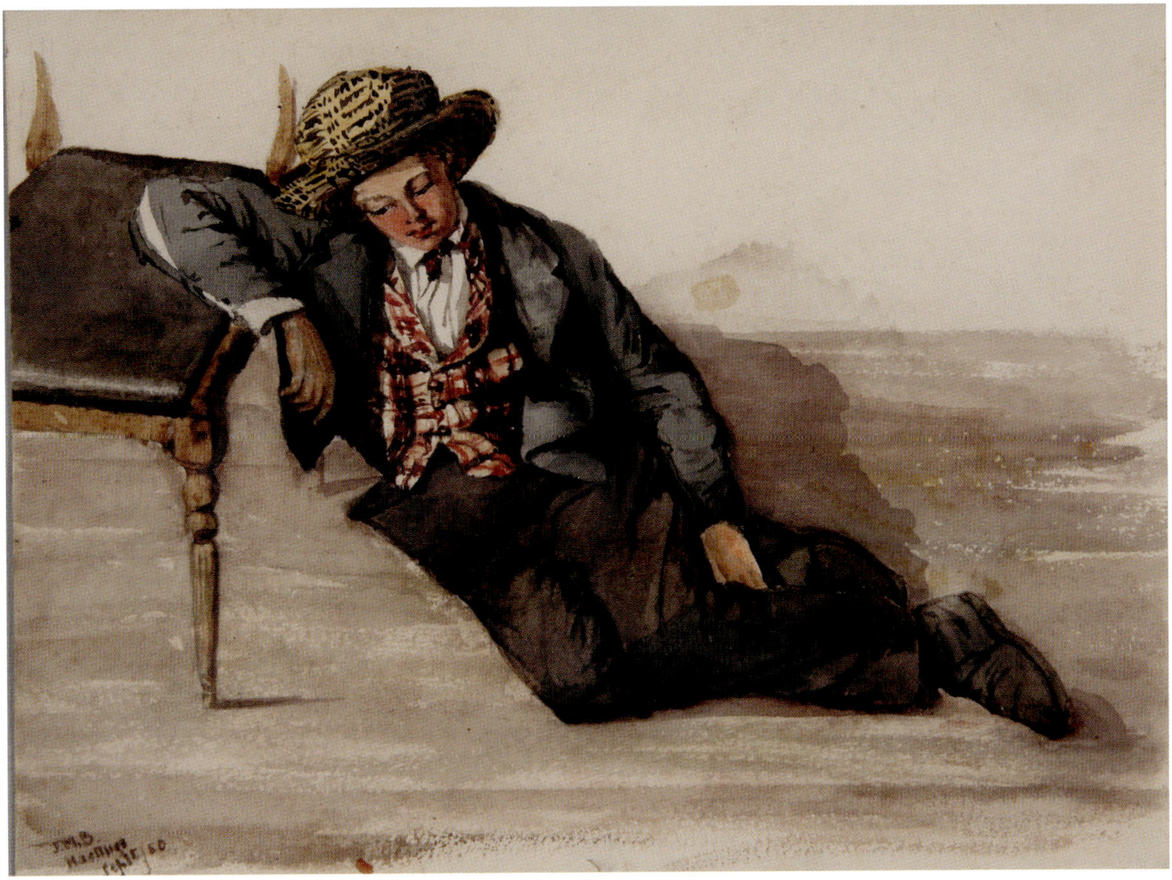

VII. *George Price Boyce at Hastings* Joanna Boyce

On 29 May 1850, George went to Hastings in search of a cure for a serious hip injury. Joanna kept him company and sketched this portrait of him. His posture, half leaning against a chair, may indicate the pain he must have been in, and Joanna also catches something of the more reserved side of his character.

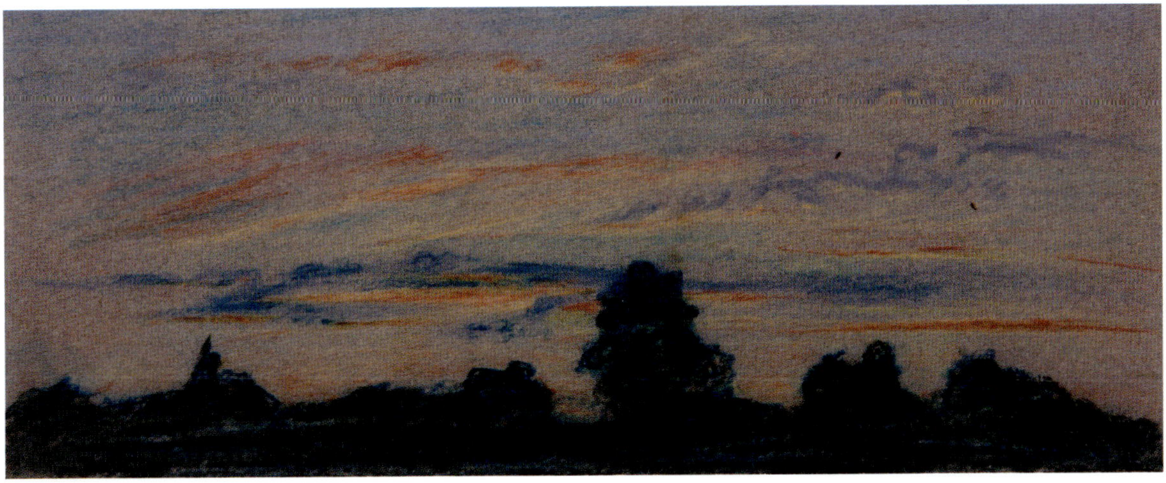

VIII. *Edgbaston* Joanna Boyce

There is no direct reference to this picture, but Edgbaston was on the route taken by the Boyce family to visit their relations in Shropshire. As early as 1845, George described to his sister the road between Stourbridge and Birmingham, where 'the road passes among numerous coal-pits, lime-kilns and furnaces'. Her evocative sketch is dated August 1851.

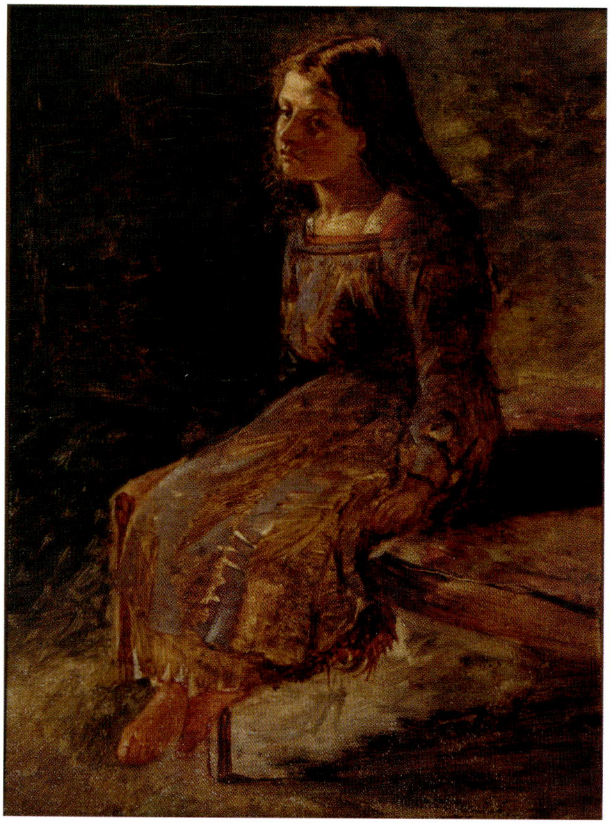

IX. *Portrait of a YoungGirl* Joanna Boyce

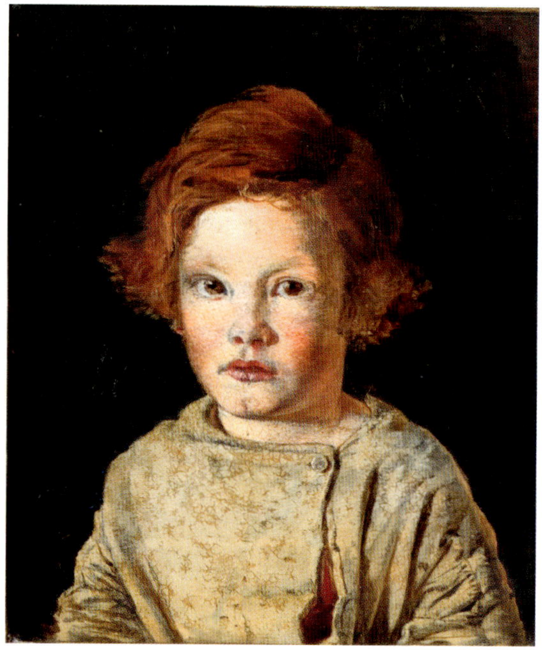

X. *Little-Red-Haired Boy* Joanna Boyce

Between 1852 and 1854 Joanna produced no less than nine oil sketches and paintings of Welsh children, with red or strawberry blonde hair. Perhaps the'Little Red-Haired Boy' was a portrait of 'Jack' – 'a very bad boy' but with 'such an ingenuous and intelligent expression'.

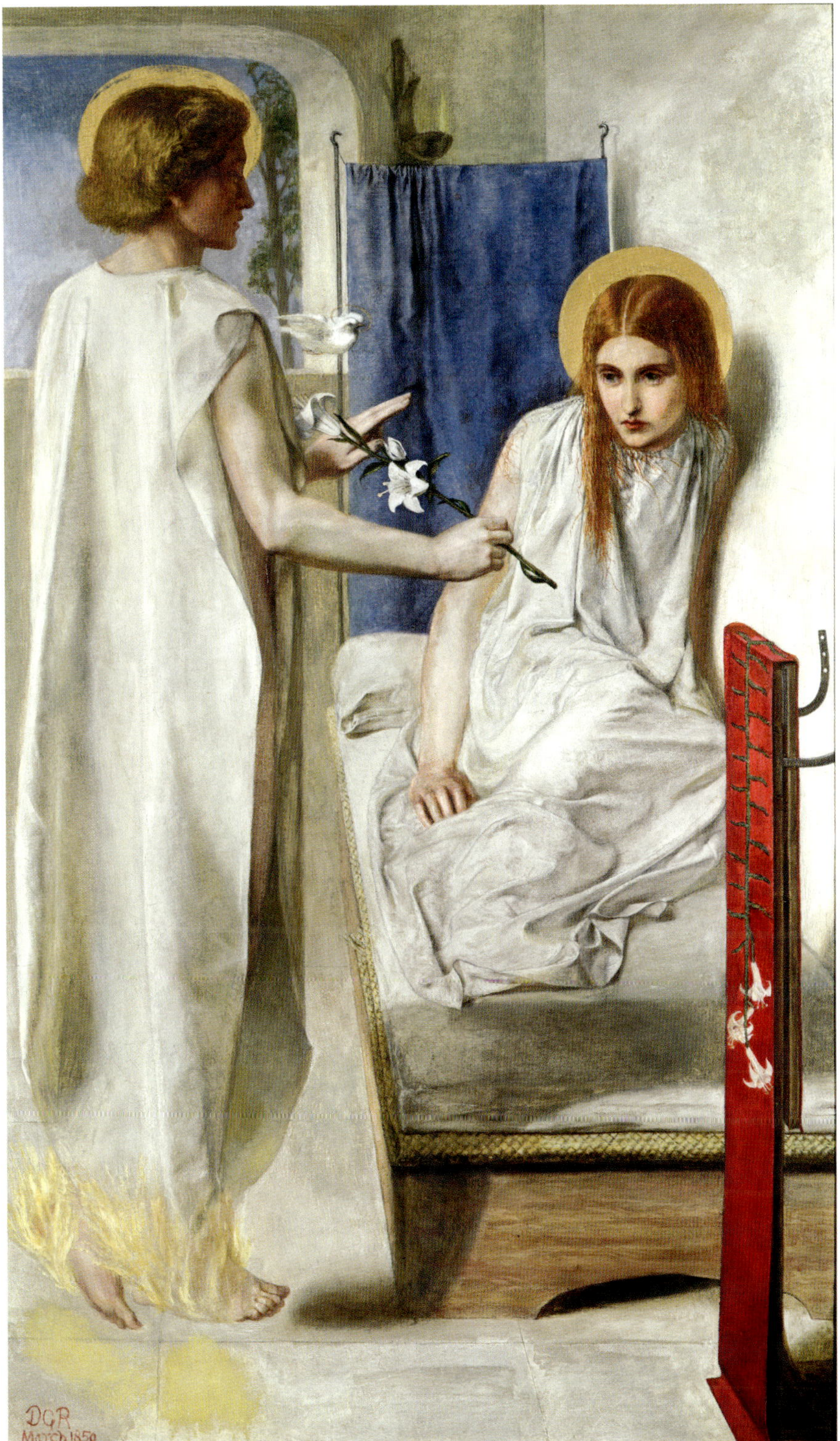

XI. Ecce Ancilla Domini Dante Gabriel Rossetti

Rossetti's unusual interpretation of the Annunciation was exhibited at the National Institution in 1850, but as was his custom Rossetti went on working on it. Visiting his studio on 28 January 1853, George pronounced: 'The Virgin one of, if not the most exquisite conception I have ever seen.'

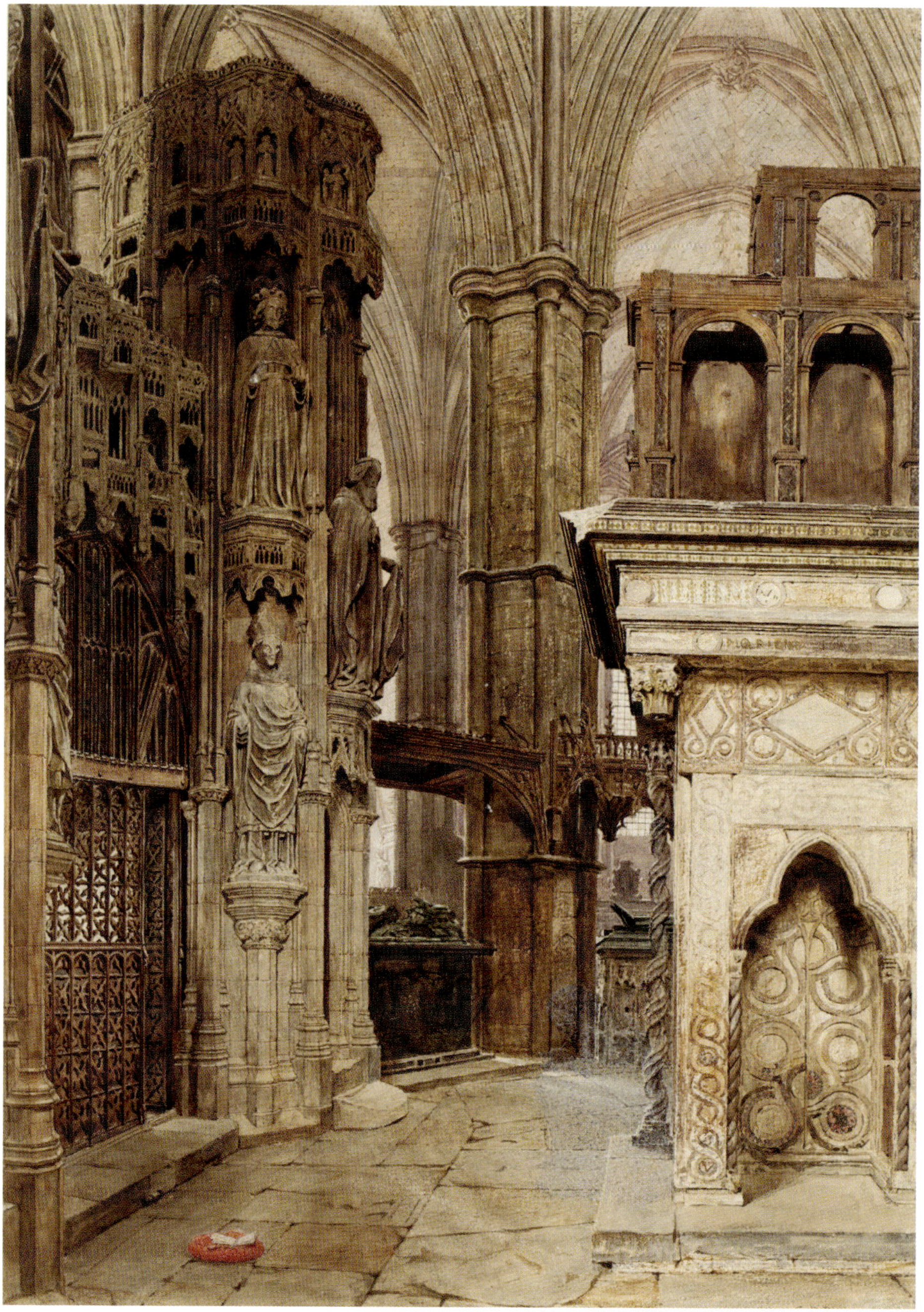

XII. *Westminster Abbey: The East End of Edward the Confessor's Chapel and Tomb, as they now stand* George Price Boyce

George began his ambitious water-colour drawing of the East End of Edward the Confessor's Chapel in 1852 though it was not completed or exhibited until 1855. It hung, with George's study of 'Beech Trees' and some paintings by Joanna, opposite their father's bed during his final illness and gave him much comfort. Henry Wallis, painter of 'The Death of Chatterton', later expressed interest in it and asked him the price. It was, said George, his '1st nibble'.

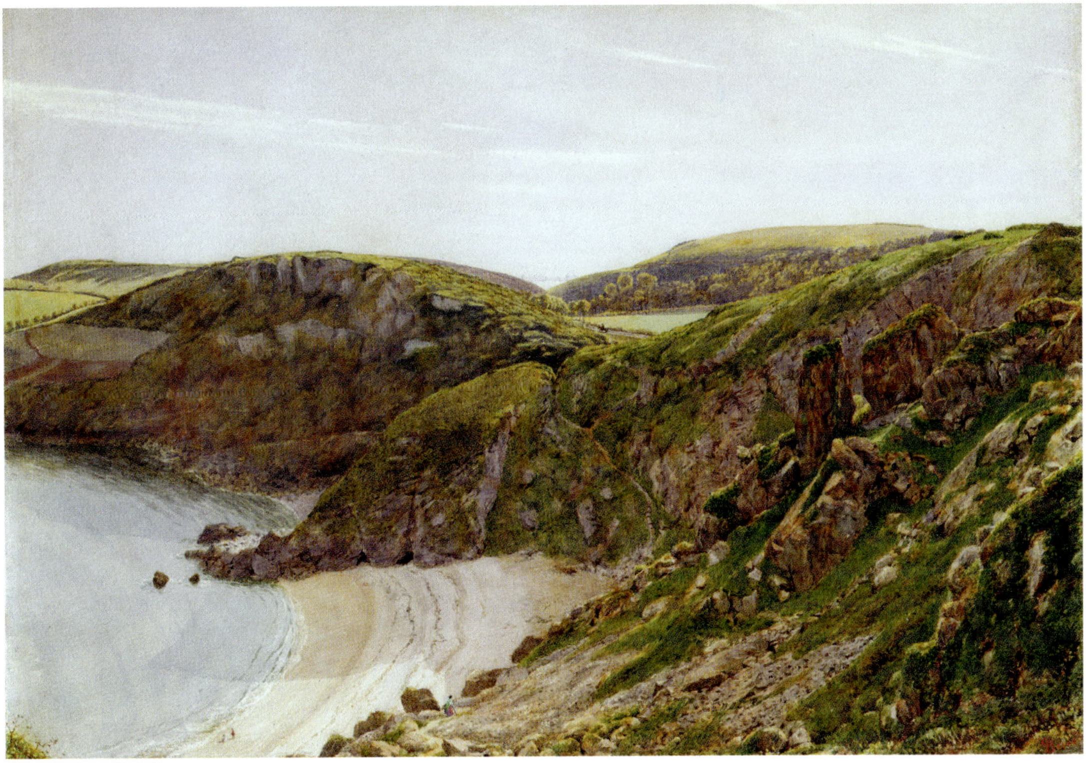

XIII. *Anstis Cove* George Price Boyce

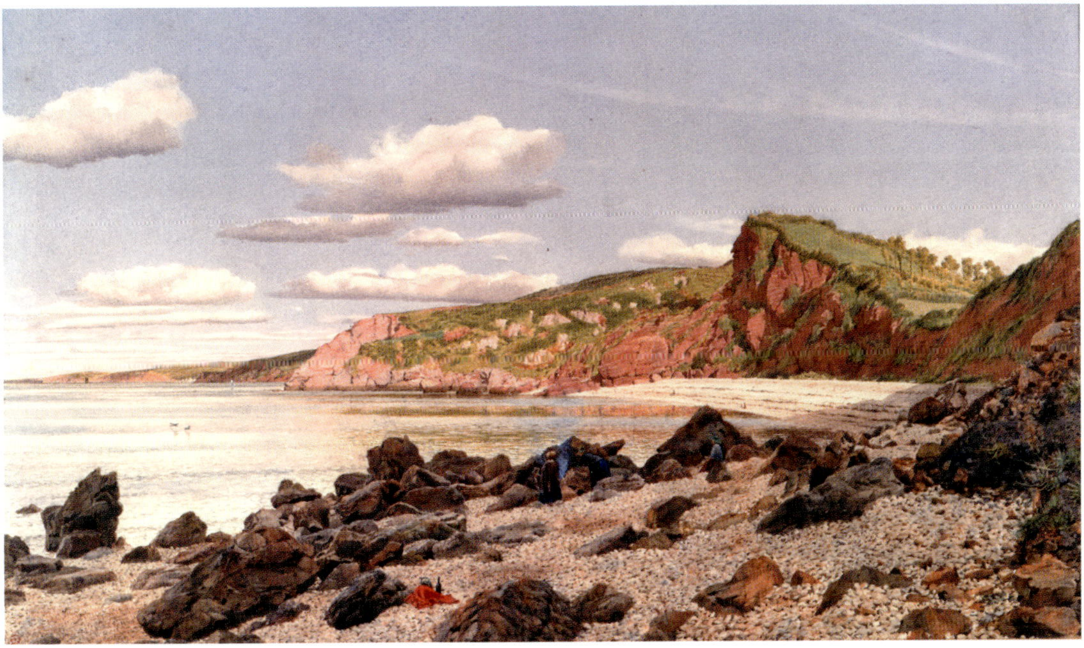

XIV. *Babbacombe Bay* George Price Boyce

These water-colours were painted during the fraught visit to Devon that followed the death of George and Joanna's father. Both pictures were exhibited at the National Institution Exhibition at the Portland Gallery in 1854, and of 'Anstis Cove' Coventry Patmore wrote: 'We do not remember seeing anything more true and powerful than this little piece.' Rossetti, who was not interested in landscape, later borrowed two of George's Babbacombe sketches 'to help him with the background of a delicate little drawing of a loving couple on a beach on a windy day'.

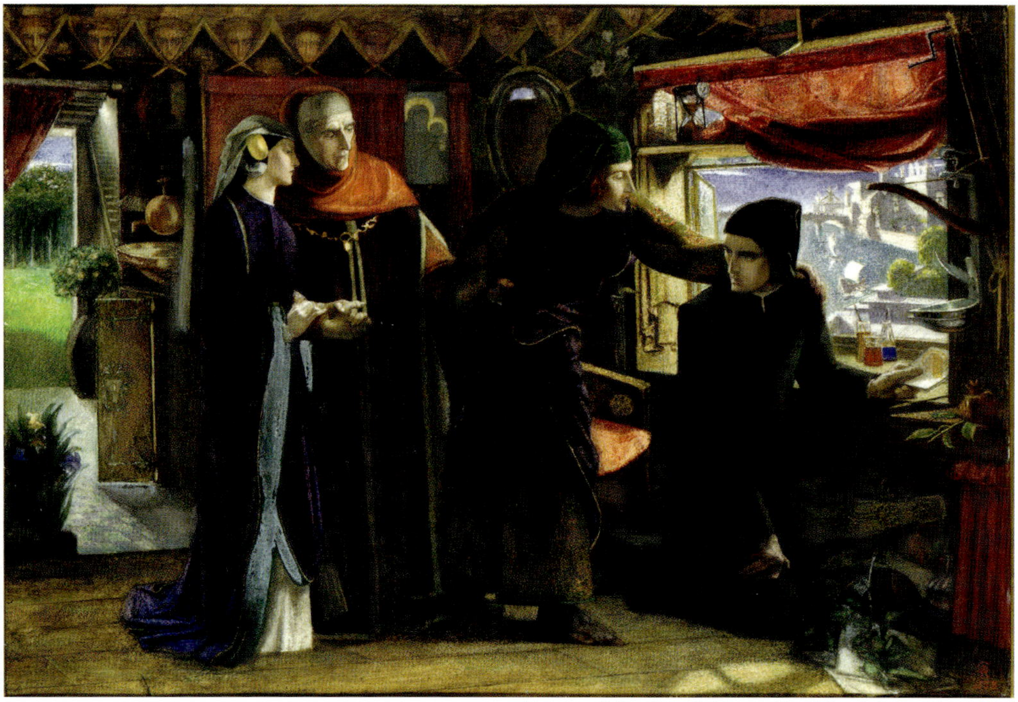

XV. *The First Anniversary of Beatrice's Death* Dante Gabriel Rossetti

On 13 March 1854 Rossetti showed George 'an exquisite drawing of his from the Vita Nuova'. Rossetti initially agreed to swap the picture for one of George's, but later said that his 'duns' – the bailiffs – would not allow it. George offered to buy the picture instead, noting that Rossetti 'would want £15 or guineas'.

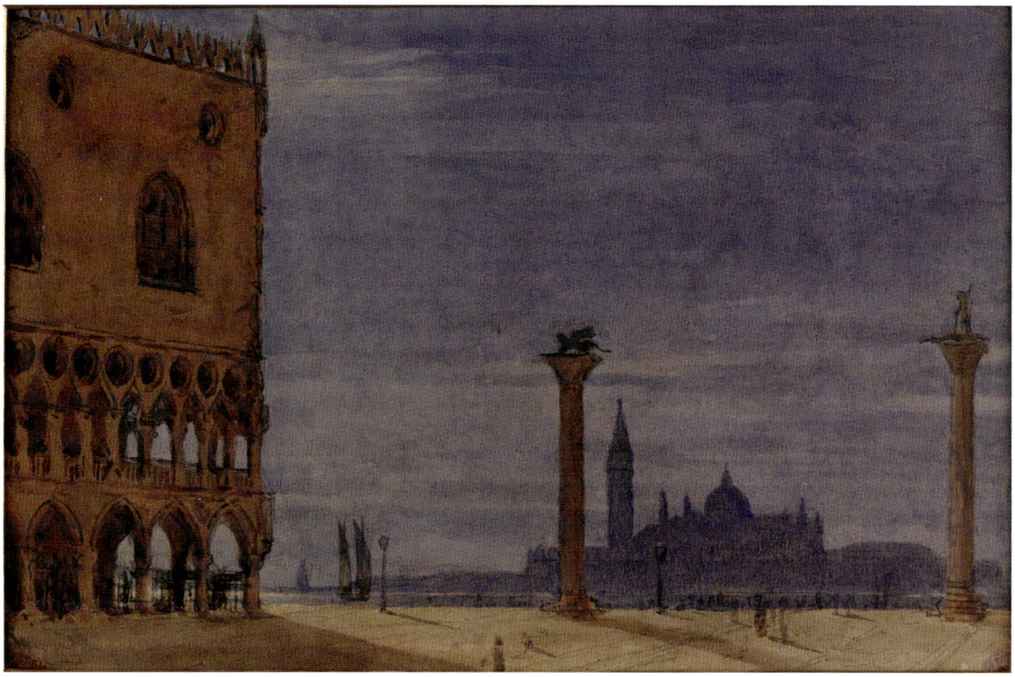

XVI. *San Giorgio Maggiore from the Piazzetta by moonlight* George Price Boyce

On 16 July 1854, Henry wrote to George saying: 'I shall grumble if you do not bring back some moonlights from Venice.' In its almost surreal simplicity, this is an outstanding example of what George referred to as his 'moonlight blots'.

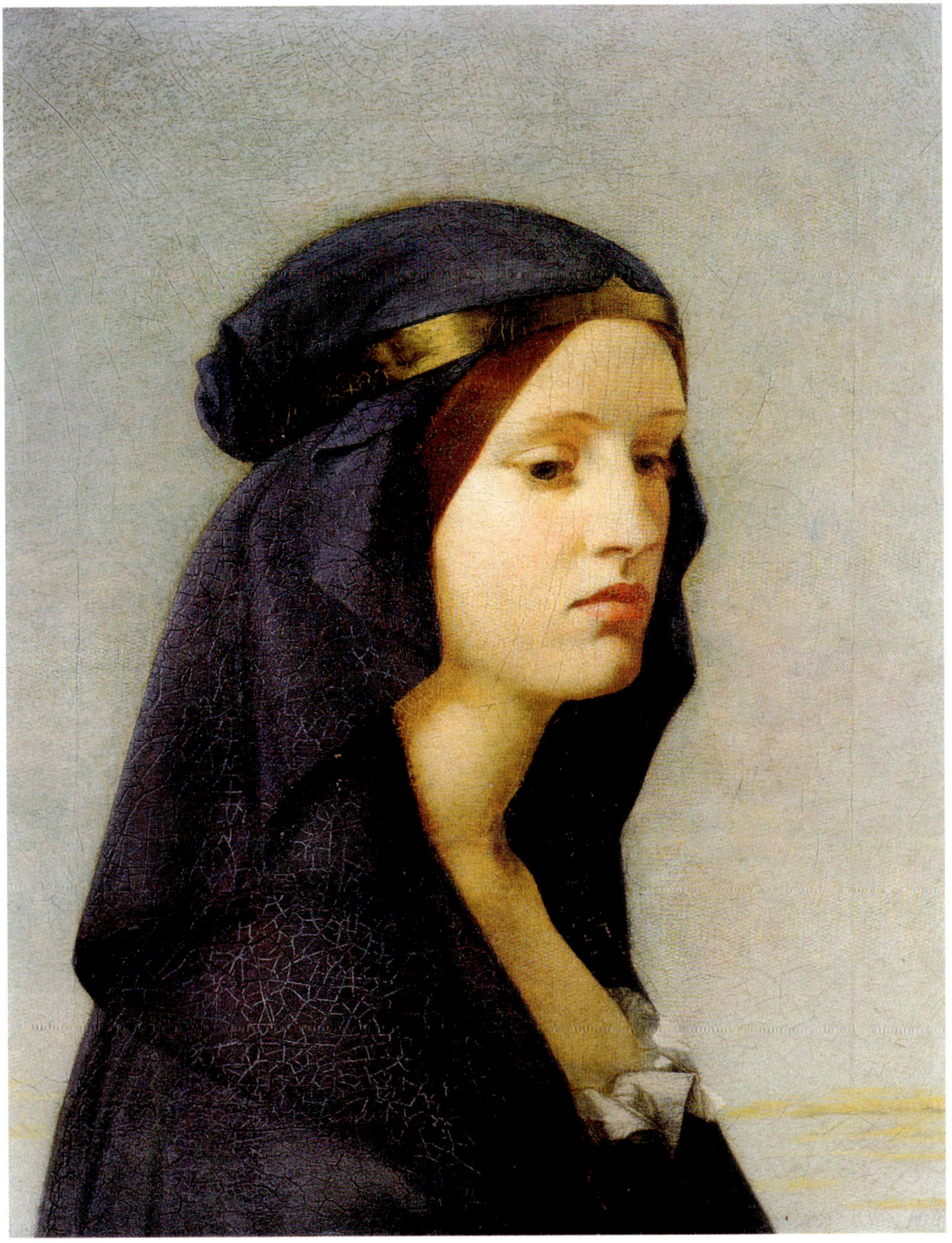

XVII. *Elgiva* Joanna Boyce

In 1855 two of Joanna's paintings were hung at the Royal Academy Exhibition – a study of Lilly Ridley in the East Room, and 'Elgiva' in the North. It was 'Elgiva' that brought her to the notice of the artistic establishment. What started out as an unsatisfactory chalk portrait of Lizzie Ridley had been transformed into a ravishing evocation, in oils, of a doomed Anglo-Saxon queen. Ford Madox Brown called it 'the best Head in the room'.

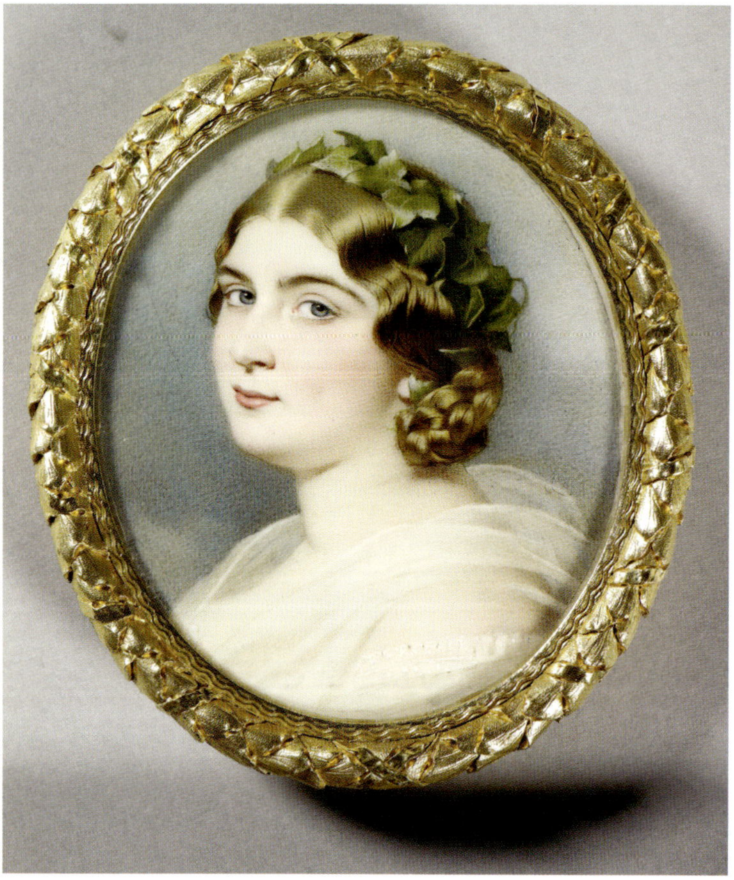

XVIII.
HRH Princess Mary of Cambridge
Henry T. Wells

Towards the end of 1853, Sir Edwin Landseer recommended to Queen Victoria that Henry be commissioned to paint a miniature of her daughter, the Princess Mary Adelaide. It was a tremendous accolade. The portrait was completed by January the following year. Henry told George that the princess was 'a gleeful damsel' and that the Queen herself had been 'gracious and complimentary, liking his miniature of the Princess much.'

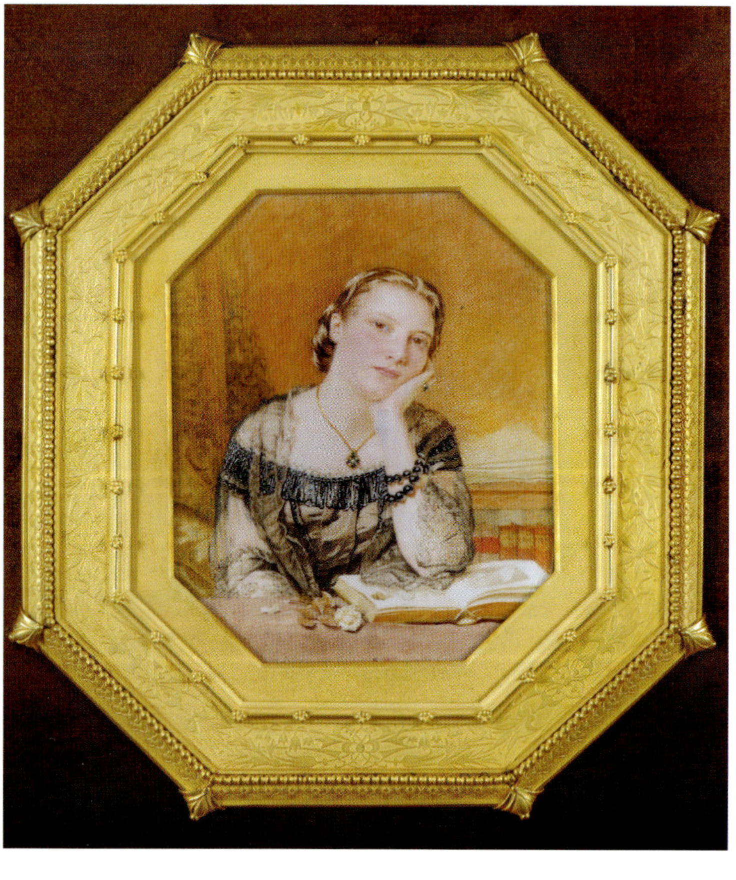

XIX. *Miniature of Joanna*
Henry T. Wells

This rare portrait of Joanna as a very young woman is undated but was painted well before she and Henry were married. It is faded now, but bears out William Michael Rossetti's description of her: 'She had a picturesque face, with a noticeable air of concentration and resolve.'

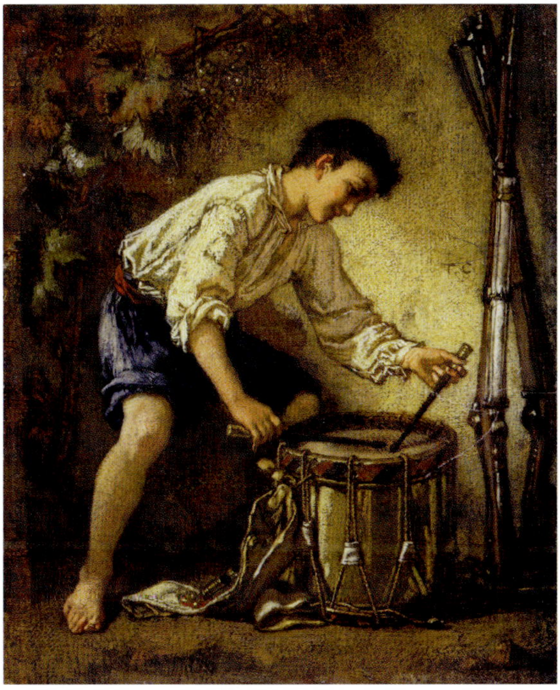

XX. L'Enfant au Tambour Thomas Couture

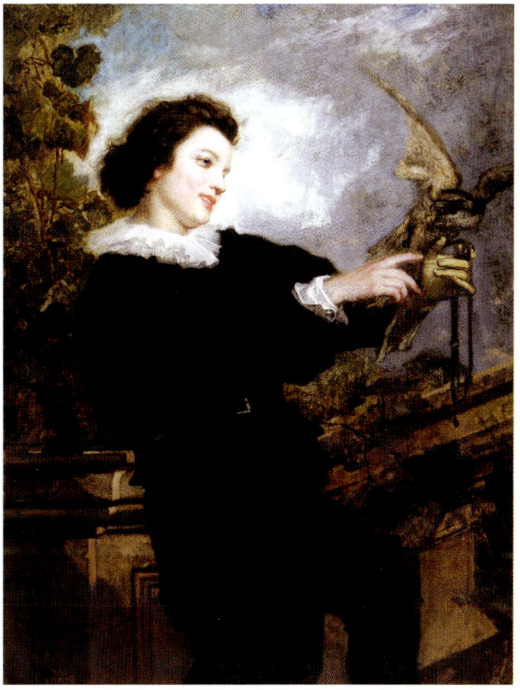

XXI. Le Fauconnier Thomas Couture

Joanna first saw 'The Drummer Boy' (1857) in Couture's atelier, and though she liked 'the action of the whole figure, and the colour of the white and blue in his dress', she thought the subject 'a bagatelle'. She preferred his 'Boy with the Falcon' (1844), which she declared the finest portrait exhibited at the Exposition Universelle in Paris in 1855 – 'a picture 'instinct with life and youth'.

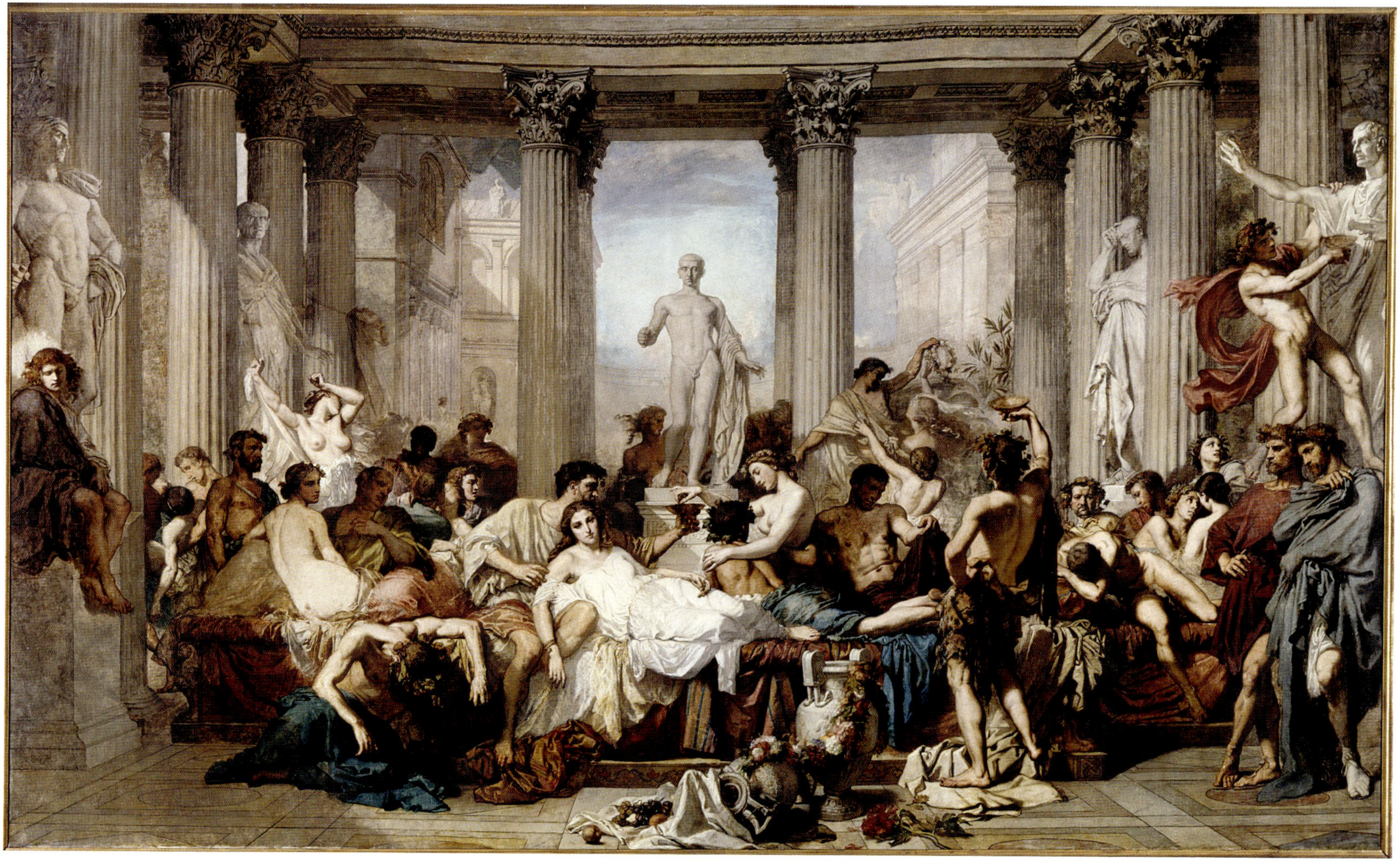

XXII. *Romains de la Decadence (Rome in its Decay)* Thomas Couture

Painted in 1847, this is generally considered to be Couture's masterpiece, and though Joanna had some reservations about her teacher's work in general, she had none about this. She hailed it as 'the finest large historical work exhibited' at the Exposition Universelle, adding that for masterly handling of colour, it 'vies with the finest Veronese at the Louvre'. For her there was no greater accolade.

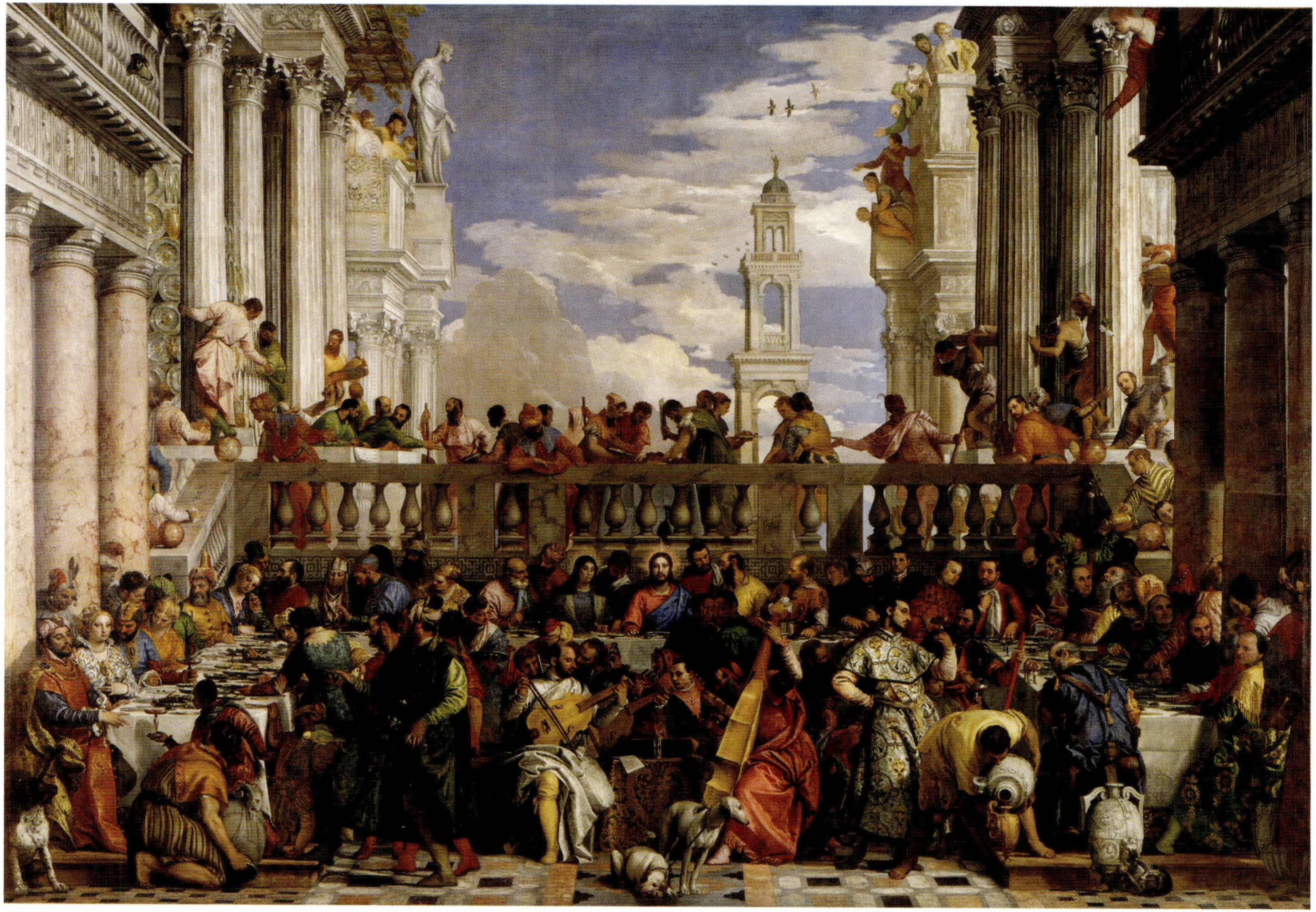

XXIII. *The Wedding at Cana* Paolo Veronese

This painting (dated 1562–63) was an inspiration to Joanna on her visits to Paris in 1852 and 1855-6 and exerted a powerful influence on her work. For her, Veronese was the supreme colourist. D. G. Rossetti went further, declaring it 'the greatest picture in the world beyond a doubt'.

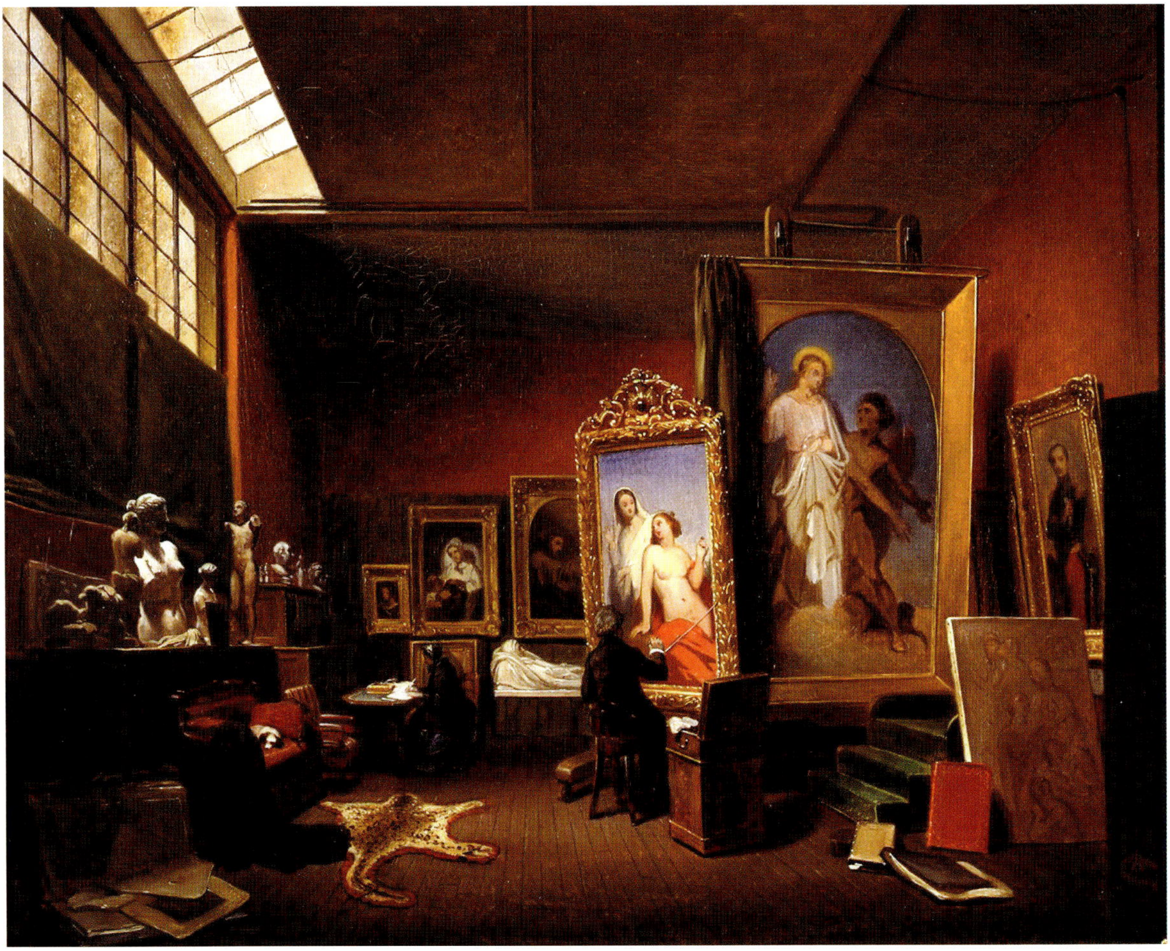

XXIV. *Ary Scheffer's Large Studio* Ary Johannes Lamme

Ary Scheffer was one of the few French painters Joanna admired, and in November 1855 she, John Cook and the Farwells visited him in his studio. This painting, by Scheffer's cousin, was executed in 1851 and gives a charming insight into the life and work of the artist. It shows his large studio, with Scheffer at work on one of the monumental classical pieces for which he was best known.

difficult to be perfectly candid at all times, but to be otherwise would be unworthy of you.

I suppose this of mine will cross a letter from you, whether or no, let me have an answer to this however short by return of post. The contents of it are of course between ourselves. Dear Mamma, Uncle and my Aunts of course believe me to be in the happiest state of mind, and indeed I am much easier now I have told you all. You will announce our engagement to the Mordans, Mat and George. As to mentioning it to others I leave it to you to act exactly as you please ... My friend Hennie Moore has been your warmest champion from the first. I believe she is still tied to her sofa. It may be a funny whim of mine, but I think it would be a pleasure to her to see you for an hour some afternoon. She thinks all is over between us. You could undeceive her.

There is wisdom, tenderness and melancholy in her letter. She recognised that her 'intense love of independence, which has often been a bane to me' was at the core of her uneasiness and a part of her longed for him to 'charm it away altogether'. But she was not prepared to leave her feelings unexamined.

Henry tried, in his own way, to understand. On 15 June he wrote: 'We are but mortals. You have no reason to entertain a jealous doubt of the direction of your feelings, because you find yourself oppressed with that weighing sensation which must be consequent upon a sudden change from a long habituated thought and determination.' It was only five weeks since he had made his position clear: 'So far from thinking you fickle or cruel, my dear Joney, I have gathered to myself the greatest happiness from your letter of this morning. You have unhesitatingly shown me your heart – for all my large possessions there I am proud and most thankful.'

He knew she was suffering profound doubts, but had unbounded confidence in his ability to counter them. He was determinedly light-hearted: 'PS I found your and my little large-eyed friend [Hennie Moore] out of town. She went yesterday to Margate ... The servant told me that Miss Moore was at home, and appeared rather surprised that she would not do as well. You must lose no time, Joney, in writing and dispelling the scandal which, depend upon it, is already surrounding Miss Hennie. A young man in a white waistcoat – 4 o'clock in the afternoon – nobody else will do – striding away with an air of disappointment – all very suspicious – very.'

For Joanna it was not so simple. Her depression increased, and 'I fear Mamma guesses all is not right'. His letters both pleased and distressed her –

'how indomitably hopeful you are.' She had been reluctant to accept his ring on her finger – 'you took me completely by storm last Wednesday morning' – and now lived in fear that she might never come to love him 'as I ought and as I must'. On a 'deliciously sunny day' she determined, 'however uncontrollable my thoughts might be, to employ my hands with drawing.'

Henry was, for once, lost for words. 'I ought never to have harped upon the thoughts which you have of late allowed to torment you,' he wrote to her on 18 June. Convinced that his presence was the best way of stopping her 'from running back into your old habit of thinking', he arranged to go and see her again. In the meantime he wrote to George on the 17th, primarily to tell him about the engagement – 'I am heartily glad that I shall have you for a brother-in-law' – but also intent on giving him the latest gossip, as well as advice on his painting. 'Tom Seddon left England last Tuesday for France and will soon return with a wife … Unfortunately he has not sold his "Jerusalem" or either of his large pictures, but he has had a nibble or two … On Monday last Millais left town for Perth. He has gone to marry the ex-Mrs Ruskin there.'[76] Smallfield, he said, was anxious that their old quarrel should be brought to an end at last, and Henry was happy to oblige – on the strict understanding that 'every injurious motive attributed to my conduct' be withdrawn: 'I will never give my hand to a man who announces his conviction that my character is such as Armstead's letters have stated it to be.'

Finally he turned his attention to George's work:

> I hope you have commenced upon some method in your outdoor painting. You must have courage to tear yourself away from 'bits' except where they are parts of an extended subject then you can paint them with all the care and reality possible. Once having decided upon a good subject I should frequent the spot and learn the scene thoroughly: after having made a very careful pencil drawing of the distant mountains, I should take a number of outlines on a reduced scale, and paint upon them when any good or unusual effect presented itself, not forgetting how the foreground objects are at such times affected by the lights and shadows. If you bring away very careful studies of the different parts of the foreground, and even the plane next removed, they will be almost as useful to you in your studio to paint from into your picture, as if you had dug up rocks, fern, road, sea and placed them bodily in your garden.

76 Millais and Effie Ruskin were married at Bowerswell on 3 July 1855. Startlingly, their union was reported in the deaths notices in the *Leader* on 7 July.

But even as Henry was telling his friends and family about their engagement, he felt Joanna's love, never certain, slipping away again. On 18 June he wrote: 'The difference of tone which three days has made in your writing would have made me most uneasy if I had not the knowledge of being so shortly with you.' It was absence alone, he felt, that drove her back into her 'old habit of thinking' and he counted on a second visit to Ashford Bowdler to reassure her. He hoped the weather might be fine enough 'to induce us to sketch'. Henry arrived on 20 June and stayed for five days, but his presence did not produce the desired effect. Joanna wrote to her brother Matthias on 27 June to say that she had once again tried to end their relationship: 'The fact was I felt he was becoming more and more to me every day, and yet I wished not to marry, so I thought the sooner I put an end to it the easier the effort would be to me and better for us both in every way.'

Perhaps it was at the Bone Well – that beauty spot 'so endeared to Mamma by many girlish recollections' – that Joanna endeavoured to convince Henry, more forcibly than before, that the love she felt for him was not powerful enough to overcome her desire to remain single and devote herself to her work. She may even have tried to give him back his ring. According to Alice, they both made sketches there, which, though 'of no great merit', were very important to Henry in later years. In letters to Matthias and Lilly, written on 27 and 28 July, she speaks of her determination to finish her 'Bone Well' picture before going on to Wales[77] – a railway journey on which Henry was determined to accompany her.

Yet even as she chafed at his – justifiable – possessiveness, she could not bring herself to break the engagement once and for all. In her letter of 1 July she wrote: 'In my determination to be sincere, I am afraid I appear callous to your suffering … My dear Henry, I know that to write you such a letter as this is like giving husks instead of wheat to a hungry man … When I picture you in the railway carriage as you left Ashford, the words "My poor boy" rise to my lips.' Of her plan to go to Wales, she wrote: 'I suppose I must let you know the day – I'm not sure that I shall.' It was not encouraging but neither was it definitive.

In London, meanwhile, a smallpox epidemic was raging, and when Henry's father and his sister Maria fell ill (mercifully with a mild form of the disease), Henry was obliged to find lodgings elsewhere in order to continue working. It was a measure of Mrs Boyce's regard that she offered him rooms at Park Place Villas for as long as she and Joanna were out of town. It must have been both a pleasure and a torment for him to feel so close to Joanna even while they were apart, and their daily letters continued unabated.

77 George was already ensconced in lodgings at Tyn-y-Cae, a hamlet near Betws-y-Coed. Joanna was to stay at Coed Fa, the Naylors' house at Betwys.

On 2 July he wrote to her: 'You now know more of my real self than any other mortal, and I can commune with you in almost the same spirit as I can with my God. Every morning as I leave my bedroom I pay a short visit to your studio ... You have left very little out for me to rummage amongst. I have turned round a canvas that was once forbidden me – "Mrs Hilton" – I am counting the days to the time when you will come and treat my studio as unceremoniously as I have yours.' On the 3rd he told her that he was painting 'with a greater zest than at any time since I left Ashford'. He had received a visit from a Mrs Bolton who wished to commission a portrait of her daughter Helen: 'I thought it unlikely that Mrs Bolton would give me my present price – 30 guineas for a small head size miniature, when I painted her own portrait a larger size four years ago for 10 guineas, and other things when I was at Dickinson's at a lower rate; but the present is a proof of how possible it is to miscalculate, for the commission has been given without demur.' Of her letters, he added: 'Your pearls are not thrown before swine. Drop me one on your work-a-days and string me more when you have leisure.'

Ever attentive, he had undertaken to retrieve the death mask of Joanna's father from Mr Thomas, the sculptor, where, much to Joanna's chagrin, it had lain uncollected for so long. On 3 July he reported that Mr Thomas had not yet sent it but there was no reason to fear it had been damaged. By 7 July the cast was in his possession – 'it is a much stronger memento than a picture or even daguerreotype could be'.[78]

As far as the smallpox went, he had been vaccinated twice,[79] he told her, and was 'without the least fear of the disease'. He had visited her sister on the 3rd – 'had a vociferous romp with Master Edgar' – and on the evening of the 4th he and Mat went to the Olympic Theatre to see 'Mr and Mrs Wigan in *Still Waters Run Deep*'.

Up to this point, the suitor, though he had had to bring all his powers of persuasion to bear upon his beloved, had done so in the full confidence that he had her mother's support. By early July, even as he wandered the rooms of Park Place Villas, everything had changed. In a letter to Joanna, Henry confessed – belatedly – to 'a short conversation we had together on the lawn the Monday evening before I left Ashford', in which Mrs Boyce had told him that she 'regretted the assistance

78 The decision was made to leave the cast unpainted, though it was returned to Mr Thomas later in the month to be mounted. It was to be delivered to Park Place Villas before Joanna's return to London.

79 Compulsory vaccination for smallpox had been introduced the previous year.

she gave me' and expressed her conviction that Henry would not have persisted in his suit had she not encouraged him.

Given Joanna's own doubts, it is not surprising that he did not admit to this earlier, but on 5 July Mrs Boyce wrote more forcibly to him: 'I have ceased to desire the union and now deplore the influence I exercised over both of you. My first impulse was to believe that the dear child's happiness would be secured by accepting your hand, but, now that I have had leisure to consider deliberately all the circumstances of the case, I have my doubts and can plainly see there are several important points we have neglected to discuss and which ought to have been duly weighed ere now by both parties. I must ask you then to let me have a little serious conversation with you on my return home and till then not to see Joanna.'

Henry was dumbfounded. 'Receiving so much discouragement from a quarter where I have hitherto received such lively help has thrown me into dejection – and I wonder whether my sanguine spirit is breaking.' Nevertheless he wrote a firm letter to Mrs Boyce, copying it to his fiancée, enumerating the privileges of an engaged man – one of which, he felt, should be the right to accompany Joanna on her journey from Ashford to Wales.

In no time at all the whole family was involved. Mrs Boyce's opposition may well have been fuelled by Joanna's own 'desponding moods', which included involuntarily confessing her uneasiness about her engagement in her sleep. Matthias, who had suffered at his mother's hands over his own engagement, wrote firmly and lovingly to his sister on 7 July: 'I have given him [Wells] my advice and my good wishes for his success in every way, but I have not forgotten to first consider you and your happiness. I can trust myself to say that I will support you in every step you may take, but I must advise you to think and act for yourself and not to yield to others', even Mamma's, wishes or commands ... You are of an age and have the ability to think for yourself.' On the same day Henry wrote: 'Do desist, my dearest girl, from asking me to end our engagement. If you asked me to open an artery – there would flow blood and life too.'

It should have been a time of rejoicing. 'Elgiva' had attracted Ruskin's serious attention in the third edition of his *Notes on some of the principal pictures in the Royal Academy 1855'* (a copy of which he sent to Henry for Joanna), and in the *Illustrated London News*:[80]

> The expression in this head is so subtle, and so tenderly wrought, that at first the picture might easily be passed as hard or cold; but it could only be so passed, as Elgiva herself might have been sometimes seen

80 *Illustrated London News*, 12 July 1855.

> by a stranger – without penetration of her sorrow. As we watch the face for a little time, the slight arch of the lip seems to begin to quiver, and the eyes fill with ineffable sadness and a look of despair.

Henry was triumphant: 'Certainly the most trumping criticism that ever was awarded to the first exhibited work of an artist. It is astonishing what a conspiracy there is just now to upset the bushel that covers Joanna's candle.' He was as proud as though it were his own work and prouder still that Ruskin himself had sent his *Notes* to be forwarded.

He did accompany her on the train to Wales, but the meeting proved a bitter one. The only promise he could salvage from their conversation was 'a short lease for three years. On 11 July 1858, if we are both living and unmarried, I shall ask you to accompany me to Shrewsbury, and there, near the spot where you granted me my request, I shall take my ring from your finger and drop it into the Severn and give you a last kiss sealing three years of gratitude. That you may withhold the ring will be my prayer from this time until that moment.'

Thus their engagement limped on. Afraid now that every written or reported word might be used against him, Henry began to copy all the letters he wrote to Mrs Boyce (something that went completely against the grain with him) in case they might be needed either as ammunition or in his defence. Joanna, ensconced at Coed Fa, wrote to him in businesslike vein on 14 July, preparing him for the forthcoming interview with her mother, and giving an unsparing insight into Mrs Boyce's character. It was clear that, even for such a lame betrothal to proceed, Mamma must be wooed and won: 'Do be guarded, dear Henry, not to use words or let slip an expression she can take hold of and use against you with apparent justice.'

Even so she was not, it seems, unduly worried. Far more concerning was her dissatisfaction with her 'Bone Well' picture: 'I have not had the courage to undo my parcel of traps yet. I dread the sight of that detestable Well – and Mr Naylor wants to bless his eyes with the sight of my "niggle" – his generic term for anything done with a brush smaller than a varnishing tool … George had the impertinence last night to propose to him to charge a musket with the three primary colours and shoot them on to the canvas[81]. He is wonderfully clever at imitations of manner and conversation and kept us on the roar last evening.'

The dreaded interview took place at Park Place Villas on 16 July. Henry reported that it had lasted three quarters of an hour and had covered every subject Joanna had anticipated 'except my health and deafness':

[81] George had by now joined Joanna in Wales.

> She allowed me to understand downright, that myself and my 'entourage' were not worthy of you, yet there occurred to neither of us the least unruffling of temper, either during the conversation or during the rest of the evening. We were exactly the same to each other as in earlier and more auspicious days. I don't know whether this was in any degree due to my tact, but certainly the principle cause was her own mood … She has brought herself to believe, that in marrying me you would ultimately have to become the support of myself and my numerous relatives, that I should thro' sickness, loss of limb or some other cause become useless in my profession and that all my sisters might become dependent upon me, or rather upon you. This is rather a sad picture, perhaps rather improbable. I tried to convince her, that my parents, altho' not rich, would leave behind them undoubted property in the shape of houses, land and Bank stock, which altho' requiring frugal management, would at least save my sisters from dependence upon others. With regard to myself I hinted that in these modern times there were such things as Life Insurances etc. … and that it would be my wish that your business friends should so secure your property that its use should never be lost to you. She then asked me the delicate question whether I thought that I was progressing in my Art – and said that she had heard Mr Cook say that he did not think my pictures were so good this year as last. I told her it was a difficult matter for me to given an opinion upon, but assured her that I still had a good deal of conceit left in me. We both of us had a laugh and she said she thought I had.

He did not attempt to convey the entire conversation, but told Joanna that he and her mother 'had hold of each others' hands from beginning to end'. He also 'thought it right to retain the remembrance that I was near a Volcano, and be circumspect'. 'As I left,' he wrote, 'Mat at the door asked me hurriedly how it had passed – and rubbing his eyes said he supposed he should be kept up another hour, but he intended to "cut it short".'

He added: 'I consider it very unkind treatment that you should withhold your "detestable Well" from my sight and yet make up your mind to show it to Mr Naylor.'

Joanna replied immediately, adding to the letter she had already begun: 'I have just received your letter. Its contents, as you may imagine, are a real relief to me. Though I was surprised, I can understand it all perfectly. You met Mamma with real affection and respect. This at once destroyed all bitterness in her feeling towards you. This is where Mordan fails. He loses his temper and says rude and even insulting things to her. These she fastens on and all is over.'

It is notable that even at times of crisis, artistic questions required answers, and that whatever may have been happening at home, Joanna was enjoying herself in Wales. On 16 July she described a climb to the top of Gallt-y-Foel, 'George being of the party', in the early evening: 'It was pure enjoyment and yet so thankless is human nature, we all complained of the sunset not being up to the mark':

> George wants to know your opinion of Antwerp blue. Whether it is serviceable in foregrounds etc… Mr Naylor is constantly teasing him about his wretched quarters at Tyn-y-Cae, foretelling rheumatism etc. Of course I take up the chorus, but he is as unimpressionable on that as on other matters. I cannot lecture him on his painting – I do not understand landscape well enough. Besides I have such faith in what he does – and a *'je ne sais quoi'* makes me silent. *A propos* of this, he lectured me well last night on two little pencil sketches of Jeannie and Arthur, (I like him to do it), and informed me that the noses were twisting on to the cheeks – naïvely adding that it was the first time he had noticed that peculiarity in my heads.

The description of Mr Naylor that follows is classic Joanna – she had an instinctive insight into the characters of others, if rather less understanding of the impression she was making on them.

> I have some hopes of getting a study of Mr Naylor. He has a very fine head; he is out of health in body and mind. His fine natural powers are wasting away and he seems like a man with little hope in this world or the next. He might get plenty of literary employment, but he is too indolent, and yet *'Ennui'* is devouring him. In his painting the reason for his failure is evident. He expects to arrive at results without using the means. He cannot draw a rock or a feature correctly and yet expects to produce fine landscapes and heads. I have been congratulating myself that he would spare me the infliction of his portraits, but I deceived myself. Yesterday he came into the drawing room and said he would show me something if I would stand at the distance prescribed. I promised obedience and forthwith there passed before me a procession more ghastly and certainly more distressing than the Kings before Macbeth, for I was

> obliged to affect complacence. I'm afraid my attempt was anything but graceful …
>
> The 'Bone Well' seems to get nastier each time I look at it. Today I shall use the scrapings of my palette in destroying a part of it peculiarly obnoxious.

She was content to be away from Henry and believed him to be happier without her. If she was aware that the widowed Mr Naylor might have an eye to her as a wife (Mrs Boyce had certainly given Henry to understand this, but he may have chosen to keep it to himself), she did not take it seriously. She was also unimpressed by Henry's attempt to woo her back to London on the strength of her special invitation to the Royal Academy at the beginning of August – 'You must not think of missing it … there will be few who this year will not have heard of J. M. Boyce' – and by what she recognised as Ruskin's belated recognition: 'The Academy have no respect for his criticisms and laugh at his discoveries – to expect or to fear exciting notice in such an assemblage would be a most ludicrous vanity.' As far as her own presence went: 'I am too conscious of my unprepossessing "physique" ever to like the notice of strangers.'

This was a recurring theme with her, and her lack of confidence in her own attractions may well have contributed to her inability to comprehend the strength of Henry's feelings. Joanna may not have been conventionally pretty, but, as William Michael Rossetti said in his *Reminiscences,* she 'had a picturesque face, with a noticeable air of concentration and resolve'. He added: 'She was probably conscious of power, but (so far as I saw) quite free from self-applause – looking upon what she had done as a mere imperfect earnest of what she might aim at doing.'[82] Certainly she was far more interested in George's paint problems than in disporting herself at the Royal Academy.

Henry replied impatiently: 'Tell George that gum may do some good to his cobalt, but cannot possibly do any radical good to his drawings. My experience of Antwerp blue is this. I used it as a background to a miniature copy I made of Thorburn[83] during my early days at Bond Street. In a few months the colour had turned the grey-greens into purples, by destroying the yellow I suppose, and committed other kinds of devilry … But why does George want

[82] W. M. Rossetti, *Some Reminiscences*, p.154.

[83] Robert Thorburn (1818–85). Scottish-born miniaturist with a soft and flattering style. His distinguished clientèle included Queen Victoria and Prince Albert, and on several occasions overlapped with Henry's. He was among those who experimented with very large pieces of ivory, such as that used by Henry for Plate I.

the colour? Why cannot he be satisfied with Indigo? – But of course George can't use what the common herd do.'

She answered him straight away: 'George says Indigo flies, and both he and Mr Naylor thought Antwerp blue one of the fastest colours – and you must admit Indigo is rather a dingy colour to use for greens in some sunlight effects. George, she said, was 'sadly desponding about his drawing – but I hope and believe it is only a passing cloud … The fear of failure in getting into the Old Water-Colour weighs upon him.'

On the 23rd Henry castigated her for her self-consciousness: 'I am sick and tired at the manner in which you harp upon your "physique". Do you flatter yourself you are a kind of "yellow dwarf"?' He told her that he had never allowed himself to tell any woman that he thought her beautiful, but that his friends were united in praise of her and thought she had a 'capital head'. He added that in his experience indigo did not 'fly'.

The bulk of his letter, however, was taken up with a visit he had made to Captain Arthur Cumming's floating battery. Ironclad floating batteries, both French and English, played a significant part in the Crimean war: they were, in effect, the precursors of ironclad warships, heavily armed and armoured, and designed to provide covering fire onto enemy shore positions. The British bombardment of Kronstadt in the Baltic from floating batteries was instrumental in securing peace with Russia. Henry, whose miniature of Captain Cumming's wife had been much admired, learnt that the captain was commanding HMS Glatton, a naval battery moored at Sheerness, and expressed an interest in seeing it. Accordingly Mrs Cumming issued an invitation, with the proviso that the battery was due to sail imminently and he would have to take his chance on the bird having flown:

> I left London Bridge by the 8 o'clock train, steamed down the Medway and landed at Sheerness Pier at 11 o'clock. I walked to the Cummings' lodgings and after some wine and biscuits we went on to the beach where the Captain's gig was awaiting us. It was very grand to sail and be rowed about by man-of-war's men in their snow white shirts turned up with blue and 'Glatton' printed in gold letters on their caps – the Captain steering … Afterwards we were rowed to the 'Devonshire' to see the Russian prisoners. The ship is kept in very clean condition and the prisoners are now in themselves very cleanly. They are allowed to ramble at liberty over the greater part of the ship, and, as far as prisoners can be, they seem very comfortable. The Lieutenant commanding spoke well of their conduct. They spend their time carving toys in

> wood, and works of great patience they are. They ask 1/6d for a piece of work that must take a man at least a week or ten days. I was most interested by the care bestowed by the Russian prisoners in forming an altar for their worship. A few bad Greek pictures have been given to them by some friends over here and also a manuscript service. They themselves have carved rude candlesticks, and on a framework have strained glazed calico to make the altar. Three little glass lamps are suspended, and the lights are burning unceasingly by day and night. The oil is purchased by the prisoners out of the money they earn by making toys.

John Cook, Henry said, was delighted to hear of their engagement, but he worried that Mrs Boyce's change of heart would end by making 'a perfect devil' of him in the opinions of their friends. He also mentions their plans to meet in Paris: 'I cannot think of breaking my promise to my sisters to take them later in the Autumn – and what is more I cannot disappoint myself of the pleasure I have long anticipated of looking at the pictures and other sights in your company.' He added: 'I have just re-perused your last letter but one and have had another laugh at your fuss about lionising … My studio is quite gay today. Mrs Vansittart gave me a sitting this morning and brought me a heap of flowers from Bisham Abbey. I have divided them into three nosegays. They make my oak cabinet look something like a Catholic Altar.'

His distrust of Mrs Boyce was well founded. She wrote at length to Joanna expressing her conviction that her daughter had been 'hurried by undue importunities' into the engagement, and had failed to appreciate the 'disagreeables and disadvantages' that would result. 'I like the man well enough, but I dislike the match. Still, my dear Joney, if you can assure me you really wish to marry, and that an union with Wells is essential to your happiness, then I will endeavour not to oppose it, but at the same time I fear I can never entirely approve or anticipate the event with pleasure.' She reminded her daughter that she had always maintained she would be 'more happy in a single life'.

Joanna replied with care, copying the letter to Henry: 'As to my engagement, I know that all you say is prompted by your anxiety and love for me. I wish to write and talk as little as possible on the subject. You need not doubt for an instant that, if I wished to free myself, Henry would not exact the fulfilment of my promise, but I do not wish to free myself.'

Henry was not reassured, having a 'presentiment' that there would be another explosion before Joanna returned to London. In his letter of 25 July, he told her that the Mordans had received 'an extraordinary and unaccountable epistle' from Mrs Boyce and that, though Mordan had countered it robustly, other friends and relations could well prove more susceptible to her attacks on his reputation.[84] 'Well, I suppose in the long run we shall be none the worse for this toss on a sea of vexation and trouble – but for itself it is not covetable.'

On 26 July he was summoned for a further uncomfortable interview at Park Place Villas: 'Scarcely a new feature in the attack ... Her ever-recurring refrain was that I had exerted "undue influence ... Why should Joanna with all her accomplishments and income enter upon an inferior marriage to her sister?"'[85] His shrewd conclusion was that Mrs Boyce had never expected Joanna to countenance marriage at all, and, finding that she was prepared to consider it, now thought only in terms of a higher bidder. Her anger with Henry arose from a conviction that he had, in some way, 'taken advantage' of the situation. 'Before and after', he wrote, 'she was nearly the same as usual – and in face of indelicate abuse, she oddly professes a sort of liking for me personally.'

In the midst of this gathering storm, Joanna's response must have appeared insouciant to a degree. Her own solution (as was habitual with her) was to refuse to discuss the matter with her mother – 'I shall speak with her as little as possible on the subject' – and she compounded her failure to understand just how bad things were by refusing to name a date for her return and giving singularly frivolous reasons for the delay:

> 11 a.m. I need the fortifications and resources of Sevastopol to resist the unceasing cannonade of solicitations and imprecations hurled against me here – more than once the moment of defeat seemed near. The Naylors have invited a certain Mr Bernard Smith to stay a few days at Coed-Fa and have made every effort to arrange that his visit should be paid during mine – as he is a clever, witty and (better than all) a magnificently bearded man! ...
>
> PS 4 p.m. Mr Naylor and Jeannie have made a violent assault this morning and I really think will force the citadel. I cannot decide before seeing George, but do not be surprised at the receipt of a letter on Monday or even Tuesday morning announcing my intention of staying till the end of the week. I suppose there is no chance of my letters being opened at Llanwst, but just notice the seal. I use that antiquated little gold ring you have noticed on the 3rd finger of my left hand.

84 This letter does not survive.

85 Augustus Mordan was the son of a wealthy jeweller.

Henry had had enough. He went to stay with Mr Wetton, 'the very tall (6 ft 4ins) acquaintance whom Clement Folkard and myself met on the Rhone last autumn'. Wetton was secretary to the Australian Pacific Steam Company who, with his wife and many children, had returned to England from Australia on inheriting a farm, Joldens, on Holmbury Hill in Surrey. A charming, if careless, man, he was excellent company and a good foil for the serious and conscientious Henry. He had become a close friend. From the sanctuary of Joldens Henry wrote to Joanna on 28 July:

> Monday will be the first day that I have entered Stratford Place with the wish not to find a letter from you. I certainly find it difficult to understand how, in face of the great interest with which you have professed to look forward to your being an invited guest to the Reunion at the Academy … you find a certain Mr Bernard Smith a sufficient inducement to change your promise and determination. Since you fixed the day of your return, I have considered every intermediate hour as something to be struggled thro' or put aside in my oblivion, and now you coolly – without the least apparent comprehension of my feelings – seem inclined to move away the date by several days. An agreeable speech will have to pass my lips when I inform your and my relatives that you have changed your promise in order that you may enjoy for a few days the society of a 'clever and witty' man.
>
> In not very thankful mood, I remain …

By then Joanna had received his account of his interview with her mother and on the same day began a letter to him: 'It is a grief and a shame to me that my dear Mother should so forget herself as to speak such unjust and ungenerous words … Your view of Mamma's motives is severe, but very near the truth. She humiliates and insults me by her present course, but she cannot see it and believes she is only doing her duty … The Naylors are so anxious for me to stay that in all probability I shall remain a few days longer. I am ashamed of having so long refused and making such a favour of it.'

His angry missive arrived as she was writing hers. She added: '*Sunday morn:* I have but a few moments, George and I have been confabulating for an hour or more this morning about our departure, and have at last decided to defer it to tomorrow week.' The weather had been wet and George wished to make the most of the fact that it had recently improved. She was amused by Henry's indignation: 'I thought you had too much faith in me and yourself to let the green-eyed monster ever creep between us. I could not forbear laughing, but indeed I am grieved if I have really given you pain – though I can scarcely credit it.' Mr Naylor, she added, had argued that the evening at the Academy would be 'by no means so delightful as I had imagined it'. All the same she hoped he would go and would give her an account of it. 'Mr Naylor has given me several sittings ... A sweet little girl named Amy Spooner has also sat or rather fidgeted to me.'

By now Henry was feeling frankly sorry for himself. On 30 July he declared that were the position reversed and he the unheeding, uncaring one, he hoped he might find in himself the strength to break an engagement 'so unequally met'. He could not be jealous of a man he had never met, he argued, but 'I feel most acutely the ease with which you can give to others a preference'. And for once she was profoundly moved by his distress:

> You have given me the most precious of earthly blessings – the deep, pure love of a noble hearted man. While life lasts I cannot cease to be grateful for it, and the memory that it once was mine – you know that my love in its <u>fullness</u> has never been given in exchange – at one time it might have been, but a shadow fell between us, which separated and yet drew us in one sense closer together. Our present relationship was the result. If you could see into my heart you would know how I value the privilege of being your solace and safeguard during these three coming years, but I am unequal to it. Within three weeks your disappointment in me has commenced.

From the beginning, Joanna seems to have regarded their relationship as a battle between Art and Love – a battle which, for her, Art would always win. The shadow she refers to is harder to interpret, but there are hints that she feared that the death of her father had, though it brought her and Henry closer, damaged her capacity to love him fully. Later she wrote to him again: 'Truly letters are dangerous things, when made the channel for the expression of our feelings. How difficult it is to find the right word, and to choose the one thought from among a hundred others, which shall best represent our state of mind at the moment. And when written how easily misconstrued – wanting the explanatory look or tone which would give it true life and meaning.'

Henry responded nobly, writing on 1 August to lift her from her 'suppliants' place' and asking her forgiveness for 'the troubled manner, perhaps spleen' he had indulged in; but the truth was that he was aware, as she was not, of the extent to which her protracted absence was fuelling the storm brewing in London. Protecting her during this 'anxious and ill-judging time', he said, was 'awkward' – an understatement, one feels.

By now Joanna and Henry were exchanging not just their own correspondence, but that of other interested parties. 'For the present', Henry told her, 'your Mamma has made a convert of Mr W. Boone.' Though Joanna reiterated: 'I do not trouble myself about the coming struggle though it may be a hard one,' she was seriously underestimating the strength of the opposition, and was even prepared to find it amusing: 'Mamma, Uncle and Aunt Robert and Mr Boone!! in array against me. The thought of "my poor boy" will be as the sling and stone in my hand.'

Henry was more acute: 'Your Mamma, besides being very clever, sees things so thoroughly like a fanatic or enthusiast, that her earnestness and the manner in which she builds on her own premises, are the very qualities to make converts, especially amongst those who are out of the way of hearing the other side of the question.'

As he had promised, he gave her news of the conversazione at the Royal Academy, which included a meeting with Leighton, whom he had not seen since Rome:

> I, of course, abused him for so easily forgetting my address. He pleaded multitudinous engagements – in short, lionising. He was conceited enough when I knew him in Italy ... He did the patronising of me in a sublimely gracious manner, taking one of my hands in both of his he said, 'and now, my dear fellow, let me congratulate you on your very charming works in the Miniature room. Being a stranger in England this is the first opportunity I have had of noticing them.' Of course I was speechless – overcome by the condescension – and took out my handkerchief to hide my blushes.

Success or not, his prospects were not good enough for Mrs Boyce. She had convinced herself that Henry's many dependents would be a drain on his own income and lead to his relying on Joanna's. Though she did not openly accuse him of wanting to marry Joanna for her money, the implication was there – and it was an implication that weighed with her friends. On 3 August he told Joanna: 'I have learned that the successful argument that turned Mr W. Boone was when she told him that I looked with complacency upon the chance of being incapacitated because I could live upon my wife's income ... I am convinced she has written in the same way to Ashford.' When Henry remonstrated with Mrs Boyce that the other members of the family did not take that view, she answered 'Oh, the Mordans take your side simply to oppose me. Mat himself confesses that he cannot help looking upon the affair with the eye of a lover. George is your friend and over Joanna you exercise undue influence.'

His plan – to write to Uncle Robert, and then call a meeting of the family to ask that Mrs Boyce cease 'her constant vexatious treatment' – was abruptly pre-empted when he received a summons to Park Place Villas that same evening. Her last words to him were: 'It is against my wish that you will see my daughter, and I forbid your visits under my roof.'

Joanna, whose main concern appears to have been that she had not allowed herself enough time to finish Lilly's portrait before her brother's wedding, returned from her Welsh haven to London on 6 August to find her betrothed completely bewildered by Mrs Boyce's implacable change of heart: 'She must remember the kisses and congratulations she gave us, when she entered the room at Ashford and found the ring on your finger.' She knew from Henry that Matthias and her mother had had a terrible scene during which she called him 'unworthy names' and told him that he ought to be rooting out everything connected with Henry's father and family. The row unhinged Matthias for the rest of the day.

For Joanna it was torture to hear Henry so relentlessly traduced (her mother had moved on from Henry's precarious livelihood to his family's lowly social position), but she still endeavoured to be 'dutiful'. Indignant and hurt though she felt, she did not think it right to leave her mother on the night of her return in order to meet him. Moreover she felt that Henry had given her mother a hostage to fortune by not making it clear right from the beginning that two of his sisters were employed as teachers. For herself: 'As to the matter of your sisters being engaged in tuition, I honour them for it.'

Now she too came under heavy fire. While her mother approved Henry's suit, she had, he told her in his letter of 15 August, gone out of her way to 'keep up my spirits by defining your character, assuring me that such was your peculiar modesty and purity of mind that she was convinced that even to a husband you would be more reserved than other women. She spoke the truth.' Since then Henry had learned from Mordan the 'shameful injurious words' that Mrs Boyce had used to her daughter and that Joanna had shrunk from telling him. 'How in the face of an estimation made upon a Mother's knowledge of your entire life can she now dare to malign you with ferocity – tearing your very heartstrings? ... You may have some faults, but I would shout to the death that want of purity is not one of them.' He became convinced that the only answer was to encourage a full investigation into his family's affairs – to be carried out perhaps by Mordan. Over the next few days he and Joanna met secretly to discuss their strategy, once at his studio, several times at the home of Mrs Ridley, now Matthias's mother-in-law, and, of course, at Corinth Villa, the home of the Mordans.

❁

It was not until 28 August that the clue to this emotional mayhem emerged. An anonymous letter, purportedly delivered to Mrs Boyce on 4 August and designed to injure his reputation fatally in the opinion of the world, was shown to Henry – probably by Matthias. He promptly took a copy of it to Mr Kinsey, his family's lawyer, whose response was unequivocal: 'There is only one person who could have written this – Mrs Boyce herself.'

No copy of the document survives, though there is plenty of evidence of the controversy that swirled around it. Joanna was horrified later to discover that, long before she and Henry were made aware of it, the letter had been shown to the Moores, as well as to Uncle and Aunt Robert. The discovery that her mother had been discussing her affairs with all and sundry – including Mrs Folkard, 'who though a very kind well-meaning woman, can keep nothing to herself' – confirmed her feeling that, to protect Henry's character and reputation, the only course open to her was to end their engagement. She realised that her instinct for reticence had done her no favours: 'I had shrunk from writing to Uncle and Aunt hoping each day matters might be more settled. I was very foolish for they having only Mamma's side of the question and being vexed at my silence began to think I was much to blame and to coincide with her.' This she determined to put right. She wrote them a long letter and Henry, hearing that they were about to leave for Southampton, went to Ashford to see them. Joanna reported: 'They were perfectly shocked to find how Mamma misrepresented many things, and then determined – partly owing to a letter from her – to come to us for a few days. Uncle has undertaken all necessary enquiries.' Though Henry had insisted upon a thorough investigation of his background and family circumstances, she was well aware that this – humiliating under any conditions – would be intolerable when carried out under the Boyce family spotlight. On 20 August she had made him take the ring from her finger, but seeing his utter wretchedness, had put it back on again. 'Not one spark of anger did he show,' she wrote to Matthias the following day. 'Only grief and unaltered tenderness for me.'

There were other flutterings in the emotional dovecote in the form of George's supposed engagement to Miss Naylor: 'I suppose it is true,' Henry wrote to Joanna on 21 August, 'if so it seems to me he ought to be heartily congratulated.' But there was no confirmation of this in George's reply of 7 September, from 'The Fish', Tan Rallt, where he was enjoying the 'luxury of a "comfortable" inn' and working on a study of the Dinas Crags – 'the only creditable thing in the careful line I've done'. He added that he was 'indebted to Uncle and Aunt for their great kindness in coming up to Town at this juncture and making enquiries, which were doubtless quite necessary, but which there was great difficulty, if not impossibility, in the way of my undertaking or even Mat'.

In the meantime, Joanna, on the strength of breaking her engagement (though she had not yet done so), extracted from her mother an undertaking to receive Henry once more at Park Place Villas. Her mother wrote: 'I will see Mr Wells – I will do anything you wish rather than this wretched, disgraceful state of affairs should prevail in our once happy family … Do as you please … Above all things I entreat you, my darling child to believe me till death your truly affectionate mother.'

Henry accordingly went, telling Hennie Moore on 3 September that 'altho' the dinner was sufficiently handsome I had no slice given me of the "fatted calf"'. He had lost no time in showing his analysis of the 'anonymous letter' to Uncle Robert who read it, folded it and put it back in the envelope saying: 'All I can say is, that I hope your belief may not be true.' In the meantime he was carrying out his investigation, and, on 10 September, wrote to Joanna from Ramsgate: 'Agreeable to my promise, I now send you a copy of so much of a note I have just written to your Mother as relates to the enquiry I have recently made at her request about Mr H. T. Wells, his property, family, etc.'

The letter to Mrs Boyce was as follows:

My dear Sister

Altho' you will know the result of the enquiry I have lately made relating to Mr Henry T. Wells, I consider it desirable in order that no mistake shall occur to inform you in writing that having seen two of the gentlemen to whom he referred you, I have every reason to believe that all Mr Wells stated in his memorandum of the 26th ultimo relating to his family, their property and income, and their respectability is quite correct.

I was particular in my enquiry on every point raised by you but more especially as to Mr Wells's moral character and conduct, past and present – and I am happy to assure you that I am so satisfied on this momentous subject that I should not hesitate to sanction his union with any dear relative of mine.

Believe me,
Your affectionate brother,
Robert Thomas

This should surely have been the end of it. It wasn't. On 21 September Joanna wrote a long letter to George, summing up all that had happened, including Uncle Robert's recommendation that Mrs Boyce withdraw her objections. 'She consented, but I knew too well this nominal consent was useless, for she hates Henry as some hate those whom they have injured.'

Henry also wrote dejectedly to George: 'My struggles have brought me no success, and so strangely timed was my ultimate defeat that I heard the announcement that my engagement must cease at the very time that any spectator would have congratulated me on having overcome the last of a long list of obstacles … You will give me credit for understanding why I ought not openly to accuse your Mamma, apart from every shade of feeling. I have a selfish stake in my silence … Although my engagement is now about to be broken, I will stubbornly hope that some future day Joney may be my wife.'

In her efforts to restore his reputation, Joanna had made of him 'a rejected man, rejected under the most doubtful-looking circumstances'.

At the end of September both families went to Paris – Henry to stay with his sisters at the Ancien Hôtel Sinet in the Faubourg St Honoré, and Joanna, her mother and Bob at the Hôtel d'Orléans, whence they planned to move into lodgings. Mrs Boyce had announced her intention of staying for three or four weeks, before leaving Joanna and Bob for a further month or two.

On 23 September, before they left, Joanna and Henry had spent a day together by the Thames. He planned the visit carefully – 'the harvest moon will be very near the full on Sunday. I wish our sojourn amidst the trees by the water could be prolonged into that "witching time" thro' and after twilight' – knowing that it could well be their last meeting.

By the time they all departed, however, Joanna had still not broken off the engagement, though according to George 'she intended doing it after the aspersions and slanders Mother has thrown upon [Henry's] character were recanted'. George, though he knew about the anonymous letter, was understandably unwilling to believe that Mrs Boyce could have written it.

Joanna, Bob and their mother were seeing Paris and its surroundings in the company of the Lahee family (the old friends with whom Joanna and Anne had stayed while Park Place Villas was being refurbished), and Joanna wrote daily letters to Henry in an effort to keep him in touch with their schedule. She was in a highly emotional state:

30 September: My darling boy – If you only knew how I am longing to see you, how utterly careless and wretched I am … If you come on Wednesday morning at ½ past 9, in all probability I could see you. Yesterday – shortly after you quitted us, we met Mr Lahee and he kindly took us to see the 'lions'. I pulled towards the fountain wherever it was possible, but never caught sight of you …

1 October: I have no idea where we shall be tomorrow – perhaps at the Invalides after 12 … If you were at the Madeleine tomorrow from 10 to ½ past I will try to be there but cannot promise …

2 October: After bidding you goodnight last evening, I returned to Mamma and soon succeeded in quieting her by telling her that I could not comprehend how she could grudge me a few hours spent with you, when she knew that in a week or ten days I should be separated from you finally … She is lying in bed sobbing and ejaculating the words 'cruel' and 'wretched' at intervals … After seeing you the Mordans made their appearance here … They can neither of them understand the decision I have arrived at, unless – they say – 'You do not love him as you ought'. I can make no answer to this … you are very dear to me, and the mere dread of separation seems to have deprived me of hope and energy …

I will keep this open till the morning in order if possible to give you some idea of our movements during the day. You had much better not call here – there would be but small chance of even a few minutes alone and a great chance of rudeness from Mamma. As to my drawing – do you think it would do for me to call on Rosa Bonheur[86] and see if I could study under her – or do you think the mere study of the head under Couture would be useful?

On 18 October, George made this laconic entry in his diary: 'Received a letter from Lilly containing one from Joanna to Mat from a boarding house – 18 rue d'Astorg, Quartier de la Madelaine, Faubourg St Honoré, where she, Mother and Bob had taken up quarters with 35 ladies – mostly ugly.'

86 Rosa Bonheur (1822–99). French realist painter and sculptor, specialising in animals. The gallery owner Ernest Gambart brought her to England in 1855, and purchased reproduction rights so that he could sell engravings of her paintings.

4

JOANNA IN PARIS

'There stands the Master. Study, my friends.'

'Old Pictures in Florence'

Joanna went to Paris at a turning point in French art. Although the École des Beaux-Arts (like the Royal Academy) championed the academic tradition in its teaching, there were already a significant number of artists – Jean-François Millet, Jean-Baptiste-Camille Corot, Theodore Rousseau, Gustave Courbet and Paul Delaroche among them – who were developing new forms of realism. Barbizon, a village near Fontainebleau, became an artistic centre where Corot and Millet went to paint, and students went to learn. They were encouraged to work *en plein-air* and to make labour a subject worthy of art.

Thomas Couture represented the *juste milieu* – in which French art, in the period following the Revolution, strove for a happy medium between the Classical Academic tradition and the Romantic Avant-Garde. Trained in the academic mode, he early determined not to allow it to become a strait-jacket, and one of his most famous paintings, 'Romains de la Decadence',[87] is a seductive mixture of classical, realistic, and (though he would have repudiated such an idea himself) romantic styles. (*Plate XXII*)

While she thought that 'Millais, Mulready and Holman Hunt were brilliant for colour', Joanna felt strongly that the English school had lost ground to the French, and was eager to learn what she could from the French masters. Not that her choice was unlimited. There were relatively few artists accepting female pupils. Rosa Bonheur, as one of the most successful female artists, appealed to her as a teacher, but Bonheur specialised in landscapes, animals and large canvases while Joanna's work thus far tended towards small-scale portraits. Under Couture, she would become versed in the tradition of the *tête d'expression*, in which students learned to depict passions and emotions in their paintings and sculptures of heads, and which had become the subject of a much-coveted award at the École des Beaux-Arts. For a young woman seeking her own *juste milieu* between the tenets

[87] Now in the Musée d'Orsay.

of the Pre-Raphaelites and academic 'slosh', Couture may well have represented the best chance of achieving it, but the fact that Henry had studied with him for six months in 1850 no doubt exerted a powerful influence – perhaps too powerful.

She enrolled with Couture shortly after her arrival, though it was not until mid-November that her studies began. This was partly because he had yet to find a suitable studio in which to teach his female students (he eventually settled for teaching them in his own studio in the Rue Cadet); but also because she had heard from Bertha Farwell that she, her mother and John Cook hoped to be in Paris in early November. Mr Cook, she said, expected Bob and Joanna to be in constant attendance on them at the Louvre, and at the Exposition Universelle, which had been in full swing since May.

She was not short of models in the meantime, sketching the inhabitants of 18 rue d'Astorg – 'Scotch girls and thoroughly British in their ideas and manners' – and persuading her landlady, Madame Héreau, who 'has a capital head, full of character and goodness', to sit for her. Bob was improving in French, was well in health and was a general favourite with everyone. George, writing on 29 October, speculated on Bob's education and the possibility of his 'making up to a Polish lady in furbelows'. He also asked Joanna to persuade their mother to stay longer in Paris, but fortunately his letter arrived too late to prevent Mrs Boyce returning to London at the beginning of November. As Joanna confessed in her reply to George: 'Our life together lately has been very wretched. I have tried conscientiously and unceasingly to do my duty to her, but she has detected a change in my feelings towards her … I do sincerely grieve that I do not love her as I did, but it is only a difference of degree.' It was far better, she concluded, for them to live apart.

We know from a letter she sent to Henry on 11 October that their engagement had finally been broken off two days before, just as he was leaving Paris. She wrote: 'I can never find words to thank you for all I owe you … My remorse for my conduct to you during the last five months is very bitter. How earnestly I wish that all the pain of the present might fall upon me – I only deserve it.' She asked him not to mention the Couture venture to anyone but George.

Henry confirmed to George that he had taken back his ring – 'at her own determined request'. He had seen more of her in Paris than he had ever dared to anticipate. He later destroyed his letters to Joanna so it is hard to know exactly when they took up their pens again but, though their correspondence faltered briefly, it is clear that it was quickly resumed. On 6 November we find Joanna writing to thank him for 'Hall's Sermons'[88] ('but remember, Henry, I cannot

88 Robert Hall (1764–1831), a Baptist minister famous for his advanced views and charismatic preaching. He was admired by William Wilberforce, Sydney Smith and Lord Brougham among others. Joanna was suitably challenged by him.

accept another present') and worrying about the number of rich and expensive dinners she was being obliged to accept from John Cook. She added: 'I do not think it right to keep up a correspondence with you though I need not tell you it would be a great pleasure to me.'

On the same day, Henry wrote to George to say that no doubt his friends and acquaintances would soon reach the conclusion that he had 'got over it'. He himself saw no probability of this: 'Mine has been no ordinary case of a man asking a wife, meeting a refusal and there an end of the affair. But at a mature age I am, for the first time in my life, moved until I am quite beside myself – it has been no dream, at the living stream I have tasted deeply and profusely.' About Mrs Boyce, he said: 'Your mother has caused me, by using the most unprincipled means, a deprivation very hard for me to bear ... but I do not forget whose mother she is.'

Whatever the reasons – Henry's inability to take no for an answer, Joanna's ingenuous habit of assuming that their correspondence would continue even though she declared each letter to be the last – by the time Joanna began her studies at Couture's atelier on 15 November, it was natural that she should tell Henry all about it:

> Emma Ringer[89] called on me a few days ago to tell me that Couture had suddenly changed his mind and had signified his willingness to give up his studio at the Rue Cadet for the young ladies. As long as Mr Cook and the Farwells were here, of course, my attendance was out of the question.
>
> Bob and I saw them off on Tuesday evening. It was doubtful up to within a few hours of their departure whether Bertha would accompany them or not. If there had been a bedroom vacant at Madame Héreau's I really think she would have stayed ... Wednesday I spent at the Beaux Arts, and after 4 o'clock went to tell Emma Ringer I should join her at the atelier on the morrow morning. Accordingly yesterday morning I set off at ¼ past 8 for the Rue Cadet and arrived a quarter of an hour before any of the others. It is a nice room (but I forgot you have seen it) and capitally heated. I enjoyed my morning's work exceedingly (drawing from the nude). So far from shrinking from it at first as I expected, I had no sooner taken one glance at the model and put my charcoal to paper, than all reluctance vanished and I am convinced that any girl may draw as I have been drawing yesterday and this morning, as free from harm

89 Emma Ringer was a friend of Joanna's and related to her cousins, the Folkards.

or any danger of it, as though they studied a bunch of flowers or a landscape. Couture I have not yet seen.

There seems to be a very ladylike, agreeable collection of girls at the atelier now. You have taught me to notice fingernails – one, I have remarked, who sits near me, with hands scrupulously clean, nails included, and another, I suppose I must confess it, exactly the reverse …

I am annoyed to find that all the studies are without exception ill drawn, and painted in something worse than the sloshy style. The great effort seems to be to makes as great a thickness of paint stick on the canvas as possible. Careful modelling seems a thing forbidden. Our model is a man of colour from Hindustan, I believe; he has a very fine head …

Yesterday morning I was again at the atelier (the third time). As I had finished my chalk study, I began a head life size … I worked my hardest and by the time Couture came – about ½ past 12, it was tolerably presentable. After criticising the study on the easel nearest the door he came to me, being the nearest, he looked at the head and Emma Ringer showed him the full-length study. He seemed not a little pleased and made me two or three compliments, which I need not repeat. What a queer looking little man he is – ugly but full of intelligence. He gave us a little lecture on drawing the foot, which amused me. Two or three had the foot foreshortened very badly. He asked for paper and chalk and said 'To draw the foreshortened foot write forty-three 'thus' which with a little shaping comes tolerably correct – not in my clumsy sketch[90], but in his it was admirable – and it was amusing to hear the gusto with which he described the drawing and position of each toe.

Couture was well established as a teacher. He had opened a studio in 1847 and usually had at least twenty-five to thirty pupils, charging them 120 francs a year. Edouard Manet was among those who studied under him and he had always accepted female students, though he taught them separately. His teaching methods were deliberately less formal than the Academy, as he proclaimed in his Prospectus:

In pursuing his goal, M. Couture opposes the spurious classical school which reproduces the works of bygone times in a banal and imperfect fashion. He is even more hostile to that abominable school,

90 Joanna included a rough sketch at this point

> known under the rubric of 'Romantic' and views with disfavour the tendencies towards petty artistic commercialism. For these reasons he expects and demands solid classical studies.
>
> His teaching is based above all on the great art of ancient Greece, the Renaissance masters and the admirable Flemish school. He believes that it is necessary to study all of these schools in order to reproduce the wonders of nature and ideas of our own time, in noble and elevated style.

A study of the Old Masters formed a central part of Couture's curriculum. One student recorded that, at the Louvre, 'he takes us only in front of Raphael, Titian and Veronese'. Another wrote in 1850: 'M. Couture prefers his students to have mastered the rudiments of drawing before they enter his atelier, as it leaves him to teach them solely how to paint.'[91] He himself explained: 'I have not made you study the masters that you should copy them. The studies were indispensable to give you a vocabulary, but now that you possess it, speak and tell of your own times.'

These tenets were close to Joanna's heart, and Veronese's 'The Wedding at Cana', in the Louvre, exerted a powerful influence over her for the rest of her life – but her relationship with her teacher proved a bumpy one. (*Plate XXIII*) She respected and admired his talent (this is clear from the review she later wrote of his pictures in the Exposition Universelle) but it was a very different talent from hers. She was always uneasy with compliments: 'I am happy to say he has not given me one word of praise since the first morning.' Later she wrote: 'As long as I was at Couture's I had no opportunity for working in a "downright" manner. Finish was out of the question. If the first painting did not produce a perfect work, no after-touching – according to theory – would improve it.' She was, by nature, a slaver-away at her drawings and studies, and though she did not entirely repudiate the importance he gave to spontaneity, she could not bring herself to adopt it. She was also aware that his conviction that beauty of outline, mass and colour required 'an incessant sacrifice of detail' differed significantly from the Pre-Raphaelite philosophy which, through her London acquaintance, she had imbibed to such effect.

Though Joanna had told Henry he could tell George about her studies, she herself was slow to confess her attendance at Couture's life-drawing classes. George had strong views about her being in Paris at all. In his letter from Wales on

[91] George Bertauts-Couture, *Thomas Couture: Sa Vie, Son Oeuvre, Son Caractère, Ses Idées, Sa Méthode par Lui-Même et par son Petit-Fils* (Paris 1932). Translated by Laurel O. Peterson.

29 October he had written: 'Be on your guard, whilst not over suspicious, against the laxity of principles and practice, often disguised under the specious air of proper freedom and experience, which prevails so much at Paris … Amongst our acquaintance we could point, I think, to several to whom a sojourn in Paris has done no good.'

Joanna had chosen the Couture atelier on Henry's recommendation, but he appears to have had his misgivings about the life-drawing classes. In addition, Mrs Boyce, who certainly knew the nature of her studies, had requested that she keep them secret. Joanna agreed, but she was under no illusions about the difficulty of sustaining the deception. On 18 November, she wrote to Henry:

> It is now ten o'clock. You are, I suppose, at Mr Cook's, or perhaps you have just left. No doubt they told you of our visit to Ary Scheffer's studio. (*Plate XXIV*) I was very glad to go, but I am afraid it very much endangers the keeping of my secret … Scheffer knows my name and he asked me how and where I meant to study. He knows Couture … For my own sake I have little or no wish to keep secret the exact course of study I am following. I do not forget your reason for objecting, but I believe there is no artist with anything approaching liberal and pure feeling who could think the less of me for what I am now doing. The fact of concealment implies something to be ashamed of. It is far better to be honest. One thing that would prevent my speaking of it is that Emma Ringer wishes the Folkards not to know the kind of study she is pursuing. I cannot speak for myself without involving her.

She had received three letters that morning – one from her mother, one from Bertha and one from Henry: 'Need I say which I seized with the most eagerness and which will be kept with the most care – but what a fool I am. I wish you to discontinue writing to me, and yet I let you know what a delight it is to receive your letters.'

> *19 November:* I have not long returned from the Rue Cadet, having been occupied nearly an hour in cleaning a palette, which I had left covered with paint … You know it is an old trick of mine – I hope I am cured now, for the labour of removing the dried colour is no slight punishment each time. Our model is a little girl with rather a pretty head. She only took off her bonnet and stockings, and I have commenced a full length small oil sketch of her …

> You have asked me more than once for an outline of my daily occupations. I get up at ½ past 7 and leave the house about ½ past 8, and reach the atelier about 9 – from 9–10 work – from 10 to ¼ past rest – from ¼ past 10 to ¼ past 11 work – from ¼ past 11 to ¼ to 12 rest – from ¼ to 12 to ¼ to 1 work – to 1 rest – to 2 work. I seldom leave before ½ past 2. I write or read or practise till dinner time ½ past 5. Sometimes I walk out again with Bob. We go into the drawing room as soon after dinner as possible for the benefit of the French conversation, and most evenings I come to my room soon after tea – about 9 o'clock, that I may have a little time to myself and that I may escape having to sing and to play. Not very amiable, you will say – perhaps not, but I have played everything I know until they must all be tired out.

By 25 November, she had come to the conclusion that secrecy was as undesirable as it was impossible, and in the course of a long letter (her father was much in her thoughts) she deputed Henry to do as he had promised earlier: 'You will be kind enough now to tell George all about my study at Couture's and quote from my letter as much as you think proper.' She had adopted the habit of leaving the room when Couture came to see her work on female models, though not on male ones:

> The little girl, our model at the atelier, has been sitting nude the last four days of the week. Both times Couture came, his knock was the signal for me to go into our second room, and not till he had left did I return to my seat. Mlle Agatha, who rather takes the lead at the atelier, manages the money affairs and is a ladylike, kind girl, asked me one afternoon, when she, Emma Ringer, and I were the only ones remaining, whether I felt any scruples. I told her exactly what I felt – viz. none with the male model, but that I would sooner leave the atelier than remain in the room when we had a female model and Couture came. She said she could perfectly understand my objection, that she was certain I should receive no annoyance from Couture or the others. She seemed more vexed at my losing time than at anything else …
>
> I dislike Couture's great picture on the easel very much as to subject. I think there were three pictures when you were at the atelier, there are but two now – the boy with the drum and scene at a mask, which has four figures. The colour seems to me fine, but the texture of parts very queer – streaky and gritty. His study for the woman's

> head, which is knocking about the atelier on an old canvas is finer than anything in the picture. The greys in the tablecloth and the dress of the Punch are lovely and the Harlequin's dress is wonderfully harmonious, but I dislike the picture for its coarseness. I don't much care for the drummer boy. His leg is good in action and modelling and not at all gritty – and the action of the whole figure I like, and the colour of the white and blue in his dress. But that such a man as Couture should make a great subject picture of such a bagatelle provokes me. And why does he paint so grittily when he knows how to get the surface in the head of the 'Boy with a falcon'? (*Plates XX and XXI)*

Her mother, back in London, had returned Joanna's picture of the 'Bone Well', with a letter stating the terms on which she would accept it. Joanna wrote to Henry: 'I am exceedingly vexed at Mamma's letter accompanying the Bone Well drawing. She might have done me this slight favour without tacking on conditions she knew would not meet with compliance.' Her mother's terms, predictably, concerned her continued correspondence with Henry, which was now everybody's business. Hennie thought it should be kept up – 'but I can't help feeling that she is very much under your influence,' wrote Joanna to Henry. She was not convinced that Matthias and George would agree.

With regard to the anonymous letter, Joanna had suggested to her uncle that her mother be asked point blank whether or not she had had a hand in it, but her uncle was concerned only to 'suppress every enquiry'. She confessed that she wished to know the truth only in the 'faint hope that she could prove her innocence ... but I fear there can be no doubt in the matter'.

Henry had evidently given her minute instructions for the artistic education of Bertha Farwell in Paris, and Joanna was anxious to reassure him that she had 'filled the office of deputy professor pretty well'. Meanwhile she had been reading: '½ past 11 o'clock: I have just finished the chapter on the "Personality of Satan". His reasoning unanswerably proves the points, which I never doubted – but the idea of the Devil being served by hosts of evil spirits has always been repugnant to me.'

George had been seeing much of the Naylors in Wales, and on 30 November wrote to Joanna in confessional mode:

> The more I saw of Miss Naylor the more my esteem for her increased. I think her unselfish, self-denying and thoughtful, tender-hearted, trusting and feminine without over sweetness. I cannot help fearing there may be much to try her in after life, as there has you, dear Joanna ...

I saw Wells the day before yesterday … I was certainly surprised to find that a connected correspondence was still kept up between you; but it seems the rupture in the engagement was not so complete as I had inferred… I must confess to have felt a good deal hurt, and I told Wells so, that such very confidential and delicate topics should be minutely entered into with him, whilst I had up to that time no further information than that you had some private sitters at Madame Héreau's. Perhaps you deemed me too prejudiced and narrow minded, but I think it would have been kinder, knowing that I am ever one to put more faith in the motive than the act, to have told me directly and not second-hand of your purposed or actual path of study …

Wells is coming tomorrow morning to run riot among my sketches. I quite dread his look of disappointment … [Anne] brought Edgar, the jolly, with her here and he walked about as if he were monarch of all he surveyed. Mother and I dine at Corinth Villa on Sunday. We tea'd at Mat's last night. We get on pretty well together but it's always under high pressure. I seem to joke, but there's pain and sorrow in it, which you well know of too well. There's one thing that I'm glad of and that is that I cannot and do not believe she was the author of that abominable letter.

Towards the end of 1855 Joanna made her debut as an art critic. Two factors contributed to this. One was the Exposition Universelle and the other was the launch, on 3 November, of John Cook's *Saturday Review of Politics, Literature, Science and Art*.

The Exposition Universelle had been two years in the making. Following the 1848 Revolution, the Emperor Napoleon III was anxious to secure lasting peace and political stability, and the success of the Great Exhibition in London in 1851 had thrown down a gauntlet that he could not ignore. Indeed, the president of the Exposition, Prince Napoleon, frankly avowed: 'The success of the London Universal Exposition impels us to emulation. Scarcely had the doors of the Crystal Palace closed when everyone began to demand that we hold a similar event in Paris.'

A long history of rivalry between the countries was put aside when France and England joined forces in 1854 to fight the Crimean War, and by the time the Exposition opened it was as a celebration of the mutual friendship and prosperity of two mighty powers. When Queen Victoria and Prince Albert went to Paris on 18 August, the *Illustrated London News* reported: 'It is not only Queen Victoria who visits Napoleon III, it is England which visits France. It is two great nations – the greatest, the most powerful, the most civilised and the most generous in the world.'

The Exposition Universelle, then, was as much a political as a cultural event. When, after much to-ing and fro-ing, the Fine Art Exhibition was installed in a specially constructed Palais des Beaux-Arts, a temporary building designed by architect Hector LeFuel on rented land behind the Palais d'Industrie, the art community was frankly disappointed. It had been hoping for the Louvre.

The exhibition itself became a major battleground. Prince Napoleon, supported by Jean-Auguste-Dominique Ingres, took the position that the show should include all works completed since 1800 by the most celebrated artists, living or dead. Eugène Delacroix, aided by the writer Prosper Merimée, managed to defeat this plan and limit the exhibiting artists to those still living on 22 June 1853. They were quick to realise that a general retrospective of nineteenth-century art would strengthen the past at the expense of the present.

Matters were complicated by the decision to have a jury which would award prizes. This led to some of France's best-known artists refusing to take part at all, as we shall see, while Ingres – from the government's view the most important artist alive – drove a hard bargain, insisting on a room all to himself with no fewer than thirty pictures. Horace Vernet, the most famous battle painter in the world, was also granted a separate salon. Decamps sulked because he had not been courted assiduously enough, and though in principle all factions – Academicians, independents and amateurs – were represented on the jury, the true independents, including Couture, Troyon and Delacroix, were hopelessly outnumbered. Thanks largely to a commission especially for the Exposition, 'The Lion Hunt', Delacroix's work was well enough installed for him to pronounce himself satisfied, but as George Sand – one of the few visitors prepared to pay five francs for the privilege of entry as soon as the exhibition opened – wrote to her son Maurice: 'Some artists got in through favouritism, some through luck.'

Joanna, always robust in her opinions, had written to George to say that as soon as she felt able, she would convey her 'crude notions' about 'pictures in Paris, ancient and modern', and in a letter to Mat's wife, Lilly, on 5 November she rehearsed some of her views:

> I am sorry to say that the English school of artists have lost ground in my estimation by their competition with the French … It seems to me that we are very unfortunate in just having let our two great colourists

> fail to contribute. They, I firmly believe, would have equalled if not surpassed the great Frenchmen – I mean [William] Etty and Turner against Couture and Troyon. Troyon is a wonderful painter, somewhat in the same class of subject as Rosa Bonheur and far finer in quality, the cattle excepted … The Frenchman, Ingres, who I am told is thought the great man by a certain set, is a very little man to my mind and usurps a whole room to himself, which his mind is by no means competent to fill, though his canvas covers the walls. Delacroix, another Frenchman, is very fine as a colourist but very extravagant in treatment of subject.

These initial impressions were reinforced on several further visits to the Exposition in the company of John Cook and the Farwells, and Cook – fresh from publishing the first issue of his *Saturday Review* – immediately recognised her potential. On 16 November, back in London, he wrote to his 'dearly beloved Johnny':

> I know I am a wretch – a very abominable wastrel – in not writing to you long before this. And worst of all, I have really no good excuse … My first duty on my return home ought to have been to thank you, and with all my heart for all your great kindness to me in Paris and I am utterly ashamed of myself that I should have left that duty unperformed so long. I admit with the utmost pleasure, and with the most perfect gratitude, that you are the best and kindest little fellow on the face of the earth. I value most highly the friendship with which you honour me, and I earnestly hope that we may continue good and sincere friends through life. May God bless you for all you have so kindly done for me, and for my darling child, Berty.
>
> I am now toiling from 15 to 18 hours a day to clear off arrears of work … The *Saturday Review* swallows up an enormous amount of my time, but I like the work, as I think we shall be able to effect much good … And you could be useful, both to the S. Review and to Art and Literature, if you would only become one of my contributors, and honour me from time to time with such papers as you can find leisure to write. Do think of this, like a good Boy, and let me have a paper from you for a very early number.

The extravagant endearments and boyish nicknames bestowed by John Cook upon his young protégées, but these evidently arose from an innocent exuberance of manner and were not taken amiss. Cook, after all, was something of a legend, even if it was a legend created largely by himself. Despatched to India as a young man, he had quarrelled with his employer and returned to England, according to him, 'on foot'. He lived on his wits until, through his influential political friends, he became editor of the *Morning Chronicle*. There he gathered together a brilliant staff of writers, including Henry Mayhew, author of *London Labour and the London Poor*, and the novelist William Makepeace Thackeray, who, in a letter written in October 1848, said: 'As if I had not enough to do, I have begun to blaze away in the *Chronicle* again: it's an awful bribe – that five guineas an article.'

He also employed women as contributors. Elizabeth Lynn (later Mrs Eliza Lynn Linton), the first newspaper woman in England to draw a regular salary, described him as 'a tall, cleanly shaved, powerfully built man, with a smooth head of scanty red hair; a mobile face instinct with passion; fiery reddish-hazel eyes; a look of supreme command; an air of ever-vibrating impatience and irascibility, and an abrupt but not unkindly manner.' He was no feminist – when Mrs Linton expressed indignation at his failure to believe that 'any mere girl' could have written one of the articles she presented to him, 'he startled me, first by his laughter and then by a volley of oaths' – but he had an unerring ear for an original voice.

The *Morning Chronicle* was a great success in literary terms, but was politically and financially a failure. It was sold in 1854, and afterwards Cook, at a loose end, made common cause with Alexander James Beresford Hope, who had inherited his father's fortune and had money to spare. Together they founded the *Saturday Review* – its aim, 'not to be a purveyor of news, the news market being sufficiently supplied', but to publish leading articles, reviews, comment and criticism that would 'address themselves to the educated mind of the country'. It was to be 'an organ of opinion, not a mountebank's platform'.[92]

Joanna's voice was nothing if not original and she certainly had opinions. She agreed to write a review of the Fine Art Exposition for him.

It was a daunting undertaking. Six hundred and ninety-nine French painters showed a total of 1,872 works – and that was before any other country was taken into account. Unable to make sense of such an enormous display, visitors were hungry for guidance which the art critics were only to happy to provide. Reviews appeared in every Parisian journal. Théophile Gautier, critic of the official newspaper of the Second Empire, *Le Moniteur*, announced that all reviews should begin with Ingres because 'it is impossible not to situate him

92 Proclaimed in the first issue, 3 November 1855.

at the summit of art'. He was, he said, more than an artist, he was an institution – heir to David and known and admired throughout Europe. The poet Charles Baudelaire did not agree, and was fired from *Le Pays*, *Journal de l'Empire*, for criticising 'The Apotheosis of Napoleon':

> I would very much like to state of the Emperor Napoleon that I have not at all recognised in him the epic and fateful beauty with which he is endowed by his contemporaries and his historians … The principal characteristic of an apotheosis ought to be a supernatural feeling, a powerful ascent towards the higher regions, a drive, and irresistible flight to the sky, goal of all human aspirations, and classical dwelling place of all great men. This Apotheosis, or rather this team of horses, falls, falls with a speed proportionate to its weight. The horses drag the chariot down towards the earth. The whole thing is like a balloon without gas which, because of its ballast, is inevitably going to smash on the surface of the planet.

Into this hectic debate Joanna lobbed her first grenade. Her 'Remarks on Some of the French Pictures at the Paris Exhibition' was published – anonymously, in the tradition of the *Saturday Review* – on 1 December 1855. After pointing out that even this vast collection could not furnish a true estimate of the relative talents of living artists, and lamenting the inadequate representation of English art – 'This may partly be accounted for by the absence of the pictures of Turner and Etty, two of our greatest men and finest colourists' – she did begin with Ingres, though not quite in the way that Gautier had envisaged, and not before she had dealt with the matter of prizes:

> It is true that two names in the highest walk of French art are not represented at the Exposition – Paul Delaroche and Ary Scheffer … The cause of their absence is well known, viz. the competition for medals and prizes. It was 'worse than a crime, it was a blunder'[93] to establish a competition; and the consequent distribution of rewards has proved, as might have been expected, but a series of minor blunders … Prizes may be useful as an encouragement to the student at the outset of his career, but never to the established artist; and Delaroche and Scheffer have wisely refused to compete with inferior

[93] Quotation attributed to the French diplomatist Talleyrand, in response to the murder of the Duc d'Enghien by Napoleon I.

> men for prizes awarded by an incompetent jury, swayed by intrigue and favouritism.
>
> Can any man with an average knowledge of art, who has made the pictures of the Beaux Arts his study, feel anything but astonishment and disgust as he runs through the list of those who have received awards? Ingres and Heim classed above Couture and Troyon. Winterhalter above Millais, Gudin above Ziem – while Holland has only an 'honourable mention' and Anthony not even that – and so on!

And so to Ingres:

> The admiration of Ingres – one of the worst epidemics to which the Parisians have fallen a prey – is, we trust, on the wane. An execrable draftsman, a bad colourist, a man with no intensity of feeling or power of the imagination, how has he attracted such a crowd of worshippers? By painting blue satin or ecstatic saints? By conceiving such pieces of commonplace melodrama as the 'Historic portrait of Cherubini, with the Muse of Music' (under the disguise of a low-bred woman) 'stretching her protecting' (deformed) 'hand over the head of the composer', who looks appropriately lugubrious? Or by the hopeless imbecility – one might almost say profanity – of the Francesca di Rimini? M. Ingres has one redeeming quality – the strong individuality in most of his portraits, which makes them valuable notwithstanding the badness of the drawing and colouring.

The admiration for Winterhalter she found easier to understand, if not to excuse: 'We may almost forgive the Parisian ladies for liking to see themselves perpetuated with those delicate complexions, and in "toilettes" the most airy and elegant ever conceived by a French mantua-maker.' But she was quick to move on to those whose works 'will repay the most patient examination', though her comments were no less pertinent for that. She marvelled at Troyon's 'Les Boeufs allant au labour' – 'the most exquisite and masterly rendering of dewy morning ever produced … The oxen, fine in chiaroscuro and skilfully foreshortened tramp lazily towards us, the breath condensed as it puffs from their nostrils' – while noting that 'his cattle are not so grand as Rosa Bonheur's – they have not the same look of weight and half-slothful power that render the group she exhibits almost sublime.'

To her teacher she paid the following tribute:

> There can be little doubt that Couture's great picture of 'Rome in its Decay'... is the finest large historical work exhibited. The subject is well chosen. If, as has been said, a picture should be 'a sermon concentrated into sight', this will well pass muster. The lesson is sternly taught. Vice is there in all its loathsomeness – the hollow frivolity of its novitiates, and the utter degradation of its victims. Still the artist has wisely abstained from making the evil so prominent as to repel the beholder at first glance, and so render his teaching nugatory. In every work of art, it is the principle of beauty that should prevail, however severe the lesson enforced, or however great the horror of the scene depicted; for it alone steals the way into our hearts and prepares a place where the truth it clothes may take root and blossom. As a piece of colour, this picture vies with the finest Veronese at the Louvre ...
>
> The whole picture is deliciously warm and glowing as the subject demands, yet not to one inch of the canvas could the term 'foxy' be justly applied. But to admirable colour and masterly drawing and chiaroscuro, Couture has added something even more valuable – rare poetic feeling. Look at the youth asleep on the pedestal of the column in the foreground, the rest in shadow! Look at the centre figure – a woman, once noble, with the plague-spot of sensuality burning on her brow. In her attitude, what languor and weariness! In her face what satiety, undefined melancholy, and half-unconscious longing for better things – for 'the days that are no more' ... And now turn to the two who have just entered. The one gazes with sternest indignation on the terrible scene before him, the other with grief and tender Christian pity – both 'hating the evil', and mourning the fall of their country, Rome, once great through the stoical virtue of her children.

Couture, she declared, was also responsible for the finest portrait on the walls – 'Le Fauconnier' – the 'Boy with the Falcon' – a picture 'instinct with life and youth'. She ended with a wry dig at a leading French journal whose remarks on the British contributions to the exposition were, 'to say the least, in a most ungenerous spirit ... Be it ours to welcome genius, and pay it our hearty tribute of admiration, from whatever land it may spring, and especially let us be above any petty jealousy of the people now joined to us in close alliance.'

It was a virtuoso performance from a young woman who had never before written for publication – the more admirable because the only thing driving her judgment was her own assessment of what was true and pure in art. There is no sense that she had been requested to take a particular line, or that she wrote with any kind of eye to her future as a critic.

Her mentor was jubilant, writing to her on 1 December:

> My dear Johnny
>
> I do not flatter you … but you must allow me to assure you in all sincerity and honesty, that I think your article very able, very true and just, and truly admirable in every way. I am very proud of it, and it was praised in the very highest terms by several very able and influential men … Of course I have told no one but Bertha who it was written by …
>
> Let me however hope that you will continue to write, and to write much … Send me as many articles as you please on the other nations who had pictures at the Exhibition, and consider whether you would undertake to review for the SR the pictures in our own Exhibitions of next year.

She complied – rather nervously – with a second review, though she had to be persuaded by Cook to 'fork out the MS like a good child … Depend upon it I will publish nothing that will not add to the great reputation you have acquired by your last article. I am too proud of you for that.' It was published on 29 December, and covered artists and pictures she had been unable to include in her first. She was particularly impressed by Léon Cogniet's 'Massacre of the Innocents', and her description of it tells us much about what she looked for in a great painting:

> Artists without number have tried to depict the horrors of the day on which Herod, in awful contempt of God and fiendish pitilessness to man, commanded the massacre of the little children throughout Judea … Some have given us wild battling groups of soldiers and women, with occasional episodes of silent grief or stony despair, rendered more impressive from the contrast with the agonised energy around. Others, of coarser feeling, have seen nothing but the fierce bodily struggle; and none have seized the moment but Cogniet. This is the one great secret of picture-making – the power of seeing and working out the moment par excellence which interprets all in itself – the moment which seems to grasp its own past and future, which is at once the casket containing precious things and the key which unlocks it. In this one still group of Cogniet's there is more of the sickening

> terror of that day than the most violent bodily action could give. Here indeed is intense action, but it is the action of the spirit, crouching in breathless fear in the angle of a ruined wall. We see the mother, with the one hand clutching the baby to her breast, the other pressed tightly over its mouth to stifle its faintest cry – her head turned round to face the intruder. With the expression at once of fear and desperate defiance, she listens, with throbbing pulse, to the wails of human agony echoing through the city. Already the tread of the woman we see in the distance, flying down the temple steps from the soldiers in pursuit, has reached her ears – they come nearer and nearer every moment – will they turn away from her hiding place or will they rush thither to seize their prey?

She went on to discuss Rousseau, that master of handling 'who appears to be of exactly opposite characteristics to Cogniet', and Horace Vernet, whose 'genius is world-wide', though she did not feel that the works exhibited at the Beaux-Arts adequately represented his powers. She recognised Vernet as 'a peculiarly national painter … There is nothing he seems to treat with such gusto as the French soldier in action or "at ease"; and we can never doubt – excepting in such mistakes as "Judith and Holofernes" – that his works are those of a *compatriote.*' That Delacroix had genius she acknowledged, but she found him a challenge:

> [He] is full of the most daring and glaring imperfections – one could fancy him rushing at the canvas with the fury of a Haydon.[94] His pictures seem like unfinished troubled dreams which he has hastened to fasten to the canvas before they have quite vanished. Magnificent in colour, full of dramatic energy, crude in execution, and coarse in drawing, they strike the eye much as the sound of a gong strikes the ear – startling yet harmonious.

In the meantime there was George to be placated. He was hurt by her failure to reveal the true nature of her studies to him and bewildered by the conflicting news he had received regarding her engagement. Earlier, on 2 December, she had written to him assuring him that she had not herself wanted to keep her studies a secret and explaining the various pressures upon her – including her friend Emma Ringer's desire to keep the Folkards in ignorance

94 Benjamin Haydon (1786–1846). Historical painter and writer, well-known for his enthusiasms and histrionics. He quarrelled with the Royal Academy in 1809, got into financial difficulties and eventually committed suicide.

of Couture's life classes. She herself had no doubt that Couture's atelier was by far the most select and his students the most hard-working. She reiterated that she had broken off her engagement; and yet she wrote: 'I love Henry Wells, it is a real grief to be separated from him, to lose an intercourse with such a head and heart as his have proved … I have refused to promise not to correspond with him because I feel in doing so I am shutting him out from all hope of marriage … oh! it is a dreadful responsibility, another's happiness or unhappiness!'

George, invited to comment, made it clear that he thought nothing good could come of keeping up the correspondence, assuming that she persisted in her, in his view 'unaccountable', determination not to marry. 'As long as he can communicate with you, H. W. will not believe in it, or rather in its unalterableness, but will always be in painfully anxious and all-absorbing hope of changing it. Is such a state of mind conducive to health, happiness or professional progress?' Mat and Mordan, he said, agreed with him, 'expressing so decided a regret at the continuance of letters between you' that he could no longer hesitate to speak out boldly.

He had only had a 'glance' at her first article and castigated himself 'that through our stupid way of dodging about the Exhibition, I missed Troyon's picture.'[95] 'The paper is really capitally written and thought, but amazingly dogmatic and confident, excuse me.' Their friends, he said, were continually asking when she would be coming back.

Henry, frustrated at missing an evening in George's company, wrote to him on 7 December – Joanna's birthday – to say that he had been tempted to throw over an invitation from Augustus Egg in order to accept George's, but was anxious, at this stage of their acquaintance, not to cause offence: 'Egg is one of the painters I covet to know more of, apart from his undoubted talent, he has an earnest, demure spirit, which means something more than play. Another reason, he is the intimate of Dickens and that group of literati of which Dickens in the chief.'

He wrote to Joanna on the same day. She answered on 10 December, telling him 'I have found it very sweet to be loved as you have loved me', but admitting that the future was dark – 'we cannot tell how widely severed or closely joined our lives may be':

> Your praise of my 'Paper' gave me far more pleasure than any I had received. You cannot think with what a quickening pulse and glowing

[95] It is not clear when George visited the Exposition. He was in Wales before and after Matthias's and Lilly's wedding, returning to London in early November. In a letter of 30 November he indicates that he had paid a lightning visit, possibly in the company of his friend, the sculptor Alexander Munro, but there is no indication in his letters to her that he and Joanna met while he was there.

> face I read it. I assure you that my fear of your judgment upon it was no sham. When I sent it to Mr Cook, I really believed it absolutely puerile, and I had to force myself to post it … On reading it through again I came to the conclusion that two or three passages were good and among them your favourite … I thought you would find the descriptions weak, the remarks trite and the language inflated. I heartily concur with you in the faults you find …
>
> Mr Cook asked me to undertake the Papers on the Royal Academy next year, and in a subsequent letter says I must do all the Exhibitions for him. I told him I should like very much to undertake the RA, if he really thought me equal to it, but I do not think I shall undertake more. If I may believe what Bertha says, you are by no means without the pale of Mr Cook's kind feeling. She has told me that he has often expressed himself in terms of the highest sympathy and respect with regard to you.

Bertha herself wrote from her parents' house in Cornwall to reinforce John Cook's admiration and add her own: 'Do try to be conceited!' She also imparted more news on the Ruskin saga: 'In justice to Mrs Ruskin I must tell you that 14 months elapsed between her separation from Ruskin and her seeing Millais. My informant said that she was cruelly neglected by Ruskin, who at one time left her in a café at Venice (I believe), which was only frequented by Austrian officers. We shall never know the exact truth of these stories, but Ruskin is "cut" by most of his old friends. I blame his wife for nothing but want of delicacy.'

As Joanna told George, she continued to 'attend regularly' at Couture's, 'but he will not have conscientious studies. He complains of my being slow and says I ought to paint a whole figure in one day. Only fancy the horror of a PRB' To Henry, she wrote: 'Couture says we ought to complete two studies in the week, and this to girls who cannot draw the simplest thing correctly. Still I am sure it is good for me to be hurried, and he does demand most strictly a certain sort of truth.'

With William Boone, who as yet knew nothing of either her broken engagement or her continued correspondence with Henry, Joanna had visited 'the house of an old Englishman, who on account of some misdemeanour cannot return to England and has settled in Paris, and amused himself by collecting all the pictures of Greuze he could get hold of – in number 65 – it is quite a monomania. He thinks Greuze the first among French artists. I was terribly disappointed. You know his sickly sentimental subjects, and so did I, but I expected better colour.'

She was well aware that even her supporters within the family – George, Matthias and Mordan – thought she should cease her correspondence with Henry. She had sought George's honest opinion and he had given it. She herself felt they should stop: 'But I have weakly put off the evil day when I should write you my last letter as long as I could.' But Henry was having none of it, and she found herself unable to insist. On 23 December she wrote to Henry to confirm that if he still honestly wished for her correspondence for its own sake, and could reassure her that it would not interfere with his making another marriage, she would comply. 'I must tell you once again, that as far as it is possible to see my future, I shall never marry.' She thanked him for sending her his first 'happy' letter.

5

MAMMA'S TYRANNY

'A bitter heart that bides its time and bites.'

'Caliban upon Setebos'

On New Year's Day, 1856, Spencer Hall wrote Joanna a letter of congratulation from the Athenaeum in London's Waterloo Place:

> First let me wish you very many Happy New Years, secondly let me congratulate you on your first appearance in the *Saturday Review*. I read your paper with sincere pleasure. I like it for its freshness, for its breadth of thought, and its somewhat solemn utterance, the intonation of which recalls to my ear, or mind, some notes of yours when singing …
>
> Let me then discourse with you kindly, if not well, upon certain minor matters. There is no doubt the 'we' is the tone of authority … 'We' is Truth, Knowledge, Reflection, Feeling, Reason, Judgment … Therefore such Judgment should be elevated and unimpassioned … Now if this be true, you have, I submit to you, sinned … 'Astonishment and disgust' are strong terms. Your handling of Ingres is bold and vigorous … but it is a fact Ingres stands well – high – amid his compatriots. This does not imply you should not give your thoughts sincere expression, but does it release you from the duty of the gentle courtesy due to opinion? … In censuring the faults of others we oft reflect our own. If the praise of Ingres be an Epidemic in France, what think you of that of Millais – of Tennyson – Carlyle and Browning in England? You are an Artist even in pen as pencil … Pray, go on: I should like to read you, not where judgment is frittered away into points of detail, but in the Historic Review of a cycle. The light of Truth is more manifest flowing from a wider Horizon.

There was shrewd judgment buried in Spencer Hall's characteristically elaborate epistle – Joanna had not yet learned how to distil the general from the specific – but from John Cook's point of view, his faith in his young protégée had been well rewarded. Her first article had excited intense interest and speculation. Joanna was still in Paris when she wrote to Matthias on 2 January, commenting on the responses to it: 'The complaint of its being dogmatic amused me – once having made up my mind to try and write I never doubted that whatever I thought, whether right or wrong, must be spoken unhesitatingly. I was not writing as Miss J. M. Boyce but anonymously, protected by the Editorial "we", in anything but a lukewarm journal.'

Her article may have been written anonymously, but the identity of the author was swiftly leaked by Cook: 'He has done the most foolish and provoking thing you can imagine,' Joanna wrote to Henry on Christmas Eve: 'He spent the evening with Ruskin some days ago. They spoke of me and Mr Cook told him I had written a paper on the Beaux Arts and sent it to him for his opinion. What an upstart Ruskin will think me.' With regard to his own opinions, she added: 'It is quite unnecessary to trouble Mr Thackeray to turn me inside out when Mr Henry T. Wells does it with such expertness and satisfaction.' Later, after telling him that she had no time to spare for any more reviews, except the Royal Academy, and 'perhaps not that', she suggested mischievously that Mr Cook might 'get Ruskin to do it'.

A letter from Henry on New Year's Eve brought the news that Anne was ill, which made her exceedingly anxious. She decided not to tell Bob, 'as he would only worry himself uselessly', nor did she tell William Boone, as he would have been sure to ask how she knew:

> Twice since he has been in Paris Mr Boone has attacked me on the subject … The first evening he began by conjuring me to give up all thoughts of you. When I said: 'Why, you know I have broken my engagement,' he was perfectly astounded. I can't think why Mamma had never told him. His evident delight at the news made me feel very angry and I changed the subject. The second night he seemed to be troubled by a suspicion that we were not completely separated. I told him plainly that the engagement was entirely broken, that I believe I should never marry, but I would do all I could to make my absence tolerable to you. At this of course he laughed. He did not exactly say I was a fool for believing that you suffer severely, but implied it and made one or two remarks which hurt, and annoyed me so much that I could no longer restrain my 'd[evi]l of a temper'. Mr Boone was really distressed – the tears ran down his face and he said he did not know what would become of him if I were unhappy

> etc. He is a very strange mixture – to warm affection he adds the most cold, worldly view of things.

Though Joanna had faced down her family and friends in defence of her continued correspondence – she had told Matthias that in spite of all the counsels of her nearest and dearest, she had taken the decision to continue writing to him on the sole grounds that Henry himself wished her to do so – she understood that Henry was thin-skinned and that letters were too easily misconstrued. She added: 'As to the "wholesome fun and quiet contempt" of my last letter, it was <u>all</u> the former and <u>none</u> of the latter ... I have often told you I am fond of teasing and it is difficult to tease you.'

Alone with Bob in Paris, her main preoccupation at the beginning of 1856, was the long struggle to improve his health. He had been so ill during December that she had seriously thought of bringing him back to England with William Boone, but Bob himself had resisted and now the plan was to try M Iriat's Gymnasium, near to the Beaux-Arts. Joanna reported back to her mother on 3 January:

> M. Iriat took Bob into a room and examined him and then fetched me. He seemed really grieved to see the injury resulting from the operation. He seemed perfectly to understand Bob's disease and said – 'convulsions I suppose, I could see that immediately. I have had several similar cases under my care and I do not doubt I shall be able to cure him, but he must have six months, the three first private.' The six months will cost £27. 2. 6. I think when he has been to the gymnasium for a month, if his health keeps pretty good and he feels himself improving at all we had better determine for him to remain the six months if nothing prevents. In that case you must come over and join us as soon as possible.

She entertained her mother with news about the boarders at the Rue d'Astorg:

> We have none so amusing as Miss Palmer but there have been some droll enough. I think it was since you left that two little women in black, old maiden sisters, made their appearance, an English girl here named them the priestesses, as their sallow greenish complexion and black dresses reminded one of Roman priests. They came from Gloucestershire and Miss Davis of course knew all their aristocratic friends. They were very vain of their musical talents and sang a duet

> one night which convulsed the whole room – unfortunately I was not there – many said it was more excruciating than any of Miss Palmer's performances. I don't speak once a week to Mrs Avry or many of the boarders. She appears an amiable ladylike woman, but it is curious she should dress so extravagantly when she is nominally here owing to poor circumstances. She confesses she is on the look-out for a husband which is unendurable to my fancy. The Polish girls are really delightful, amiable, full of play; the beauty is so witty and good natured. During the last few weeks an old woman with a very short waist, springy and active in all her movements appears in the room – I believe she whisks through the keyhole, she is the very impersonation of the wicked fairy in the dear old fairy tales, who introduces herself in that aerial fashion at the christening of the baby and by one black gift poisons the 'little blessing's' future existence. I long to put a black stick in her hand and high-heeled shoes on her feet. We have another English family – a Mrs Cleeve and her son fresh from Cambridge, where his fond mother informs everybody he took the first prizes – which everybody finds difficult to believe. He has a strong dash of Leech's[96] young England and speaks with the orthodox nasal drawl. A niece of Mrs Cleeve's – a Miss Rawlings – is with them. On New Year's Day she presented me with a splendid bouquet, which overpowered me with astonishment, as I had not exchanged a dozen words with her.

It is touching that in spite of the rift between them, Joanna was as generous with her wittily lethal pen-portraits to her mother as she was to her other correspondents. A day or two later, she wrote gleefully to Henry about Spencer Hall's 'labyrinthine effusions': 'A "permiscuous" mass of deep-sounding words – you know his style. But the worst of it is, that in one of the few sentences in which I could find head and tail, he demands an answer. An endless string of his letters are looming in the distance – woe is me.'

The news concerning Hennie was worrying: '[She] is now under severe trials of mind ... that seem sapping her life away'. Joanna doesn't, at this point, say why Hennie was in such distress, though the reasons – emotional as much as physical – did emerge later. In the meantime Hennie had evidently confided in her, and in her anxiety – Hennie was never strong and Joanna was protective of her – she had told Henry something of what was happening. She added: 'I

[96] John Leech (1817–64). Caricaturist and engraver, who regularly contributed to *Punch,* and was well known for 'social commentary'.

tremble when the fear of losing her comes over me … I do believe that such a friendship as ours rarely exists between girls … She has a most rare intellect that has often put mine to complete rout, and the most sensitive womanly feeling.' Anne, thankfully, had made a rapid recovery. Of Bob's progress at the Gymnasium, Joanna remained hopeful – M. Iriat's treatment included exerting a form of magnetic power over him, which gave her immense satisfaction: 'Iriat does not make any manifestations, but while he is helping Bob to do different exercises, he gives him power and will, a portion of his own health and strength into him.' But she was apprehensive that she would 'soon have to live in the same house together and the same room' with her mother. She had received two 'much nicer' letters from her during Anne's illness, 'and I was beginning to feel quite different, when yesterday's scrap has undone all. There are but twenty lines which she has contrived to poison by one most gratuitous remark.'

Of William Boone she wrote: 'You describe him truly – a warm and true friend he has always proved himself to us; but if possible I will never refer to him in a question of right and wrong – his moral sense is perverted.'

As far as Joanna's correspondence with Henry was concerned, her family's principal anxiety seems to have been her disregard of the proprieties. In one sense they had cause to worry: Joanna's letters were enviably unconstrained, demonstrating just how engaging, flirtatious and loving a non-love-letter can be. She even referred to her appearance – telling him that she had snipped off her 'bell-ropes' to hang even with her chin. Whatever her reservations about marriage, she had no reservations about the intimacy of their correspondence. Henry was the person with whom she was most herself, and her letters brim with confidence and wit.

She was working regularly at the atelier again:

> Couture's visits have lately been very irregular, indeed he talks of turning us out and coming to paint himself. He says that in the six weeks' holidays he gave his pupils, he made 7,000 francs by the work he got through. From that time he has not made a penny. He has praised me these last two or three weeks – not, as far as I can see, because I have worked well, but because I have worked more in his own way. I have been amused at a little silent battle we have had over the points of light in the eyes. He is very fond of saying to us, '*Soyez näives, soyez simples, peignez ce que vous voyez*'[97], but he never will let us be so in reality. In obedience to my own instinct and to his precept,

[97] 'Be naive, be simple, paint what you see.'

I always try to paint what I see, and consequently put in the high lights on the pupil of the eye, the first time I saw them. As soon as he saw my study he indignantly ordered the extinction of the aforesaid lights, though they were very bright in nature. The week before last the model's eyes were raised, and there were the high lights glaring before me. I audaciously put them again on the canvas, but it was useless. This time he smeared them out and even extended his correction to the high light on the nose, which was really hardly perceptible in my study. He said such littlenesses were never to be expressed, and that Raphael generally indicated the eye by the shadow of the lid without marking the pupil at all. I think someday he will be surprised to find himself indulging in his exterminating hatred of details, until he prefers a face without features or a hand without fingers …

I am grieved to think about George and his painting. I believe your advice is good, but doubt his ever taking it. I do believe the only thing that would force him to make a start would be the loss of every penny in the world. If he woke one morning and found himself beggared he would cast off his indolence and fear of failure, and we should find him making pictures. But what besides will move him? I have for some time suspected he was growing fond of Jeannie Naylor. If you recollect, you and I talked it over that day at Betws … Jeannie is a truly good and intelligent girl, and I think she would not find it difficult to like George, but I know she will not marry unless her father does. She has often assured me she would never leave him and her little brother unless there were someone to fill her place. But in all probability he will marry again in a year or two …

Hennie writes she is much better … I reproach myself for having told you so much, not that I doubt your secrecy for an instant, but I fear it was in some slight measure a betrayal of her trust, and it pains me to think I should have once been guilty in that way.

Now I'll tell you what I should like, if you are not angry, a little sketch 3 inches by 2 of the studio, which is now daily honoured by your presence; and you can note down at the back, whether such a curtain is chintz or silk damask and such a piece of furniture deal or rosewood. Do you think me impertinent to ask for a sketch from the hand of a Master? In return for this one precious little scrap, I will perhaps send you a sketch every week of the model of the preceding week. Am I not generous in giving you such opportunities for 'hashing' my weeknesses?

Mrs Boyce was havering about returning to Paris, but insisting, if she did so, on sharing a room with her daughter. This would have been torture for Joanna who, though she was taking her usual line of refusing to discuss Henry with her mother, was nevertheless under extreme pressure from her. In a letter dated 21 January, in an attempt to underline her position, she wrote:

> This is the direct answer to your question, 'Are you under any promise to Mr H. W. never to marry, if you do not marry him.' He ... has never asked such a promise of me. I should like to answer many other things you say but am determined as I told you in my last letter to restrain myself from doing so as long as possible, and I again entreat you not to write to me on this subject as I assure you nothing could be more inimical to our mutual peace.

And again, on 25 January, she wrote:

> Since arriving at my present decision I have never wavered. I did not at all forget that acquaintance who might hear of my correspondence with H.T.W. would probably not be very charitable in viewing my conduct, but this consideration did not weigh with me for an instant. I was earnestly striving to find the right path and not that which would ensure me from animadversion ... I long to be the same with you as I used to be and the only way is to let this unfortunate matter sleep.

She knew, she said, that Henry would never have mentioned their letters to anyone outside her family: 'I would like to know which of my friends made the remark you have repeated to me – he (or she) was quite right – "I am one of the last girls to play fast and loose".'

Though Matthias and Anne were prepared to accept Joanna's decision to continue the correspondence, George remained unconvinced that she had chosen the right course, but as Henry (unlike Mrs Boyce) was preserving a dignified silence, he was prevented from broaching the matter with his friend. By then, George was sitting to Henry regularly for a water-colour portrait (attending what he referred to as 'séances' with him every Thursday morning), so this must have been frustrating.

George held out the hope of being able to 'send as a Candidate to the Old Water-Colour Society', but was concerned that he had not produced enough suitable work. He wrote to Joanna on 26 January:

> [Tom] Seddon tells me that Holman Hunt is on his way home. He has sent one picture over, which I've heard spoken disparagingly of – a ragged, worn-out goat by the shores of the Dead Sea, entitled 'The Scapegoat'. (*Plate XXV*) Rossetti seems to be entirely working for Ruskin at present and has an exquisite drawing of the Passover in hand, which I've not time to refer to farther than to say the boy Christ in it watching the blood trickling down the doorpost is a most heavenly realisation or idealisation rather … If you should see in the shop in the Gallerie Vitrée or elsewhere a well modelled cow or sheep grazing, please buy it or them for me, and take advantage of the first opportunity of transmission …
>
> I like your second contribution to the *Saturday Review* quite as much, perhaps better, than the first, especially the excellent criticism of Cogniet's pictures. I didn't like the words 'execrable draughtsman' and 'hopeless imbecility' etc, applied to Ingres, nor the general tone of that criticism, for altho' in great measure true it wasn't entirely so, and calculated to give the notion of the writer being actuated by some personal spite, and so defeat the good object in view. It will surprise you perhaps to hear that when I asked Anthony whose pictures had struck him most in the exposition he replied: 'Those of Ingres'.

To this Joanna sent a pert riposte: 'I can understand Anthony being struck with Ingres's pictures, they struck me by their stiffness, flatness, ugliness etc, etc. But if Anthony was interested by them I should very much like to hear him talk about them.'

A further problem now presented itself in the form of the Naylors who were planning a visit to Italy, and, through Mrs Boyce, extended an invitation to Joanna to join them. Jeannie Naylor had made it clear that she would not consider George or anyone else as a husband until her widowed father had found a new wife, and – as Joanna well knew – Mr Naylor had considered making her an offer. She had never taken this seriously, dismissing it as one more ploy by her mother in the battle against Henry, but she now realised the danger. If she went, she risked Mr Naylor's taking it as a cue to propose, yet because of her friendship with Jeannie, a refusal to accompany them could easily be misunderstood – especially if Jeannie's pleasure in the trip depended on having Joanna as a companion. She told Henry:

> I can unhesitatingly assure you, Mr Naylor could never persuade me to be his wife, even if he wishes it, of which I have no incontrovertible

proof… Setting aside the question of regard, of itself an insurmountable obstacle, I would never marry him, because he is too old – because he has a spoilt child,[98] who will at least be a great trouble to his family – because he is exacting and indolent – because I would never place myself as Mamma over a girl only two years younger than myself, etc, etc, etc, ad infinitum.

Her life in Paris was, in any case, about to change. On 1 February she wrote to her mother: 'The study from the life is over at Couture's. I go to him this month for composition. Had I not better now tell Mme Héreau and the ladies that I am under Couture?' To Henry she wrote:

For the last three weeks we have all felt that a break up at the Atelier was impending. Couture came but twice a week, and then seldom took the trouble to look at our studies. On Tuesday he told us he wanted the Atelier for a month, or rather that we must not have models for a month, but we might come and copy and watch him paint. This was not at all to my taste, so I made up my mind to stay away altogether. On Wednesday he came again to paint on his boy with the drum and he asked if I intended to come. I said No, I wished to paint a portrait and to go to the Louvre and should take this opportunity. He seemed vexed and said he would set me to work to compose and paint pictures, as I was quite advanced enough. This made me prick up my ears, and I said 'would you really, Sir' – 'Yes, I would', 'Then I shall try and manage to come.' Afterwards, when there were but two or three of us left, he told us that the fact was he wanted to get rid of all but those who were advanced and that three or four was the utmost he wished to keep … I have decided to go for this month at any rate and see whether the work he gives me is of use as to a picture for the R. A. If Madame Héreau will sit she would suit my purpose very well, but I much fear she wants to get out of it …

Hennie is in great trouble – I wrote to her on Sunday. I think she will tell you herself all she wishes you to know of her grief when you see her, give my very best love to her. To see Edgar and to comfort Hennie are the two wishes that draw me to England. I am seized sometimes suddenly with a longing to see his merry little face and hear his laugh. He is just at the age when boys are so delightfully comical.

98 Arthur Naylor, Jeannie's wayward brother.

> If he forgets my name I shall be dreadfully vexed – I can't expect him to remember my face.

Henry, who had always harboured 'bright dreams' of their visiting Italy together, was profoundly disturbed by the prospect of Joanna's going there with anyone else, never mind the Naylors. He pressed her hard to refuse, and though she would not make him any promises, she did write to her mother on 10 February to say that, should the invitation be forthcoming, she could not accept it. She added that the gymnastics were not benefiting Bob as they ought, not least because of his own 'dawdling habits', whether while dressing, eating, walking or praying: he spending an unhealthy amount of time on the last.

To George, on 13 February, she explained: 'I could not accompany the Naylors. Mamma ignores the reason, but she knows it … If you wish to know it I will tell you … before I went to Wales, before my engagement, in a letter to H.T.W., Mamma told him that she had heard Mr Naylor intended to make me an offer.'

'At last the old carthorse is in the stable', wrote Joanna to Henry. She had succumbed to a serious asthma attack, returning from the atelier 'in style in a *remise*' because she was unable to walk. She confided to him that she had heard nothing from the Naylors, but had received another invitation to Italy, this time from her friend Margaret Piotti[99] and her Italian husband: 'No letter could be more urgent. She sets before me every inducement and anticipates every objection, and she assures me that the Dr joins his sincere solicitations to her own. She says she has been received in a way far outstripping her expectations, that they move in the best English and Italian society and that her husband is exceedingly respected in Rome.'

She hoped that he might be more in favour of this proposal, if only on the grounds that it would give her an excellent reason for refusing any subsequent one. 'I know that you still hope (at any rate until very lately), that we might visit Italy together. I cannot see the remotest probability, for it would be impossible unless we stood in a closer relationship to each other. Do you wish me for the sake of this possibility to refuse this and every other chance I may have of visiting Italy?'

Her study with Couture was faltering, though she was still attending classes: 'I am perfectly at a loss how to accomplish a finished head,' she wrote to George, 'everything done in Couture's atelier is so detestably "slap-dash".' And

99 Margaret Daniell was a fellow student of Joanna's at Cary's Art School, and her parents were friends of the Boyce family. She had married an Italian doctor and was now living in Rome.

to Henry she said: 'It is impossible for me to send anything to the R. A. I have quite lost the power of painting a finished head, and I seem to have lost in a great measure the eye for colour. The last head I tried to paint at the Atelier was bad in every respect, but execrably [so] in colour – and I really think now I should do better to return to my own way of painting.'

She dreaded the strength of Henry's feelings with regard to the Piottis' invitation, and was more than ever convinced that he should 'break every tie that unites us': 'Oh Henry,' she wrote, 'why will you waste the whole strength of your life upon me? How I wish Lethe were no fable – I would hold the cup to your lips, which should drown every recollection of me.'

Poor Joanna! Fated always to be cast in the role of the less loving one, constantly to be reminded of the use she was making of him, and yet determined not to let a longed-for opportunity pass if – between Bob, her mother, and the logistics of the journey – it could be managed. Apart from 'the present unhappiness of my life with Mamma' and her desire to learn Italian, there was her health to consider. She was still suffering from shortness of breath and was smoking belladonna cigarettes to alleviate the symptoms. But underlying all was her profound conviction that if she could not love Henry enough to bear the restraint of an engagement willingly, she would never make him a good or lovable wife. As he had, for the moment, softened a little on the subject, she dared to add: 'I think you know in your own mind that I should prefer you as a companion into Italy to anyone … nevertheless I shall if possible accept Margaret Piotti's invitation.'

On 18 February she wrote to her mother, almost pleading for permission to go. Needless to say, the plan she outlined was not convenient: Mrs Boyce was not prepared to leave her house and servants for more than three or four weeks at a time and was therefore unwilling to take over the care of Bob in Paris. She opined that the visit would be far better postponed until the autumn. 'Thus what you so much wish to avert', she wrote wryly to Henry, 'will be averted not through my unselfishness, but Mamma's.'

On 23 February, George joined the growing chorus of those who did not wish Joanna to go: 'Mother bids me say the travelling so many miles alone at this season of the year would be quite enough preventive strength. It appears the Mordans and Mat view the matter in the same light, and so, truly, do I.' He added triumphantly: 'Not only Anthony told me he liked and was greatly interested with Ingres's pictures, but Dante Rossetti has told me the same thing more than once. *Mettez-vous çela dans votre pipe.*'[100] And, by way, of redressing the balance:

[100] 'Put that in your pipe [and smoke it].'

'The Brighton Committee were so overpowered by the contribution of a picture which had been publicly recommended by Mr Ruskin, that they have your portrait of Lizzie Ridley starred and the pamphlet placed beneath it – Realise your greatness now, if you can!'

He had bought the third volume of *Modern Painters* for her: 'It's the most erratic and puzzling book with regard to previous assertions and theories [Ruskin] has published – but very interesting withal.' He gave Henry sittings every Thursday morning (the 'séances') 'but sit and yawn and fidget considerably, so he says. Somehow or other he can't help taking the florid and lusty view of my phiz, as he did in the miniature. It's its worst phase, I think, which is saying a great deal indeed. His unfinished portrait of little Bessy Topham,[101] just dead, was beautiful and very like.'

As Italy was out of the question until the autumn, Joanna proposed returning to London at the beginning of May to undertake the Royal Academy reviews she had promised to John Cook. She wrote to her mother: 'I have not returned to the Atelier and am uncertain whether I shall. I have made a chalk life-sized sketch of Mme Héreau which elicited the easily excited admiration of the "womenites" in the salon, but which is very poor both as a likeness and a drawing – altogether I am in the bluest of blues about my painting.' She was convinced that 'if I sent a head this year to the Academy folks would think someone had painted "Elgiva" for me'.

Towards the end of February Bertha Farwell wrote to her friend to tell her that John Cook, who had been seriously ill, was recovering. She was humbly aware of Joanna's superior artistic talents: 'I have loved painting from quite a child but I shall remain an amateur, whilst you, Joanna, have a grand career open, and genius to light your path ... Are you jealous of Millais? I am sure you are not, and in the same way I feel no jealousy of you.' Mrs Boyce had paid them a visit, and Bertha's grandmother, old Mrs Wade Browne, had expressed her high opinion of Henry. 'Mrs Boyce then justified her own conduct and gave it her own colouring.' Bertha, to whom Henry had been giving lessons, thought him 'embittered'. She added that Holman Hunt had returned from the East with four pictures: 'He has gone through unheard of hardships and was shipwrecked on his way home.'

Joanna had a sad commission to undertake before she left Paris. The nephew of one of her French friends, Mlle Cazeaux, was dying of consumption and the family wanted her to make a portrait of him: 'The photographers have failed several times. I feel very nervous about it in fear of failure, but if they

[101] Probably the daughter of Francis William Topham, George's friend and mentor.

continue to wish it, I shall try.' She succeeded in making a life-size charcoal sketch 'just in time', and was particularly struck by 'the most remarkable resemblance' between him and George, which convinced her that there must be a hidden link between the two families.[102]

Looking after Bob was a constant worry – his unstinting devotions, which in normal circumstances would have pleased her, exacerbating her anxiety: 'It must really be injurious to his health to kneel so long every night in the cold.'

She was again struggling with her portrait of Madame Héreau – 'one of the weakest attempts I have ever made,' she told Henry. 'I commenced an oil portrait tolerably, and knocked a hole through the canvas the next morning.' She was also making studies of the two Polish girls who were staying at the house with their mother – the elder 'plain but interesting', the younger 'a beautiful girl with a most exquisite complexion'. She was, she said, in 'a mist' about her painting: 'I have been making at Couture's daubs so horrid in colour that Emma Ringer's were delicious in comparison. I blame my own stupidity and not your advice, which I believe was excellent, and which has at any rate been of this great use – it has taught me my exceeding weakness.'

Details finally emerged of the reasons for poor Hennie's tribulations. Her fiancé, Henry Warton, had been caught up in a law suit concerning the Paris Chocolate Company, and had lost his entire investment. Though he had 'acted with the sternest honesty throughout' and even Hennie's father admitted that his only fault was 'in not being sufficiently a man of business', Henry had offered to free Hennie from their engagement, and this had been accepted by her parents. 'It has been full of torture to Hennie; when she wrote she had fallen back to the weakness of her worst times ... I do really despond about her health now.'

Joanna was in a quandary about the Royal Academy. She had recommenced work on 'Madame Héreau' but thought she would not have the courage to send it. In a letter to Henry she said:

> So far from being at all like my old painting, it is at present more gritty than Couture's grittiest chef d'œuvres. I can fancy your burst of laughter if you could see it now. I am afraid it is rather grotesque in costume and coiffure <u>vide</u> sketch, grey hair brushed up with rather a wild look about it, white frill, black velvet dress and a very dark background. It does not look very absurd to me, but I am afraid it will strike others so.

102 There was a family tradition that the name Boyce derived from 'Bois', and that they were of Huguenot descent.

> Madame Héreau proposes, if I exhibit it, to call it 'Portrait of Madame Héreau, Reader to her late Imperial Majesty, Marie Louise' – This might stand as some apology for the antique look of the costume? but would be making much ado about nothing …
>
> I am worse than George, I think. I have even a greater disinclination to do anything beyond studies … The little flute-player I send you is, I know, execrable. Why have you such a predilection for pen and ink? I do nothing (but) scratch and blot with it.

Worried half to death by news of Hennie's decline – ('I fear she will never recover') – she planned, on her return, to spend as much time as possible with her friend. She added: 'We were awakened this morning – (Palm Sunday) – at 6 o'clock by the cannon announcing the birth of a prince – they fired a hundred times; for a princess there would only have been twenty-one. The firing continued so long Bob confided to me he began to fear the Empress had presented the nation with twins.'

❈

Henry was profoundly unhappy. Though he lived in hopes that his tenacious pursuit of Joanna would eventually bear fruit, there were times when everything conspired to throw him into the slough of despond. His letters veered between affection, anger and resignation. Joanna, having restrained herself from answering one of his more intemperate letters immediately, told him gently: 'I am sorry for being the cause of it, and I entreat you to forgive me.' She blamed herself for his misery. For his part, he simply could not accept her view either of herself or their relationship. Had he not love enough for both? She did what she always did in such situations – backed away, exhorting him to concentrate on his work, at least until 8 April, when entries had to be submitted to the Royal Academy.

Nevertheless she continued to keep him apprised of her doings – visits to the Louvre, where Henry's 'favourite little girl of Vandyck's seems more exquisite each time I see her', and progress – or lack of it – on two portraits, one of Mme Héreau and the other of Isabel Borzewska, one of the young Polish girls who would eventually become 'Rowena'. 'If I could, I would give up my painting utterly,' she told him: 'but spoiling canvas seems as necessary to my existence as eating and sleeping.'

On a lighter note, Henry sent her a copy of the *Saturday Review*, directing her to Charlotte M. Yonge's *The Daisy Chain* – a novel that began as a series of conversational sketches in that august journal. She replied: 'I obeyed your directions with the utmost docility and read [it] over very carefully, but if

Hennie had not informed me before that I was "exactly described in it", I must confess my obtuseness would have hidden the lesson you have given me. I can picture you two gloating over the hideous picture of my foibles – your solemn intonation, her quiet edification – how delightful!' She assumed that they had put her down as 'the clever girl (very flattering this) who refused to marry', but was not convinced by the parallel.[103]

Joanna had no intention of seeing Henry on her return, and had said so, but she knew perfectly well that this would not stop her mother preparing for battle. 'I cannot be ignorant that [Mamma] herself has spread all the information, true or untrue, that could give rise to gossip about me,' she wrote, and in a further letter: 'I am in no little dread of her handwriting, as I expect one of those letters of hers, of which she keeps a copy.' Anne invited her sister to make her home with them on her return. Her stepdaughters were away, but she was determined that Edgar should not join them until he had been reunited with his doting aunt. She also proposed that Joanna stay at Corinth Villa while she and Mordan went on their annual holiday to Wales.

Meanwhile Joanna worried away at her portrait. She was coming to the conclusion that she would send it to George and let him decide whether it was good enough to submit. She herself was unconvinced. 'I do not think want of perseverance is the cause of my failure, so much as the wearying dissatisfaction everything I do causes me … I painted Madame Héreau's left cheek eight times determined not to be beaten and the last was worse than the first … I have not heard from Mamma.'

The rest of the family had heard plenty. Matthias wrote to Joanna, saying:

> You will no doubt have heard that Mamma and self have had a serious outbreak … she tells me that she does not mean to visit me until I leave off visiting and seeing Wells, which I shall not do … It may be unfilial but my home will be all the happier for her absence. Anne tells me that Mamma is trying to exact a promise from you not to stay in London more than three weeks … I think you will do wrong if you make any such promise, and if you do not at once assert your independence and prove it. Otherwise your yoke will indeed be heavy and Mamma more self-willed than ever. She has no right to take advantage of your affection for Bob … Does Mamma propose to pay the extra expenses of your voyage to return to Paris and then back home, for if she will, as she ought to, stay with Bob till he can come back, you could now

[103] The parallel is indeed unconvincing, but it is a nice insight into this three-way friendship.

come over for good … Lilly and self are looking forward to your being with us – stop as long as you can – absolutely free … Lilly is likely in a few months to be a Mother.

On 6 April Joanna wrote to Lilly saying that she did not see any possibility of accepting either the Mordans' kind offer or theirs. It would be different, she said, if her mother did not believe herself the injured party: 'If I were to leave her it would only confirm her in this belief of my undutifulness and her own blameless martyrdom.' She went on: 'I hear on all hands of Mamma's good looks. Mr Naylor said "your Mamma was looking exceedingly well – quite larky".'

To Matthias, on 8 April, Joanna let rip:

By the same post came a note from George and a hateful letter from Mamma … Yours came to hand last. I blessed you from my heart as I finished it. Mamma does not even show me the deference to ask the promise of me you mention – she simply, after expatiating on the inconvenience and expense to her of her visit to Paris, says 'and please bear in mind that longer than a month I cannot, will not remain from home so you will make your arrangements accordingly. I certainly would not inconvenience myself etc, etc'. She goes on about H. T. W. with the usual patchwork of melodramatic and false expressions. She denies that after Uncle's enquiries she was obliged to withdraw her opposition – I call upon Uncle and all my family to witness that she was obliged, and that she invited him and received him at her dinner-table more than once and would have been obliged to have received him until any future period or until I was married, if I had not chosen to break my engagement … I told her in the presence of Uncle and Aunt that I would at any time renew my engagement myself if I found H.T.W. was suffering from her misrepresentation. Not a fortnight (I think not a week) had elapsed before she had begun again. She has no sense of honour, for I know from Bertha Farwell that she has been trying to set Mrs Wade Browne and the rest of them against him, they being his particular friends and it is to him she is indebted for their acquaintance, and besides I know also that she retails her view of the affair to Mrs Campbell the dressmaker – why, she knows better how to publish a thing than Moses with all his advertisements. I burn under her treatments and I thank you my dear brother and Lilly (your little jewel) for the part you take …

As to my yielding to Mamma's tyranny, for I can call it nothing else, I scarcely see a way to escape. Only think what a splendid case

> she would make of it to all her sympathetic friends and dressmakers if being in London I were to imprison her in Paris ... I shall tell her if her stay is absolutely to be confined to a month I shall certainly leave the day after she arrives instead of staying a week with her and return the day before she leaves.

George had his own problems. He wrote in his diary on 29 March: 'Mother in a very bad temper – addressed me as Sir. Home wretched indeed!' For four or five years he had gone regularly to his studio in Great Russell Street, to paint in peace, see his friends and occasionally, no doubt, to stay the night, but it was too small a space in which to live, and on 5 April he began the move to new chambers at 15 Buckingham Street, off the Strand. That same day Joanna wrote to say that she would, after all, send her portrait of Mme Héreau for him to submit to the Royal Academy on her behalf: 'A lady who is going from here to London on Monday will take charge of it. She expects to arrive at London Bridge by 9 o'c Tuesday morning and she will leave the picture at Buckingham Street about 10 or 11 o'c the same morning.' George replied immediately:

> I've little doubt you've done quite right in sending it. I've scarcely seen any pictures for the Academy this year. Hunt showed me a month ago his drawings in Egypt and Syria, two of which are intense in expression of light and heat and reality – sunny and beautiful into the bargain. He sends 2 pictures – 'The Scapegoat', and an Eastern incident – a man feeling the features of a girl through her veil before popping the question. I've bought Tom Seddon's drawing of the Sphinx. (*Plate XXVI*) Neither Miss Howitt nor Miss Smith have sent anything to the Portland or elsewhere. I find a gentleman of the name of Cavendish of Belgrave Square has eased me of the Venice Sketch of the narrow street and water-carrier which I sent to the former place. I called with Fred Warren on Ruskin a week or two ago. We had a long and delirious inspection of his Turners. After a few words of preliminary talk he enquired after you.
>
> I've moved at last into my new rooms, part of a 3rd floor with 3 windows overlooking the river (at foot of Hungerford Bridge) and like 'em much. I've only seen Mr Naylor twice during his stay in London. He has been lodging at the Gt Western Hotel, so that I've not met with Miss N. at all – nor am likely to, I suppose for years.[104] I've just

[104] Perhaps he had proposed and been refused by her, or perhaps (characteristically) he had had second thoughts about committing himself.

> had a chat with Hennie Moore. It was painfully touching to note the eagerness with which she watches the breaking up of the winter and heralding of the spring in the budding trees and bright and showery skies, believing them, as she seems to do (and we would how willingly believe to be the case), to symbolise the renewal of her own health and strength … H. T. W. will be very hard pushed to get all done for the Academy. I like most of all his little water-colour drawing of a child of Alfred Corbould's, which is very beautiful in expression and colour.

On 7 April he recorded a visit from Ruskin:

> He was in haste as usual. Showed him some water-colour studies and sketches, which he commended; said I had an exquisite eye for colour etc, that I chose my subjects very oddly, should paint the distances and mid-distances freely, but carefully and truthfully, and relieve upon them a faithful bit of foreground Preraffaellite work. He was most unceremonious and friendly in his address, as a master with his pupil.

The following day both he and his mother were at Buckingham Street to receive Joanna's picture. He was clearly taken aback, writing in his diary: 'It rather staggered me by its roughness and coarseness of painting and carelessness of drawing, and by its contrast with all she has done before. It is less refined and tender – a taking largeness about it – and on the whole effective in colour. H. T. Wells came in just as Mother left.'

It was not until 13 April that he wrote a long letter to Joanna to acknowledge delivery of the picture. Unpacking 'Madame Héreau' – hedged around as she was 'with a frightful array of spikes' – had, he told her, put him in mind of exhuming the departed: 'I laboured like a very demon at it and when the lid gave way with a crash, that seemed to bring upon one unprepared all the horrors of extraction of a hook-fanged double tooth and I caught sight of the severe and imperious dame within, I thought I should have fainted … Fooling apart,' he added, 'I don't like your new style as well as your old. The old was less pretentious, more simple and direct and characteristic of yourself … Mind you I'm not blind to the breadth and vigour … and the many "precious passages" of colour.' Nevertheless he had lost no time in 'cabbing' both Joanna's picture and his own – a 'meagre and spectral drawing, part of the North side of St Mark's' – to Trafalgar Square, so Joanna's letter of the 15th, begging him to get the picture away – 'I am heartily ashamed of it' – arrived too late to be acted upon. It's possible that on this occasion George's tardiness as a correspondent was deliberate. (*Plate XXVII*)

Joanna was planning to return on 26 April. Her sister Anne, plainly worried by the toll their mother's behaviour was taking on them all, wrote:

> Mamma is certainly behaving most abominably to you, but, as Mordan observed at breakfast this morning, he wonders, being so totally independent of her and supported as you are by all your family, that you allow yourself to be worried by her. If you would like to come and live with us for two or three months or longer we shall be most happy ... Surely if Bob cannot be left alone at Paris (as Mamma told me herself last Sunday), she – as his Mother – is the most proper person to be with him ... As to her letters I should threaten to return any that had the slightest unpleasant allusion, and without answer. Unless you make a stand now, you will indeed lead a wretched life with her – she certainly has not the slightest regard for truth; the different versions of the same occurrence she gives to different people are really remarkable ... Mat, Lilly, Wells and Denny dine with us tomorrow. We asked George, but he did not like to accept on account of Mamma. What do you think of her and Wells meeting at George's new rooms on Tuesday last, where they had both gone to see your picture? George tells me you have quite changed in your style of painting, that there are some very fine parts about it etc, etc ... I quite long to see it ... I wrote to congratulate Mamma on her birthday, as I knew if I called we should have a scene. The next day I had a letter thanking me, but making herself out quite a martyr, and saying she had intended to ask us to dinner on the 10th. It may be the truth ... I thought Mamma had promised not to talk about your affairs to anyone, but I don't think she keeps it ... Mamma is not satisfied with quarrelling with Mat about the business, and Wells, but she must make rude, unfeeling remarks about his marriage and behave very rudely to Lilly ... She fancies that Mat will pass it over in case of being left out of her will. My belief is that she will survive us all. Every one notices how REMARKABLY well she is looking. Quarrelling is her life blood. She thrives and fattens upon it ... For appearance sake we have asked her here, when we have had friends, but she really always spoils the evening. She is sure to make some sneering, unpleasant remark.

One would have loved to know Henry's reaction to 'Mme Héreau'. Whatever he said it amused Joanna:

> How I did laugh over your letter – it was so odd to see my picture (fiasco?) through your eyes. You have said far more in its praise then I expected, and yet I am surprised and vexed, if George thinks with you,[105] that he has sent it to the Academy. I still hope it may be turned out. If it should be hung low or near the eye, you must do me the favour to drop a palette on to it on the varnishing day or kick a hole through the canvas. The nose weighs on my conscience. It seems to grow larger and thicker and heavier and heavier. I knew how bad it was and knew you would pounce upon the horrid thing immediately …
>
> On Tuesday I received by the same post letters from Mamma and Mat and a note from George. Mamma's one of the worst – Mat's so kind and staunch. I had a letter from [Bertha] two days ago. Mr Cook evidently wishes me to review the other exhibitions, but I shall not. I shall have but too little time for the Academy… I cannot write about the sculpture – I don't understand it. The Naylors are in Paris. I shall be with them as little as possible. If George does really care for Jeannie Naylor, I should think he will come to Paris.

For all his teasing, George was actually sanguine about 'Madame Héreau'. He thought that if her picture were hung a little above or under the line it would 'tell capitally'. 'I am sure', he added, 'that when you see Millais and Hunt's pictures this year, your faith in the excellence of French handling and colour in general must be shaken – at least I hope it will.'

He was particularly struck by the strange behaviour of Ruskin, who had called on him on 'the first of the Academy days' and 'whilst jerking out at intervals a few commendatory exclamations with respect to some sketches I showed him, deprecated strongly or rather censured my not taking up and working out some real and worthy subject – and in oil':

> All the way down the stairs – three flights – he was muttering 'them, them (?) you be losing time as you did last year, and in Venice etc, etc, etc … It made me mad and melancholy by turns. It was too true to be laughed at or forgotten, and I'm in a more profound state of 'sulk' even than usual …
>
> Probably H. T. W., with whom I had a short stroll today, has told you about Millais's and Hunt's things. Our likings don't quite coincide. For interest and pathos of subject, the former's lovely blind

105 She had not yet received George's letter when this undated reply to Henry was written.

girl plucking the blue bells at her side unconscious of their beauty and of that of a vivid double rainbow, which spans the dark rain-filled sky and gleaming bright landscape, is to me by far the most noticeable. And then the little wounded child is almost as touching. For gorgeous colour and solemn effect and for a sort of spell-binding power his 'Autumn Leaves' stands alone – almost – in Modern Art, I should think. (*Plate XXIX*)The two former tell of more thought in the painter, but the latter induces most thought in the beholder. But you'll see in time and perhaps set us both right. Hunt's 'Scapegoat' is marvellous in intensity, thoroughness, and expression of down-weighing desolateness. Arthur Hughes has an interesting picture of St Agnes' Eve, full of happy effect, and passages of lovely colour. (*Plate XXVIII*) Rossetti, whom I see pretty often and with whom I passed a most pleasant hour in Lord Ward's gallery yesterday – the 2 Angelicos coming in for all the superlatives we could master – often asks after you under the significant appellation of 'the stunner' a term he applies to all – male or female of high or low degree – in whom he takes an interest …

The lady who brought your picture, brought us also the unwelcome news that you had lost your purse with some considerable amount in it.

To both George and Henry Joanna endeavoured to explain the new style she had adopted. To George, in the letter in which she tried to persuade him to extract her picture from the Royal Academy, she wrote: 'For more than a year I have been trying to change it and to paint more thickly … When I set to paint Mme Héreau I found that I must either paint it in the old slimy or the new gritty manner, and chose the latter … Now it flashes upon me with all its weak extravagance and I shall be really ashamed to see it at the R. A.'

The portrait of Mme Héreau has unfortunately not survived in any visual form, though the struggle Joanna had in achieving it comes vividly to life on the page. As with 'Rowena', and in accordance with Couture's precepts, she had painted a layer of bitumen between the grounding and the final coat, and the condition of the picture deteriorated alarmingly. It affected both pictures, but, according to Alice, in the case of Mme Héreau, it had distorted the features and given the portrait an 'almost diabolic expression'. She and her sister, afraid that it would affect their mother's reputation as an artist, decided to burn it, though they later regretted having done so. 'Rowena' suffered less, though it too was much disfigured, it was among the paintings eventually destroyed in the air-raid, but a photograph by Philip Street survives to give an idea of its strength and energy.

Joanna remained in a quandary. To Henry she said: 'I feel certain that all that is good in my present manner I shall lose in adopting my old method – but I am disgusted with what I do.' She added that with regard to Jeannie Naylor, her brother George's behaviour was 'certainly odd'. She hoped that he would not lose her – 'I believe there are few like her' – but was optimistic that Mr N., if he had ever inclined towards herself, no longer did so: 'Perhaps the greyness of his beard now in a state of bristly growth has enlightened him as to his antiquity.' She thanked him for his 'orthodox sermon' on the loss of her purse, adding that if she had Fortunatus' purse, then 'the delightful French lady', Mlle Cazeaux, and Henry Warton should be rich tomorrow. Her mother, she added, was expected on Thursday afternoon: she would leave for England on Saturday: 'I fancy she will occupy Friday with one long scene and cry for a week afterwards to the intense sympathy and commiseration of the old ladies.'

From John Cook, to whom she had promised articles on the Royal Academy exhibitions, she received a characteristic note: 'My dear Johnny: Of course I pay your travelling expenses, you little ass. So let me know what it costs you in coming from and going back to Paris.'

It was a wretched homecoming. Though based at Park Place Villas, she stayed there as little as possible, spending her time with the Mordans, with Matthias and Lilly, who had made her welcome at Clifton Road, and with Hennie. She was delighted to see her nephew again. To Henry, on 27 April, the day after her return, she wrote: 'Edgar is a perfect boy, and with his funny ways and roguishness has made me laugh, but my head and eyes are aching, and I am very unhappy.' The crossing had been rough and Uncle Robert had remained in town specifically to see her and to advise her most strongly not to see Henry. She herself had determined not to see him while she was in London. Yet in that same letter she wrote: 'I should like to see you with George the first day you can arrange it.'

It is clear that she had yielded to pressure from him: 'When I consented to correspond with you, it was with the undoubted understanding on my part (and I then thought you fully shared it) that we should not meet when I returned from Paris … You ought not and must not expect me to make appointments with you.' In the event they arranged to meet at Hennie's at 4 Maida Hill West – 'even now you and Hennie alone think I am acting rightly' – and once again Joanna seems to have reassured herself that it would be for the last time. On 6 May she wrote to George: 'I saw Henry Wells as I told you I should and I decided that I would in no way object to meet him as a friend at Mordan's or Mat's or anywhere where we both visit, but I will not by word or by letter make appointments with him or arrange meetings. It is useless entering into an explanation or defence of my conduct.'

6

LEAVING HOME

'Let this old woe step on the stage again!'

'The Ring and the Book'

'Madame Héreau' was accepted for the Royal Academy Exhibition. Joanna observed to Henry: 'I am delighted with the position of my picture – 1st advantage – it can't be seen – 2nd – I'm somewhat of a martyr. I am very sorry some of yours are not well placed, and very pleased about Bertha's. I am to go with her and the Foleys on Friday to the Private View.'

This she did, writing to him afterwards: 'I have just returned from the Academy. Your little Corbould is in, but too high to be well seen. I like your portrait of Mrs Oliver immensely – all the rest I had seen before, except the original of Miss Hammond – the Astley children are capital.' She added: 'I think the green dress of the woman in Bertha's picture and her attitude very nice indeed, but I had imagined the whole thing better – still it is a great advance.' Her own picture, she said, was one of the worst in the room but somehow she couldn't be annoyed by it: 'I am afraid this indifference is a bad sign – I do not understand it.'

She was extremely busy preparing her articles for the *Saturday Review*, writing to George on 6 May: 'You are a great deal among the PRBs – if you have heard much of Holman Hunt's "Scapegoat" and could give me a clue to any hidden meaning there may be in his picture or any explanation beyond that given in the catalogue I should be exceedingly obliged to you.'

In the event Joanna more than fulfilled her promise to John Cook. She contributed five articles between 10 May and 7 June covering the painting, portraiture and sculpture on display at the Royal Academy. Her Parisian experiences were much to the fore and her assessment of the Pre-Raphaelites and their contribution to English art was both shrewd and enlightening:

> This is the moment to form some idea of the existing state of English art in and by itself. With the somewhat disappointing result of our last year's competition with the European schools fresh in our minds, it is

> no small consolation, in walking through the Academy, to feel – and we trust without self-deception – that our greatest men were simply not understood by our neighbours.

She went on to define the French notion of 'high art' as consisting of 'an enormous canvas, life (or larger than life)-sized figures, and an historical incident – if horrible so much the better.' The English, for whatever reason, had chosen to operate on a smaller scale, but in her view pictures like Millais's 'Escape from the Fire' and Holman Hunt's 'Claudio and Isabella' were expressive of 'a higher genius and purer feeling' than most of the gigantic canvases produced by the disciples of 'high art'. 'Such pictures as these are truly things of beauty and joys forever.' Landseer use to paint such poems, she said, but rarely of late, enervated as he was by court favour.

Joanna had hoped, in her review, to restore the reputation of English painters as 'colourists', but had to acknowledge that many who might have been honoured with such a title had been knocked from their pedestals during the previous year. The Pre-Raphaelites were an exception, and to them she paid tribute:

> The Pre-Raphaelite movement has done good, and will do more and the extravagances that its leaders fell into in some of their first pictures, such as Millais's 'Carpenter's Shop', were but the necessary results of a great change. The history of all reforms, whether in religion, literature, or art, has told the same tale – men fly from one extreme which they know to be bad, to fall unconsciously into its opposite. Moreover, there was probably, among the PRB's, a seeking for notoriety at any risk, and a consciousness on the part of two or three, that, public attention once fixed on their works, they could command admiration at will. We may well forgive this, for they have taught us by their pictures, aided by Ruskin's words, that an artist's strength lies in a child-like sincerity, and in the shunning of pride ... The great men in the group have walked calmly onward, heedless of the strife of critical tongues, and the walls of the Academy during those last few years have been but the theatre of their triumph.

She praised Millais's 'Autumn Leaves' for the 'solemnity and gorgeousness' of its autumn twilight and the simplicity of the subject matter: 'It has the spell-binding power of nature.' 'The Blind Girl' was almost as impressive, and though she had reservations about 'Peace Concluded, 1856' (in which a young

English officer returns from the Crimea, which she felt to be slovenly in parts) she described 'L'Enfant du Regiment' as 'a gem of colour' and his 'Portrait of a Gentleman' as the best portrait in the Academy. Having a particular talent herself for painting children, Millais's ability to catch 'child nature' so brilliantly enchanted her: 'There is the most comical, puzzled look on his sturdy little face imaginable.'

Joanna's first article was ecstatically received, not just by John Cook and Bertha, but also by Henry, which pleased her: 'It was no small relief to me to find you liked my review. I feared I had written great nonsense.' Her silence on the subject of his own pictures was as much a matter of delicacy as anything else: 'I feel ashamed to speak my praise to you because praise has sometimes a twang of patronage in it, and I am a pretty specimen of humanity to take that position towards you … Your paintings are really beautiful and mine bad.' She told him that she had written a paragraph on the English school of portraiture to come before her critique of Millais, in which the best miniature painters, Henry included, had been mentioned, but had thought better of it and had reserved it for a later review.

Her second article appeared on 17 May and again the Pre-Raphaelites predominated. The symbolism of Holman Hunt's 'The Scapegoat' so repulsed her that she struggled to address the picture at all, yet she could not deny the sheer visual power of this 'fundamental error of taste':

> The scene is so strange and new to most of us that we must take its truthfulness on trust from the artist … The sky, glowing like an opal – the distant range of hills, with their heights flushed and burning in the sunset light, and their base in shadow – and the livid, green of the level, lifeless water stretching far away – are inimitably fine in colour, drawing, and gradation. Coming nearer to the foreground to the 'salt-encrusted shallows', we are surprised to find the reflections from sky and mountains brighter than their realities; but even this we are inclined to take on faith from Mr Hunt, as it seems almost impossible that he could have made a mistake in such a matter. The goat, feeble and exhausted, and soon to be counted among the skeletons already strewn upon the desolate shore and faintly lit by the sun's last rays, is finely felt and successfully rendered … Take it for all in all, it is a wonderful picture, and must amply repay the artist for his toils.

She was particularly moved by 'a quiet grey picture', hung too high up in the corner of the East Room. Painted by William Windus, the subject was taken from an old ballad called 'Burd Helen', but the story Joanna read into the picture – that the young woman was about to be deserted by her treacherous knight – was not the story told in the ballad, in which a homesick heiress tries to escape from her fiancé by plunging into a river. The knight, trying to follow her, is drowned. That the painting is 'a touching episode in the endless history of the struggle between the true and the false heart in man and woman' makes sense however one reads the ballad, but it is interesting that Joanna, given her own struggle to break free of a true heart, chose to read it as depicting the false heart of man.

Several paintings took the Crimean War as their subject – Joanna picked out Frederick Barwell's 'London Gazette' and Noel Paton's 'Home' as being the most touching – and this was the year in which, within a few days of the opening of the exhibition, 'young Wallis' found himself famous:

> His 'Chatterton' not only gives promise of great things in the future, but is itself, though not faultless, a picture of high achievement … The sad history of Chatterton's misdirected genius and boyish vanity is well known. Wallis has chosen for his subject the morning after the poet's mad deed, and has painted the corpse stretched on a bed in a poor cottage. The morning light streams on to the figure, which is simply and exquisitely drawn – the head and right arm fall over the side of the bed, the hand clenching some fragments of a manuscript – the poison-phial lies empty on the floor.

She had kind, though not uncritical, words for Arthur Hughes's 'April Love' – 'there is too much fondness for crude colour, purple especially'[106] – though 'the fine conception of the picture makes us almost forgive and forget these defects'. The sting, with Joanna, was always in the tail, and even the much-admired Millais did not escape censure for his double rainbow in 'The Blind Girl':

> Almost everybody knows that in nature the order of the colours in the secondary rainbow is the reverse of their order in the primary. Millais has painted them, however in precisely the same order in both rainbows. It is curious he should have made such a blunder, but still more curious that Mr Ruskin should not have noticed it in his new pamphlet. One can imagine the vehemence with which so gross a scientific heresy would have been denounced in a painter of the older generation.

[106] Purple was one of the relatively new pigments with which the Pre-Raphaelites were experimenting and several of the pictures, 'The Scapegoat' included, displayed its fascination for the artists.

In her third article, published on 24 May, Joanna turned her guns on the Academicians. Those who had exhibited, she declared in her opening salvo, 'have apparently made little effort to compensate for the inaction of so many of their body'. There was nothing by Mulready, one of the few Academicians she admired as a colourist, and Leslie, whose 'capital scene' from Don Quixote had so enlivened the exhibition the previous year, had contributed a 'Hermione', from Shakespeare's *Winter's Tale*, which, in Joanna's view, should never have been hung, never mind in the 'place of honour in the East Room'.

She was no kinder to Landseer or to Frith. Of 'Saved' she wrote: 'That the child and dog ought to be wet, and are not, is so staring a blunder that Landseer must have been told of it by all his "good-natured friends",' while ' "Many Happy Returns of the Day" by Frith falls below his usual average'.

Only one thing infuriated Joanna more than a great painter resting on his laurels, and that was a painter who frittered away his talent on an unworthy subject. She regretted that Abraham Solomon's 'powerful painting should be wasted on such trivialities as "The Bride", which is moreover full of affectation, and "Doubtful Fortune",' while Edward Leighton sadly disappointed her with his 'Orpheus': 'The only thing which at all gives proof of latent power is the figure of Eurydice, which well expresses the irresistible drawing of an unseen power. The rest of the picture is almost too ridiculously bad to provoke criticism.'

Bertha passed the test: 'Miss B. A. Farwell exhibits a clever little picture entitled "The Invalid",' and Joanna was charmed by Mrs Webbe's white owl, 'warming his five wits – humorously characteristic and capitally studied'.

On 31 May, she turned her attention to portraiture and landscape. The former she declared was 'at a very low ebb', and the proof – a portrait of 'The Lord Mayor of London' by S. A. Hart – was hanging in the place of honour: '*Punch* has done much to make the Lord Mayor and Corporation ridiculous,' she observed, 'but Mr Hart has done more.' Leaving aside the masses of canvases that were there only because their sitters 'have titled names tacked on to them', and lamenting the lack of a Velazquez, Van Dyck or Reynolds, she yet allowed that there were some deserving exceptions, the miniaturists Sir William Ross and Robert Thorburn among them. Ross she saw as a painter who made up in truthfulness and simplicity for what he lacked in the power of idealisation – 'Nothing could surpass the little miniature of the "Countess of Lichfield" for tenderness and purity … and delicacy of modelling' – while Thorburn's picture of 'Lady Elcho' demonstrated 'a lack of grandeur' which she found gave a quietly harmonious feeling to the whole. And having doffed her cap to the two giants among miniaturists, she was able at last to turn to Henry, 'next in rank to

Thorburn'. She described 'a lovely group of children,[107] forcibly painted, and very harmonious in colour. The baby is admirable as flesh painting, and there is a delicacy of drawing in the children's hands rarely seen.'

Among the landscape artists she detected more signs of life than for several years past. From the marine painters, she picked out Clarkson Frederick Stanfield, who had originally been pressed into the navy at the age of fifteen, and Frederick Richard Lee, whose pictures 'are among the most earnest and successful studies from nature in the Academy'. Her choice of the best landscapes included 'The Cucullen Hills' by John Inchbold – 'marvellously careful in drawing and detail, and the sky fine in colour and gradation; but the foreground reminds one of a geological map from want of mass'. The only picture exhibited by Anthony she felt to be 'quite unworthy of his powers', while those of W. F. Witherington were dismissed as 'dead in colour and altogether commonplace'.

Her final Royal Academy review, on sculpture, appeared in the *Saturday Review* on 7 June. She had told John Cook that she did not feel equal to the task, but in the end addressed the subject with even more than her usual brio. This may have been because she was not as well acquainted with sculptors as she was with painters, but it was also because she recognised that, as an art, it was stuck. Moreover the Royal Academy treated it like a poor relation in terms of exhibition space: 'The merits of a Phidias could scarcely be appreciated within its scanty limits,' she declared, acknowledging that though her comments might seem severe, she would readily concede that any individual piece would look infinitely better elsewhere than in that 'cruel "black hole" in which the vigorous or lucky cling to the solitary window, and live, while the weaker or less fortunate are left to perish, huddled together in a forced and fatal proximity'.

That said, she rode into battle. The problem was the crushing weight of the past:

> Why should our sculptors assume, as one or two of them have this year done, that naked men with classic swords and shields, or burly masses of brawn half covered with armour, could possibly call up the sympathies of the present age for deeds of valour? Are there not acts of heroism, of daring, of endurance, done in the nineteenth century, as worthy of record in undying bronze or marble as ever were the feats of arms of Cannae or Thermopylae, of Cressy & Agincourt? Yet, in all this year's exhibition of plastic art, there is not one single incident selected for representation – with the exception of Mr Thomas's

[107] This was Henry's painting of the Astley children.

> 'Boadicea' – the reality of which could affect the heart of the spectator, or give his pulse one additional throb. Some naked nymphs – each one 'startled' at what is generally impossible to discover – are, with the above exception, absolutely the only representatives of emotion or dramatic energy in all this waste of platitude and prettiness. Surely it needs no artistic perception, nothing but a grain of common sense, to see that all this is not as it should be?

The reason for this lack of aesthetic aspiration lay, for Joanna, in the way sculpture, which should be among the highest and purest of arts, had been subordinated to the requirements of decoration. 'Our furniture is unworthy of the age we live in, and so fine art is dragged down from monuments, civil and ecclesiastical, to drawing-rooms and boudoirs to supply the shortcomings of industrial capability.' There were works in the exhibition, she said, that might have been got up 'by that celebrated French cabinet-maker who produced *des meubles antiques dans le goût le plus moderne*'.[108] With some glee she observed that 'in the head of his "Rebekah", Mr E. Davis was certainly lit by a spark of inspiration, but as soon as he descended to the bosom, it went out', while 'Mr G. G. Adams's colossal "Duke of Wellington" would be impressive if it were not for the smirk upon the mouth.' Not everything was to be condemned. Some of the portraits were excellent, and a tribute to the legacy of Roubiliac, Nollekins, and Chantrey.

She closed her review of 'the condemned cell' with her conviction that England's sculptors were not short of technical dexterity, but needed to refresh their inspiration – opening their eyes (as the Pre-Raphaelites had done) to 'the warm and earnest sympathies strewn in the path of every man's daily walk of life', harking back to the spirit, not the letter, of the antique, and to the faith and purity of the Middle Ages, not to its quaint and occasionally grotesque features.

❁

Almost all Joanna's letters to Henry are undated, but in early June, perhaps a week or so before she was due to return to Paris, she told him that she had spent a quiet half-hour at Kensal Green cemetery paying tribute to her father: 'The sun was shining and the slab looked brilliantly white with the blue shadows of the high grass and buttercups upon it ... You have often accused me of sentiment, but I feel that in this, the one real sorrow of my life, there is not the faintest trace of it ... You have bound yourself more strongly to me by the love you felt for him,

[108] 'antique furniture in the most modern taste'.

and the sincere respect you have paid him than in any other way. That cast[109] is more valuable to me than I can tell you.'

The family's differing opinions on how she ought to behave were exacerbated by her homecoming, not least because Henry was a good friend of the Mordans and Matthias, as well as George. The news from Paris that Bob's health had taken a turn for the worse was an additional worry. Joanna fretted that the gymnastic exercises, in which she placed such faith, might be a casualty of his ill-health, or even the cause of it.

She had told her mother that she and George would travel to Paris on 11 or 12 June. John Cook wrote her an affectionate letter before she left, hoping that she would soon return to 'labour hard for the S. Review'. Joanna had wanted to see her 'darling Henry' once more before her departure, but the meeting did not take place. She wrote to him: 'I shall not loiter in Paris. My Italian visit is still uncertain. We shall be blown across the channel pretty briskly tonight.' On arrival she sent word that though Bob was 'very pale and weak and very much thinner than when I left', his liver and lungs were healthy and gentle gymnastics had once again been prescribed.

They were in time for the baptism of Eugène Louis Jean Joseph Bonaparte, the Prince Imperial,[110] on 14 June, which was celebrated with a great procession: 'George and the Naylors came,[111] and we all started for the Tuileries Gardens to see the cortège ... the Empress we saw exceedingly well and very lovely she looked – the baby was invisible when the carriage passed us, but he was seen by many bowing in obedience to the *gouvernante*'s coercion and screaming as only babies do scream. In the evening Mamma, Bob and I went out to see the illuminations.'

George later described the scene in a letter to his friend William Allingham: 'On the illumination night, it was quite the "*belle de nuit*". The vast bodies of military, mostly mounted and well-costumed, rendered the scene infinitely more effective in its way, than anything we can do in London ... Perhaps the prettiest sight was the Seine, where it reflected the brightly illuminated *quais* and the undulating blaze of a barge covered with lamps and moored in the centre of the stream.'

Several of the Exposition pictures had been acquired by the Imperial family and hung in the Luxembourg – very badly, according to Joanna: 'They

[109] The death mask of her father that Henry had recovered between 3 and 7 July 1855, while she was away at Ashford Bowdler.

[110] He had been born on 16 March 1856.

[111] Whether George had come to Paris with the Naylors is not clear, but they were evidently socialising together. George may have resumed his attentions to Jeannie and it soon became apparent that her father still had designs on Joanna.

have bought the largest and finest Troyon and put it in a wretched dull side light – it is scarcely to be recognised, and I was the more provoked because George was triumphant in condemning it as part and parcel of the unhealthy school of French landscape.' She had heard about Couture's commission from the Emperor to paint the baptismal ceremony. (*Plate XXX*) 'Already he has finished the portrait of the Legate. The sketch for the portrait is decided on – it is to be as large as the "Decadence" – how he will revel in the white draperies'.

On 21 June her article on the minor exhibitions held at the Society of British Artists, the National Institution and the New Water Colour Society appeared in the *Saturday Review*. It was not quite her final outing as a critic, but it was her last review of an exhibition. 'As usual [there are] an immense number of bad and hopelessly weak pictures,' she observed, and though she managed to find a handful that demonstrated originality, beauty and power, she was soon in fractious mode: 'Mr Hurlstone continues to paint drawing-room imitations of Murillo – simpering Italian boys with large eyes and treacly complexions ... It must be confessed,' she ended, 'that wading through these collections is rather weary work.'

As for life in Paris, she told Henry:

> I shall be very glad when the Naylors are gone. They were to have left for certain on Saturday. George is the oddest boy I ever came near – he evidently avoids all sorts of opportunities. The Naylors are very anxious to persuade us both to accompany them to Auvergne. Mr N. came yesterday when I was out and represented to Mamma the advantages for me etc ... Fortunately Mamma wants me at home, and so she did not encourage the idea ... Of course she sees through Mr Naylor, but she has never said a word to me about it. I thought he had altered his mind, but suppose it is not so.

George left for Strasbourg soon after, on the first stage of his journey to Giornico, in Italy, where he intended to spend some months. He had, according to Joanna, taken 'no oil colours with him'. She confessed to Henry that she had lost her purse again, and intended from then on to carry her money loose in a pocket. She worried about Bob's increasing obsession with his religious duties and 'fidgeted' for news of George, though this arrived soon enough: 'He is all right – in ecstasies about the skies, mountains and wild flowers.'

For some time Madame Vernet, wife of the distinguished painter Horace Vernet, had been anxious to introduce Joanna to the painter Paul Delaroche. Joanna was initially reluctant, largely because she knew that Delaroche did not approve of Couture. But now she gave in, describing the visit to George in a letter on 25 June:

> I had seen Delaroche's eldest boy the day before, he was to have introduced me to his father and I was to have gone over his atelier – I arrived too soon – Delaroche had a gentleman with him, however I was ushered up into a kind of boudoir – presently Delaroche came in, he is thin, pale, a rather small man, past fifty, with rather a keen look in his face – he was very polite and kind and looked at what I showed him, praised them and said he would always be happy to give me any help he could, I thanked him and retired. Madame Vernet was dreadfully annoyed to find how badly I had managed, and wanted me to go again to see his atelier on Wednesday, but I think my courage will fail me.

As far as Mr Naylor was concerned, she continued to be remarkably obtuse – cheerfully assuming that he had given up any idea of courting her, only to find that she had deeply offended him. Her letter to George went on:

> I was trudging off alone to change your hat when I met Mr N. also alone. I was not far from the St Eustache Bureau d'Omnibus ... He said would I not just walk down the Boulevards with him for three minutes. I said I must take my ticket ... During the few minutes I was obliged to wait between taking my ticket and the arrival of the omnibus he stayed by me – if wishes could have made wings they would certainly have sprouted from my shoulders – as it was I turned a cold ear to what he said, which, though by no means ambiguous in meaning, was rather carefully undefined in language. I jumped into the omnibus the instant it arrived; the next communication I had from Mr N. was a rude sarcastic note ... (But as Toots says 'it's of no consequence'[112]) while I believe he was in fact full of repentance and annoyance at having in some measure compromised himself on the Boulevards. I answered by a polite good-natured note, quite ignoring his temper. Before this reached him, not satisfied with his first note, he sent me another much ruder, cowardly I think it; this he sent by Jeannie when she came to bid me good-bye, she of course being quite innocent of its contents. The next morning came a third and last epistle, manly and kind as befitted his age. He seemed sorry for the other two, but still tried to make me believe they were written in kindness to correct me of my faults ... I think he is a man who

112 Mr Toots, in *Dombey and Son* by Charles Dickens.

> under no circumstances would admit himself in the wrong, who with very great difficulty can forgive anyone who hurts his vanity … Prudishness is one of the faults he accuses me of – I hope it will be a very long time before I see him again, but shall be very grieved if Jeannie and I are in any way alienated.

She was looking forward to returning home with her mother and Bob on 3 July, and wrote to Henry on the 2nd to let him know the hours of her departure and arrival. She was anxious about Hennie: '[She] may look cheerful but I am sure her heart is very heavy. Her one wish now is to get strong and earn some money somehow – and there is Henry Warton earning nothing, but waiting for a government appointment.' And she was still extremely concerned about Bob. She had promised to take him to the Comédie Française before they left Paris but at the last moment he refused to go:

> When we were alone I asked him to tell me his reasons – he said he thought it was wrong to imitate nature… that it wasn't truthful. For the same reasons he objected to novels etc. I said, if he had objected to the theatre because he might see immoral pieces or encourage immoral people, I should have understood and respected his reasons. If we could find a clergyman with commonsense and true vital religion who would take charge of Bob, I should be very glad. Mamma says she will not leave home again.

George, who had reached Airolo in Switzerland, was not entirely surprised to hear about 'the awkward and unfortunate affair' with Mr N. 'Knowing something of his moods and temper, I foreboded some little unpleasantness, but not such a crisis as you narrate.' The weather – changeable – had make sketching difficult: 'It is the nature of the place they say. I await the clearing up to move down at once to Giornico, where I must work like a horse to bring home anything at all finished … Please send me (at my own expense, mind) a much more open tie of about the same width of thick dark blue silk – netted I believe – and without a stiffener. I remember well having seen such in the best West End gentlemen's hoziers' shops … Addio!'

❋

Family tensions engulfed Joanna immediately on their return home. 'I and Mamma have just had it out in the old style,' she told Henry. 'I asked her about telling you of Mr Naylor being likely to make me an offer. She denies having written, and requests to see the letter. Send it to me at once. If possible it shall be read in Uncle and Aunt's presence – they dine here today. Bertha Farwell has written to me to propose accepting the invitation I and Mamma have long made [for] her to come and stay a week here. Mamma says she won't have her. Pleasant is it not! – I have not once since I have paid Mamma an annual sum – supposed to include that privilege – had a friend to sleep here.'

She added that she, her mother and Bob would be dining at the Mordans with her aunt and uncle the following Thursday. She also expressed her determination to visit 'poor Anne, laid up again with rheumatism', and it may have been on that visit that she ran into Henry by mistake, as she was soon writing to tell him that he should not be blaming her: 'The Mordans never hinted to me, that you were likely to be there last night and I had no idea that it was possible':

> I want to see you very much, and I wish some good fairy would arrange matters – I cannot. My life is constant strife. Mamma loses no opportunity – and Uncle and Aunt are her staunch allies just now … I do not think they came up on purpose to alter the state of things, but now, as Aunt told me, it is their hope, that before they leave London matters may be arranged on a more amicable footing. I told her no one could be more anxious than myself but nothing could make me alter my determination. We very nearly quarrelled … But I am forced to acknowledge, however mistaken her views may be, her anxiety is unselfish and she and Uncle are really kind, and all that they say stands out in strong contrast to Mamma's false accusations and unbridled invectives. I never felt so calmly determined in my life.

She added a PS: 'I have heard of a clergyman living at Sidmouth, who educates a few boys … He is a very superior person, is married, and has a beautiful house near the sea. Perhaps sea bathing might be desirable for Bob.' Her mother, she told Henry, had refused to allow Bob to visit the Moores – not because she thought he would be present, but because she has 'no respect' for them and 'won't have Bob tampered with and taught to be undutiful'.

On 16 July, Joanna, her situation worsening by the day, wrote to George to acquaint him with the latest news about Bob. 'Coming home in the train,' she wrote, 'I could see his lips moving in prayer continually and since he has been home even in the midst of amusing conversation I have seen him force his thoughts away and begin praying.' Mrs Boyce, initially in favour of sending him away, had suddenly changed her mind, saying she did not see the necessity. Joanna despaired: 'He ought to be with boys and men – nothing can be worse for him than the dreary objectless life he is leading now.' Her mother, she was convinced, was trying to force her to leave home.

The good news was that Henry's portrait of George had been much admired by the Mordans, and as a result Mordan had commissioned one of Anne. Also 'Hennie Moore is really much better – she walks about a little and begins to get rosy … H. T. W. sends his kindest regards to you. Millais's pictures look finer than ever – "Autumn Leaves"'

On 5 August she wrote to George again, miserably aware that he did not want to think badly of his mother, but determined that he should understand that a crisis had been reached:

> It is all very well for you to say that her words are not believed, but do they not inevitably leave a stain behind? In Uncle and Aunt's presence she told me I must leave home if I would not give way about H. T. W. and then recanted it in their presence, and when I asked her whether she wished me to go, answered then and several times since in this way 'I know what you want me to say but I won't say it' and the other morning she offered to let me the house! And in a stormy conversation we had the other evening she said 'I can't live with you any longer, the sooner we part the better' – I have just been down to dinner and during it she again began on the old subject in the old way and said 'I repeat what I said the other night, you say you have places to go to, I can't live with you any longer, you had better go,' and I turned to Bob and told him he was witness of what Mamma said – so now there is scarcely any other path open for me.

It was a devastating blow. The Mordans offered her a home while she looked for somewhere to live – 'I suppose it must be some family with the requisite rooms' – and both they and Matthias proved staunch, true-hearted friends. With regard to her mother's refusal to receive Bertha Farwell, the reason she had given was 'Mr Wells' "insolent pertinacity"'. As Joanna paid her mother £170 a year on the express agreement that she should be allowed to receive her friends, this was intolerable. It occurred to her that her leaving might force her mother to change her mind about Bob: 'She continues to maintain that it is best for him to stay at home – he goes upstairs every night at ¼ p 9 and is seldom in bed before 11 o' c. This hour and ¾ is spent on his knees or reading his Bible, and in the middle of the day sometimes I find him on his knees.'

Henry had left London on 4 August to visit his friend Francis Astley, in Arisaig, Inverness-shire. Though Joanna wanted him to 'have a "holiday feel about him"', she could not resist telling him about her mother's latest attack, precipitated by a row between Matthias, her mother and herself on the subject of income tax. Even though she saw it as her only course of action, she still could not make up her mind to leave: 'You are surprised at my irresolution, but wretched as I am at home it requires a great effort to make up my mind to leave it altogether.' She was concerned to do nothing until Mr Boone had been informed – a hint at the power wielded by this friend of the family. Matthias was a tower of strength and Mordan 'very kind', though it galled her to think how dependent she was on him: 'I know the whole affair bores him.' She added: 'Bertha Farwell put me a rather startling question the other day: "Do you think Mr Armstead is fond of either of the Miss Wells's? – I turned it off as well as I could … She is not slow at putting two and two together.' So evidently the rift between Henry and Armstead had been healed, and Armstead's interest in Henry's sister Sarah (they later married) was not news to either Henry or Joanna.

By now the various members of the family were consolidating their positions. Joanna herself put copies of several letters in a packet, inscribed 'Letters connected with my leaving home'. One was from George, in Giornico, to Matthias:

> I received yours and Joanna's letters yesterday, and with the one exception of the prosperous advent of your little boy, on which I congratulate you and Lilly most heartily, their contents were painful enough. I feel very much at a loss to refer strongly and directly to many of the points therein, being absent from home and unable therefore to bear ocular testimony to facts, which would be denied probably by Mother, but of which I have no doubt myself, judging from what I have already seen and heard and from what I now hear. If Joanna's health and spirits are suffering, as I greatly fear is the case, from the unhappy life she is leading at home, it is certainly most desirable she should leave it, and I shall not for a moment set myself against it.

He was sorry neither the Mordans nor Matthias and Lilly had room to offer Joanna a permanent home, but was grateful that they could provide a temporary refuge: 'It gave me real distress to find that you think Mother has in some degree alienated Bob's affection and respect for his brothers and sisters, and especially for Joanna, who has thought and done so much for him.'

On behalf of herself and Matthias, Anne wrote the following letter to Joanna. It is long, even pompous, but is worth quoting at length because it was evidently intended for public consumption – to defend Joanna's actions in the eyes of their extended family and friends:

> We have observed with deep regret and sympathy your present position at Park Place, and as there appears no hope of it mending it becomes our painful duty to offer you without further delay a few words of advice.
>
> We understand that the principal causes of disunion between you and Mamma are: firstly, that you, having on a certain point after much reflection determined to pursue one course, she wishes you, and in fact endeavours to coerce you, into pursuing another. 2ndly. That contrary to the arrangement between you, and in consideration of which you have been paying her very liberally for your board and lodging, she has refused on one or two occasions to have your friends to visit you.
>
> On the first point we cannot but feel that you have a moral right to act on your own opinion, and that Mamma cannot expect from you at your age a greater degree of obedience than your own sense of affection and duty prompt you to yield. The refusal to have your friends to visit you is not only unfair, but very hard on you, as it prevents you returning kindnesses already received, or to receive others in the hope of returning them.
>
> Mamma has told Mordan that she is leading a miserable life, and that the mutual affection once existing between you has entirely gone (we know however yours has not). She has also told you frequently that the sooner you part the better.
>
> Under these circumstances your existence must be a wretched one ... and this occurs just at that period of life when youthful hope and imagination usually combine to clothe it in its most brilliant colours ... Again you are blessed with warm affections and keen sensibilities, and the scenes you are now almost daily subject to, cannot fail to be injurious to you both morally and physically and your health injured. We therefore, after mature reflection (for of course Mamma cannot be expected to leave Park Place), advise you to seek a home elsewhere, where you can have that freedom of thought and action, which you are qualified and entitled to enjoy. Until you can find such, our houses are at your service ...

You will, we are sure, feel pained at leaving her, but your consolation will be that you do it for the best, that your motives are pure, and that you will be supported by the opinion of nearly all your relatives and friends. We and they all know you have been an affectionate and dutiful child, and that nothing short of necessity could induce you to leave home.

With respect to leaving Bob, to whom you have ever been so loving and self-denying, we fear the good influence you once had over him is for the moment in abeyance … We earnestly hope that Mamma will see the necessity of soon placing him with a superior Country Clergyman to discipline and prepare his mind for the active duties of life. This can never be done at home.

You will be glad to hear that Mordan joins us in advising you as above.

With our kind love, believe me,
Your very affectionate sister & brother,
Anne Elizabeth Mordan,
Matthias Boyce

Both George's letter and Anne's are undated, but on Wednesday 13 August Joanna moved out of Park Place Villas.

7

LIMBO

'How is it under our control To love or not to love?'

'Two in the Campagna'

On Thursday 14 August, Joanna wrote to Henry from Corinth Villa, Anne and Mordan's house. The family was away in Buxton but had, as promised, made their home available to her:

> Yesterday afternoon I left Park Place and came here. At length the step is taken. I believe I have done the right thing, but at present I am wretched – it really is a terrible thing for a girl to leave her home in such a way and to leave Bob too. I am too miserable to write about it, but I must tell you how it came about. On Thursday morning last week, as I was starting for Highgate [to see Hennie], Mamma called me up the steps and said, 'If you are thinking of acting on what I said yesterday … remember that if you will give up respecting Mr Wells, I am willing for you to stay.' I did not remain to have a quarrel; from that moment on I have been trying to make up my mind to leave. I saw Mat the following evening and he again repeated his intention, if I did not object, of writing a joint letter with the Mordans advising me to leave. This, owing to the necessity of sending a copy backwards and forwards to Buxton, did not reach me until yesterday morning. In the meanwhile Mamma's manner to me has gradually and completely changed, having become quite kind and avoiding all dangerous topics. From what Mat says, this change is perhaps in consequence of a letter from Ashford to her, and perhaps she was a little frightened by my unvarying depression. Whatever the cause it made me hesitate about leaving; but after some conversation with Mat on Wednesday night, I determined, as she had in no way retracted what she had said, and as I know so well by experience that she was likely to resume her former treatment of me at any moment, to act upon her words and their letter without

delay. About six o'clock I left, telling Bob I should not be home to tea – walked here, had tea and then went to Mat's, who gave me pen and paper, and I wrote a short letter to Mamma … Mat also enclosed to her with a few words a copy of the letter he had sent to me in the morning. I walked back to Corinth Villa and sent Elizabeth with the two letters to PPV telling her to take a cab from the Maida Hill stand and fetch my box etc. When she came back, I asked if there was any letter for me. She said no – that Mamma had kept the cab, while she read ours, and had then sent out a message 'her love and she could only express her astonishment'. Up to the present moment this is all that I have heard from her …

In the evening there was a great fire towards Westminster. You know, I suppose, that it was Broadwood's manufactory,[113] which is burnt to the ground. On Monday afternoon I went to see Mr Cook. He made me stay and said he wanted to talk to me particularly. He asked me how I was getting on with Mamma etc. I told him exactly how the case stood. As almost everybody else has done, he did all he could to persuade me to give up corresponding with you. I answered him as I have everyone else. Finding he could not move me, he desisted … I have not heard again from George. I have never heard from Jeannie Naylor since last I wrote more than a month ago. I should not wonder if Mr Naylor has forbidden her. If they cut me, I suppose George will receive the same treatment. Will he be glad or sorry? Of course my painting is at a standstill.

Bertha wrote, as directly and lovingly as ever, inviting her to join the Farwells at St Martin's in Cornwall – 'away from everything that can remind you of home.' About Bob's rejection she added: 'Bob's heart may be turned from you but … he cannot forget the tender care with which you have guarded him from every evil – at least he cannot forget it long.'

In the meantime Mrs Boyce had shown a copy of Anne's and Matthias's letter, advising Joanna to leave, to 'Messrs Boone and Hall', who promptly wrote to Matthias a letter that, Joanna later confided to George, 'were it not very absurd, would be very offensive'. She, Mordan and Matthias were convinced that though it was signed by William Boone, it was undoubtedly composed by Spencer Hall (who, as we have seen, was given to grandiloquence), and was sent preparatory to

113 The Broadwood Piano Factory, in Horseferry Road, Westminster, was one of the twelve largest employers in London, producing 2,500 pianos a year. It burned down on 12 August. Only about 200 pianos were salvaged from the fire, but production continued elsewhere until the factory could be rebuilt.

Mr Boone's calling on Mordan at Corinth Villa. Its contents can be inferred from Joanna's reply, written to await his arrival:

> If in this letter which I am about to write to you there should be any word or expression which seems in any way disrespectful, forgive me, for it will only be apparently not really so.
>
> The perusal of your letter to Matthias surprised and shocked me much. I thought you would have waited to hear some explanation before pronouncing so decided a judgment. I had read the letter from Anne and Mat many times, and knew of the copy being sent to Mamma. Had Mamma shown you my short letter written to her on the evening I left home, you would have known who was responsible for my leaving home …
>
> I hope to see you this evening, but I will go through your letter on paper and answer it as though it had been addressed to me … Indeed, dear Mr Boone, you do <u>not know the true facts of the case</u>. 'The original cause of our most unhappy family disunion' was by no means Mamma's refusal to consent to my engagement. At the time Mr Wells first expressed a wish to enter our family, Mamma permitted him to be the medium (or at least to try) of healing differences <u>then</u> existing between herself and the Mordans. With Mat also she had long been at variance, and there are those who know how much my life had been one of endurance.

She pointed out that her uncle, Robert Thomas, had undertaken a thorough investigation of all the objections raised by Mrs Boyce to her daughter's suitor, and had been sufficiently satisfied to inform her that 'she no longer had any right to continue her opposition'. She added that although her uncle had since denied giving this advice, she had found the letter that proved he did so, and she enclosed it for Mr Boone's perusal. She went on:

> I told Mamma in Uncle's and Aunt's presence, that if she continued to spread injurious and false reports against Mr Wells, as she had when I was engaged to him (and has since), I would renew my engagement at any moment were it only in vindication of his character.
>
> You tread on dangerous ground when you refer to my dear and honoured Father. If I were to follow implicitly his plainly expressed wishes to me on his sick bed, irrespective of my own, <u>I should marry Mr Wells</u>. The 'one course', which you find so ambiguous is simply

> this. I will not object to meet Mr Wells as a friend at any house, at which we mutually visit; I will continue to correspond with him – but I will make no appointment with him by word or letter … I have no intention of marrying, and this he knows better than anyone else. For any wrong others may think I do to Mr Wells, I am amenable to him only. To show you how little my brothers and sister (I do not speak here of Bob) have been actuated by party spirit or one-sided views, they have all told me they do not think me prudent in having thus decided, but acknowledge I must be best able to judge for myself, and have never thrown a doubt on my conscientiousness in the matter.

She rehearsed the exchanges that had taken place between herself and her mother before she finally left Park Place Villas, citing the constant quarrels and her mother's oft repeated: 'We can't live together any longer, Joanna – the sooner we part the better.' Though Mr Boone evidently felt it was within her power to restore the affection that had once been between them, she reminded him that it was her mother who had lost all affection for her, and not the other way round: 'I still love her as a child must love her Mother, but it is with the deepest pain I confess, that my respect for her has during the last few years been fearfully lessened and love must wane with respect.'

She ended her letter with renewed gratitude for the 'kindness and courage' demonstrated by Anne, Mordan, Matthias and George in supporting her in a step 'which must appear undutiful to those who do not know the truth. About Bob I am extremely anxious.'

Mordan, who was evidently commuting between Buxton and London, received a belligerent William Boone alone, and subsequently 'fought manfully and skilfully' to persuade him to alter his opinion. He succeeded to the extent that by the time Joanna and Matthias joined them at Corinth Villa they were very cordially received. Joanna told Henry that when he left he understood the state of things better, and opined that 'Mamma must be bound over to keep the peace'. She admitted that she had been very angry over the Boone/Hall letter at first, but seeing Matthias and Mordan roaring over it 'I joined in the laugh and am at this moment joining the chorus with Hennie over pet morsels'. She wanted Henry's news too: 'Tell me about your sister and Mr Armstead. Tell me how you get on with your large subject. Don't go sitting out in the wet.'

The comfort she received from Henry's letters during this agonising period was frequently compromised by the vagaries of the post between London and Arisaig. Joanna fretted that her replies were at cross-purposes in tone with the letters she then received. She also fretted about the problem of moving her possessions out of Park Place Villas. Bob had paid a few visits, but had surprised Mordan in particular by the extent to which he was infected by Mrs Boyce's notions. 'He seems to think', wrote Joanna, 'he is to be constantly on his guard against me, and that everything I say or do is likely to proceed from wrong motives. Mordan', she continued, 'is parting company with his head traveller' – she hoped that this might open up the prospect of a job for Hennie's suitor, Henry Warton. From the Naylors she had received two letters, one from Mr Naylor and one from Jeannie: 'Hers kind as ever, his more savage and more cowardly.'

A letter from her Aunt Robert in response to her leaving home can't have made her any happier: 'Your intelligence, although not unexpected, caused us great sorrow. I too well know, my dear, dear niece what you have had to endure, but you could so easily have removed the cause by giving up the obnoxious correspondence ... We have heard from your Mamma on the subject. Your Uncle answered her letter, but I feel not to her satisfaction.'

'And so', wrote Joanna to Henry, 'Uncle, like a bad servant, is giving satisfaction to no one.'

She determined to send for her things the following Wednesday 'that is to say all my things besides pictures and casts and lay figure ... I shall write a note for Ellen Milner to take with her on Wednesday morning. I do not think Mamma will refuse to let her take away the things, but there is no knowing what she may do.'

Mamma meanwhile had evidently written to Joanna, who forwarded the letter to Anne in Buxton. She replied bracingly: 'What an abominable letter ... Did you require anything to justify the important step you have taken and to reconcile you to it, this charitable epistle would afford you abundant grounds for both; for a more vulgar, base and unnatural insinuation than the one contained therein cannot be imagined.' She returned it in order that Joanna could show Mr Boone the kind of accusations levelled against them all: 'He is a true friend, but too apt to judge without hearing all particulars.'

Anne was convinced that Joanna should, if at all possible, accept Margaret Piotti's invitation to go to Rome. She also commiserated over their mother's refusal to hand over all Joanna's possessions: 'Mamma had undoubtedly no right to refuse you the chest of drawers and work-table – they were given unconditionally ... It is quite as well Bob does not call, as with his present feelings, it would only be to act as spy.'

To Joanna's great disappointment, Henry Warton was not offered the job. She wrote to Henry: 'Watkins has engaged another gentleman as traveller ... Poor Hennie – her heart has long been sick with hope deferred.' She also regaled him with her efforts to secure her possessions. Her mother, besides refusing to hand over the chest of drawers and the work-table – a bone of contention which dogged their relations for months – had also retained the oil portrait of herself that hung in Joanna's bedroom and which, Joanna contended, belonged to her. Then there was the locked drawer full of letters about which Joanna was justifiably concerned. Ellen was sent with a lock-up box in which to bring away the contents, and there was an anxious moment when she was obliged to ask Mrs Boyce to show her where the drawer was: 'Mamma actually said she'd find it and told Ellen to leave her the key. But Ellen was too much on her guard for that, made an excuse and never let the keys out of her hand, and if I had sent anyone else the fate of my poor letters was inevitable.'

As it was, they were got away safely – ammunition, if it were needed, against Mrs Boyce and her many allies. Joanna determined to ask the faithful Wilday, their picture-framer, to undertake any further removals. She had seen nothing of either Mr Boone or Mr Hall: 'I agree with you in thinking Mr Hall will avoid us, but I do not believe he can really be wishing to marry Mamma. I think they would both be too much afraid of Mr Boone. If Mamma does marry again it won't be Mr Hall.' She felt that 'his stupid interference' arose solely from his cowardice in the face of Mr Boone and her mother.

Thoughts of escape from London consumed her, though she was afraid that if she accepted invitations both to Cornwall and Italy, her 'poor Rowena picture' would suffer. This was another in her series of illustrious women, for which her model was Isabel Borzewska, the pretty Polish girl from her Paris pension. She had begun it in April, but had only just taken up work on it again. In the interests of her work, she decided to accept the Piottis' invitation but to remain in London until the time came to set out.

'Edgar comes tomorrow,' she told Henry (the Mordan children were to return to London ahead of Anne). 'I hope they have cured him of this dreadful habit of saying "d---- Papa, d---- Mamma" etc, etc. Of course they laughed at first, and so he childlike repeated the entertainment, as he found it successful.' She planned to send him her mother's latest – 'a disgraceful letter even for her' – but needed it to show Mr Boone and those 'dear friends and relatives' who were taking her mother's part. 'Better success with your sketching, and destruction to the midges.'

In a letter to George, dated 2 September, Henry described his problems with the mail in detail. It was a subject that tended to obsess him – understandably, given the extent to which his and Joanna's relationship depended on it: 'The post is only delivered here three times a week and as the postman has to walk from Fort William (38 miles) it does not reach here until about 6.30 p.m. At that time the dressing bell rings and at 9.30 our letters are sent to the village to be ready for the postman when he starts on his return about 3 o'clock in the morning; there is as you will now understand no opportunity for replying by the return post and we are caused all sorts of awkward delays.'

George had evidently confided in Henry that he was ill, but had sworn him to secrecy. Henry was greatly concerned – worried that George was laid up 'in rough quarters among strangers' and that 'the long illness to his hip' could recur. He begged George to tell his family but also offered, generously, to go himself to Giornico to take care of him. Of his own work, he wrote:

> I get awfully disgusted with my doings, for I find myself in the midst of the most perfect material a landscape painter could desire, and yet I am producing four commonplace looking scenes … I have not at all accounted for the beauty and vastness of the country.[114] Over the sea from all parts of the coast you see on the Western horizon the bold mountain-islands of Skye, Eig, Rhum, Muck etc, and in the gaps between them the full expanse of ocean. My only weekday pleasure has been yachting with Mr Astley. One day all the party went to Eig and lunched there, we fell in with three whales on our return, so near did one of them come to us that the ladies were alarmed …
>
> You carefully avoid all mention of Joanna, although a great deal has happened to her lately. Between us there is nothing to discuss, but I shall introduce her name to prevent as far as I can its being a skeleton between us. I hope she will know more peace and happiness now than she has for some time past. The treatment grew worse and worse until it preyed upon her health. I think the heaviest blow to her is Bob's change of feelings and conduct towards her … it is hardly his fault, yet I could wish he had been less impressionable.

It seems Henry allowed jealousy to get the better of him again, this time on the subject of John Cook, because in her next letter Joanna chided him:

> You certainly are under some strange influence, or have 'suffered a sea change' during your stay amongst the seals and whales and green waters. Mr Cook, instead of being the kind-hearted, fatherly old bachelor he was when you left London for fatal Arisaig, is now in your distorted imagination a young marrying man, a very improper person to be my adviser, and moreover one who dares to find pleasure in my 'soothing presence'. Really Henry, you have written a great deal of nonsense, which

[114] One of these scenes survives; Henry's self-criticism is fairly accurate.

more than verges on the offensive. I do not joke about the Italian visit – I know it is a real grief to you. I wish you could think differently about it.

One of the abiding fascinations of Joanna's letters to Henry is the way in which they map the shifting emotional tide with such sharp observation and psychological acuity. Joanna did not spare anyone, including herself, and the result is often sharply comic. The saga of the chest of drawers and the table was designed to run indefinitely:

> [They] are undoubtedly mine, but I can't force Mamma to surrender them. It is astonishing that she is not ashamed of the meanness of keeping them with the immense superfluity of furniture now left to her in that house – beside the two pianos. If she sells the grand piano, as I suppose she will, it would bring more than twice as much as the chest of drawers and work-table are worth together. But worse than the meanness is the dishonesty, for she knows they were given freely and unconditionally. The way she tries to make out they were not, in the beginning of her letter (which is still looked up), is really amusing. She tries to prove that the position of the chest of drawers is altered by my connection with you. This is more wonderful than table-turning.

She had received a 'most worrying letter from Aunt Robert', revising their family history to the extent of saying that Joanna had told her how happily she and her mother had lived together 'before Mr W.'s declaration of his unfortunate attachment'. In fact her aunt used to condole with her on the difficulty of living with her Mamma:

> The only difference was this – she had no motive for persecuting me. Storms we had in plenty … but my plan was always to forget what she had said and done as soon as the passion was past, and to behave to her the same as before. Aunt knows perfectly well, no matter who the miserable wretch might have been who fell into my snares, the results between Mamma and myself would have been the same. How I wish she would marry and leave Bob to my charge. I believe Captain Murray[115] did propose to her and was refused. I wish some good fairy would put it into his head to try again. I almost think she would change her mind. Mr Hall is an enigma, but I feel certain he has never thought of marrying her.

[115] Not identified.

In the midst of these upheavals, Joanna found time to write what would be her last article for the *Saturday Review*. It was on the subject of Ruskin's *Harbours of England* – 'a mere bagatelle', opined Joanna, 'compared with the ponderous volumes he has not long since published', but full of charm and interest for its investigation of a subject 'hitherto almost untouched by writers on art – viz., the sea and ships as represented by painters, ancient and modern'. The book was built round a series of twelve engravings from pictures by Turner – a series cut short by Turner's death, but one that nevertheless inspired Ruskin to flights of poetic rapture on the subject of his genius: 'The surface of quiet waters, with other painters, becomes FIXED. With Turner, it looks as if a fairy's breath would stir it, but the fairy's breath is not there. So, also, his boats are intensely motionless, because intensely capable of motion.'

Joanna loved it, believing that the very brevity of the book saved Ruskin from his more perverse eccentricities and dogmatic pronouncements. And she agreed that at the heart of Turner's genius was the shipwreck he had witnessed in 1816 and had never forgotten: 'He had seen more than the death of the ship. He had seen the sea feed her white flames on the souls of men.'

Her review, enthusiastically trumpeted by John Cook, appeared on 27 September. In the meantime, following Matthias's advice, she made her will (her lawyer was John Neate, who had also drawn up her father's will). She left £700 to Hennie, £300 to Mlle Cazeaux, her Parisian friend, and the rest (besides some small legacies) divided equally between Bob and Matthias. She told Henry: 'Two thirds of what I have from Papa's estate must go to be divided equally between my surviving brothers and sisters [sic]. I have no power over it. I have fixed Bob's majority at 27. If George were to marry, or if Anne's circumstances were altered, I should change the distribution immediately … On Monday eve I am going to Mr Cook's (may I?) to meet Bertha, who returns today.'

Henry did not scruple to advise her. He thought she had been unfair in leaving George out. This she had done, she said, only because she was sure he would never marry. If he married, she would change it. If she died before he married, she knew that Matthias would share his portion honourably and equally with his brother. But she conceded: 'If I have not left for Italy when John Neate returns, I will see him and consult with him about it; and indeed I am very much obliged to you for warning me from ignorantly doing an injustice.' Anxious that he should not misinterpret her decision, she added: 'For two or three years before the loss of my dear father, George and I did not get on well together, for some reason not very easily determined. From that time we have been more and more to each other. Of this I am certain, he has been more and more to me. There has been a change in him, and beside that I understand him better and I honour and love him deeply. I would not wrong him in any way.'

With regard to Hennie, she was much more sanguine: 'Hennie is really wonderfully better. I was there last Tuesday. She walked, ran, danced and skipped about, till I – and I believe she too – forgot how ill she had been.'

Her aunts had written, begging her to be reconciled to her mother before she went to Italy: 'Letters from Ashford are constantly recurring vexations. I avoid nearly all my friends, and those I see expect me to talk – that is to say, they ask me questions on the very subject I most wish to escape.' Mrs Boyce had sent her 'one very shameful letter', but she had determined to go with Anne to call on her. George wrote from Giornico, begging her not to think of travelling to Italy alone and offering himself to accompany her 'if I can get over Passport and other difficulties'. He confessed that he had been laid up for ten days with further hip problems, but had 'got all right again', and repeated his reservations about the continued communication between her and Henry: 'I am sure it is not only an irregular but an unwise proceeding.' He added: 'I am glad to see that Madox Brown's "Christ washing the disciples' feet"[116] has gained the Liverpool prize.'

Henry was now staying with Millais and his wife at Annat Lodge in Perth. Joanna wrote that she had been with the Farwells to see 'Mr Armstead's things': 'How very beautiful that pen and ink drawing of Godiva is. The group he is now doing of mounted huntsmen seems capital to me, but I feel very ignorant of this sort of thing ... His "Desdemona" promises to be very beautiful.' She liked what she saw of Armstead – 'earnest and kind'. He had promised to lend her a book of early Saxon costume to help with her new portrait: 'I want to have a cup made for my picture and could find no book at Mr Boone's that would help me at all.'

The cup had a role to play in her 'Rowena picture', which, like 'Elgiva', was based on an episode in Anglo-Saxon history. The story this time concerned the warrior Hengist who helped King Vortigern defeat the Picts. At the victory banquet, Hengist's daughter Ronwein (Rowena) was instructed to present the Wassail cup to the king. Geoffrey of Monmouth describes the scene in his *History of the Kings of England*: 'Ronwein came out of an inner room carrying a golden goblet full of wine. She walked up to the king, curtsied low and said: "*Lauerd King, was hail!*" When he saw the girl's face Vortigern was greatly struck by her beauty and was filled with desire for her'. The picture, along with other drawings, casts and materials, had only recently been removed from Park Place Villas – hence the delay in completing it.

[116] 'Jesus washing Peter's feet', now in Tate Britain, London.

'Last Friday', she wrote, 'Wilday removed my things from PPV – some of them to Mat's, some here and by far the greater part to the room Mr Angell has kindly put at my disposal.'[117] These did not include her 'small portrait of dear papa out of my study. I told him to ask for it particularly. She [Mamma] refused to give it up, saying that I had given it to Papa, that I had no right to it or the frame either.' Wilday did manage to extract Joanna's large chalk portrait of her father and an oil one of Anne. 'As for the smaller portrait, I intended giving it to Mat and shall do so now, and leave him to get it away from PPV.'

'On Wednesday', she told Henry, 'I hope to begin at my new room, though I have very little hope of finishing my picture with any satisfaction to myself. I find there is no doubt Saxon girls always wore tight sleeves to the wrist. Am I to sacrifice truth or beauty? I mean to work as quickly as possible and start for Rome directly I have finished it, if I can find a family or a lady travelling at that time.' She had painted a small portrait of Ada, one of Mordan's daughters by his first marriage, as a surprise for him, but 'it is very indifferent as a likeness and thoroughly nasty in colour'. Her sketch of Mordan's other daughter, Clara, was, she thought, infinitely better.

As for George, she declined his kind offer to serve as her escort: 'As I mean, if possible, to finish my Rowena picture (you saw the commencement at Paris, it is that large study of the Polish beauty) before leaving England, I shall not be able to start before the middle or end of November.' She agreed not to travel alone – 'as you all so strongly object' – but was sure she could manage it very well. She took him to task for raising the subject of 'the correspondence' – about which she had informed him and the rest of the family six months before: 'What then is the use of opening these questions over and over again? It is like constant ploughing of a field – I can get no peace ... With reference to my leaving home, I am more and more convinced I was right in every respect in doing so.'

Sensing that Henry was becoming increasingly dissatisfied with their bargain, she reminded him that he had promised to let her know of the slightest change: 'If it has come – and I fancy I have detected a difference in your recent letters – say so now. I shall probably be long away in Italy. By the time I return, if entirely severed from me, you might feel able to form other ties, and a happy home might be within your reach.'

George had made his reservations about their correspondence as clear to Henry as to Joanna (he told Henry he thought it 'not only an irregular but an unwise proceeding') and on 13 October Henry replied, putting George firmly in

[117] Joanna's studio was at the North Star inn, probably the one in the Finchley Road, close to Corinth Villa. The Angells were friends of her sister Anne, and Hennie later became a daily governess to their children.

his place: 'I have not lost all my self-respect, and when I am convinced that your sister's conduct towards me is to be considered in the light of Charity, I shall cease to trouble her for it.' Joanna, however, accepted that they had arrived at another moment of truth. She wrote to him at the Sea Horse Inn, Shalford, Surrey:

> I dare not trust myself to write unreservedly on the one subject uppermost in both our minds. When you say 'If you could love, Joney, what a wife you would be', it is like saying to a lame man 'if you could run, what a racer you would be'. And yet the anticipation of the total separation we have mutually agreed on affects me more than you have any idea of. But perhaps it is merely a selfish grief. Do not lament for my sake the troubles brought on by our engagement – they must have come sooner or later, and the happiness it has brought me has been far greater. Looking back now I can earnestly tell you, I would not exchange the certainty of having once been fervently and faithfully loved by you, for years of quiet happiness. Unloving as you know me to be, I am greedy of the love of some few …
>
> Besides weak thoughts troubling me, I have weak eyes and a weaker will. The sight of 'Rowena' disgusts me. I paint slosh, and then curse myself for my laziness … I think I must leave now without finishing my picture. Each day finds me farther instead of nearer to its completion.

She was expecting to see him on his return to London: 'Be sure to bring me your miniature of your sister and your Arisaig sketches on Sunday – I really want to see them … As soon as I have finished [Volume IV of] Modern Painters you shall have it.' In a brief subsequent letter, referring to their meeting at the North Star, she added: 'I saw you yesterday morning. The two omnibuses stopped a minute close to each other, and I quizzed you leisurely reading the paper.' This is lovers' talk.

By 25 October Joanna's Italian journey was again under threat – this time because Bob was seriously ill with an abscess. The abscess lanced, and Bob on the road to recovery once more, she worried again about her inability to be of practical help to George and the emotional harm she had done to Henry. She had compounded this by including with one of her letters to Henry, a further frank epistle from George, and Henry had taken offence. Now she felt that she had betrayed George's trust and that as a result Henry might withdraw his offer to go and accompany him home. She wrote to him daily, and all the indications are that she was seeing him too – though she claimed to maintain her rule about not making actual appointments to do so. There are references to 'that little book of Robertson's I showed you the other night' which he had snubbed, and though there had been much talk of parting, the actual moment had not yet come. One Wednesday, 'past midnight', she wrote that she had been ' "mooning" this last half hour (or hour – I don't know at all how long it is since you left) in my room'. The meeting had perhaps been unsatisfactory, for although he had only just gone, she told him: 'I want to see you alone very, very much, to talk with you about many things … Goodnight, Henry, I wish I could send you happy dreams now, for by day it seems I send you wretched ones enough.'

Incredibly, as she told George, she was still being harassed by Mr Naylor, to the extent of having received several letters from him. George asked if it would be too much to see the 'paradoxical and startling epistles', saying: 'It must have been a very much stronger revelation than you had yet had; and yet I can't see how you can be amused and entertained at discovering him to wear only the mask of a gentleman and at his having written what you think I would call insulting.'

Joanna was far more preoccupied with saying goodbye to Henry. In a letter written to him at the beginning of November, again late at night, she wrote:

> There is but one way for me to bid you goodbye as you wish and as I wish and will. I will come to Stratford Place … Would you like me to do this? Your letter is a great blow to me. Although we have but so lately decided on what to do, I was unprepared for your sudden determination … I wish you really to understand that it is from no wish to escape from our present intercourse that I have determined to end it. Believe me, Henry, I value it too much … I needed your faithful heart to lean upon …
>
> It is dreadful to me to hear about your painting. (Not, as you well know, that the money question can in any way affect me, but as affecting you). But I do hope and believe that the want of commissions is quite a temporary thing, for you have given unmistakable proof of increase of power in the miniature of your sister, not to mention the Arisaig drawings. Do try and work heartily and not give way to despondency, Henry. Don't let me feel I am to be a curse to you in every way …
>
> Keep my letters and all else; I wish to do the same and I know it is your wish also. If ever you want your letters, I will return them all.

> My little painting of the rocks I will bring you on Wednesday, and the little sketch I made at Highgate the other day, if you would like it.

In a subsequent letter she added: 'In the case of the Farwells, if we separate, I must be the one to retire. It was you who introduced them to me, and it would be quite reversing the order of things for you to break with them on my account. Besides, there are other reasons why it would annoy me for you to discontinue seeing them.'

On 6 November, she wrote to George exhorting him not to travel alone. Not only were Matthias and George's friend Fred Warren more than willing to go to him, but Henry himself had said to her: 'I could wish exceedingly to go and see what I can do to help him. I want to see in it no connection with our troubles, and if he were to write and tell me to join him I should think it one of the friendliest things he had done for many a day.' Joanna added to George: 'I did not intend to mystify you about Mr N., you shall see all the letters I have had from him – 4 in all.'

Her meeting with Henry at Stratford Place solved nothing. He had tried, and failed, to persuade her resume their engagement: 'I cannot engage myself to you now,' she wrote, 'so either our present intercourse must continue or we must separate entirely.' She then went on to talk about her work: 'When I returned from my painting this evening, I found that Wilday had sent my 'Housemaid'[118] ... The whole painting is completely spoilt. The face looks smeared, and there is a large dark mark on the nose. When Lilly saw it, she exclaimed with the most delightful candour 'What a nasty smeary thing – it isn't worth anything. I should throw it away' ... I am staying in now on the chance of Wilday coming. I wish he were not so meek; I could scold him so much better ... I see you laughing again.'

No wonder he thought her 'cool'. He never really understood how important it was to her to tease away emotional stress. In the same letter, she told him:

> I had hoped to leave you happier on Wednesday, and am very sorry I failed, but I can say no more ... I claim no allowance for my unusual character. Selfishness and caprice are common traits enough, and you will know they are prominent in my character. But now you are asking a sacrifice which would dishonour me and you in the granting, viz, if I were to marry you feeling as I now do ... You know this is no new fear with me. I have tried to conquer it and I cannot, and though

118 'Our Housemaid.' This was intended, with 'Rowena', for the Royal Academy exhibition of 1857.

> sometimes – as on Wednesday – I forget it and try to fancy myself, if I loved you, a happy wife, the old dread returns more strongly than ever – a proof that it is not groundless.

His own letters to her veered between 'vicious little missives' and 'thick good-humoured looking packets'. He had dubbed her, not altogether kindly, his 'representative girl'. The reference was to Ralph Waldo Emerson's 'Representative Men', published in 1850 – a series of lectures on Plato, Swedenborg, Shakespeare, Montaigne, Napoleon and Goethe which they had both read, and which, in her case, had attracted and repelled her: 'I think [him]the most dangerous writer I have ever come across. I have two volumes of his essays. They are like the forbidden fruit. I long to taste them and dare not … It was the spirit of supreme self-reliance that seemed to me to run like a subtle poison through his writings; not the independence of man of his fellows, but of God.'

Otherwise there was little change. Bob's recovery after a second operation on his abscess, and the prospect of George's being well enough to travel, put Joanna in a more ebullient mood, though she was anxious on Henry's behalf about his commissions. His sojourn at Vale Royal, in Cheshire, whither he had been summoned again to paint the Cholmondeley family, was not proving a happy one. Joanna wrote: 'It is very vexatious about the Cholmondeleys. I did not think that you, as one of the very few good miniature painters, would feel so directly the effects of photography. You must feel and know what is best for you to do, but this I know, that if miniature painting were forbidden by law tomorrow, I should not have the slightest uneasiness as to your success in some other branch or branches of your profession.' On the following morning she added: 'I hope the photographer will make ugly portraits of the children. I am afraid I am spiteful, but the Cholmondeleys have not behaved well.'

The situation recovered, to the extent that Henry was given the 'little Miss Cholmondeley' to paint. In the meantime Matthias travelled to Paris to accompany George home, only to find that the latter had decided to stay there for a fortnight to take advantage of the curative powers of a certain clairvoyant who had been recommended to him by his landlady.[119] Matthias spent a single 'wet, dreary day' with his brother before returning on his own. Joanna, meanwhile, struggled with 'Rowena': 'I am dreadfully dissatisfied with my picture altogether. Each day it seems to me more sloshy and pretentious … Yesterday I received a letter from Jeannie Naylor from Florence. As I expected Mr N has forbidden her

[119] The skills of clairvoyants in the nineteenth century were not restricted to spiritualism and fortune-telling but embraced healing and mesmeric powers.

to write to me. She says she is committing an act of disobedience but could not bear to leave my last unnoticed.'

Joanna was now staying with Matthias and Lilly at Clifton Road. Henry returned to London from Vale Royal at the beginning of December, and on the 5th Joanna wrote to him at Stratford Place, confessing that she was less at ease with them than with the Mordans:

> Lilly is very different to Anne, and Anne's worth a hundred of her. She wounds and irritates me constantly without knowing it, and yet I should find it very difficult to explain exactly how. She is a good loving little wife to Mat and satisfies him, and so she satisfies me completely in one sense – as if I had any right to expect satisfaction in any sense – but she has neither very sensitive nor very deep feeling. We are excellent friends though in a way. Mat never chafes me, and I believe with Lilly the fault is more than half mine. My mouth is getting a 'little soured about the ends'.

She was of course sharing a house with two happy newly-weds: 'Mat and Lilly are rattling the dice in a distracting manner over a very loving game of backgammon', she wrote, and, when she was reading Elizabeth Barrett Browning's *Aurora Leigh*:[120] 'I was glad when Mat and Lilly left me, for insane exclamations would burst out at the fine passages.' As a great admirer of the poet, Joanna loved *Aurora Leigh* for its passion, its beauty and 'its salt of truth'; as a critic, she thought it 'a great pity it is so spun out at the end, and the conversations, though full of good things, are so absurdly unnatural for lover's talk'.

On her recommendation, George took advantage of his sojourn in Paris to visit Couture: 'He received me very kindly tho' unceremoniously – patted you on the back very considerably and said he was '*enchanté d'avoir des nouvelles de Mlle Joanna*'[121] – showed me several very excellent studies.' The Empress had already given him a sitting for his picture of the imperial christening. 'We talked over the English Pictures at the Exposition. He spoke admiringly of Mulready, W. Hunt (the ancient Water Colours), Millais, and some painter of hunts, whom I couldn't think of ... I'm as inimical as ever to Troyon and Rosa Bonheur's colouring, electric, unnatural light – heavy, dirty and monotonous shadows, and leaden mineral skies.'

She riposted: 'I am glad you saw Couture and his pictures – so he patted me on the back? He paid me tremendous compliments when first I went and

[120] *Aurora Leigh* was published in November 1856, though dated 1857.
[121] 'delighted to have news of Miss Joanna.'

used to congratulate the atelier on making a grand acquisition in me, but I used to fight him a little ... He likes immensely doing the master in the midst of a group of awed and admiring disciples.'

From her letter to Henry of 5 December it is clear that Joanna was seeing him, if only occasionally. She invited him to come to her studio at the North Star that day, in the company of Anne, to see how 'Rowena' was progressing, and in her letters throughout the month gave him wounding glimpses of her life as a waif and stray, while steadfastly refusing a closer tie with him. 'Long ago I told you it was my firm belief I should never marry. I repeat it now ... Letters of this kind seem to occur periodically in our correspondence – each time with less hope of its being the last and with less result.'

Yet they could not give each other up. He challenged her to make the decision for him. She responded by offering to let him go if he wished it, and then assuming that somehow they would go on. Every impassioned outburst – 'Whether you believe it or not, that I am very, very far from being indifferent to your present unhappiness, and yet I cannot avert it. I know that I have been and am the curse of your life' – came wrapped in the common currency of what interested them both – their work: 'You have told me nothing about Wednesday evening. I want to know, who you had there and all about it. So you are doing a miniature of Anne. How do you get on with Miss Close? and what are you doing with Mr Fowler? ... I am disgusted with my picture. Mrs Newman sat for the arms one day last week – and when she had gone I took it all out again, excepting some browner smears on one arm, which is of course worse than before.'

She had found employment for Hennie as a daily governess, but was concerned that Hennie's father, in his 'pompous indignation', would not take this well: 'I shall call there probably the Sunday after next in order to receive rebuke or coldness in person.'[122] She ended her letter: 'When I esteem you I love you; when you disappoint me, the fairy light fades ... I hope I have not hurt you, Henry, by what I have said. At this moment I would like to feel my head against your faithful old heart. God bless you.'

George had decided to return in early January of the following year. He sent bad news: 'I was very shocked and pained to hear today of the recent death in Cairo of Tom Seddon – of diarrhoea. Poor fellow, just at the time there was every chance of his making way, and spending many happy years with his young wife ... He will be very much missed in our 'set', of which when present he was ever the enlivening spirit and the *bien venu*.' He signed off with a warning: 'Don't touch Isabel-ski's face.'

[122] In fact, Hennie did not take up the post, though whether this was her father's doing we do not know.

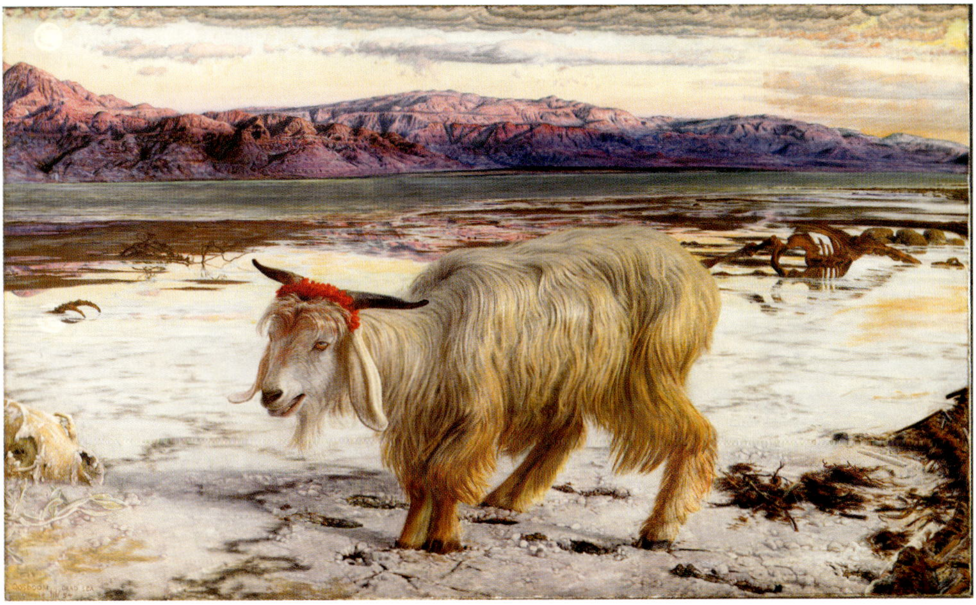

XXV. *The Scapegoat,* Holman Hunt

Early in 1856, George heard that Holman Hunt was on his way home from the Middle East, and had sent a picture ahead to the Royal Academy depicting 'a ragged, worn-out goat by the shores of the Dead Sea'. He found it 'marvellous in intensity, thoroughness, and expression of down-weighing desolateness'.

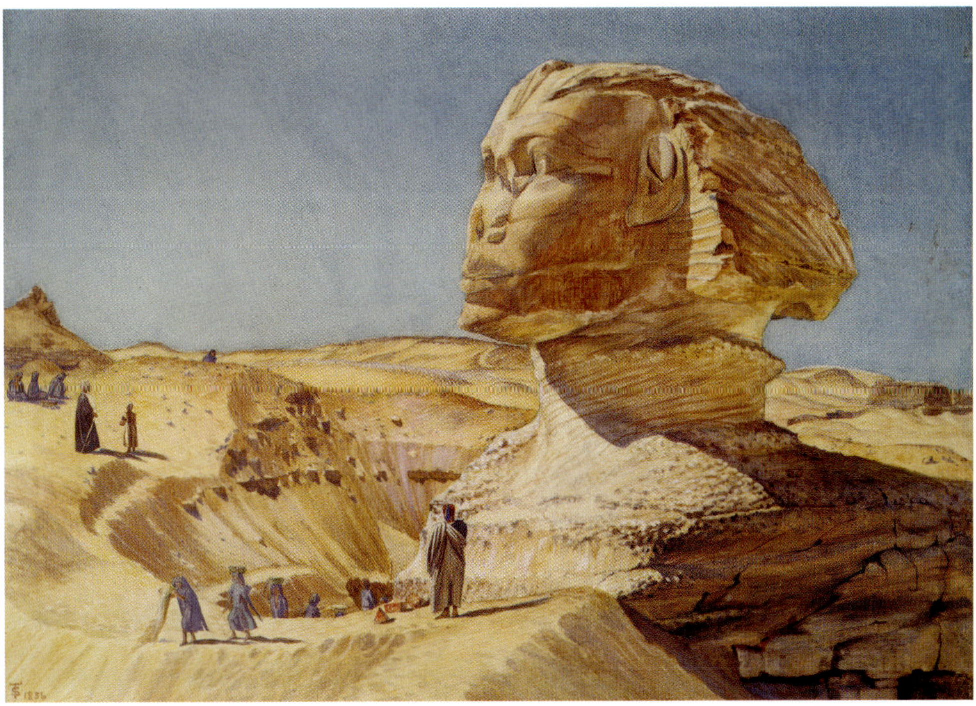

XXVI. *Excavations around The Sphinx,* Thomas Seddon

Tom Seddon made his first journey to Egypt and the Holy Land in the company of Holman Hunt, and the two of them spent some time camped in the vicinity of the sphinx. 'Both pyramids and sphinxes, in ordinary daylight', wrote Seddon in 1854, 'are merely ugly, and do not look half as large as they ought to look.' This water-colour, which is far from ugly, was bought by George in April 1856

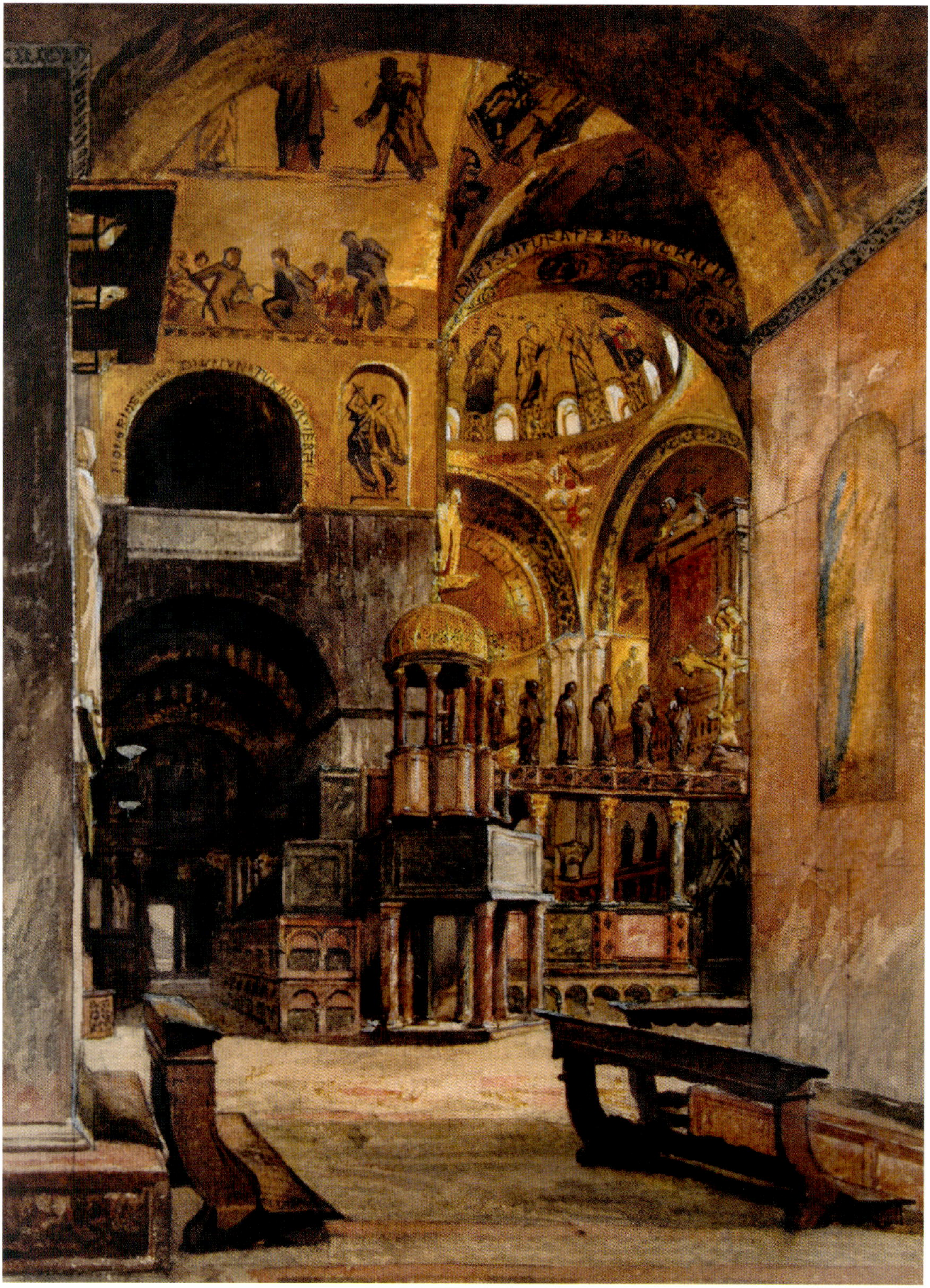

XXVII. *The North Side of St Marks, Venice* George Price Boyce

When George visited Venice in 1854, Henry hoped he would make 'at least one drawing of the interior' and on 'a large-sized paper'. George himself described this beautiful water-colour as a 'meagre and spectral drawing', but submitted it to the Royal Academy in 1856, where it hung in the North Room.

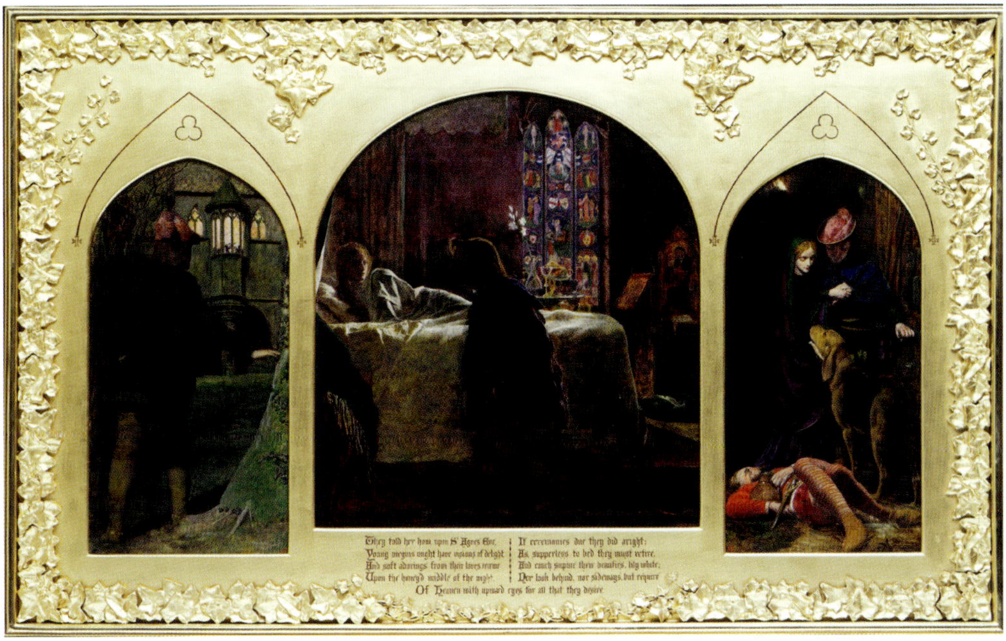

XXVIII. *The Eve of St Agnes* Arthur Hughes

Hughes based his picture on John Keats's poem, which had been published in 1820. It shows Porphyro coming to the castle where a feast is taking place, awakening his beloved Madeline from her dreams, and the escape of the lovers into the night. Ruskin thought the face of the awakening Madeline 'exquisite', while George described Hughes's picture as 'full of happy effect, and passages of lovely colour'.

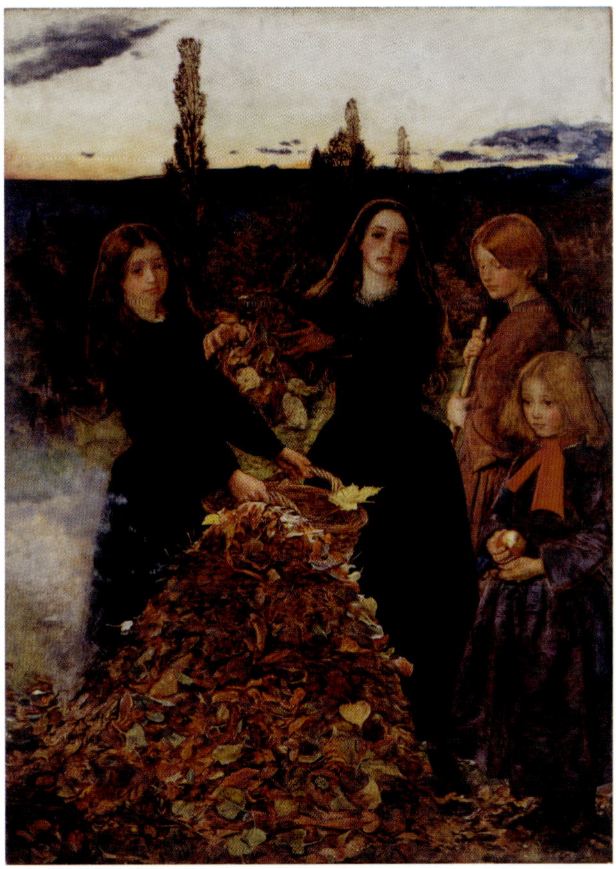

XXIX. *Autumn Leaves*
John Everett Millais

Millais's 'Autumn Leaves' was exhibited at the Royal Academy in 1856. Joanna praised it in the Saturday Review, 'for the solemnity and gorgeousness' of its autumn twilight. It has the spell-binding power of nature.'

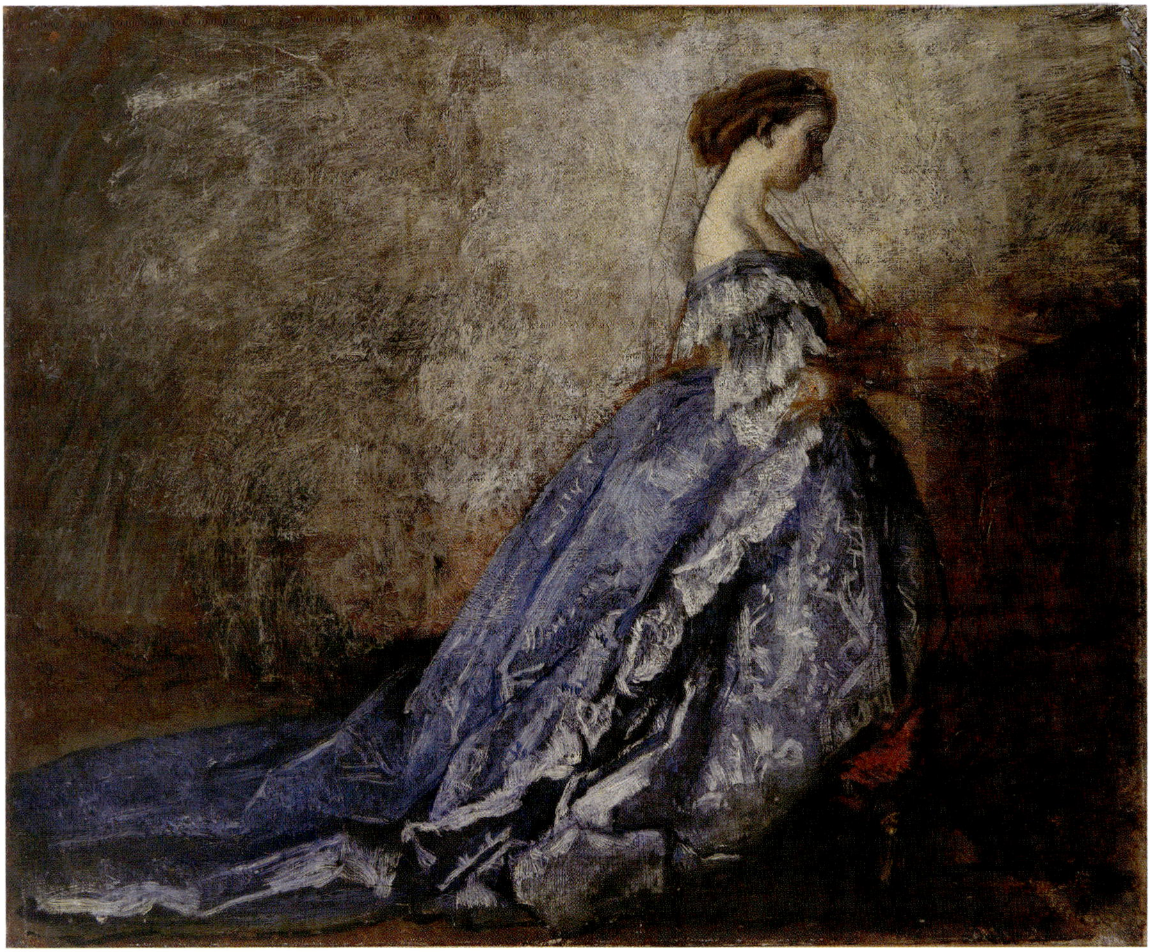

XXX. *Empress Eugénie at Prayer* Thomas Couture

In 1845, Couture won the prestigious commission to commemorate the baptism of the Prince Imperial, which took place on 14 June. The picture, which Joanna said 'was to be as large as the "Décadence" – how he will revel in the white draperies', was never completed, but Couture did produce a number of studies for it, including this dramatic and impressionistic painting of the Empress Eugénie at prayer.

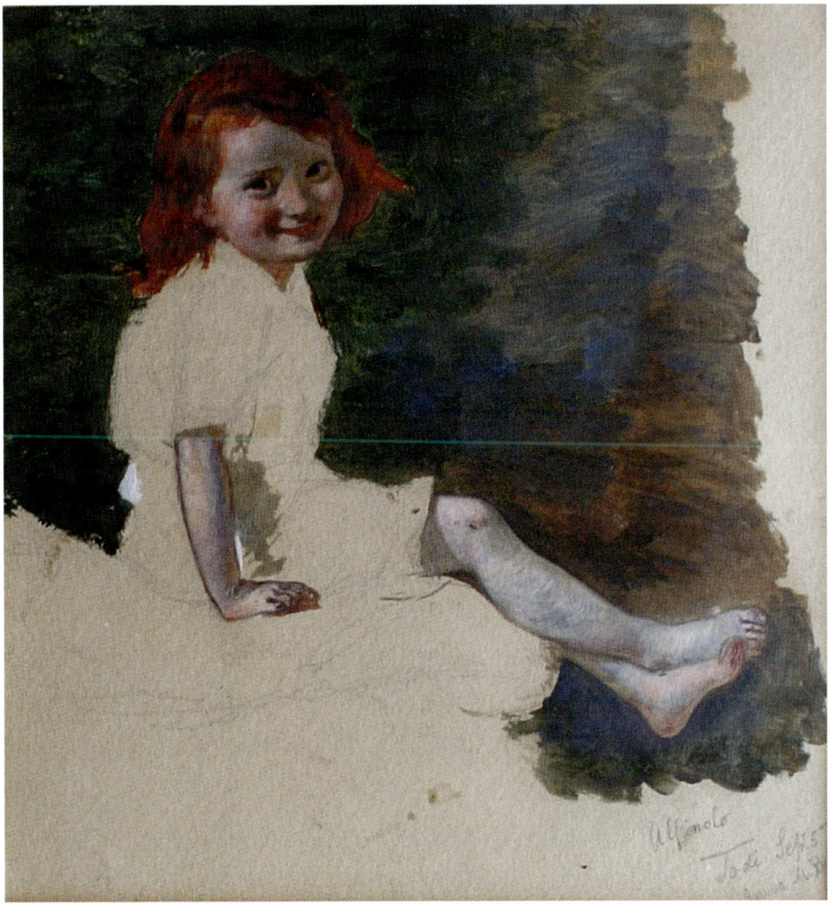

XXXI. *Alfrinolo at Todi*
Joanna Boyce

Joanna and her friend Margaret Piotti rented a studio in Todi where they worked industriously, in between enjoying the entertainments the town had to offer. This is one of the many water-colour sketches she made of local children

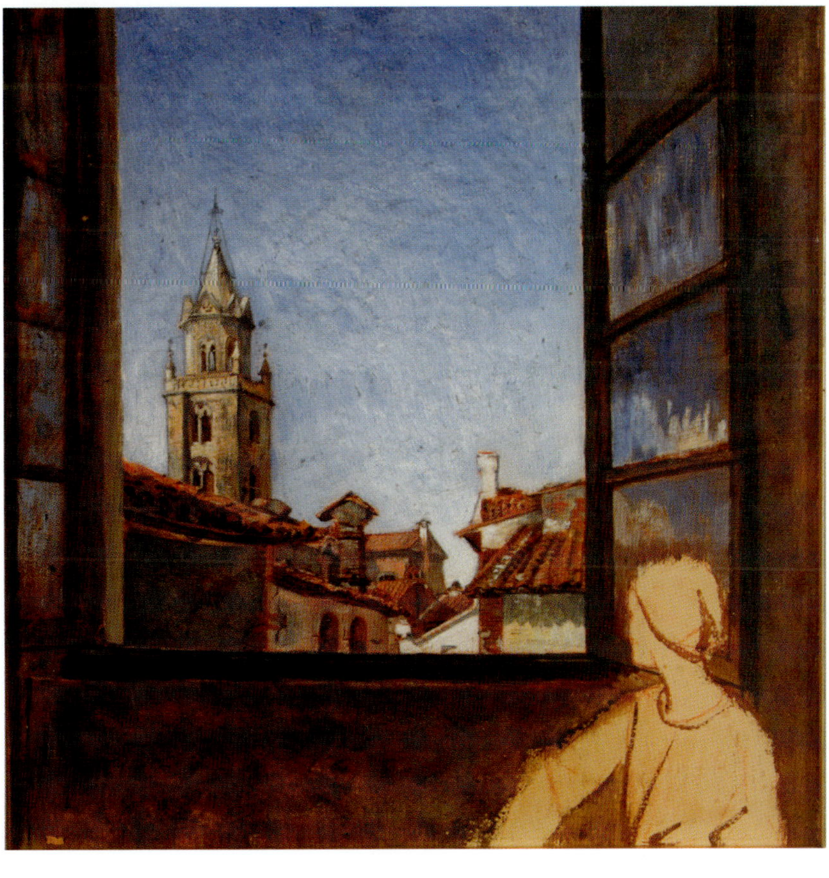

XXXII. *Woman at a Window in Italy*
Joanna Boyce

In August, Joanna and Margaret set up their easels in the passage of the Commune and sketched 'the sun-lit roofs and chimney pots seen through the open window.'

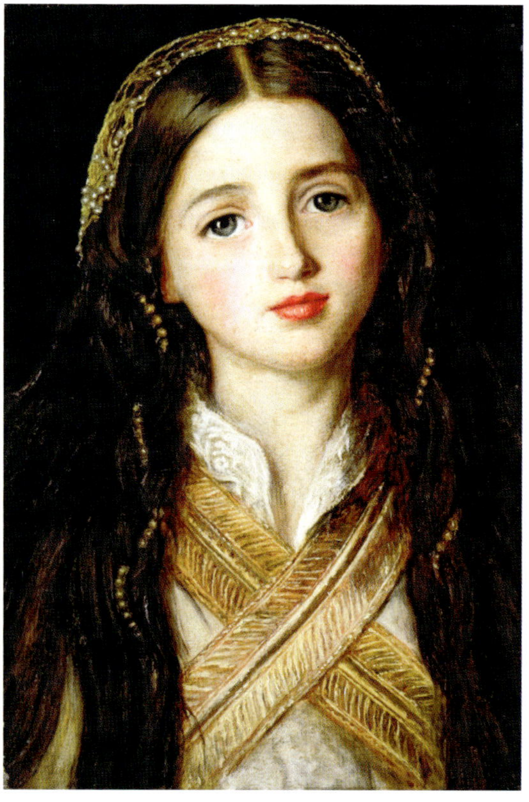

XXXIII. *Alice Gray* John Everett Millais

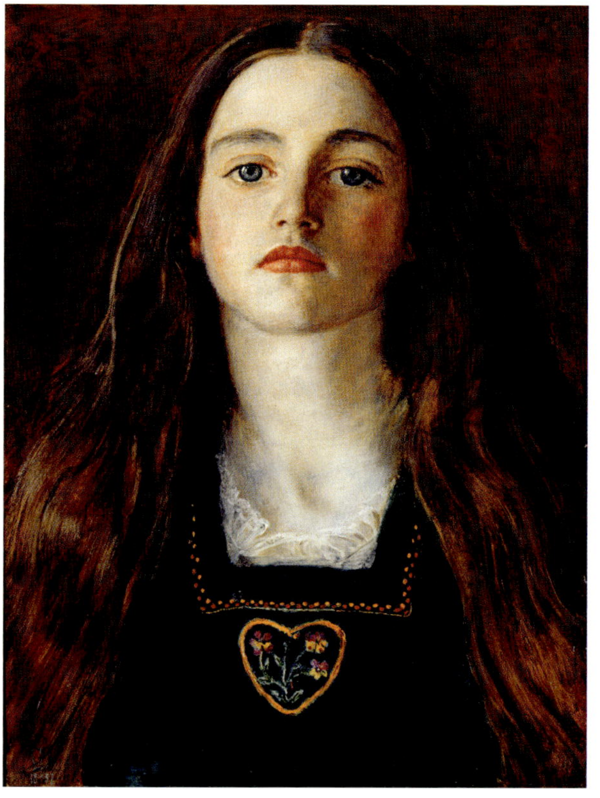

XXXIV. *Sophie Gray* John Everett Millais

These are the pictures commissioned from Millais by Joanna and George. George wrote to Joanna in Italy on 19 November to tell her that one girl 'was perfectly bare-headed' and the other with 'but a line of gold and pearly fretwork on the crown of the head and a few pearls entwined in the hair.' He preferred the bare-headed one (Sophie), but was fretful that as their tastes so often coincided, she would feel she had got second-best. She was determined upon Alice: 'Let Millais know at once that I wish to have the head he has painted for me. I think it would be foolish for us both to have studies of the same head.' Besides, she added, 'Henry has a predilection for the second sister's head.'

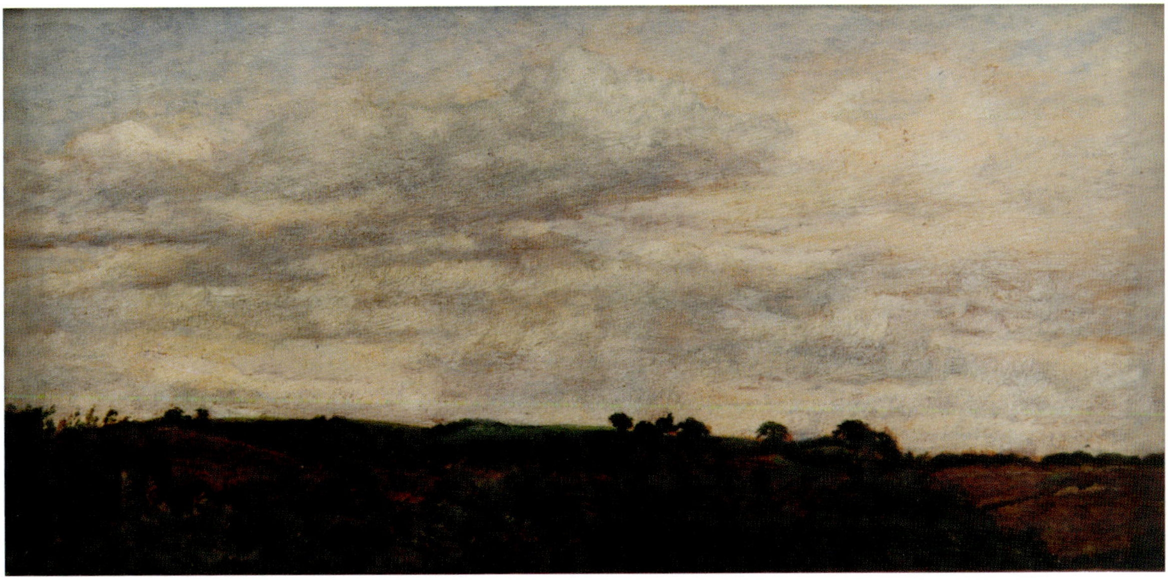

XXXV. *Holmbury Hill* Joanna Boyce

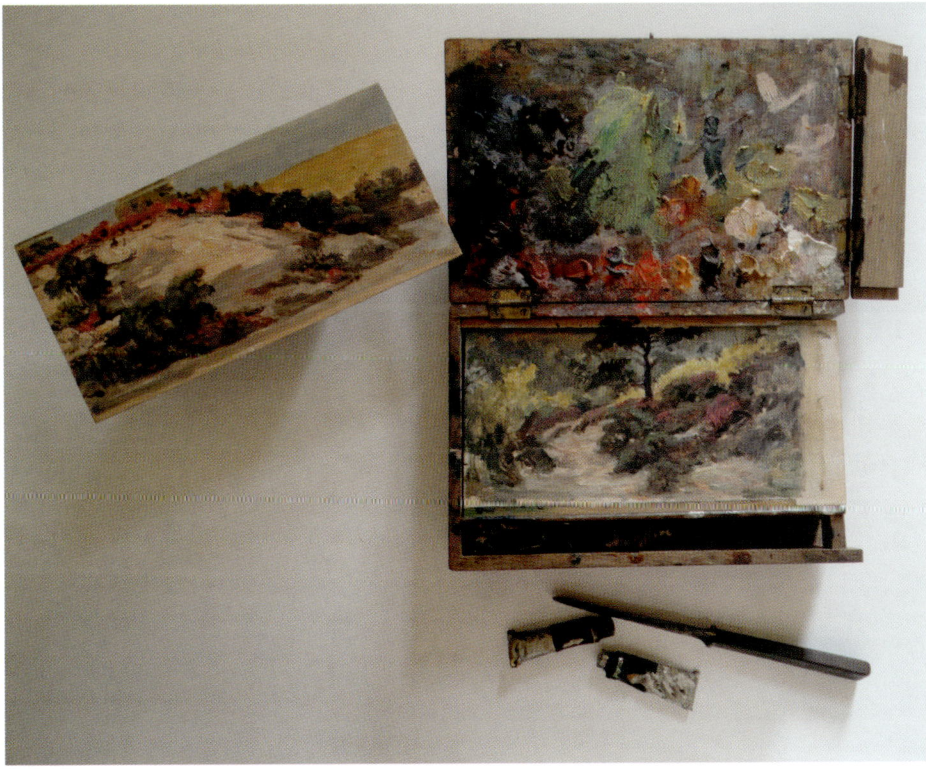

XXXVI. *Photograph of Joanna's paintbox*

Joanna and Henry spent one of the happiest periods of their married life at Joldwynds, a house on the south slope of Holmbury Hill. 'We have a magnificent view before us, stretching right over Sussex away to the sea, immediately below us the plain is richly wooded and behind us rises the hill, almost one flow of purple heather.' Her painting of Holmbury Hill and the three energetic sketches that are still with her paint-box are wonderfully evocative of the surrounding landscape.

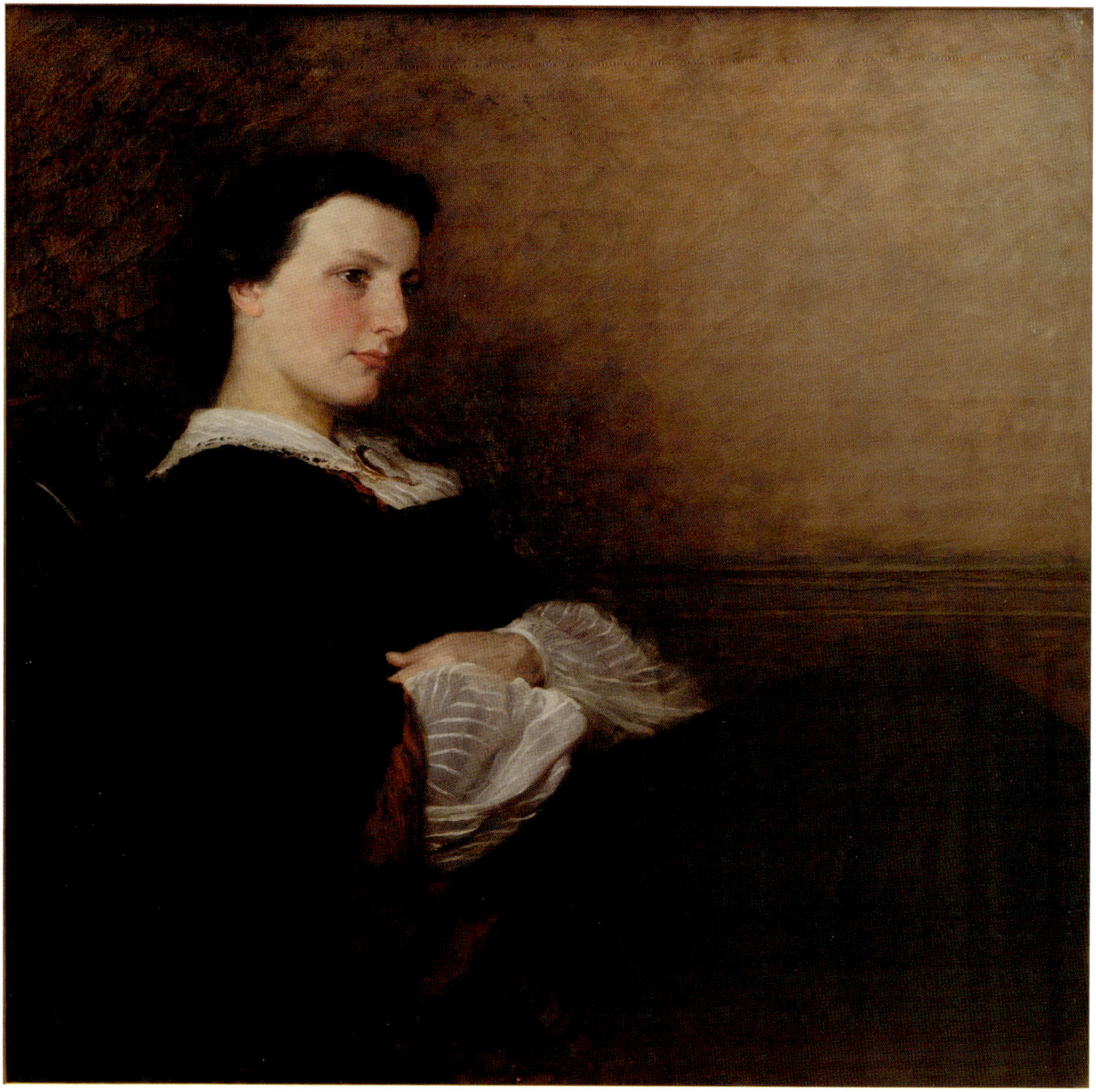

XXXVII. *Joanna* Henry T. Wells

'A thoughtful head'

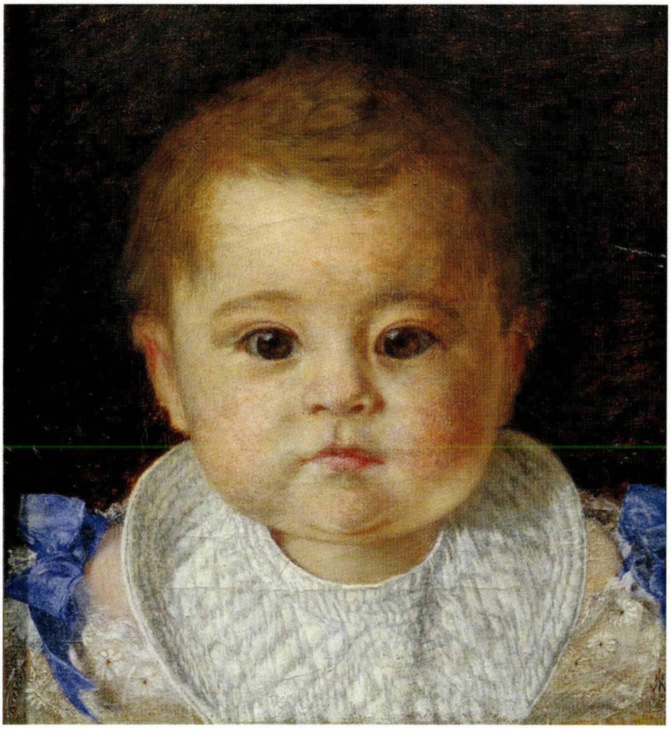

XXXVIII. *Sidney*
Joanna Boyce Wells

Joanna's and Henry's first child, born on 19 January 1859, was, according to his mother, 'a little tiny Puck'. Hennie Moore described 'his large eyes, dear round little face, his briskness and his intelligence' – qualities which Joanna caught in her portrait of him.

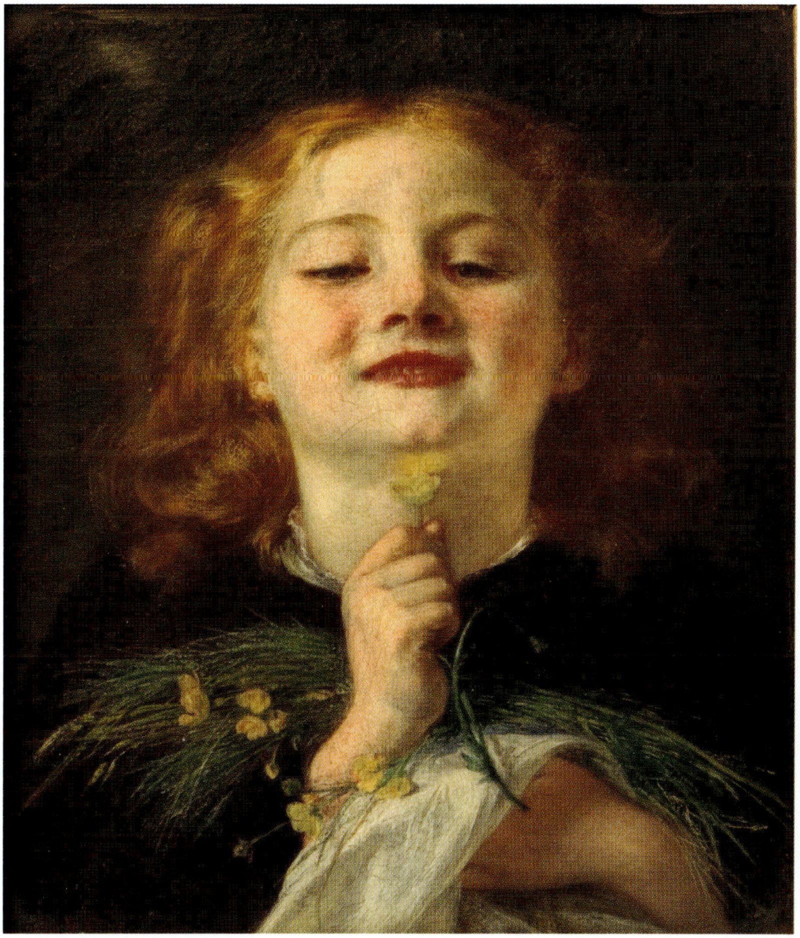

XXXIX. *Do I Like Butter ?*
Joanna Boyce Wells

Joanna's 'little buttercup picture' was completed in 1859 in spite of her recent confinement. Her marriage to Henry prompted her to take what steps she could to boost the family income, and 'Do I Like Butter?' was exhibited at Ernest Gambart's Winter Exhibition and purchased by Thomas Plint, a Pre-Raphaelite enthusiast from Leeds.

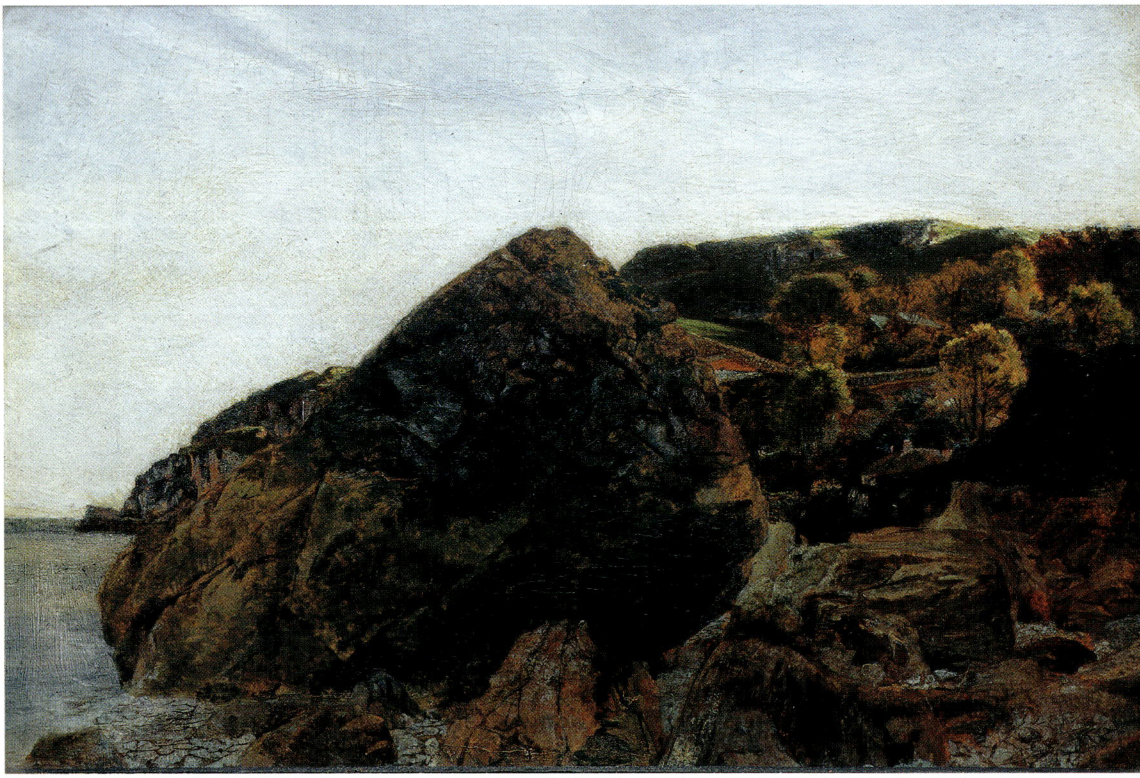

XL. *Shanklin, Isle of Wight* Joanna Boyce Wells

When did Joanna paint this picture? It is usually dated 1859, but though George was in the Isle of Wight painting the 'Undercliff' towards the end of that year and early in 1860, there is no evidence that Joanna was also there, either with or without Henry. She was, in any case, heavily pregnant. Perhaps she made the picture from sketches or photographs supplied by George, to occupy herself during the late stages of pregnancy, or perhaps it is a much earlier work, undertaken on a family visit of which no record survives

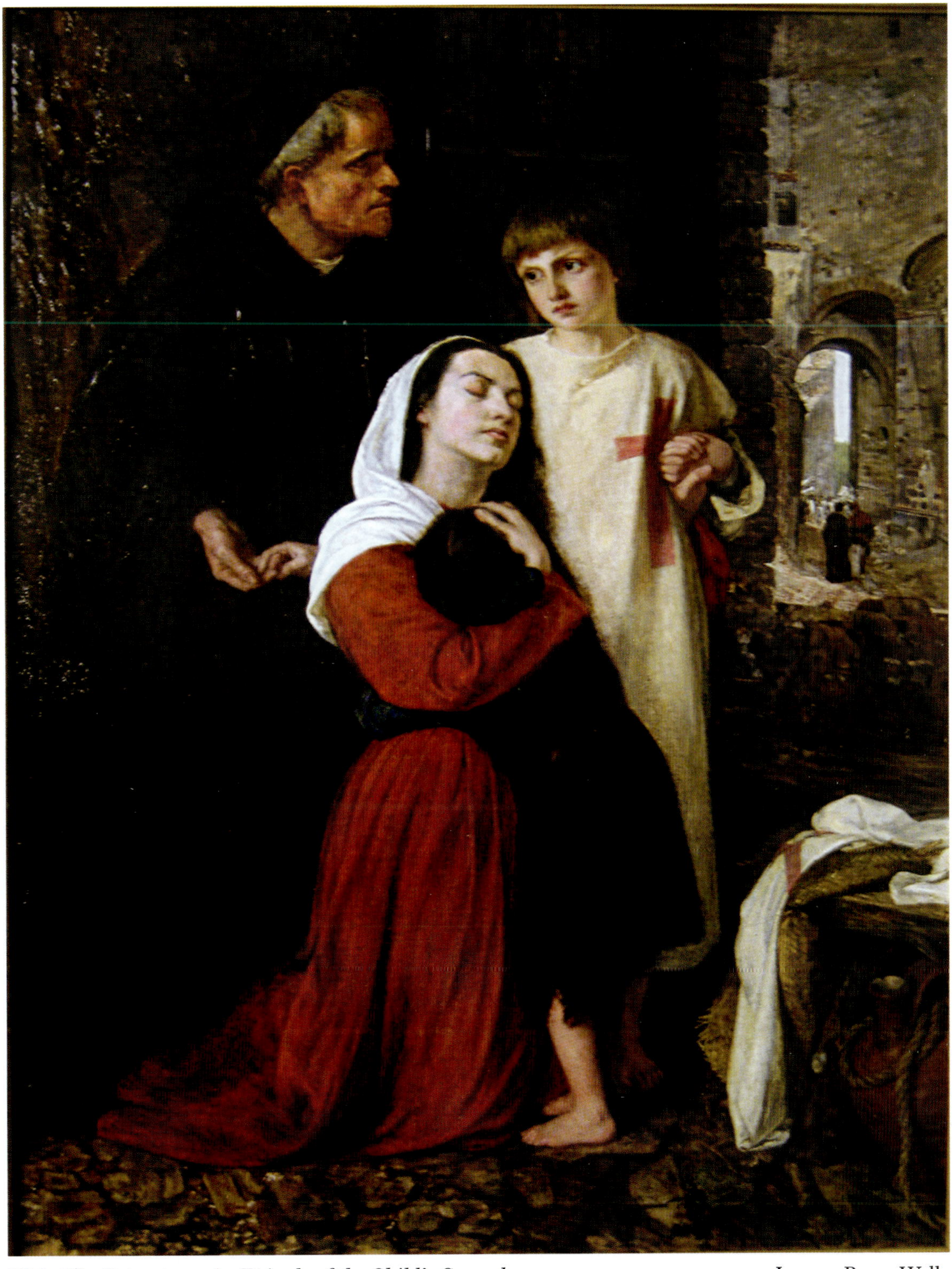

XLI. *The Departure: An Episode of the Child's Crusade* — Joanna Boyce Wells

Joanna began this picture (1857-60) – her only 'history' painting – while she was in Todi, making numerous sketches there and taking several local children as her models. It was accepted for the Royal Academy exhibition in 1860 but was, according to George, 'most shamefully and unjustly hung'. 'My poor "Crusade",' wrote Joanna. 'I only wish it had shared the fate of "Sidney".' The latter had been rejected.

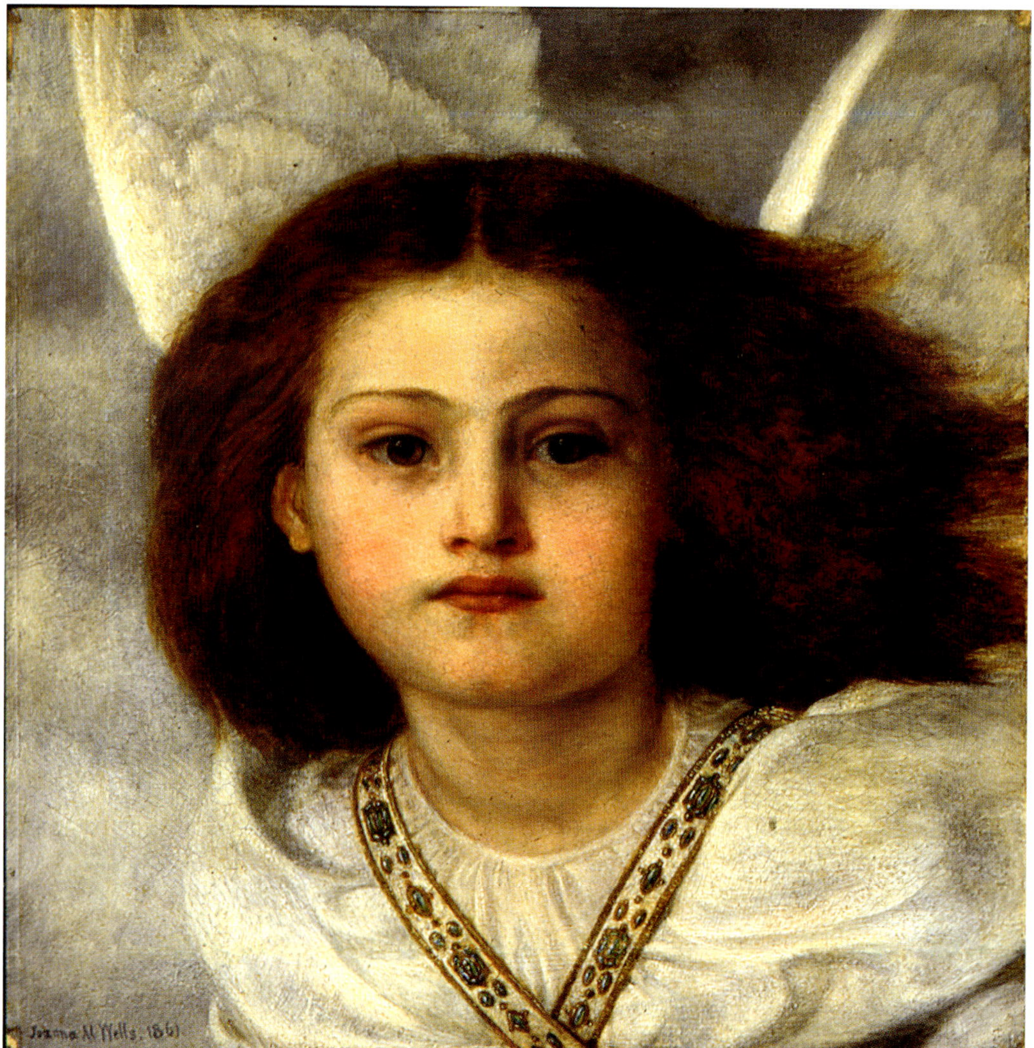

XLII. *Bird of God* Joanna Boyce Wells

'I shall feel thee guarding me, out of all the world,' wrote Browning, and Joanna believed, with him, that artists and poets aspired to 'the wings of a dove – the bird of God'. Her most 'Pre-Raphaelite' painting was exhibited at the Royal Academy in 1862 prompting this comment from an anonymous reviewer in the *Spectator*: 'A few weeks before her death she finished a lovely work... the head and bust of an angel...Full of the tenderest and most loving work.' It was hung on the line, against the door of the South West Room.

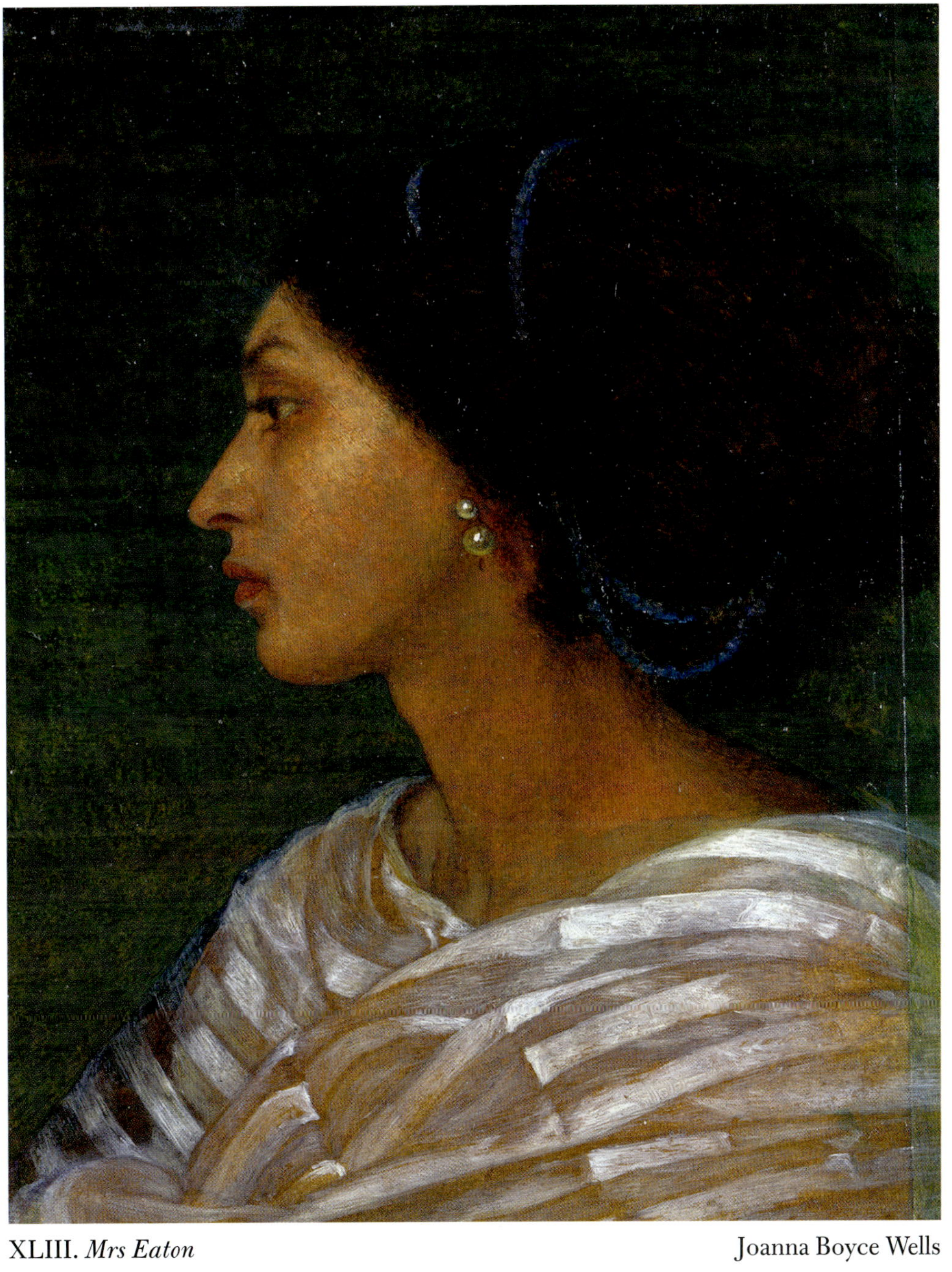

XLIII. *Mrs Eaton* Joanna Boyce Wells

This arresting portrait of Mrs Eaton wearing Joanna's wedding shawl of white and dull gold was produced during Joanna's researches for 'The Sybil' – a painting she was planning for the Royal Academy in 1862. The Cumaean Sybil, consulted by Aeneas before his descent into the underworld, was thought to have come to Italy from the East and Mrs Eaton, who also modelled for Rossetti and the Solomons, was appropriately exotic.

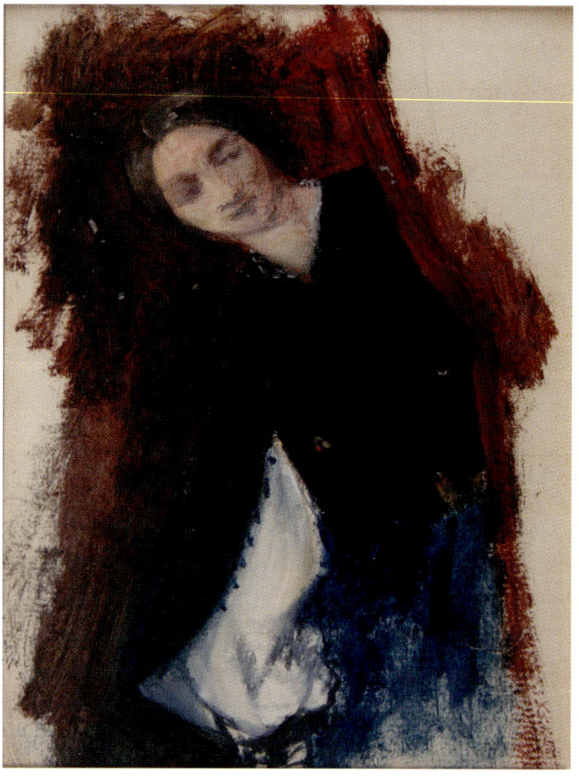

XLIV. *Oil sketch for 'Peep-bo'* Joanna Boyce Wells

The original idea came from a sketch she made of her sister Anne, with her baby and his nurse, when they stayed with Joanna and Henry at Joldwynds in 1858. She turned it into a self-portrait in which the mother, in a rich Titian-green gown, surprises baby Alice on her nurse's knee. The finished painting, was destroyed in 1942, but a photograph and this delightful sketch survives.

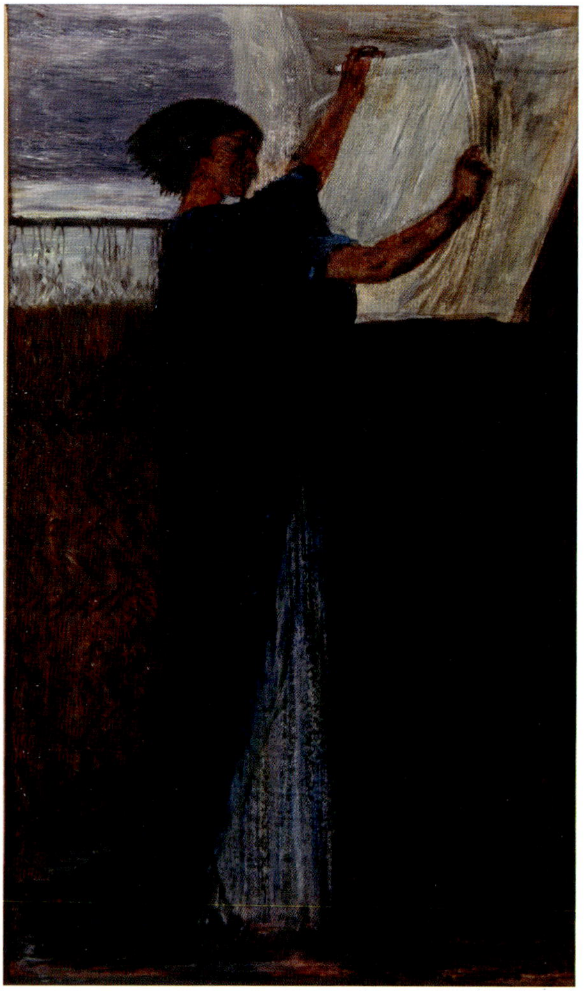

XLV. *Oil sketch for 'Sybil'* Joanna Boyce Wells

Joanna worked on 'Sybil' throughout the winter of 1860-61, and though the painting was never finished this sketch, which shows the Sybil absorbed in an enormous book of prophecy, is among the finest of her incomplete works. The *Critic* considered 'the head exceedingly fine', while the *Athenaeum* pronounced it 'masterly and grandly mysterious'.

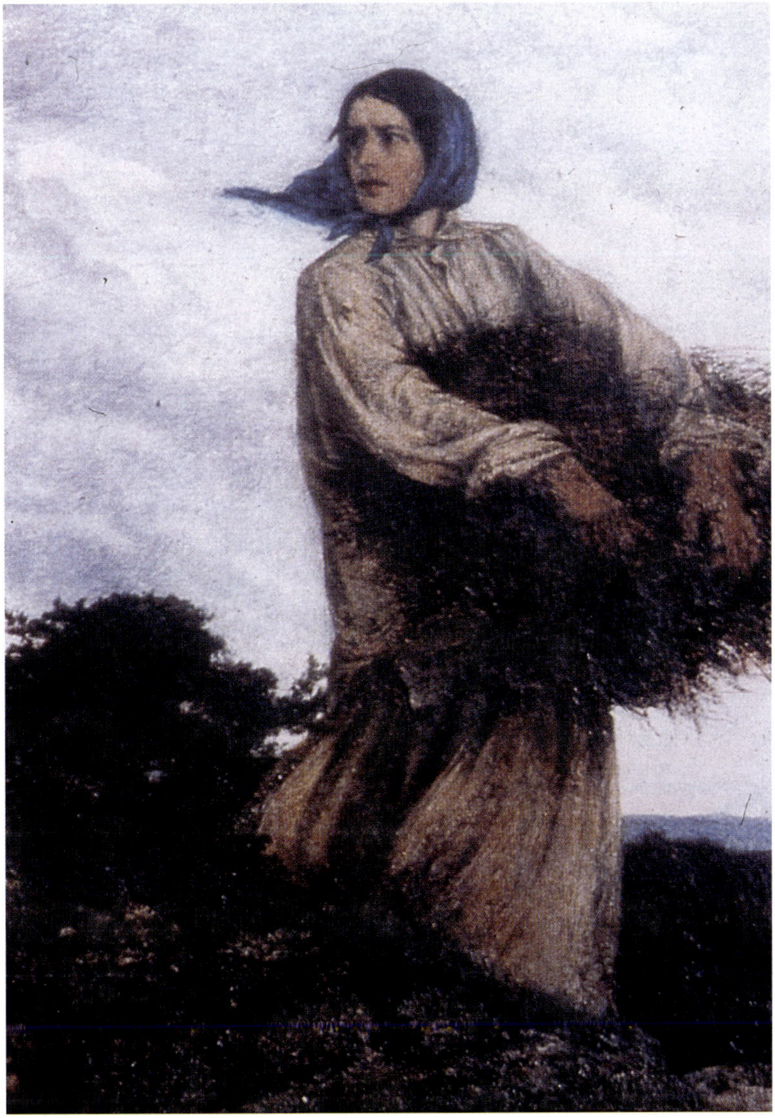

XLVI. *The Heather-Gatherer: Hind Head*

Joanna Boyce Wells

Joanna developed a talent for portraying solitary figures in outdoor settings and 'The Heather-Gatherer' was much admired by her peers. Rossetti, writing to her in January 1861, said: 'I am especially disappointed in not seeing your faggot picture, of which I have heard so much from Watts and the others.' After her death, it was one of the pictures chosen to represent Joanna at the 1862 International Exposition.

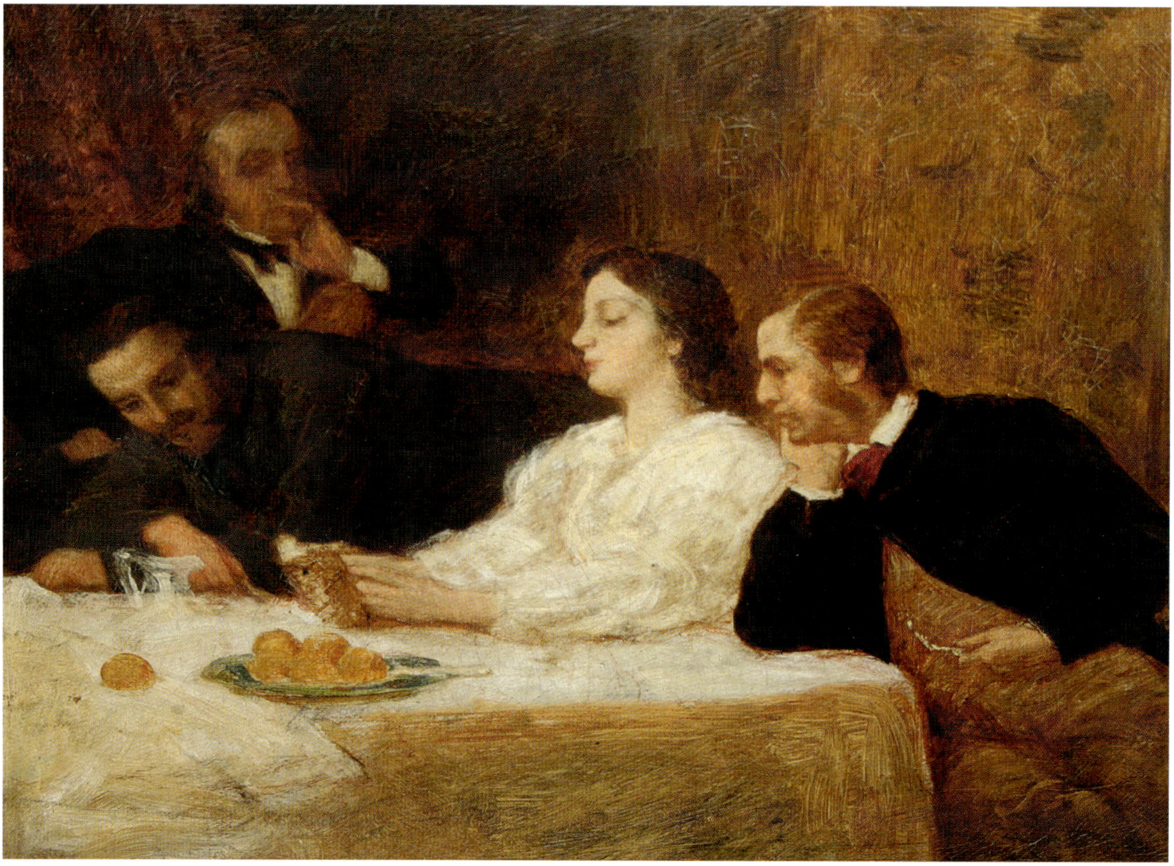

XLVII. *Conversation Piece* Henry T. Wells

George, Joanna and Henry sitting at a table with John Clayton standing behind. They are listening to Joanna reading aloud – from a book by Robert Browning, according to Henry, who had left the table to fetch it, and was struck by the composition of the group on his return.

She already had. In a letter to Henry, written on Christmas Day, she observed: 'I was much relieved by your telling me you did not think I had spoilt Rowena's "figure head". What of the background etc?' To George on the 28th she confessed: 'I have touched Isabel Borzewska's face. I could not possibly exhibit the picture without painting on it.'

By the end of the year she was bowed down with the strain of it all. She told Henry: 'I am too selfish, too proud, too nervous, in one word, too unloving, to marry.' She had left home to live peripatetically as a guest in her brother's and sister's households in defence of a correspondence which was no longer giving either of them much happiness. They had agreed to meet again, but she had missed him – another accident of the post. In despair she wrote: 'Oh Henry, I wish I could go home to my father.' She had spent the early morning of Christmas Eve reading his letters, and longing for him during those quiet hours. Most of all she longed for peace.

❃

George eventually arrived in London on the morning of 7 January 1857. Joanna went to Buckingham Street to oversee preparations for his return, and thence to the station to meet him. The ministrations of the clairvoyant had not cured George's damaged hip, and on 9 January they both went to Brighton to seek help from Henry Harrap. George settled at Bellevue Mansion, in King's Road, where Joanna spent extended periods of time in between visits to London. Before they left, however, a meeting at the Mordans gave rise to another accusatory letter from Henry about Joanna's hurtful behaviour, precipitated by George's reiterated strong views on their continuing correspondence, some 'ignorant rudeness' on the part of Bob, and Joanna's failure (in Henry's eyes) to defend him. Joanna responded with real anguish:

> As to your repeated complaints of my conduct when we meet, if you only once could put yourself in my place you would feel that you are unreasonable. We meet as friends – and the sort of "*equivoque*" there is in our relationship makes those around me closely observant and critical of my behaviour. You not only are angry because I do not behave to you as though we were engaged, but you feel you have a right to reproach me for not suppressing every sign of pleasure at being with George again (he cares little enough for my 'fondness'); while you pointedly separated yourself from all of us and read a book during a great part of the evening …

> There are but three or four persons now living, whom I feel I can depend upon, and you have ceased to be one, Henry. My friends drop off as fast as leaves. The disease is, I know, not in them but in the tree. I knew then and know now, that the blame is mine only.

'Bob', she added, 'is completely Mamma's tool. He merits pity rather than anything else.'

She was, by this time, utterly wearied – and most of all by being repeatedly obliged to restate her case. 'I am tired', she wrote to Henry, 'of analysing my own feelings', but went on to explain, as clearly as she had yet done, her feelings about the married state:

> I believe that married life for man and woman is a higher life (especially if a woman is a Mother) than single life, if it is what it ought to be. But I set this standard very high. The slightest falling off from it would be dreadful to me. If mutual tenderness or mutual honour grows less the poetry and purity of marriage are no more. You may think I write like a silly, sentimental girl, but I feel this very deeply and I hope I always shall.

In spite of Joanna's adamant – and naïve – refusal to make 'appointments' with Henry (and the evidence that she did not always stick to this), it was not surprising that they ran into each other rather often in London. He was a close friend of all her siblings and a frequent visitor in their houses. She, no longer immured in Park Place Villas, was much more available to him. One can hardly blame Henry for his passionate belief that the 'higher life' was theirs for the asking, or for his using every weapon in his armoury, however unfair, to overcome her resistance. He meant either to succeed or fail, and when he accepted any kind of compromise, it was only as a means to an end – marriage. To his bare-knuckled attacks on her long-postponed Italian journey, she could only answer that it might enable him to forget her. Her preparations for the trip had been few enough – 'my big portmanteau (my most expensive purchase) will be chiefly filled with old dresses everyone is tired of here' – and for the rest she just wanted to be gone:

> This I know, Henry, if I loved you as dearly as my nature would let me, I would leave England now. My going to Rome simply depends on this, that I have a friend there who offers me a home and a loving welcome. I long for rest, and not excitement or pleasure. I long to be away, to find myself among strangers, with whom at least my past

will be a sealed book, where no one can have a right to expect my confidence, or to pry with loving or unloving curiosity into all that is most sacred to me, where I shall be beyond Mamma's reach and the unnecessary annoyance she has the power to inflict. And now you say 'self' again. In doing this I do not forget you, Henry. I firmly believe that if you can forget me and marry another girl your life will be happier than I should ever make it.

Emotional exhaustion consumed her. Her eyes were giving her much trouble: characteristically, she had read articles on the subject by the eminent Sir David Brewster,[123] and consulted her own doctor, before deciding, also characteristically, to follow her own instincts and wear a green shade.

Brighton, however, was not entirely devoid of social life. On 3 February she wrote:

Thackeray[124] has given his lectures on the two last Georges down here. George and I attended both. He has disgusted almost all sets down here with his treatment of George IV, which I thought only too merciful. I think the Brighton townsfolk are staggered at a stranger coming into their Town Hall and coolly knocking their idol from his pedestal – and the aristocrats, of whom there were plenty present, were disgusted at his irreverence for royalty and rank. His jokes were for the most part very pale – wonderfully so for a man *par excellence* a humorist. One of the best things he said was that in trying to find what stuff George IV was made of, to get at his character, he came first to a coat, then to a waistcoat – then under waistcoats – more under waistcoats – then nothing at all.

Two days later she wrote to him again – a relaxed and chatty letter: 'If I may express an opinion, I am sure Browning is much the greater poet of the two, and that he has written things which a woman could not have written. I am equally sure there are things in Mrs Browning's books – and those its finest touches – which no man could have written.'

She had evidently already informed Henry that she had commissioned a picture from Millais and he had taken umbrage because she had not consulted

123 Scottish theologian and physicist whom we met earlier conducting scientific experiments on table-turning (n.42 above).

124 From 1855–57 Thackeray lectured in Britain and America on 'The Four Georges'. The lectures were later published in book form.

him first: 'I do not think there was much ground for annoyance about Millais's picture. I had often wished to have one before, as I have wished for a Titian or Velasquez. I was thinking about it at breakfast one morning, and I determined I would spare any sum short of £100 to procure one; and at once I asked George if he would write to Millais. George very readily consented.' She had been unwilling, she said, 'to let George's consenting moment pass', and added: 'I forgot to tell you that Mr Surgey was down here the first week we came. He seemed pretty constantly in the society of one lady. He called one day and we thought he rather inferred that this lady was the lady. He said he had called on you lately, and that you had asked him why he was so much at Brighton, and then he laughed and looked dreamy. Symptoms conclusive?'

Millais sent a cordial note accepting the commission, which prompted a further letter from George 'stating especially that it must be strictly a business transaction, and that we knew well the market value of his works'. This second letter was – typically, it seems – ignored. It was Henry who advised George to insist on an answer:

> If Millais does not answer a business letter, write another. I expect he looks upon this second letter of yours as an order for a ditto ditto, and as letter writing is not one of his propensities, he is not slow to satisfy himself that as he has replied to your original order, an affirmative to your second order is 'understood'. Nevertheless I think I would make him answer the letter and thus give him a lesson in civility. When I left him early last October he had not commenced a picture – but he had promised himself to get four ready for the exhibitions.

Millais did eventually reply, saying that he would with pleasure paint a small picture for Joanna when his winter work was done, and adding 'the price won't be ruinous'. At some point, George, on the strength of his admiration for 'Autumn Leaves', also commissioned a painting from Millais, though it is not clear exactly when.

Joanna remained in a continual state of apprehension about her eyesight and worried about the lack of improvement in George's health. Though she still hoped that Harrap might 'put him right', George's hip was, if anything, worse. He had kept her in the dark about the reason for this latest problem, but confessed all in a letter to William Allingham, written from Brighton on 9 February:

> At the very time you were writing to me 'how happy you travellers are? How I envy you!', your humble servant was lying on his bed

at Giornico suffering the consequences of an innocent bit of fun, namely, scrambling over a wall and giving chase to a trio of country lasses, who were wont to come and sit by me as I worked, and sing quaint ditties of the country to me. In the excitement of the moment I quite forgot my first 9 months lying up some 5 or 6 years ago from an injury to the same part by overwalking and skating, or should not at this very time be still paying the penalty of my folly. For, in fact, after resting and breaking off my work at Giornico and following professional advice in Paris for a month without benefit, I have at length been obliged to come down to this miserable place, accompanied by my sister as nurse, and put myself under my old doctor, Harrap (a quack as the faculty chooses to call him), who so wonderfully set me on my legs the first time. You will easily conceive what a sore trial this is to me, fond as I am of independence and freedom of movement … For months I've scarcely touched a brush or pencil, and it's impossible to say when I shall be able to take to either vigorously again. All is not, you see, *couleur de rose* with us artist ramblers. There's poor Seddon, whom we have lost altogether, and dying away from his wife and relatives at Cairo; and young Herbert,[125] a painter of promise, cut off in the Auvergne. I hope in the meanwhile you have been blessed with good health and spirits and that these have found vent occasionally in song of your own genuine, quiet stamp …

Your references to Tennyson and Browning were very interesting … What wonderful things there are in *Men and Women*[126] – especially 'In a Year', 'Fra Lippo Lippi', that letter from the Arab Student, and 'Blougram'. What I've read of *Aurora Leigh* I don't like nearly so much as these.

I didn't meet with Ruskin abroad. By a letter just received from my friend Warren, I find he was present at the meeting at Hunt's about poor Seddon's works and spoke very feelingly and sympathisingly. His *Letters to Beginners in Art* is announced and some notes on the Turners in Marlborough House have appeared. There's some excellent stuff in the latter and many fine passages, especially one about the old Temeraire at Trafalgar – too long to quote entire – in

[125] Arthur John Herbert (1834–56). Historical painter.

[126] *Men and Women* by Robert Browning was published in two volumes in 1855. Interestingly, though the book was passionately admired among the Pre-Raphaelites and their circle, it had little wider impact until after the death of Elizabeth Barrett Browning in 1861.

which he speaks of those triple ports, whose quoirs of flame rang forth in their courses into the fierce revenging 'monotone, which – when it died away – left no answering voice to rise any more upon the sea against the strength of England etc …'

Rossetti, I hear is hard at work on the Tennyson illustrations.[127] I know nothing of what the rest of the brotherhood are doing. I am very glad that 'Anstis Cove' continues to please. It is so much more than I dare to hope for my drawings in general.

On receipt of a letter from William Rossetti, George and Joanna had each contributed five guineas to a subscription for the purchase of Tom Seddon's 'Jerusalem' picture, undertaken when he was travelling in the Holy Land with Holman Hunt in 1854. The subscription had been organised by the Rossetti brothers, Madox Brown, Mark Anthony and Holman Hunt, and supported by Ruskin (who had made, as far as Joanna could tell from friends' reports, 'a very mawkish speech'). They raised £600 to buy the picture and provide a pension for Seddon's widow and child. It became the first Pre-Raphaelite painting to enter a national collection, and is now in the Tate Gallery in London.

Henry had evidently read both *Men and Women* and *Aurora Leigh*, and was seduced into expressing himself prettily, though not wisely, on the subject of women, love and intellect. Joanna was not prepared to let him get away with it:

What had love to do with the intellect of Catherine, the late Empress of Russia, or of Rachel, or of Mrs Siddons, or Mary Somerville, or George Sand, more than that increase of power which it always gives to man and woman?…

If Mrs B[arrett] B[rowning] had been your wife, you would have said 'It is not your duty to engage in the strife of the world for public fame instead of ministering at your own home, sew on my buttons, darn my socks, make my puddings and write no books.' Yes, but Mrs B. says, 'I have a mind, which wants food and exercise'. Answer 'Converse with me, soothe <u>me</u> with thy lighter fancies, touch <u>me</u> with thy finer thought'. But I have talents or a talent and with it the constant impulse to employ it – not for notoriety or fame, but for the love of it and the longing to work.

[127] The publisher Edward Moxon had commissioned Rossetti, Holman Hunt and Millais, among others, to illustrate what became known as the 'Moxon Tennyson'. It was published in the spring of 1857 and though it was later regarded as a landmark in the history of book illustration, it lost Moxon a great deal of money and the stress involved in its production is thought to have contributed to his death a year later.

She was distinctly amused by a letter from her aunt relaying 'the tattle of country folks': 'She believes it is considered that I continue a correspondence with you in order that I may marry you, if Mr Edwards[128] does not propose.'

As Henry's skin was by now paper-thin, the joke was lost on him. Once again she found herself apologising, though she reminded him: 'I have had satirical letters from you, "flaying" letters that have proved me foolish and ridiculous. And to tell the sober truth, though they have galled me they have pleased me. I liked to feel you my master. I liked to feel you could be unsparing while you loved me.' She added: 'Strange that we should so long have misunderstood each other. There are two or three things I can't reconcile. A week or two ago you read Mrs Browning's poem, and compared me to her heroine with loving and admiring words. And yet this *Aurora Leigh* is certainly one of that set of women which you "from your heart abhor".'

On 18 February she wrote: 'I am not going to the Ridleys on Thursday – though I don't think I should object to a *valse à deux temps* with you – or any good dancer – in a good room with good music. I have heard of your flirtations.' She added a PS: 'Let us try and keep the peace for one week. I believe we require a police officer to keep us in order.'

The lack of improvement in George's health and her own inability to distract him made her nervous, though they were both working: 'An old fisherman has been sitting to us today … he amuses us a good deal for we keep him talking to prevent him sleeping. On seeing my sketch this morning, he exclaimed in high glee "That's he, that's he. If the old 'ooman could see that!"' In the meantime they needed money. Joanna wrote to Matthias for funds in the middle of February – £20 for George and £30 for herself (she had not yet received a promised cheque from the *Saturday Review* for her article on Ruskin's *Harbours of England*). The intention was to move out of Brighton to a village from which George would commute for his treatment.

The cheque from the *Review*, for £21.40, arrived and with the funds from Matthias a 'very comfortable domicile' was found for George in Lindfield, near Haywards Heath. Joanna wrote to Matthias on 27 February: 'It is a pretty village and I should think there is very good sketching about.'

She also wrote to Henry who, she had heard, complained constantly about her, her conduct and her letters: 'Mordan and Mat and George all tell me you are no longer what you were, and they all say that I must look to myself as the source of this change.' Once again she tried to 'put a stop to a correspondence and an intercourse which have ceased to bring you anything but anxiety and

128 The identity of 'Mr Edwards', if he ever existed, must remain a mystery.

disappointment'. She had asked that this should happen after she had left England: now she felt it should happen immediately. In the same letter she looked forward to seeing his miniature of Anne, with which he had professed himself dissatisfied.

The news from Matthias was troubling, and included a packet of letters between him and their mother. 'You can imagine their character,' wrote Joanna to Henry: 'She is trying to break up the businesses. If she succeeds – according to Mat's calculation – she will reduce each of our incomes from the estate from more than £400 to £60; her own of course remaining intact.' To Henry she wrote: 'You know that I do not want to "get rid of you", and that I have determined after all that has passed that our present intercourse shall only be broken by you[129] ... It is a shame and grief to me to know that my influence over you has been for evil.'

Joanna and George intended spending a week in London before moving to Lindfield, but were delayed in Brighton by a boil on George's neck. This was eventually lanced, the surgeon ordering him 'lots of port wine and meat'. She was particularly concerned that George should be present to take 'a more decided part in our business matters', partly because it was unfair that everything should rest on Matthias's shoulders and partly to 'prevent Mamma effecting the pretty little coup d'état she meditates'. They arrived in town on 12 March, after yet another explosion between Joanna and Henry, this time the result of Mordan's having caused offence. Joanna wrote: 'I cannot understand Mordan speaking to you as you relate. It must have been one of his sudden inconsistencies, from which none of his friends are safe. But I do not think you are right or even kind to lay any blame on me because of it.' She wanted to know about his painting: 'I always have to beg for studio news like any Scotch terrier.' The good news, however, was that Henry's sister Sarah had become engaged to Henry Armstead.

It was a relief, no doubt, when preparations for the Royal Academy Annual Exhibition took them all over, though Henry continued to give Joanna a very hard time – as evidenced by several short, pert replies from his inamorata, once again installed with Matthias and Lilly at Clifton Road:

> I would with pleasure have accepted the theatre ticket from you, had you been in a different mood, but you must admit that money, fierce looks and almost-rude behaviour do not go well together. They are too much for my digestion. I hope you have finished or are finishing all for the Academy satisfactorily.

[129] This was disingenuous, as she had only recently tried to put a stop to the correspondence herself, though one suspects that she never intended Henry to take her up on it.

Will you be so very good as to bring me a tube of crimson lake this evening and one of yellow ochre? I did next to nothing on my picture on Monday and not very much yesterday. I found I must throw a shadow from the front piece of drapery on to the fold that turns back, and even now the piece that ought to go back will come forward. By the same post as yours came a letter from Mlle Cazeaux. She says much prettier things to me than you do. I have half a mind to quote them. Goodbye…

I wish instead of coming to my study tomorrow morning you would come as late as you like in the afternoon. I can't spare ten minutes of the morning light. Lizzie Ridley will probably sit to me some time tomorrow for the ear etc. You are very 'ridiculous' about 'Mr Solomon & others'. You know there is no one's advice I care for a bit compared with yours.

My picture is in much the same state as when you saw it. That piece of white display over the shoulder I painted in and out 10 or 11 times yesterday – wasting two or three hours over it and leaving it much as it was before – and the boy Solomon came and wasted another hour for me.

I did very much wish you to see my picture (as I foolishly believed you thought it no trouble to come) in time for me to take any advice you might be kind enough to give me. I preferred this afternoon to this morning for several reasons, principally because I thought we should both waste less time. I shall work on my picture all day Monday. By all means I wish to avoid causing you 'inconvenience' and am very vexed I have already trespassed so far.

Wishing you a very good dinner, and hoping you may not be kept a moment waiting for it.

Quarrelsome they were, but they were seeing each other all the time, and, on 9 April, something happened that fundamentally changed their relationship. Joanna hinted at it: 'I felt much as you did, and notwithstanding the contrary experience of the last months, I believed nothing could happen to estrange us.' She wanted to meet him alone, though not at her own studio or at Stratford Place. 'Can you think of any other way in which we could meet?' Significantly, one of the things she wished to discuss with him was her mother's desire to break up the businesses 'in which case my income would be reduced from between £500 and £600 to between £100 and £200'.

On 18 April, D. G. Rossetti wrote to her with news of the Royal Academy exhibition:

> Let me beg herewith your acceptance of what I have been meaning to send ever since I saw you – 3 photographs from my drawings. The two on large paper are from the Palace of Art – 'St Cicely' and King Arthur 'in the Vale of Avalon' – the smaller one is from the 'Lady of Shalott' … My brother was yesterday at the RA One of your pictures only is hung[130] (more shame to them), and that I fear not as it should be, since my brother only saw it in the catalogue … the exhibition he says is a poor one. By the by you are not the only glaring instance of shameful exclusion, since they have rejected the only picture sent by Arthur Hughes.

Perhaps Joanna did not mind too much. On 20 April she agreed to become engaged to Henry again, though predictably her surrender was not unconditional:

> My dear Henry
>
> Before I tell the others of our doings today, I want to tell you seriously and in writing that I really am determined not to marry for four or five years – I want you to know this now, that you may if you like run off with the ring.
>
> Yours very sincerely
> Joanna

[130] 'Our Housemaid' was hung – 'Rowena' was rejected.

8

SLOPING TO ITALY

'And we slope to Italy at last And youth, by green degrees.'

'By the Fireside'

The engagement was to be kept secret (apart from George, the Mordans and Mat and Lilly) until after Joanna departed for Italy. Whatever had changed between her and Henry, their misunderstandings persisted. She was in Bertha's bad books for her treatment of him, and was sufficiently unnerved to accuse her fiancé of ignoring her while he was playing billiards – a rare case of the boot being on the other foot.

Henry was triumphant again, writing to George, now installed at Lindfield, on 24 April – during painting hours too – to say that 'Joanna since Monday last holds herself engaged to me'. He was reconciled to her Italian journey only in as much as he hoped to 'gain his wishes' abroad if not at home. Besides, Joanna had set her heart on it, and for her the flurry of preparations began in earnest. She wrote to him:

> [The Mordans] start on the 14th, so I shall be in a perfect nightmare of hurry-skurry. Lilly's portrait, I fear, will be unfinished. I do not like making you so useful but I must ask you to be so kind as to get me a Bradshaw (continental) … I owe you a lot of money for colours, varnish, tooth powder, etc, etc, etc. I am afraid I have given you much trouble about my picture. If you go or send to the RA, do ask again about George's. He comes up probably on Saturday.
>
> Don't get the Bradshaw. I must have it for June not May.

The Royal Academy news was disappointing, as Rossetti had already imparted in his letter to Joanna. Henry, so blithely confident that all their works would be accepted that he made no early enquiry, found himself, on 1 May, obliged to send the following letter to await George in his Buckingham Street chambers:

> Now to the Academy news – they are so bad that I trust I am not the first reporter of them. Neither of your drawings are hung – and Joney's

> 'Rowena' is turned out. It is an infernal business and looks very like some spite against the name … I think the treatment both of you have received is shameful – but in the case of the 'Rowena' there seems to be a crime beyond the injustice. Were it not so, men in their position would have felt that a girl who displayed such power (I say – genius) had a peculiar claim upon their care. And they turn the picture out!

He was peeved, too, with Millais. Henry had won an Art Union prize[131] which entitled him to select a fifty-pound picture from the Royal Academy exhibition, and he had asked Millais to search him out a good one. 'He promised faithfully – and apparently with heartiness, but his carelessness of others is supreme. He never went.' As a result, Henry expected that all the good things would have already been purchased and that he would be left with 'some rot not worth hanging'.

George came up to town on Saturday 2 May to find that one of his drawings had, in fact, been accepted, and one was 'doubtful'. On 6 May, before returning to Lindfield, he attended a conversazione at the Society of Arts where, he noted: 'Ruskin speaking ramblingly and nearly broke down.'

Finally Joanna left for Paris, staying briefly with Madame Héreau at the Rue d'Astorg before setting out with the Mordans for Pau – 'the first place, I should think, where a letter could reach me'. From Blois she wrote to tell Henry more about what had happened to her after 'losing sight of you and your white flag on the pier'.

> We have seen a great deal that is very interesting, especially the Château at Blois, the scene of the murder of le Balafré by Henry III (our old friend). Catherine de Medici's suite of rooms is particularly interesting, as the wall decorations have been very carefully restored, and they are very beautiful of their kind. I asked if Delaroche had been to the château to study the locale for his picture[132] – yes, he had; but the actual room and the one represented in his picture are about as unlike as could be. There were some splendid things in the exhibition of his works at the Beaux Arts – my old favourite, the Marie Antoinette being the grandest to my fancy; and after it the Duc de Guise picture

131 The Art Union was a nineteenth-century institution of art patronage that originated in Switzerland and rapidly spread to Britain and other countries, including the US. The Art Union of London was the first and largest such union in Britain: it distributed prize coupons annually which could be exchanged for works of art.

132 'The Assassination of the duc de Guise at the Château de Blois' by Paul Delaroche.

and the Napoleon at Fontainebleau. There was a very striking picture of Beatrice Cenci,[133] of which I have never heard before …

Mordan talks of leaving here Sunday evening or Monday morning. We shall go straight through to Bayonne and sleep at Biarritz. On to Pau the next night. The next ten days we expect to be scrambling about the Pyrenées and on to Toulouse, thence to Montpellier, Nismes, Arles – Marseilles by tomorrow or this day fortnight. We have been looking out and talking about the steamers today, and Mordan and Anne both think that those which stay a few hours at Genoa and Leghorn will be the most agreeable … Be sure let me know about your miniatures – all about Lilly's and of any fresh commissions … Mordan is writing to Mat and to George about the businesses. We think that as an interview between Mat and Mamma is the last hope of preventing a break up, and as there must be someone else present, George is the proper person. He unfortunately thinks a great deal of paying 16s for coming up to London, forgetting that he spends it to ensure £400 a year.

While still at Lindfield, George had replied to a worried Joanna regarding the family business. As usual, Mrs Boyce was proving impossible to deal with and 'those unhappy Estate troubles' seemed almost insoluble. He was concerned to impress upon her that her recommendations were not going unheeded:

> For example, I have constantly urged Mat to see and confer with Mother more frequently and to bear her anxieties and humours more patiently, and to adopt the tact of conciliation and non-resistance in non-essentials … And with what result, do you think? To his and my own detriment, I thoroughly believe. For Mother in consequence looks upon me as partly foolish, ignorant and negligent and partly as culpably servile to Mat. So that what influence I might have had with her is now to all appearance utterly gone and my powers of persuasion null.

He did not feel he should be a trustee, partly because he knew he was unfit for the office, 'but principally that as I intend to make landscape painting my life-

[133] Beatrice Cenci (1577–99) was a noblewoman who was executed in Rome, along with her mother and one of her brothers, for the murder of their brutally abusive father. As a result she became a symbol of resistance to the arrogance of the aristocracy. The most famous portrait of her, by Guido Reni (1575–1642), is of doubtful authenticity and hung, in any case, in Rome, where it proved an inspiration to the poet Shelley. It may be that the picture Joanna saw was a copy.

occupation, and shall in all probability be very much on the Continent in pursuit thereof'. He was, he said, a 'muddle head at figures', but was more than willing to be present at Matthias's proposed interview with their mother, should he wish it.

Quite apart from brotherly solidarity, George was well aware that the financial consequences of breaking up the businesses would affect him as much as anyone, 'considering that my profession has hitherto been, and likely still to be for some time, a losing game', but he felt that Joanna overestimated his powers of persuasion as far as Mrs Boyce was concerned.

❁

Towards the end of May, Henry heard that an exhibition of Pre-Raphaelite paintings was to be held at 4 Russell Place, Fitzroy Square.[134] He wrote to George on the 25th:

> I have just returned from a foraging expedition – and your rooms at Buckingham Street are robbed of two drawings. Next Monday they will be seen in exhibition. Now let me narrate the cause and manner of this cheeky proceeding: Yesterday I had to lunch with some people in Piccadilly, and on my road I met Rossetti, and he turned and walked about a mile with me. He told me of an Exhibition, which is about to open, of the works of the fraternity we know so well – Rossetti, Millais, Holman Hunt, Madox Brown etc, etc. He said he should like to get some things of yours, and he also showed a wish to have the 'Rowena', but this for one reason at least could not be.

Since Rossetti and Ford Madox Brown were unable to wait for permission (they had to write the catalogue copy that evening), Henry, believing that George would want to be represented, went with Rossetti to Buckingham Street: 'Most of your drawings must be locked up,' wrote Henry, 'but he has got two.'

The works selected were 'The Crypt of the Church at Giornico' and a small drawing of a sunset in Wales that hung over the door. George was distinctly ungrateful, commenting in his diary on 26 May, 'They will look ridiculously small and mindless by the side of Rossetti's, Millais's and Hunt's works. I'm very vexed I wasn't in town to have contributed better things.' He also wrote to Joanna, expressing himself more strongly: 'To my unfeigned horror, found that

134 This was a semi-private exhibition, organised by Ford Madox Brown. The exhibitors, who included Rossetti, Millais, Hunt, Lowes Dickinson, Collins, Hughes and Martineau, paid £10 each to take part.

[Wells] and Rossetti had been round to my studio and seized upon that dowdy Giornico Crypt and a little red sunset sketch to represent me there. My ill-luck has followed me in this, the news coming too late to admit of my substituting better things. Just conceive the figure they'll cut on the same walls as Rossetti's wonderful works.'

Henry must have had his own misgivings, for later he added: 'Rossetti thought of taking the "Babbacombe Bay", but I preferred the "Crypt" – moreover I could find no frame to fit the Babbacombe altho' we looked for one. The beaches I should have liked to have sent, but Rossetti didn't seem to think them interesting. With contrition I must confess to being a great fool and worse for forgetting the "Campanile" and the little interior of Mordan's.' Though it was late in the day, he tried to make amends by sending two additional pictures round to Rossetti's.

George left Lindfield on 27 June and attended the exhibition that same day, noting crossly in his diary: 'To PRB Exhibition in Russell Place … I found my little "Sunset" sketch in North Wales mounted in a preposterously wide gilt flat, whereas I had left it in my room mounted on white paper. A lot of the foreground is covered by the mount which completely spoils the sketch.'[135]

This unsatisfactory episode was concluded by Madox Brown who wrote to George on 30 June, asking that all pictures be 'cleared out' of the exhibition rooms by the following day, and adding:

> Rossetti it was who first brought two of your drawings, one of which was very inferior & the other 'in north Wales' was so badly mounted that I thought it necessary to order a gold mount for it, which is a great improvement; if you are not satisfied with it however I must pay for it. After this two more drawings of yours were brought also without your knowledge, I believe by Wells – Of these two latter ones the Venice I esteemed a very fair specimen of your work I thought, but the little one I did not fancy as it looked an old and very inferior work.

No wonder George was miffed. He had, however, enjoyed a visit to Hogarth's, a print-sellers in the Haymarket, where he saw 'a rather clever caricature-etching founded on Millais's "Dream of the Past" picture'. This painting, one of Millais's submissions to the Royal Academy and subtitled 'Sir Isumbras at the Ford', depicted a knight on horseback helping two peasant

135 Virginia Surtees comments that George was ahead of his time in preferring a cream or white mount to a gilded one.

children across a swollen river. It had caused much consternation, and Ruskin had gone so far as to deem it a 'catastrophe'. In the parody, entitled 'A Nightmare', 'Millais himself is the old Knight, Rossetti the girl in front, Holman Hunt the child behind. Ruskin is the ass on which they are riding, and which is by far the best thing in the etching in every respect.' The artist, George later discovered, was Frederick Sandys, and his satire had just as much to say about Ruskin's advocacy of Pre-Raphaelitism as it did about Millais.

He also went to Petworth to see the Turners, noting dismissively in his diary: '[They] are of the crude yellow sort. The Chain Pier at Brighton being the best. He introduced into the foreground of it a broken basket with some floating turnips, carrots etc.' But he was evidently glad to be back in the swing of things. On 2 July:

> W. Allingham and Alex Munro came and breakfasted with me. Afterwards skirmished and rhapsodied and ecstasied over the new Tennyson, and Millais's and Rossetti's illustrations. A. said that when Tennyson was reading 'Maud' at Oxford, [Thomas] Carlyle, as he himself said, 'went out into the fields; I didn't want to hear his "Maud", I have read it before. Besides, I don't like to see a noble fellow like that letting himself out through such a gimlet hole' (meaning poetry).

❁

Joanna, meanwhile, was doing some rhapsodising herself, relaying every step of her journey in joyous detail to her 'dear Henry'. Apart from the odd personal aside – it is 'dear Papa's' birthday, she is convinced that George must make more effort to help Mat and their mother resolve the business problems, why did Henry fail to take advantage of getting a letter to her at Bordeaux? etc – she was, on the whole, content to share her delight in being a tourist with him, and even express her longing for his actual presence. Yet her doubts about her own ability to love were never buried very deep: 'My old horrid fear, that you will dislike me when we are married, has been haunting me incessantly … I cannot help knowing that I am quite destitute of much that is (I fear) necessary to retain a husband's love.'

She had not taken her water-colours with her: 'A sketch book and pencil, an execrable BB of Mordan's, have served my few wants.' She sympathised with him over the lack of sitters: 'Have you heard nothing from Millais? It seemed probable he might give you a commission … I hope Mr Boone's letter may miscarry. I expect he will attack me much the same way as Bob did.'

And subsequently: 'I have just received your second letter … I do not see any objection to my little picture[136] being engraved in the *National*. Millais, Windus etc, etc, have not objected on the score of caricature, why should I?'

The engraving of their pictures for books and magazines was welcomed, or at least accepted, by most artists as a way of spreading their reputations, though not all were easy to deal with: Rossetti had quarrelled violently with the Dalziel brothers, among the best known engravers of the day, over his illustrations for the Moxon Tennyson – a quarrel that gave rise to the following sarcastic quip from the artist:

> 'O woodman, spare that block,
> O gash not anyhow!
> It took ten days by clock –
> I'd fain protect it now …
> (Chorus of wild laughter

George did not agree:

> I had a hasty glimpse today at King's in Brighton of the new Illustrated Tennyson, and was delighted to find the cuts from Rossetti's so much better than one could have expected. Hunt too seems to have some splendid designs. On the whole I thought, as I turned the leaves rapidly over, finer than Millais's. I have not yet seen Ruskin's pamphlet, but in a recent extract from it in *The Times* severe comment is made on Millais's irregularity and slovenliness and worse exemplified in his Academy pictures this year.

❁

Joanna had reached the Pyrenees and was in heaven. George had sent her off with Murray's handbook and he himself had visited some of the places that she and the Mordans were passing through. She wrote to Henry:

> The scenery as we neared Cauteret was very grand and more rugged than any we had yet seen. Directly we arrived we hired a guide and horses, and started on a mountain excursion to the Lac de Gaube … to me it was a perfectly new and absorbing enjoyment, and constantly

[136] This picture will have been 'Our Housemaid'.

> I wished you had been with me to share it. Mounted on a first-rate little horse, I was carried up a very precipitous, rough path without ever any fear or discomfort and very little exertion through the most magnificent scenery I can imagine. Until I see Switzerland I cannot believe that in the Alps there is anything more perfect in its way.

Cette (now Sète) provided a less pleasurable travelling experience:

> Last night was the horror of horrors. We left Toulouse about 6 p.m. and reached Cette about 12. I was just ready to take my rest and had begun to read your letters again before lying down, when I heard a kind of whizzing in my ear, which I instantly recognised as the war cry of the mosquito. From that moment till ¼ p 4 in the morning I paced my room and only ceased fanning myself to dart at the little wretches on the wall or on the curtain. Then as it was daylight and I thought Anne and Mordan might possibly be suffering the same martyrdom, I went down and knocked at their door – fortunately they had not been plagued. They advised me to open my windows, as it was daylight and go to bed – as I was dreadfully tired I did so – I fell asleep, but the detestable humming woke me time after time. The mosquitoes got to my hands, but almost spared my face. I laughed outright many times in the midst of my desperation at the recollection of Doyle's cut of Robinson[137] sitting in blank despair with the mosquitoes buzzing round him.

Having taken in the Pont du Garde at Nîmes, they arrived in Marseilles as planned, where Joanna parted company with the Mordans and set sail for Italy. Just before she embarked she wrote to Henry: 'Yes, yes, yes, do, if you can, spend the winter in Rome, portrait painting.'

Henry was still being made to feel badly about the Russell Street exhibition, though he defended himself to George stoutly: 'Your Campanile drawing looks one of the best things in the Exhibition; such was the criticism Clayton, Smallfield and self agreed upon.' The Society of Female Artists, which had been founded in 1855 to enable women to exhibit their work more freely, had just mounted its first exhibition. Henry thoroughly disapproved, remarking:

137 One of Richard Doyle's engravings from *The Foreign Tour of Messrs. Brown, Jones and Robinson*, published in 1854 by Bradbury & Evans. The series illustrates the adventures of an artist and his two friends on the continent, and includes many scenes with which Joanna, Henry and George would have identified, including no fewer than eight on the scourge of mosquitoes.

'In the first place I am convinced it is not worth a shilling … and in the next I entirely disapprove of the principle involved. Men make no distinction … it is merely a question of talent, not of sex.' His attitude was at best disingenuous – it was never 'merely a question of talent' – at worst it smacked of that inherent chauvinism that may well have fed Joanna's reservations. All the same, Joanna was never an 'art sister'. Throughout her short life she allied herself to men and – whatever the obstacles – competed with them too.

Most of the letters Joanna wrote to Henry on her travels are undated, but they add up to a colourful picture of the people, the places, the pleasures and hardships of this long-awaited escape:

> Fortunately I had the first class ladies' cabin to myself. At the table d'hôte, where I was the only lady, I made acquaintance with a gentleman (advanced in years!), who proved very useful during the rest of my journey. He managed everything for me at Civitavecchia, luggage, douane, passport etc, carriage to Rome etc … Margaret was of course delighted to see me, and does everything to make me comfortable. The Doctor improves on acquaintance. It is almost cool here, and the atmosphere seems so delightfully light and pure.
>
> Yesterday morning we went to St Peter's. There seem to be no such things as 'first impressions' in Rome. I have heard so many descriptions and seen so many photographs of all the most remarkable monuments here that as yet nothing astonishes or appears new. I had even anticipated the apparent smallness of St Peter's compared with its real gigantic size. One of the things that did surprise me was the badness of most of the pontifical monuments in the church. But how splendid Michael Angelo's Pietà is, and how shamefully placed and disfigured – dirty candles rising before it and little brazen cupids hanging over it … Last evening almost an hour after sunset we walked down the Corso to the ancient city by Trajan's column, the Forum, arch of Titus to the Colosseum. It was a bright starlight, but not moonlight night, so we could see very little – still if all detail was lost, dim light increases size and the Colosseum seemed stupendous, and completely dwarfed the amphitheatres of Nismes and Arles, which at the time appeared colossal … Today we go to the Sistine Chapel and the Vatican. We are to stay in Rome about a fortnight, and then go to

> Todi, where the Piottis have taken apartments for some time. I expect we shall do very little in the way of excursions. I hope they will be left till you come …
>
> Talk Italian I must and will. I find I can understand a little what they say. I have told Margaret I am engaged. She seems very pleased … She is very little altered. I think you will find her very 'exaltée' and rather tiresome in consequence. She always used to tire me in that way and does still; but she is very kind and very intelligent. Her husband is devoted to her, and she seems to have gained a great many real friends. Oddly enough the very first persons who called on her I knew – a Mrs Phelps and her daughter Madame Valleri. The former is an Italian, her maiden name Garovalini, a rather high family here. Her husband was a thorough reprobate and she, when in England, taught singing and Italian. She gave singing lessons at the first school I went to. I recognised her instantly, and her daughter – then a pretty little girl – now a mother. They did not know me, so I held my tongue till they had left – thinking it was just possible their antecedents were not known. On the contrary I found that Margaret knew just all that I did. The daughter is beautiful and has sat to Winterhalter by his express request.

Several such letters found their way to Henry from 35 Via Ripetta during this time. In them Joanna expressed her customary anxieties about the family business and about Bob but they had become almost rhetorical. Her fears for Henry's work and future were more keenly felt, though for his sake rather than her own: she had absolute faith in his artistic abilities.

Her last week in Rome was crammed with two visits to the Vatican, the first to see the statuary – 'After the Apollo and the Torso, I think the resting quoit-player pleased me most' – the second to see the Sistine Chapel: 'I took your opera glass with me and followed your example as we were the only visitors, and lay down on the floor and studied each subject at my ease. I expected to enjoy them and was not disappointed.' There were walks, dinners, galleries and churches, including the Church of Sta Maria Sopra Minerva – 'do you know it? The only church in Rome at all Gothic in architecture. It was quite a relief to see something besides that sickening Renaissance.' There was also a visit to the dentist to have a recalcitrant nerve dealt with using a hot wire – 'the English method'.

Henry must have confessed his money worries to her for she responded immediately and generously: 'If you really are outrunning the constable, will you refuse to borrow of me instead of touching the capital? Don't say no – I can't bear for you to be cramped for money, while I am in luxury.' She urged him to 'keep a brave heart about the future': 'I sounded Margaret the other day as to the likelihood of portrait commissions in Rome. She says that last winter was a first rate season for the portrait painters in Rome owing to the visit of the Russian Royal family. This winter may not be so good – still she seemed to think it not unlikely a portrait painter of high standing might find work during the winter.'

About her host, she opined: 'I like Dr Piotti more and more. He is ridiculously hot-tempered, but devoted to his wife, and very clever and good. Ever since I left England I have been the one "*de trop*" with a married couple perfectly happy in each other. You could hardly have wished me differently placed if you had had your choice. It is perfectly delightful to me to see Mordan get fonder and fonder of Anne; but I cannot, though I try, persuade myself for an instant it would be so with you and me.'

They remained in Rome until the end of the month, so that Joanna could witness the St Peter's Day celebrations on 29 June, with all its illuminations and fireworks.

> On Monday last, St Peter's day, we packed up for our journey, and at 6 in the evening went to hear the vespers at St Peter's. The music was overpoweringly beautiful – the voice of one singer especially, an alto … St Peter's is like a woman who is immensely improved by an elegant toilette. Unadorned it has none of the simple, naked grandeur of a Gothic Cathedral, but on feast days, what with the crimson and gold draperies, the incense rising and (sometimes) the sun pouring in, the crowds of people in gay costume and on this day the brilliant line of Cardinals and more sober Monsignori, one forgets the absolute bad taste of the sculpture and ornamentation and feels only its relative worth from its seeming so much in harmony with the scene altogether. The Madeleine in Paris has some resemblance in effect to St Peter's – both are like Pagan temples – and seeing the people energetically kissing the gilt toe of the black apostle dressed up in Pontifical robes helps the illusion. In the evening we went to the Piazza del Popolo to see the fireworks or Girandola as they call them here.

Hennie Moore wrote to Joanna on 2 July. She was glad to hear that her friend was leaving a sultry Rome for the countryside – 'don't forget you are a Dove of Peace and a Comforter and a blessing to one solitary little owl in this wide world'. Confessing that she was not at ease with her own family, she was inclined to look for a post either as a resident or daily governess (the post Joanna had found for her had not proved acceptable): 'I should like to be away – among fresh faces, and people, who know and can say nothing about the past.' She added that she had heard from Henry that, as far as the Boyces' financial affairs were concerned, things had improved. For Joanna's sake, she hoped this was true.

Joanna had begun a letter to Matthias on 25 June, before she left Rome, and completed it after their arrival in Todi. She made anxious enquiries about his progress, or lack of it, with regard to the business (the continuing lawyers' expenses, the need for financial security), before bringing him up to date with her own adventures:

> We are in delightful apartments. The town is very picturesque, the people primitive and kind hearted, the country round tolerably interesting, and the air is much purer and cooler than in Rome … The wine is wonderfully cheap and as good as it is cheap.
>
> We had rather an interesting episode in our journey – (of this Murray will tell you nothing so I will). Our first halting place after leaving Rome was Civita Castellana, a small town situated on the top of a height; the most conspicuous building in it is a fortress, once the residence of some despotic Italian noble, now converted into a prison for political offenders. We obtained permission to go over it through a friend of the doctor's; the most remarkable among the prisoners is a certain Gasparoni – a splendid old fellow 63 years of age. When he was 20 in a fit of jealousy he killed the girl he loved and finding a price was set on his head by the government he turned brigand and for ten years he made himself the terror of travellers. So well known was he for his wonderful daring and agility even among foreigners, that very few English passed through Civitavecchia, where he was first imprisoned, without going to visit him. When he was a little past thirty he gave himself up to the authorities, and he and his 16 men have lived together in prison ever since, more than 30 years, a happy quiet life. The commander of the prison, a gentlemanly intelligent man, seemed really attached to Gasparoni, more, he seemed really to respect him. A nobler looking old man I have never seen, with a wonderful fire in his eyes and a long snowy beard. He sat for me to make a quick pencil sketch of him, and it is possible I may have an opportunity of painting him.

To Henry, after describing the journey to Todi, she wrote: 'Dr Piotti is a very funny man with the kindest heart and first rate abilities. He is like a child for want of self-control. 20 times a day he flies into passions and is sorry after. It is

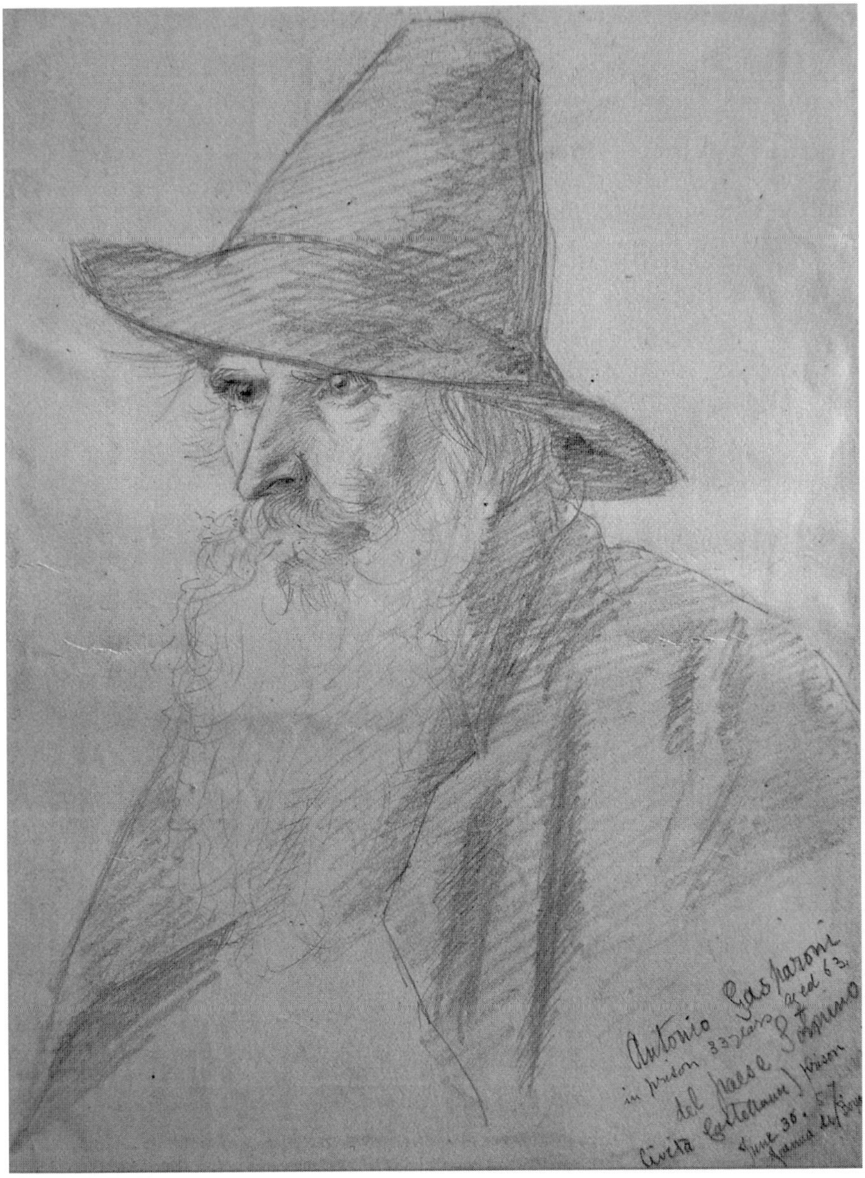

Head of Antonio Gasparoni — *Joanna Boyce*

Gasparoni and his band of brigands were confined in a fortress prison at Civita Castellana, where they had become a tourist attraction. Joanna's sketch shows the 'wonderful fire in his eyes'.

very hard for Margaret to bear sometimes, but she is as good as gold, very patient and cheerful with him … Is the day for your sister's marriage fixed? … I want very much also to hear how Bob is.'

On 8 July, she wrote to George to confirm that she and the Mordans had indeed been to Gabas on their way through the Pyrenees, and had recognised it as 'George's village'. They had ridden there from Les Eaux Chaudes: 'It was an exquisitely clear morning and the Pic du Midi looked sublime, his awful jagged snow covered crest glittering in the sunshine.'

She was impatient for news, complaining to Henry that she had had to wait thirteen days for his letter (the vicissitudes of the post were again becoming a subject for mild bickering). On the other hand, she said, she was delighted by Todi and she and Margaret could not wait to start work:

> The town itself is the quaintest and most paintable I have ever seen. Being placed on the summit of a very steep pointed hill all the streets are precipitous and wind about with the most perplexing irregularity … This is the harvest time, and at intervals during the day, when they rest, you can hear the young men singing in chorus to their sweethearts and the clear treble echo of the girls. I hope we shall be able to make some street sketches, but at present, even in our quiet rambles, we are such objects of wonder to the natives that easels and campstools in the middle of the road are not to be thought of … My poor tooth is still only temporarily stopped with gutta-percha. (*Plates XXXI and XXXII*)

In another undated letter she wrote:

> Thanks for the little sketches – the Lady Margaret and baby pleases me extremely. Lilly not quite so well. It is impossible to judge rightly from such a tiny thing, but it seems to me that with the sleeve falling as it does, you can hardly get that look of slenderness and falling in at the back of the waist, that is so peculiar in her … I am very sorry commissions are so 'backward in coming forward'. Have you done or are you doing any chalk heads?
>
> There are plenty of glow-worms here and fire-flies. You must have seen plenty of the latter when you came to Italy – they are so lovely when seen in numbers and against the sky. The only insects that really trouble us are fleas and the common flies; the latter are the worst here, the former in Rome. There are no mosquitoes, for this I am heartily thankful.

Back in London, little things conspired to upset Henry's equilibrium and she could not help teasing him: 'Your lectures I deserve and feel, but your quizzing is quite another thing. It reminds me of the coal-heaver, who when asked by his crony why he let his wife beat him, answered "Lor, it pleases her, poor thing, and it does me no harm". Certainly your shafts are blunt and your aim bad, but if shooting pleases you why shoot on – I am not afraid of being struck.' She was suffering badly from nettle-rash – 'my face is like a gigantic nutmeg grater, and my hands are spotted all over'.

Henry had sent her a photograph of her 'Rowena' which she liked, except that it appeared to show up some damage to the surface of the picture. Her anxiety was well-founded. 'Rowena', like 'Madame Héreau', had been painted according to Couture's precepts, which dictated a layer of bitumen between the grounding and the final coat. While bitumen did initially lend a lovely quality to the paint, it tended to break up later, disfiguring the picture with cracks and darker patches.Joanna never adopted the process again, but was sufficiently satisfied to ask Henry to send the 'most delicate and pretty' of the photographs to her model, Isabel Borzewska. In the meantime, she told him, she had begun work on the picture that was to become 'The Departure: An Episode of the Child's Crusade', and was employing local children as models. Her nettle-rash continued to ornament her in the most 'florid style – I could tear the flesh off my bones with the irritation'. It did not stop her working. She and Margaret had found room in a large public building to use as a studio and, as she told Henry, 'this is how we have been passing the days. Up at 6 – breakfast at 8 or ½ past – to our studio at ¼ past 9 – painting until ½ past 1 – dinner, nap, sometimes a short Italian lesson – back to the studio at ½ past 4 – at dusk (at 8) for a little walk – supper at 10 and then to bed, but rarely to sleep. Today I have actually commenced my picture, and I think I have been very fortunate in getting a good model for the tallest boy.'

They were finding plenty of people to paint – the Countess, her maid 'wearing a scarlet headdress peculiar to Todi', and the local apothecary among them. She wished Henry could join her – 'much more ancient than Rome,' she told him:

> Every evening we go and see the rosy and golden light turn to grey and the stars come out, and the landscape fade slowly out till nothing but the outline of the hill, the gleam of the river and the night fires of the reapers can be seen; and then, do you know, oddly enough from beginning to end of this pleasant hour (and never of course at other times) I want you to be with me instead of Margaret. If you could just flit over every evening and pass it with me, we would shake hands at the edge of the

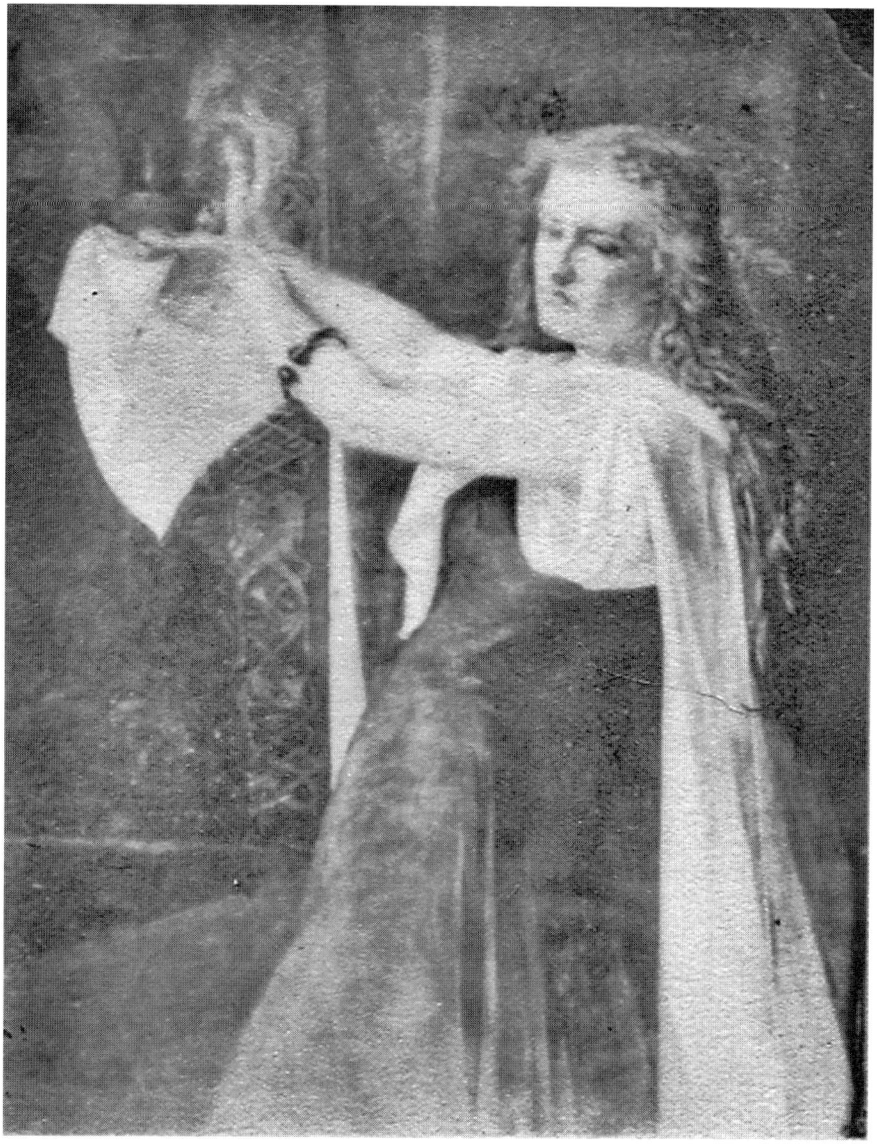

Rowena Offering the Wassail Cup to Voltigern *Joanna Boyce*

The original painting, based, like Elgiva, on an episode in Anglo-Saxon history, demonstrates Joanna's increased confidence as she found her own path between Pre-Raphaelite exactness and the loose, grittier juste milieu *style she had learned from Thomas Couture. As her letters make clear, it cost her much and she constantly worried about every next step, writing to Henry: 'I was very much relieved by your telling me you did not think I had spoilt Rowena's "figurehead".' The painting was destroyed in 1942.*

> ridge and you should disappear until the next sunset. You'd look so funny flying off like a great bat, that I should laugh all the romance out of our meetings; simply vanishing into thin air would be simpler and a better arrangement. What do you think about it? Will you come?

All her efforts to establish from Dr Piotti exactly how the Italian post functioned were fruitless and tended to precipitate outbursts of temper on the part of her host, so Henry's natural irritation on the subject remained unassuaged. 'This one fact is quite certain,' she wrote, 'be as regular as we may in posting our letters, they will not arrive regularly.' She was glad to hear that Henry had a new large commission, but sorry that the subject was not more promising: 'Painting dead babies is certainly not a cheerful occupation. The Piottis hold out brilliant hopes of your getting plenty of work in Rome through the winter … Will you be such a very good boy as to accept from me a copy of the new Illustrated Tennyson? Get a copy with proof impressions if possible.'

George was now installed at Malt House Farm, at Godalming. He was still very lame and very dissatisfied with his lack of progress in painting in oils. Henry wrote to him on 25 July, proposing a visit. In the meantime he proffered the following thoughts:

> It is difficult to help you out of your painting troubles with advice. After all it is want of practice, not faultiness of system, which is thwarting you … I think that perhaps in your present dilemma it may be useful for you to remember, that all light parts should be painted opaquely and thickly, that in the deeper tones and shadows all warm colours should be more or less transparent, broken and modified by greys or greens etc, etc, painted into them …
>
> Lick the pale, pure transparent colours rapidly over the wet (or dry) opaque surfaces, as you would a wash of water-colour, and drag with the most delicate handling the grains of opaque colour over the surfaces of the wet warm colours. This kind of thing is what you must aim at, in contradistinction to the pasty, japanny way of painting. But, as I have said, all rules are foolishness.

There had been a review of the Russell Place Exhibition in the *Saturday Review*. Henry offered to bring the article with him if George had not seen it: 'It was evidently written by a friend of Rossetti's.[138] The praise was good, because

[138] The review was by Coventry Patmore and dated 4 July.

the writer had entire sympathy with the painter, but it was out of all proportion … You were not by any means the only good name omitted.'

In Todi, the heat increased day by day: 'Margaret now bears me company in the nettle-rash,' Joanna told Henry. Sketching out of doors was impossible, but though she and Margaret were beset by fleas, flies and gnats, they were not short of entertainment: 'We get tolerable music even in this outlandish place. There is a theatre, where they have operas in the season. Twice or three times a week I am serenaded (it is against Italian etiquette to serenade a married lady) – it is a little compliment, that is usually paid to unmarried girls newly arrived in a place. Fortunately one of the musicians is a beautiful violin player, self-taught and a genius. They come about eleven at night. We go out on the balcony and can only just distinguish their dark forms in the street.'

She was not impressed by the exterior of the Church of the Madonna della Consolazione, describing it as 'a facsimile of a certain blancmange mould at Park Place', but was delighted to have extracted an invitation from 'Professor Vallery from Perugia', on behalf of Margaret and herself, to watch him painting frescoes in the cathedral:

> Accordingly we went and stayed some little time watching him and talking. A better sight than his angels and Madonna was himself. He has a very fine head, over massive perhaps but unusual in character, and with a brilliantly clear olive complexion. I longed to paint him. He was working on a scaffold near the ceiling in an arched chapel. There was an Italian boy waiting on him with a shock of long hair parted down the middle and cut straight at the ends, who reminded me of Rossetti's drawings; and the scene altogether of his design of Giotto drawing Dante's portrait on the plaster.

There were firework displays, a moonlight picnic and a grand feast day 'of general pardon': 'A great number of peasants from the neighbouring villages came crowding in … In the morning they confessed and got remission. In the afternoon they danced and drank, and began in good earnest the score against themselves for the next day of pardon.'

Henry's sister Sarah was to marry Henry Armstead on 8 September. Joanna had decided to give her a little rosewood worktable, and asked Henry to buy it for her. She was hungry for news of him and of home: 'What

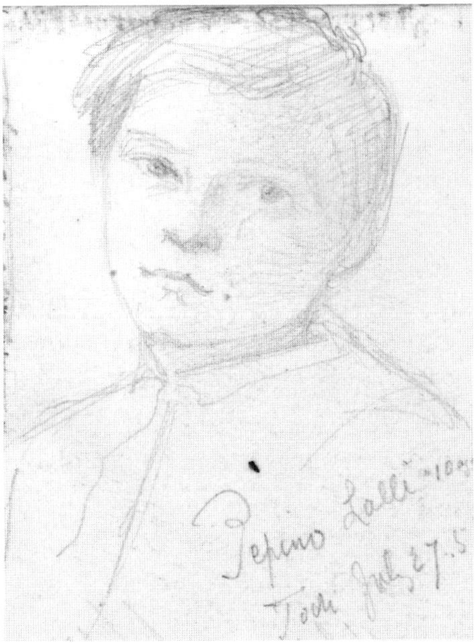

Peppino

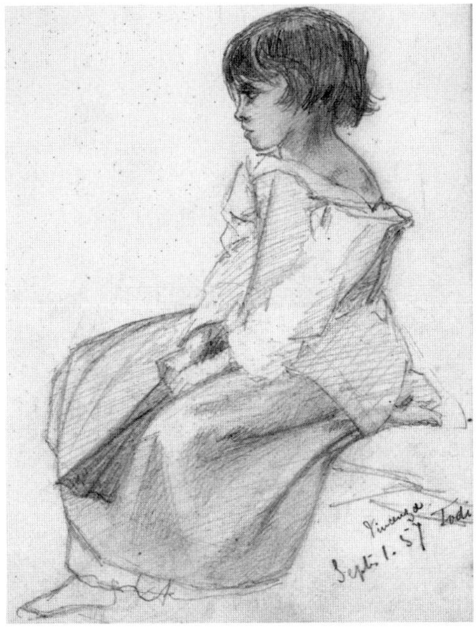

Vincenza

Two of the local children employed by Joanna at Todi

decision has the fat lady with the defunct baby come to as to the size of the miniature?': 'Have you seen Bertha Farwell lately? has she been working again in your study? and how has she gone on with her picture?': 'Have Mr Cook and the rest been to Manchester? and how are poor Mrs Browne's eyes and when is the operation to be?': 'Have you met Mr Boone since I left, if so, was he friendly?' She longed, she said, for 'a quiet hour alone' with him.

He, meanwhile, chafed at their separation, but even as she rehearsed once more her own feelings of inadequacy in the face of his love, it was in a calmer, more reconciled spirit. It was clear that she missed him – 'How I long for you of an evening on the rock, when the light fades away and all is silent and peaceful' – and he in turn was doing everything he could in his letters to hasten their marriage.

The Piottis planned to return to Rome at the beginning, or at the latest by the middle, of October, thus further complicating Joanna's and Henry's already complicated arrangements. Henry sent news of the recapture of Delhi on 21 September,[139] for which she was grateful – 'The Dr brings home confused

139 Delhi had been stormed by sepoy rebels the day after the Indian Mutiny began on 10 May. The battle to regain it was long and costly, with as many lives lost to disease as in the fighting.

reports more aggravating than none' – but most of her letter was devoted to the problem of where to meet him and when. 'I don't see why you should not make off immediately after your sister's marriage,' she wrote, adding: 'Of course you are quite wise not to expect commissions in Rome, and of course you may get none, but I think there is a very fair likelihood. Margaret says you should if possible get introductions to the foreign ministers, and better than any, to the noble Russian families here.'

Henry had asked Joanna's advice on the subject of further art training for his sister, Augusta, and Joanna took this seriously, writing several letters to him as new thoughts occurred to her. At first she recommended the Female School of Design in Gower Street as the best place for drawing, but later wrote: 'I am inclined to think with Miss Osborne that Cary's or Leigh's are on the whole better places – there is more varied work going on in the same room, and Mr C. is I think much more strict than he used to be, and at his worst more particular than Mr Leigh ... Miss Osborne is mistaken in imagining they only draw flowers at Gower Street.'

On 14 August Hennie wrote to her, full of anxieties about her future as a governess, the debts she was incurring, and, more than anything her fear that 'intercourse with superior intellects and hearts as warm as mine should make me slide into my rightful place ... I do want to be your best loved friend even though I don't deserve it.' She had hung Joanna's photograph opposite her bed. 'I call it "my star of strength" ... Most people think it so stern, but I would not have it other than it is.'

Daily life at Todi continued to entrance Joanna. A cattle-fair attracted crowds of visitors, many of whom took advantage of a travelling dentist: 'Tooth after tooth was held aloft, the ensanguined proof of victory. Great strong, country loons going up one after another with the utmost docility and gravity to be operated on.' She had not been idle, she told him, yet she had done very little. She was afraid that the boy's head in her picture was 'dreadfully morbid in colour'. The wife of the Gonfaloniere, 'a very beautiful woman', had agreed to sit to them, and Joanna could not resist making a study of her:

> She sits in a room in her own house instead of coming to the Commune. It is the funniest interior I have seen; I don't mean the rooms, but the people. There are five women servants, who seem to have each and all nearly as much authority in the house as its mistress. When there are visitors, they come into the room if they like and talk with them, and make no ceremony of offering fruit or any kind of refreshment on their own account without a word from their lady. You would imagine that

> being allowed to make so free with visitors, they would be made to keep themselves tidy and clean. By no means, and Domenica, the cook, the dirtiest and scrubbiest of them all, thinks nothing of coming and taking me or Margaret by the arm and staying to talk all the time we are in the house. The stairs, as in most Italian houses, are very dirty; and the other day as we came away we found a donkey occupying one of the landings with the perfect serenity of an animal that knows no one will dream of disturbing him.

Feeling that she had dealt too hastily with the matter of Augusta's art training, she gave Henry her final opinion on the choice between three options for a beginner:

> I have attended at Gower Street, Cary's and Leigh's and I have come to this conclusion. As a beginner the choice lies between the two former. The grounding is much more severe and thorough at Gower Street than at Cary's, but it is intended more for designers than for artists and is perhaps too tedious; but it is first rate of its kind and the students have free *entrée* to very useful lectures on anatomy etc at Marlborough House and there are Perspective classes at Gower Street ... The one advantage of Cary's over the School of Design is that it is more thoroughly for artists, and while Augusta is outlining from the cast, she will see others painting from the cast or from still life, and drawing and painting from the model and from pictures – enlivening and spurring sights to the beginners.

On 21 August, she once again confronted her feelings for him: 'You are unhappy simply because, loving me, you are separated from me, while I, loving you (and I think I do love you Henry), am wretched under the constant dread, that after all this time of pain and anticipation, I shall bring you misery instead of happiness.' She was seized sometimes, she told him, with 'a sort of rabid longing for someone to tease. I have never fully enjoyed the luxury of teasing since Mordan took Anne away from me.' Teasing the Doctor was hopeless – he simply 'flew into a rage and began to call on the Madonna and less pretty people'. But it seems she had, at last, made up her mind: 'All I can say now is, come to me as soon as you can, and I will try in the months that are coming to make up for the months that are past.'

Henry's plan was now to leave England on 21 September and meet Joanna and the Piottis in Florence. Every possible contingency had to be covered, and there were last-minute errands for him to run: 'I hope you will be able to get a proof copy of the Tennyson – don't play me any tricks. I should like to give George a copy of the poets of the Nineteenth Century. Would you be so kind?'

On 1 September, Hennie told her: 'Your boy looks very well and very nice. He seems to have a quiet heart within him and full of happiness.'

Millais, meanwhile, had written to George about their commissions: 'Dear Boyce, I have painted one head for you and am painting the other for your sister. I will send them in the course of a week to you, if you will give me directions. I am sure you will like them, as they are as good as I can turn out.' (*Plates XXXIII and XXXIV*) Joanna told Henry: 'What we shall have to pay is still an awful mystery. I am preparing myself for the worst.' She added: 'I shall not forget Sarah on the 8th. I am glad she is pleased about my present. Mind, I shall blame you if the ornaments are ugly.'

He would also be blamed, Henry realised, if he did not present the *Nineteenth-Century Poets* to George in a 'presentable' state. Mindful, perhaps, of his last well-meaning attempt to second-guess George's aesthetic tastes, he suggested that George go to Bumpus's,[140] select whatever pleased him in the way of impressions, paper and binding, and put it on Henry's account.

The Millais pictures were finished. He had produced portraits of his sisters-in-law, Sophie and Alice Gray, who had been his models for 'Autumn Leaves'. On 14 September Millais wrote to George from Bowerswell, in Perth, to say that he would bring them to London at the end of the month: 'You must decide with your sister which is to belong to which. All who have seen them show no particular preference. They are in thin frames and have glasses before them. I shall ask you to let them be exhibited next year at the RA.'

Now that they were to meet again, Henry wrote a heartfelt letter to Joanna, lamenting the time already lost to them and urging their swift marriage. Hennie later indicated that Joanna had finally accepted that arrangements for their future should be placed in his hands. Joanna took his accusations (and these they certainly were) in good part: 'Your last letter has been constantly in my thoughts if not in my hand … the severest as well as the tenderest parts are precious to me.' And yet she could not regret the delay, feeling that they would have a better chance of happiness because of it. She wrote cheerfully:

> I am afraid that both I and Margaret will shock your prejudices in the dressing line very much at Florence, and unavoidably. We are as vexed as you can be – all our presentable apparel lies safely locked up at Rome … You are so irreproachable in your own dress – with

[140] J. & E. Bumpus, a bookshop favoured by the royal family which undertook binding commissions.

> one notable exception – that I don't think I should venture into that domain. Do you know the exception I refer to? Cloth boots on a man – I have a spite and hatred against them and the feet that wear them, which I could find no adequate way of expressing, but by taking my scissors and snipping them (the boots) deliberately to shreds.

A further missive from Henry was delivered while she was writing this amiable epistle. It is hard to imagine exactly what he might have said – after all, things were finally going his way – but it was unsparing, and over a 'remark of which you have completely twisted the meaning'. She resented it 'to the uttermost' and was profoundly hurt: 'Until now I longed anxiously to meet you at Florence – now I dread it … I did not think you could have wounded me so wantonly.' She told him roundly that the words, 'though they had been ten times true' should never have been written.

Too late. Henry was on his way and would, as he said to George, 'lick the post'.

❁

From Florence, on 1 October, Joanna wrote to her brother Matthias to say that she was 'determined no longer to oppose Henry's earnest wish for our marriage'. The plan was for this to take place in Rome, and soon. She hoped that 'some unpleasantnesses would be escaped by being married out of England'.

Hennie wrote immediately to say that how pleased she was, adding: 'I don't like your being married without one of your own family by your side … Could not George or Mat come over for the occasion? Let me know when all is settled.'

No one liked the idea of Joanna's marrying so far from home, and letters from Anne (who was pregnant) and Matthias both gave the impression that they suspected Henry of bullying her into it. It was Henry who replied, writing to Matthias on 23 October, offering immediately to abandon the plan of marrying in Rome and leave the place and time of their marriage to fate or fortune. 'I hope I do enough,' he wrote, going on to explain that the decision had been reached at least in part so that they could see Italy together, at the right time of their lives, and without too much extra expense:

> You must not think that I am indifferent to Joney's wish to have some of her family at her marriage, or your wishes in the same direction. I sincerely wish it could be so, but it is evident that as we are

> circumstanced we cannot have in this matter unalloyed good fortune… I was unhappy at her leaving England at all, and I should never have dreamed of marrying her abroad, but now that she is willing to marry me, she is abroad, and I am disappointed at finding an impediment to my marriage when I might have expected it was left for her to remove the last.

He added: 'If you or the Mordans could have come to Rome how delighted I should have been. I trust dear Anne will get through her confinement well this time.'

This latest upheaval did not stop Joanna enthusing about Florence to George, on 1 November:

> I don't want to set you longing too much, but there can be no place like Florence for seeing the grandest of the early Italian masters in perfection, the frescoes of Giotto, Masaccio, Filippo and Filippino Lippi, Orcagna and Ghirlandaio, and the oil pictures of Botticelli are things that thoroughly delight one in every way. I had in some very slight degree anticipated their wonderful power and simplicity but I had no idea they were so fine in colour. The Fra Angelicos too, especially one in the Uffizi and two in a church in Perugia, have the purest loveliness conceivable, one wonders how it could get through the brushes. In sculpture Luca and Andrea della Robbia and Donatello are the great fellows.

George's stay at Godalming came to an end early in October, and he had since visited the Art Treasures Exhibition in Manchester. Joanna wrote: 'Of course you have gloated over the Turners and Constables, Linnells, Holman Hunts, Millais, Velasquez, Vandyke and Reynolds etc. Did you know that H. Hunt had worked on the girl in "The Awakening Conscience"? I should like to know what you think, but to me and Henry it seemed dreadfully injured by the change. The "Hireling Shepherd" and the "Valentine and Proteus" are certainly things that no early or late masters can snuff out.'

She went on to explain how she and Henry had arrived at their decision to marry in Rome, adding that unless he saw some real and hitherto unexpressed objection, 'I shall do as Henry wishes … It is now more than two years and a half that his life has been quite unsettled and the fact of my being in Italy is the result of my own will, indulged in opposition to his wishes.' She had realised at Todi, she said, that she had been ungenerous and selfish in leaving him thus after their engagement, and had written then to tell him that she was in his hands.

She asked that he, Mat and Anne should let all their friends know. She herself would write to her mother, Aunt Robert and Aunt Mary. Henry, she said, had taken a studio in the Via Ripetta, near the Piottis at no. 35: 'He expects his sitter Lady Margaret Beaumont and her baby and intends to finish her miniature in Rome and he hopes to have other sitters. What did you think of the miniature of Lilly? Has Millais sent in the pictures and the bill yet? I am waiting to know. Pray keep my picture until I return. Mat will pay for it. I did not forget to drink your health on your birthday, or Anne's on hers.'

From Hennie, on 4 November, she heard that her friend had finally taken a post as daily governess to the Angell family (the introduction had been effected by Anne) at a salary of £40: 'Harry is seriously annoyed that I should be "making a menial of myself to people whose equal I am".'

Her letter also cast more light on the family's objections, to which Henry had understandably over-reacted. His nerves, during this period, got the better of him more than once. Anne, she said, had told her: 'Oh, we have no objection to its taking place out there, only if she could come nearer some of us might be present.' Mordan had added that they thought Henry might have met Joanna in Paris but that was before they realised he meant to stay on in Italy: 'For my part', he said, 'I am expecting cards and cake every day.'

Certainly Henry's letter of 11 November to Matthias was cordial, calm and businesslike. He was now in his element, planning the wedding and enjoying the foretaste of married bliss that their days together in Rome were affording him: 'Our life over here is quite that of old-fashioned people. We trot about together and are so constantly in each others' society that I think it is impossible for Joney to feel like a girl.'

And once the decision had been made, the Boyce siblings were generous in their support and good wishes. Anne wrote to her sister on 21 November: 'We wish you both all the happiness you could yourselves desire, and we think, all things considered, you have decided wisely … Mordan went to Park Place on Thursday evening, and told Mamma you were very shortly going to be married to Wells.[141] Of course she is as much opposed to it as ever, but that can't be helped … The children are quite well, particularly my darling pet boy … They all send kind love and kisses to "Aunt Doney" and "Unchi Wells" as Edgar kept calling Wells before Bob last Sunday.'

Mat followed this with a letter dated 23 November: 'It is certainly time that you both were settled in a way that will put an end to all the doubts and uncertainties that have so long distracted and tormented you. It would

141 It is not clear whether Joanna's letter had reached her mother before Mordan's visit or not.

have been most pleasant to us as well as to yourself to have been present at your wedding, but you must console yourself with the reflection that we have all along entirely approved your marriage with Wells … I need not say how glad, nay proud, we shall be of having Wells as a brother-in-law, for whilst his abilities, self-reliance and perseverance command our admiration, his moral qualities have secured our respect and esteem.' The papers needed for the marriage to take place in Rome would, he said, be sent off the following day, 'so I hope I shall give satisfaction to Wells on the score of speed'. The only thing that troubled him was how to give them a present they would admire, 'as neither Lilly nor myself make any pretensions to taste'. He was 'particularly pleased with Wells's miniature of Lilly, having begun to despair of ever seeing a good likeness of her'.

George had already written to Joanna on 19 November. He was 'in a fix' with respect to the two Millais heads. Both paintings, one of the girl holding the leaves and the other of the little girl holding the basket, were 'very beautiful, and the latter, according to Halliday and Millais himself, is the favourite with most, but I like the first the most … It is perfectly bare-headed … The other too is almost bare-headed, there being but a line of gold and pearl fretwork on the crown of the head and a few pearls entwined in the hair.' Millais had asked him to decide at once on Joanna's behalf, but he was nervous 'as we generally agreed in our likings' that she too would prefer the first picture. 'He pressed me ultimately to write to you at once and get a decision without delay. I promised to do so.' He thought Millais would charge them about £70 each.

When Joanna replied, it was decisive: 'Let Millais know at once that I wish to have the head he has painted for me. I think it would be foolish for us both to have studies of the same head, besides Henry has a predilection for the second sister's head and from what you say it is quite up to the mark in painting.' She was certainly not about to ask Millais to do a further version of the picture George preferred.

George told her he had spent a pleasant evening chatting to Mrs Millais before dinner and with Millais after, and that Millais had shown him an exquisite little picture, just completed, called 'Pot Pourri': 'And now,' he continued, 'as to your approaching and, as I take it, finally resolved upon marriage with Wells at Rome, I agreed in the main with Mat, Mordan and Anne, that altho' in several respects it was desirable it should take place there, or at some distance from London, yet it was most unfortunate that no old and tried friend or relation of yours and ours could be present on the occasion … But whichever way you decide, my sincerest and most brotherly wishes and prayers will ever accompany you both.'

He added: 'I like the promised little head of James Jasper,[142] which you most kindly left for me with the by no means to be sneezed at little snowdrop study, as much, aye more than ever.'

On 24 November, Henry wrote at length to George. Much of his letter was a progress report, some of it an exculpation of his decision to press for their getting married in Rome, but it also contained a note of apprehension. Though Joanna had at last realised, he said, that 'it was not kind to run away from me and do all sorts of mad things and keep me waiting' and was, finally, 'quite in earnest about marrying me', he had learned not to underestimate her capacity for losing her nerve. The sooner the marriage could take place the better.

There were financial considerations too. He had made arrangements to be away from England for a long time, had spent a good deal of money and had taken measures to obtain work while he was in Italy – including making several appointments with potential sitters. He did not deny employing this 'flood of reasons' to persuade her to marry him in Rome. Everything, he wrote, now depended on Matthias. 'I cannot give notice at the Consulate until I am advised by Mat of the advent of the parchments – so I shall be all expectation during this week.'

'Let me assure you,' he added triumphantly, 'I have every confidence in being able to walk with untrembling legs, when I go to be "turned off". I never was in such good spirits with my "venture" as I am now, and with good reason; for since Joney has ceased to fight me and look upon me as an artful antagonist, she has become none the less lovable etc, etc.'

They intended, he told George, to go to Naples, Amalfi and Paestum for a fortnight after the wedding, before returning to Rome, when he would begin work in earnest. Then, having expatiated at length on the artistic glories of Florence, Assisi and Perugia, he described a scene that had made a poignant impression on them both, highlighting their mutual passion for faces and their love of children:

> At Spello we found some good Pinturicchios, but the town is remembered by us because of two beautiful children we saw there. One a little laughing cherub face. The other, when we caught sight of her, looked like a young Velida. From a blank wall, flush with the façade of a Church came a fountain of water – the trough being a long, ancient sarcophagus. The child had put her pitcher to the fountain and

[142] This study of James Jasper, the old fisherman was painted by Joanna on 20 February 1857 when staying in Brighton with George.

> was standing in some sort of monumental pose flat against the wall on one side of the sarcophagus – staring at us with her loose flaxen hair drooping over her forehead – her dress blue, worn, dusty with some drapery about her neck – her feet bare. She looked altogether dusty and stony – her features more beautiful and impressive than any that remain in my memory ... Joney left Spello in an uneasy state of mind (we were only there an hour). I think she would have liked to carry the child to Rome.

He ended: 'Tell Anne that we shall be married on the 7th unless Mat disappoints me ... The wedding dress is bought (a white moiré antique) and everything will be ready by the middle of next week.'

But the promised papers, to their dismay, failed to arrive. For Henry, after such a long campaign, it was more than flesh and blood could stand, and on 30 November Joanna, unnerved by the prospect of further dissension between her fiancé and her family, wrote to Matthias herself: 'Either the letter has miscarried or you have not written to Henry, as he requested. He is dreadfully annoyed at the disappointment and so angry that he will not trust himself to write to you. I too am very vexed. Such complete uncertainty at such a time is to say the least very annoying. I cannot let my Aunts or Hennie know the day and if it cannot be on the 7th probably none of you will know it either, also Henry's family will be in ignorance.'

Needless to say, Matthias's letter arrived two days later. Joanna replied immediately: 'I am so savage with myself for writing to you as I did yesterday.[143] I am determined never again to write under high pressure from another person be it who it may.' There was no doubt as to who was exerting the pressure. Henry disliked very much being out of control: 'I was vexed', Joanna wrote, 'to see him so dreadfully out of sorts.'

Hennie, on the other hand, was full of joy: 'I am glad your birthday is to be <u>the</u> day ... How lovely you will be – that Bernouse[144] could not be better, and I find a pleasure in thinking that something you and I chose will be worn by you then.' Mordan, it appeared, had spoken firmly to Mrs Boyce: 'It is a relief that you will henceforth be shielded from all attacks.' He had also tackled Mr Boone, and their talk had been 'more satisfactory than any previous one'.

[143] The letter dated November 30 must have been finished on December 1 to fit this remark and Henry's response.

[144] This bernouse (or burnoose), Joanna's wedding garment, was not the hooded Arab cloak normally understood by the word, but a soft, shimmering shawl, perhaps worn also as a veil during the ceremony. In her painting 'Mrs Eaton' (1861), her model is wearing it. (Plate XLIII)

Henry was in a quandary – unwilling to relinquish his self-righteous fury but aware that, once again, he had over-reacted. He wrote to Matthias on 2 December: 'Your letter of today makes me feel the dilemma of my rage very much. You have done your best in respect to speed, are so full of good thoughts and kindness, and write so utterly innocent of having given me the least cause for uneasiness that I am thoroughly pulled up, and I hope you will forget all about the rumblings of anger that may have reached you.'

There was a small delay, occasioned by Joanna's catching a cold, but on 9 December 1857 she and Henry were finally married.

9

MAN AND WIFE

'So the year's done with (Love me for ever!)'

'Earth's Immortalities'

The deed was done at last. On 9 December Henry wrote exultantly to Matthias: 'We are really married and are off to Naples.' He asked his brother-in-law to advertise the marriage in *The Times* thus: 'At the British Consulate, Rome, and at the Protestant Church, by the Revd F. B. Woodward, Henry Tanworth Wells Esq, 17 Stratford Place, London, to Joanna M. B., second daughter of the late G. J. B. of London.' Anne, meanwhile, had received a letter from Margaret Piotti saying that Mr Freeborn, the Consul, was an ill-bred and distasteful man, but that the Revd Woodward had 'performed his part most sympathetically and impressively'.

The year ended in drama. On 16 December an earthquake struck the Naples area and for some time no word was heard of the honeymooners. Joanna's Aunt Mary wrote to her on 29 December, an endearingly flustered letter: 'I am MOST anxious to hear of you and your dear husband's safety, and God grant that you are both spared to us for many, many years. The account of the earthquake in the neighbourhood of Naples is awful and we are all with intense anxiety wishing to hear from you. I should have written to you before, but have been, and still am, suffering from boils.' She had made them a bed quilt as a wedding present, to await their return.

The family's anxiety about the earthquake was well-founded, as was borne out by Joanna's letter of 6 January to 'dear Aunt Mary'. By then she and Henry were safely back at the Via Ripetta in Rome, but, she said: 'I'm sure you will agree with us in thinking our escape most providential, when I have told you all.'

She and Henry had set out on the morning of 16 December to see the magnificent ruins at Paestum. They had intended to spend the night at Salerno, 'but it occurred to Henry that it would save both time and expense if we could get on to La Cava that night, which we accordingly did':

> At a little after 10 o'clock the first shock occurred. I immediately recognised it as an earthquake – Henry would scarcely believe it, but after a minute's interval came the second and much more violent shock. It was not a sudden shake, but a slow pendulum-like movement increasing in violence at every vibration; and it seemed to both of us as the motion increased, as though the walls had a strange gutta-percha like tenacity which alone prevented them breaking to pieces. We immediately dressed and went downstairs, where we found all the inmates of the hotel assembled; and as another shock might come on at any moment, we went for a short time right out into the road. After an hour or two, as all was quiet, we returned to our room. In the morning we found an arch spanning our sitting room was cracked up the centre.
>
> We took the rail early in the morning for Pompeii and in the evening reached Naples. The shock was much more violent at La Cava than at Naples, yet not only had the people turned out of their houses at the time of the earthquake, but as they expected a repetition of it on the following evening at the same time, the city presented a very curious sight. We walked out from half past nine to half past ten and found groups of the Neapolitan peasants squatting round charcoal fires and crowding round the shrines chanting prayers to the Madonna to avert the earthquake, and in the grand piazza we found numbers of people settled for the night. We were also told afterwards that numbers slept in their carriages sooner than trust themselves under roofs. Yet all this alarm was occasioned by a much less violent shock than we had suffered at La Cava. There we were close to the worst, and had in fact within a few hours of the time passed over the very ground where such numbers have perished – that is to say if what we hear be true.

There had been, she said, little or no information in the local papers and they were anxious to get a copy of *The Times* with a detailed account of it. The first report in *The Times* appeared on the 24th, in a telegram sent from Marseilles, and there was a longer account on the 26th bearing out Joanna's description of Neapolitans camping out in the streets or staying in their carriages rather than trust themselves to buildings. It was only much later that it became clear that half the villages in the Basilicata area south-east of Naples were completely destroyed, and the number of fatalities, estimated at between eleven and twelve thousand, was almost certainly far greater.

Nevertheless Joanna and Henry remained for a further five days in Naples, even making an ascent of Vesuvius which, in the circumstances, carried insouciance to the level of recklessness: 'Here we were most fortunate in getting a rather dangerous but most splendid view of the two craters, which both shot out immense volumes of steam with occasional showers of red hot stones while we were there. Of course we had a trusty guide with us, who knew how to take care of us, and we got down to Naples safe and sound. An eruption of the mountain was expected every day.'

They arrived back in Rome on Christmas Day. Henry, she said, was 'dreadfully busy': 'Three full length miniatures to finish for the Academy, and a number of new commissions – they are coming in every day. I am painting too in another studio ... We are very grieved that you are still suffering from boils.'

She thanked Aunt Mary for the bed quilt, adding that as yet she had received no communication from her Aunt Robert. This arrived soon after, written on New Year's Day 1858, with Aunt Robert wishing Joanna and her new husband 'a long and happy union, with health, prosperity and all earthly comforts'. Joanna's shrewd earlier comment, that by attempting to please everyone, Uncle Robert had ended up by pleasing no one, was borne out by her aunt's plaintive comments on the continuing stalemate at home: 'I do verily believe and have often told your Mamma, that if once reconciled to Mr Wells as a son, she would find him kind and most attentive to her reasonable wants and wishes ... I feel sure, dear Joanna, that a reconciliation between you and your only Parent would add to your happiness ... I have had no letter from Bob since last spring, and I begin to think your Mamma has cut me as a correspondent.'

Henry was aware that Matthias needed their support in London to solve the problem of Mrs Boyce and the businesses, but was anxious that he would have to leave many commissions unfinished if they returned in March. He had hoped to complete 'three large miniatures for the Exhibition. Lilly's is nearly done; Mrs Vanderbyl's has not been touched since I left England, Lady M. Beaumont's I am now painting upon'. That morning he had received a commission for a full-length miniature of Mrs Popham of Littlecot Hall, for 130 guineas, which he could begin in Rome but would be able to finish in London. He had more commissions than he could cope with, including, Joanna told Lilly, 'a half-length portrait of a princess Obelinska'. As Hennie remarked, on 29 January, 'How delightful it must be to see your husband's talents so recognised! The croakers won't see him bankrupt yet!'

It was not Henry's work that delayed them however. On 26 February Joanna had a miscarriage. On 3 March, Henry wrote to Matthias with a dramatic account:

Joney's illness commenced last Friday afternoon: at that time she was put to bed and suffered a miscarriage, which had doubtless been caused by a frightful shock she received during the Carnival a fortnight before. During the eight days of Carnival we were the guests of M. and Madame Dalloz (I am painting her portrait); opposite to our balcony was a large one filled with numerous English. They were bent upon having fun, so were we, and on the afternoon of Saturday, 13th February, towards the end of the day, we succeeded so well that a dense crowd collected between our houses, quite filling the road. Excited and quite entering into our frolic of the moment, which was hoisting a basket filled with nosegays, toys, etc. by way of a cord which I had succeeded in throwing into the opposite balcony, the people below shouted and tried to upset the basket by pelting it with nosegays. At the moment when it was midway and everybody's attention was upon it, the party of twelve dragoons whose duty it is to clear the Corso for the horse race, came on in full career. There was no time for pulling up – (they were so badly arranged) so they went over and thro' the crowd – it was a frightful thing to see the mass of fallen creatures mashed and stamped on as the horses went over them. Joney caught sight of the dragoons just a second before they were upon the people, and my first notice – for I was engaged pulling the basket over – was her shrieking and clinging to me. Very many people were injured. Six were immediately taken to the neighbouring hospital, and to two boys extreme unction was administered. The next morning I was called out of my dressing room to be told that these two boys had died. It was done in so bungling a manner that Joney surmised what was being told to me. It was fortunately a false report, but for many days it was thought impossible that one of the boys could survive. I am happy to say that they are now nearly well and will soon leave the hospital. The Government I believe made enquiry into the matter. The dragoons, officer and men, were put in prison, but what has since happened it is next to impossible to learn in a place like this. Of course no fault rested with the people in the balconies and very little I think with the dragoons; we think the blame attaches to the soldiers and police whose duty it was to clear and guard the course, and in this they so utterly failed that they allowed the dragoons to come up, without even raising a cry of warning.

For three days after the miscarriage Joanna was unable to leave her bed, and her ills were exacerbated by 'violent toothache', but Henry was hopeful that she would soon be stronger and able to take drives with him. They expected to be in London by Good Friday, from which time he would be kept busy until his pictures were safely delivered to the Royal Academy. He was anxious, however, that Matthias should keep an eye open for a suitable house for them – preferably in Bayswater or Kensington.

George wrote on 7 March to say that Anne had been safely confined ten days earlier: 'I never saw her look prettier nor more interesting than when nursing her little one in bed a few days after. It was a picture you wouldn't have forgotten and would have wished to paint – with the softest and tenderest of brushes.' He had collected the second head ('Alice Gray') from Millais and paid for it with money Joanna had left with Matthias for that purpose, but he was still worried that she would not like her picture as much as his. He went on to give her news of their :

> Millais is working very hard to get his big picture done for the Academy. Our heads will go, and another lovely little picture called 'Potpourri'. He has lately done too a splendid woodcut of the 'Finding of Moses' of which I luckily came in for the last proof, and I hear much of a still more recent one of the Devil sowing tares. You know that I got him to meet Clara and Ada[145] here to see the former, as he was in want of a beautiful little girl's head, he said, for his big picture. As ill luck would have it, I wrote for her just as she and Ada and Edgar had moved to Brighton. He was very much struck with her. Rossetti has not been in town for an age, is still at Matlock doing I know not what, and will go thence to Oxford to finish his distemper of 'Sir Launcelot before the "San Graal"', which they say is very beautiful. Several of the other preraffaellites are painting compartments in the same room, which is destined for the use of a Debating Club. The subjects are all from the life.

It was Rossetti who had persuaded Benjamin Woodward, architect of the new Oxford Union library and debating chamber, to allow him to decorate the walls above the gallery with a series of Arthurian murals. He had met William Morris and Edward Burne-Jones when they recruited him to contribute to their *Oxford and Cambridge Magazine* in 1856, and the three became prime movers

[145] Mordan's two daughters by his first marriage. Clara was acknowledged to be a great beauty.

in the venture. Among others who joined in were Arthur Hughes, Spencer Stanhope and the young Val Prinsep,[146] who, with lavish praise, summed up Rossetti's charm and charisma: 'What fun we had in that Union! What jokes! What roars of laughter … [Rossetti] was the planet around which we revolved – we copied his very way of speaking. All beautiful women were "stunners" with us. Wombats were the most beautiful of God's creatures. Medievalism was our beau ideal and we sank our individuality in the strong personality of our adored Gabriel.'[147] Ruskin, who paid a brief visit to Oxford in October, wrote to George Frederic Watts: 'The worst of it is that all the fun of these fellows goes straight into their work, one can't get them to be quiet at it, or resist a fancy; if it strikes them ever so little a stroke on the bells of their soul, away they go to jingle, jingle, without ever caring what o'clock it is.'[148]

The project was not altogether a success. Rossetti and his merry band of painters had no idea about the techniques involved in fresco painting, and as they painted directly onto the wall, their Arthurian odyssey began very quickly to decay.

Holman Hunt's 'big picture' – 'Christ and the Doctors' – George had not yet seen:

> He called here some while back and said he would write to me to come up. What think you of Frith getting £3000 for his picture of 'Epsom races' and some £300 or more for the sketch?
>
> Solomon's picture 'The Lion in love' is clever and amusing, but the subject is flimsy. Simeon delivers a lecture at his brother's house on Saturday next on 'Colour and its poetry'. 'Cheek' is the order of the day. I would go though, were I not engaged.
>
> I have heard nothing concerning your painting since you wrote to me. Will you bring home something for the Academy with you? I hope so. 'Rowena' is at Stratford Place whither I got Ryan's men to remove it with every care some time back. Do you propose sending it again this time? 'Our Housemaid' was sold a few days back by Leggatt at Porter's rooms … Your two little heads of James Jasper and the Betws 'Rufus',[149] which were hung up, are much admired by the élite. I wish I could speak with any satisfaction of my own doings,

[146] Valentine Prinsep (1838–1904). Born in Calcutta, his parents made their London home, Little Holland House, the centre of an artistic circle. He first exhibited at the Royal Academy in 1862.

[147] Quoted by Oswald Doughty in *Dante Gabriel Rossetti: A Victorian Romantic* (London 1949) p. 227.

[148] Letter dated 18 October 1857, in the Bodleian.

[149] Both the tiny study of Rufus, a fair haired urchin, which Joanna painted at Betws in 1855, and her study of James Jasper, the fisherman were passed down to her daughter Alice.

> which have been culpably small this winter. I have sent 3 drawings to the Portland and, having seen them there, wish them heartily away again …
>
> Ruskin is busily engaged in the National Gallery, arranging and having framed the Turner sketches left to the Nation. He showed me some most interesting relics there the other day, consisting of some sketch books of the painter crammed with outline memoranda on every page and on both sides … R.'s last book was *The Political Economy of Art*, which I have not yet read, and which is more animadverted on than any of his previous works.

The rest of the gossip George intended to keep for their return, but could not resist a last minute errand – which he scribbled on the flap of the envelope: 'Should you have time to buy me 2 or 3 sets of shirt studs of glass colour-mosaic on a black ground of about the size of the sketch I shall be glad. Burges,[150] who wants one of the sets, said he gave 4 or 5 shillings for a set he bought in Rome. Your choice will quite satisfy me. Don't trouble yourself about them if you are pressed for time.'

The correspondence now became businesslike – and somewhat self-absorbed on the part of the newly-weds. When Matthias offered to rent them his family's house in Clifton Road for an extended period, Joanna made it clear that this was only acceptable if they could have it for four months rather than two, 'because in the first place our move from your house to another in the beginning of June would come just at the height of Henry's busiest time, and secondly because Henry intends leaving town in the middle of August'. She had heard from Mordan that Matthias, were it not for the expense, was anxious to leave town in early April with Lilly and the children, and calculated that he would be glad to extend his family's stay at Richmond if it could be afforded. Matthias proved only too happy to oblige and Joanna and Henry were able to move straight into Clifton Road on their return. Joanna was delighted to make the acquaintance of Anne's new arrival 'who is a fine baby absurdly like Mordan with a quantity of fair hair, that stands up from his head like a top knot.'

From her mother and Bob she had heard nothing, but was pleased to know from Hennie, whose brother was at the same school at Ilfracombe, that Bob's master 'gave a first-rate account of him, both as to his abilities and his

150 William Burges (1827–81) – an architect, according to William Rossetti, 'with chubby face, like a cherub on a tombstone' – was an old friend of George's, having lodged in the same house at 15 Buckingham Street. He had a passion for medieval fantasy, which he brought to bear on his most famous creations, Cardiff Castle and Castell Coch.

conscientiousness and perseverance.' Of George she said 'I never saw [him] look so well in my life. He is amusingly disgusted with himself for getting so fat.'

After Joanna and Henry's marriage, their path and George's inevitably diverged. Though their mutual friendships and shared love of art ensured that the bond between them remained strong, George became steadily more independent of his family and correspondingly closer to the Pre-Raphaelites, who visited each other constantly, shared models, helped each other in times of crisis and were patrons of each other's work.

George's talent as a painter was respected by his friends. In *Some Reminiscences*, William Rossetti noted that his landscape water-colours 'are, for delicate observations and well-harmonized diligence of execution, not easily to be surpassed'. He added that 'his vocation for art, though not of extensive scope, was highly genuine'. With regard to George's reputation as a collector, Rossetti commented: 'Boyce had a taste for collecting objects of fine and decorative art, and had a very sound judgment in the choice of them; whenever one went to see him there was something fresh to look at;' while Alice later observed that George's eye 'never missed anything lovely or of old and truthful craftsmanship', and from the moment he could call a place his own, 'many a charming or quaint bit of china, many a relic of past days or some old world costume ... would find its way into his snuggery'.

In spite of his documented, and ultimately unsatisfactory, interest in Lizzie Ridley and Jeannie Naylor (among others), George's private life was also increasingly a Pre-Raphaelite affair. On 21 January 1858 Holman Hunt called on him to discuss a portrait George had drawn in 1854 of Annie Miller[151] – a model whom Hunt intended to mould into a suitable bride for himself. To this end, he had a favour to ask of George:

> After that her education both of mind and manners shall have been completed, he wished to destroy as far as possible all traces of her former occupation, viz, that of sitting to certain artists (those artists, however, being all his personal friends, Rossetti, A. Hughes, Stephens, Egg, Holliday, Millais, Collins and myself), and as mine was the only

[151] Annie Miller (1835–1925). Holman Hunt had found her in a Chelsea slum and hoped to marry her once she had been 'educated'. Before travelling to the East in 1854 he made out a list of artists for whom she could sit, which, for the most part, she ignored. George's drawing is the earliest known portrait of her.

> direct study of her head, as it was, he would hold it a favour if I would give it him and he in return would give me something of his doing that I might like. At first I resisted him stoutly, but finding that it was a serious point with him, and that my refusing would be in some degree an obstacle in the carrying out of his wishes with regard to her (which it would be both selfish and unkind and foolish in the remotest degree to thwart) I at last reluctantly assented to give him the study, the most careful and most interesting (to me) and which I prize the most I have ever made. He thanked me heartily for my compliance. He gave me real pleasure by telling me that she always says I behaved most kindly to her.

In spite of his professed 'chilliness of heart', George had a reputation for kindness and for generosity in his praise of other artists' work. Though 'Little Simeon Solomon' had 'called and stayed a long while and jawed and bored us considerably' on 13 February, George was happy to attend a reunion on the 19th at which he partook of 'tea and fish, wine and cake' and was 'much interested with a book of sketches by young Simeon'.

But his closest friend was always Rossetti. On 22 May he described a typical meeting between the two:

> We went off to his rooms in a cab and had tea there. While I was looking at his excellent drawings he read aloud to me several translations of his in the metre of the original early Italian Sonnets and other pieces before and contemporary with Dante. Several of them most touching and graphic, terse and simple. Admiring a little pen and ink sketch of a little girl wheeling a child along in a go-cart, he gave it to me. He came back with me in a cab to my place and there we sat and read and talked of Browning. He recited also 2 excellent little pieces by Morris. He spoke of [Burne-] Jones being 'an angel on earth, and too good for this world'

A letter from Joanna on 26 May, asking fretfully when they might catch sight of him, showed that George was only too well occupied elsewhere. In his diary he recorded a visit from Rossetti on the 29th, during which he made a drawing of Annie Harrison, the landlady's daughter:

> He told me some amusing anecdotes about Thackeray and repeated some ludicrous exclamations of Morris. He read a lovely little MS

> poem of Browning's about a portrait of a golden-haired beauty on a golden ground that he copied from some lady's album[152]... Burges asked him how he would lay in a head in oil colour. He said 'begin by modelling it thoroughly in pure blue, tempered with white where necessary. For the darkest shadows use it very purely and thinly, and perhaps in hatchings and in reflected lights omit it, leaving them for the local colour of the second painting which may be taken up as soon as the first is dry and can be scraped smooth.' I made a slight sketch of Annie while Rossetti was doing this.

Four days later Rossetti was again at Buckingham Street: 'He told me further particulars about Dickens, who it appears had left his wife and taken to Miss Fernan,[153] an actress with whom he is infatuated (platonically, as he pretends).'

On 10 June he had found Holman Hunt 'hard at work on some drapery in his "Christ and the Doctors" picture, which is a noble and wonderful work and intensely expressive and realistic. Every single head full of meaning and worthy of study. The head and legs of the boy Christ not finished. All the flesh had first been modelled in bright blue.' At 7.30 the same evening he dined with Hunt and others where 'Boxing was the principal topic discussed and Hunt communicated the doctrine that it was on account of our ancestors' pugnacity and warlike propensities that England had become great. Now we were degenerating into a generation of milksops.' Hunt and several of the others were arranging to take boxing lessons with Alec Reid, a well-known retired pugilist who was a room-manager at 'The Cambrian', a public house near Leicester Square. 'After some time,' George went on, 'he mooted the subject which was the cause of the gathering, viz. the importance of supporting the old Liverpool Academy.'[154]

Little wonder Joanna was finding it difficult to tie him down. In a letter written on 9/10 June, she invited him to join them on a weekend in the country, remaining overnight and with permission to 'make off as early as you like in the morning.' She also told him: 'No occasion to bring nightshirt or brush or anything. I will furnish all, and in case you are very good, you shall have one of

152 The poem is 'A Face'. 'If one could have that little head of hers/Painted upon a background of pale gold.'

153 Ellen Ternan (1839–1914). Actress. Dickens was forty-five when he and Wilkie Collins employed her to perform in their production of *The Frozen Deep* in 1857. He fell deeply in love with her, and later separated from his wife Catherine, though he did attempt (not very successfully) to keep the liaison secret.

154 The Liverpool Academy was founded in 1810 as a northern counterpart to the Royal Academy. Controversy flared over the awarding of prizes to Pre-Raphaelite painters (especially to Millais for 'The Blind Girl' in 1857) and the ensuing split threatened the Academy's survival. Hunt determined that his friends should support it by sending as many pictures as possible to the 1858 exhibition, and George, Joanna and Henry all contributed work.

my frilled nightgowns as a treat.' On 17 June, she suggested they meet for tea before she and Henry went to the Solomons – evidently the best that could be managed.

The inauguration of the Hogarth Club was taking place at about the same time. This venture, though relatively short lived (it was dissolved by the end of 1861), proved particularly important to artists like George, who, while respected within his circle, outside it remained for the most part unrecognised. On 6 April he had received a letter from Arthur Hughes proposing 'an Art Club (of professionals and non-professionals) of about fifty members, with facilities for exhibition of works, etc, and asking me to join'. On 10 April an initial meeting was held (it included Ford Madox Brown – generally agreed to be the driving force – William Morris and Burne-Jones) and on 4 May George joined his fellow artists in Morris's rooms in Red Lion Square to establish the club's aims in detail. According to William Rossetti, it was Madox Brown who decided to name it after William Hogarth, 'a painter whom he deeply reverenced', and Holman Hunt also recorded: 'We fixed upon this name to do homage to the stalwart founder of Modern English art.'[155]

The club's premises were initially in Piccadilly and later at Waterloo Place, and its membership was made up mainly of PRBs and their adherents, though it also embraced a wide variety of painters, sculptors, architects, writers, collectors and patrons. Honorary members included Carlyle, Thackeray, Browning and Tennyson. In addition to the founding members, several more candidates were proposed, some of whom were blackballed. George wrote: 'Would have proposed Wells, but felt certain he would not join, and thought I knew one who would be likely to blackball him … I was asked first to be a trustee, and then a member of the committee, but declined both on account of being so long absent from town.' Blackballing became something of a blood sport at the Hogarth, and contributed to its premature closure.

Three of George's pictures had been selected for the Royal Academy that year, and he was particularly pleased that Ruskin had picked out one of them, 'At a Farm House in Surrey', for praise: 'Full of truth and sweet feeling. How pleasant it is, after looking at Mr Frith's pictures, to see how happy a little girl may be who hasn't gone to the Derby.'

Joanna, increasingly concerned about the family finances, castigated herself in a letter to Matthias for not taking more account of the sums she had already received, and for accepting it as her due, without taking a proper interest

[155] William Michael Rossetti, *Some Reminiscences*, p.224 and William Holman Hunt. *Pre-Raphaelitism and the Pre-Raphaelite Brotherhood* (London 1906–07) pp. 142-43.

in the safe working of the business: 'The £500 per annum is of great moment to us, but I assure you honestly the great feeling in my mind now is that indifference and neglect about the businesses is wrong to dear Papa's memory.' She stressed Henry's willingness to become more involved.

Matthias replied with a note of the accounts, reminding her that he had often asked her to keep a record. He also added, tactfully but firmly: 'Altho' I am afraid I cannot make Henry useful, I shall be most glad to explain to him thoroughly the working of the businesses and the state of Papa's estate generally. I only wish Mordan also would take the time and trouble to master the matter.'

While Henry replied immediately, offering to meet Matthias in his chambers to look over the books relating to Joanna's property, George, characteristically, expressed no concern whatsoever. He set off for Lynmouth in Devon (which had been recommended to him as a picturesque spot by a fellow artist) on the evening of 21 June, thus missing the inaugural meeting of the fully-fledged Hogarth Club on 2 July. Before leaving, he had lent Rossetti '2 sketches of mine on the coast of Babbacombe as a help to the background of a delicate little drawing of a loving couple on the beach on a windy day that he is doing for Miss Herbert'. (Virginia Surtees notes that Rossetti detested working out of doors, and was in the habit of 'borrowing' backgrounds from his landscape-painting friends.) George had also visited Rossetti to see 'a large head in water-colour he is doing for [Miss Herbert] and a splendid design of Mary Magdalene meeting and jeered at by a lot of gay women on her way to the house of Jesus who is looking earnestly and absorbingly at her'.

Joanna now worried that the steep roads and gorges of Lynmouth would not only damage his hip but would make it difficult for him to reach the best sketching places. To add to her anxieties, she and Henry were having problems finding a suitable house. They had determined on Kensington, where many eminent painters already lived. Headed by George Frederic Watts and Frederick Leighton, this group of fashionable artists, known as the Holland Park Circle, centred on Little Holland House where Thoby and Sara Prinsep hosted regular salons and proved adept at finding patrons for their protégés. These included not only members of the aristocratic establishment, but also the newly-rich industrial magnates of Birmingham, Manchester and Liverpool. Patronage opened doors, and during this unique period, favoured artists could and did earn fortunes.

Joanna and Henry's first choice of house, on Campden Hill, had fallen through over the terms of the lease, and they were in constant touch with Matthias over possible alternatives. On 24 July it seemed that their second choice was well-advanced: Henry wrote to Matthias declaring: 'I am going to buy Burton's house',[156] and asking that £320 of Joanna's settlement should be invested in buying the ground rent. 'The house I can pay for besides having a little money to spare for the furniture.' As their tenancy of Clifton Road was coming to an end, they decided to move at once to the country, and by 17 August were installed at Joldwynds,[157] in the Surrey Downs, which they had rented from Henry's old friends, the Wettons.

It was, Joanna told Lilly, 'an old tumble down place; already we have been obliged to have workmen here to prevent the dining room wall falling in', but they were completely happy there. 'The house is placed on the south slope of Holmbury Hill,' she wrote to George on 19 August. 'We have a magnificent view before us stretching right over Sussex away to the sea, immediately below us the plain is richly wooded and behind us rises the hill, almost one flow of purple heather … Of course we have been sketching but the wind which has been very high unsettles me considerably, in fact I was nearly blown over yesterday, easel and all, my great hat which is tightly tied to my head acting as a sail and holding too much wind for its tiny freight.' (*Plates XXXV and XXXVI*)

She asked for news of his painting, lamented that he had not been able to spend a week or two with them – 'although we are supposed to rough it a bit, having very few tea-spoons and a cook who describes herself and very correctly thus: "I be no a genteel cook'm".' She told him: 'My "Peep-bo" deserves no approval, Maria's face which you saw and a piece of tablecloth painted from your mediaeval hangings being the only tolerable things in the picture – in fact almost the only things in it at all.'[158] (*Plate XLIV*)

To Hennie, on 31 August, she waxed lyrical about their country idyll:

> No visitors or tourists and very few human beings at all within a mile or two of us, but plenty of other beings, numerous from their being so seldom disturbed; partridges, hares, snakes, adders, ferrets, field mice, frogs, toads, moths, dragonflies etc. out of doors, and rats and mice indoors; which list you may think longer than pleasant, but the only things that really trouble me are the rats and mice when they help themselves to the contents of my larder. An adder fled out of my path the other day and tried to get up a bank. Having nothing but a canvas

[156] The purchase of a house proved very difficult. It is not clear where this particular property was situated, but as Burton owned the leases on at least two houses in Upper Phillimore Gardens where Joanna and Henry eventually settled, it may have been one of those. In the event they purchased number 9 which was owned jointly by a builder, Joseph Gordon Davis, and the landowner Charles Phillimore.

[157] The Wettons had let Joldens (presumably to provide an income) and had taken up residence in the nearby Joldwynds, which they lent to Joanna and Henry while they were in Australia.

[158] 'Peep-bo' was not finished until after Joanna had given birth to her second child. By then the characters in the picture had become the artist, Alice and Alice's nurse, Susan.

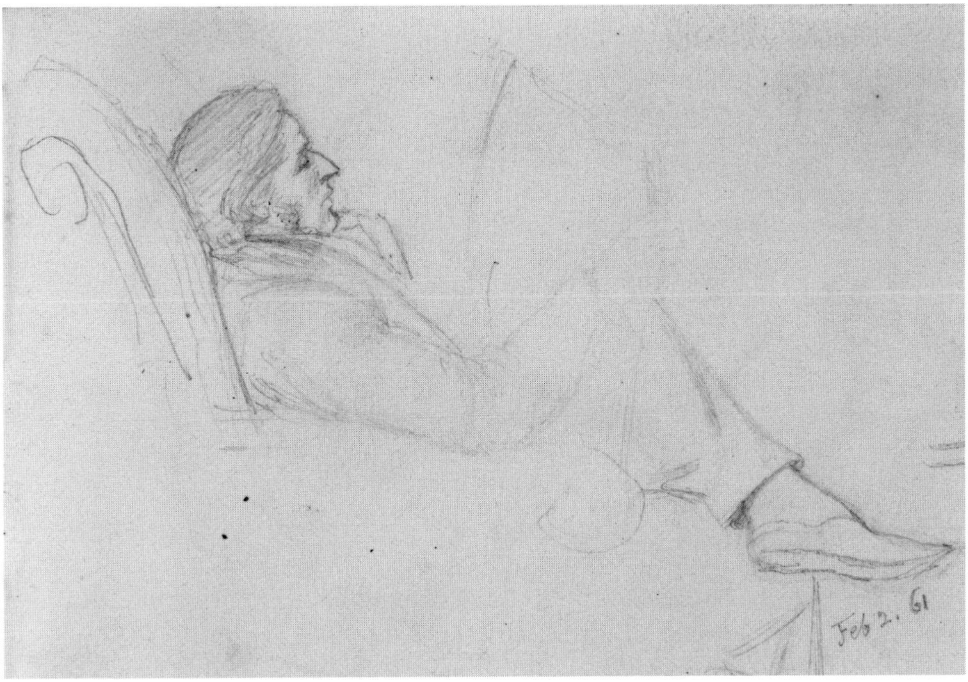

'Henry is full length on the sofa reading.' *Joanna Boyce Wells*

> in my hand I knocked him down three or four times with that and hit him with a large stone but he escaped at last down a hole. We have read Eliot's *Scenes from Clerical Life* and are delighted with the book. He [sic] has great humour and fine tender manly feelings.

Mindful that she might, in the light of her own happiness, appear indifferent to Hennie's old grief, she added: 'I did not know as I do now, how far better it would be if you and Harry were married; and my heart bleeds for you often when I am on the point of telling you how happy I am in my married life and how thankful I am to God for having over-ruled all my wicked selfish purposes as he has.' (*Plate XXXVII*)

She was indeed blissfully happy. To Matthias, on 4 September, she wrote:

> Annie, Nurse, baby and Edgar (the last unexpectedly) came down on Wednesday evening and Mordan yesterday. They all leave today about three o'clock. I hope, dear Mat, you will not feel hurt that I do not, (as I find it is possible to accommodate so many) ask you and Lilly to bring down the two boys and nurse, but though I would not

> on any account the Mordans should know it, we are scrupulous about having so many… Not only are we anxious not to take over-advantage of Mr Wetton's kindness, but we are in some degree at the mercy of his servants here, who may report all to him or his family, with their own views and exaggeration. Such things as this for instance; we have been obliged to turn the drawing room into a nursery these last few days – of course I had every care taken, thick drugget laid down etc.

If Henry was not quite as happy at Joldwynds as his wife, it was largely because his work was not progressing as he had hoped: 'Part of my disappointment at the result of my stay here arises doubtless from the fact of my using oil instead of water-colours. I paint slowly and of course badly, but this I ought to be somewhat prepared for.' Their visitors made demands upon his time, 'demands which have been duly honoured by this poor weak Ego, who has so much of the schoolboy still left in him that the sight of bowls on the lawn is always sufficient to turn him from the straight but narrow way which leads to his sketching stations'. 'Joney', he added, 'has quickly stepped in and secured one subject, the possession of which would have made me happy.'

He described how she had simply sat down at the side of the road, where a broad sheep-track led up a steep embankment crowned with gorse 'which waves about in the wind like giant hearse plumes'. There, he said, 'Mistress Joney does the very best thing possible, she paints it late in the evening, with a stormy sky and howling wind, up the steep bank a poor haggard woman and tired child are toiling. I think this is real poetry, it is by far the best subject she has ever hit upon, in my opinion.'[159]

For Joanna even the omnipresent rodents had their charms. She wrote to George: 'Augusta Wells, who is stopping with us, has been gone to bed some time, and charmed by the silence, the rats are frolicking about above and around, not in the room: they are supposed all to be dead by the rat-killer who came and poisoned them as he thought last week, but the drug seems to have acted like a mild dose of strychnine and given new strength and elasticity to their muscles.'

She was nearly five months pregnant when she wrote to Hennie on 10 October: 'It is a wet Sunday afternoon. Henry is full length on the sofa reading. He has been twitting me with neglect of you … The fact is he is an absurd boy.' Impending motherhood had not stopped her working, nor had it entirely banished the bouts of depression which frequently overcame her where her art was concerned:

[159] This picture was later entitled 'No Joy the Blowing Season Gives', a quotation from Tennyson. It was destroyed in the Bath air-raid, but a photograph survives (Plate 21).

> I am ashamed to say during the last week I have given way to a shameful fit of despondency about my painting… I have often thought before and do still think it is a kind of monomania… Henry is very good and patient with me and has cured me for the time, but I know the enemy will return, but at longer and longer intervals I will hope. One of the thoughts in connection with these things that stings me most is that I, who am so soon to be a mother, cannot even command myself, and another that while I do earnestly try and I believe in a great measure succeed in being a good wife to Henry at every other time, then I miserably fail …
>
> And now to tell you soberly what I have been doing. The principal thing is a landscape subject with largish figures which Henry wants to send to the Academy next year in default of both my figure pictures or in addition to one. It is a very simple subject, merely a barren sandy bank crowned with old nodding gorse, and a woman and child toiling up the path against the wind, time chosen being evening and a rainy sky. I am painting a study from nature of it and repeating it at home on a larger canvas changing the effect to what I want. Henry is delighted with the subject and I disgusted with the execution of it, but hope that patience will not fail to carry it out to the best of my power.

They still had nowhere to live in London. There were looming problems with the second house they had planned to buy, and yet they needed to leave Surrey. Joldwynds was draughty and damp and there was scarlet fever in the village: 'Do pray for my coming little one … the responsibility of having children seems to me very, very great, and through God's help only can a mother hope to fulfil her duties in any measure. I know you will pray for me too and for my husband.'

And then there were the plans for the family business. On their return, she and Henry went to live with Henry's mother at Stanhope Terrace and, once installed, Joanna again took up cudgels on the subject of their mother's objections to how it was being run. The exact nature of the argument is unclear from the surviving correspondence, but it concerned the payment of income tax. The idea now was to offer Mrs Boyce an indemnity which would protect her income while leaving the rest of the family free to conduct affairs as they wished. Mr Boyce's will, as labyrinthine a document as ever lawyer penned, can't have made the position any easier. Joanna told Matthias that, sooner than go to law or have the estate thrown into Chancery, she would let the matter go, but she was still hopeful that a solution might be found without resorting to litigation.

Other old quarrels died hard. In a letter to George on 19 November she wrote: 'I have just written a letter to Mr Boone asking him to try and get Mamma to give up my chest of drawers and worktable. Success very doubtful.'

By 10 December their second house purchase had fallen through and they were 'all adrift again.' Not until the 23rd, by which time her baby was imminent, that Joanna could report that they had at last obtained possession of a new house, 9 Upper Phillimore Gardens. With a permanent residence finally in sight, she braced herself once more to write to her mother, keeping a copy of her letter:

> Furnishing is now the one thing to be thought of. I should be much obliged if you would let me know the earliest day on which it would be convenient to you to give to the carrier, whom I will send, my chest of drawers and worktable. As I have not forgotten that when I applied for them before, you refused to deliver them, although they were the distinct unconditional gifts of my father. I have communicated with Mr Boone on the subject, and he has expressed his willingness to me to speak with you about it, if you wish.
>
> Please give my love to Bob. I manage to hear of him pretty often, both as to his health and his progress in his studies. I was delighted to hear of his great success at Dr Munro in the summer, and should have written him a few words of congratulation, but as I had received no acknowledgement whatever of my previous notes to him and to you, I was silent.

To her aunt Mary she was much more affectionate: 'I shall put your quilt on the bed the very first night we sleep in our own house. Everything in the room will be new and beautiful of its kind, and so, well in keeping with your cunning handiwork.'

Needless to say, the reply Joanna received from her mother was profoundly unsatisfactory. It elicited from Joanna this steely and determined response, which of course was also carefully copied:

> I shall without delay give Lanning an order to make a chest of drawers and worktable in every respect precisely like those you withhold from me, and of which I believe Lanning was the maker. I will send him to Park Place trusting you will allow him to make the necessary

> measurements. You will thus replace property, which I must repeat is mine, being the unconditional gift of my father and as entirely my own as any book or article of jewellery he gave me, and so any allusion to his will is quite irrelevant to the subject ... When Lanning has finished the furniture, I will send in the receipted bill to you ... Perhaps you may then change your mind and, permitting me to have the old ones, take the new ones in their place ... The matter will then be ended between us.

Mrs Boyce now defended her failure to acknowledge her daughter's existence since her marriage by saying that she had not known her address. Joanna dismissed this with the contempt she must have felt it deserved – she had after all been in constant touch with other members of her family. She sent her love to Bob: 'I think of him much and often, and wonder whether your keeping him separated and estranged from me and all of us can be to his advantage.'

To Bob she wrote crisply (again keeping a copy): 'If you would give me news of yourself, your studies or anything that concerns you, instead of advice, of which I do not stand in need and which you ought to feel diffidence in offering, I should be delighted to hear from you.'

Though George had left London before the Hogarth Club was officially launched, it was his first port of call on his return. After his five-month sojourn in Devon, where the birds enchanted him – 'there are plenty of my old favourites, the water ouzels, and I have seen one splendid kingfisher' – he meandered back to London, arriving at the end of November. Rossetti had been busy. George visited him on 15 December:

> The new things that I noticed were an intensely impressive water-colour of the Virgin in the house of John, the latter seated at the window and striking a light and looking out upon Jerusalem at twilight. The Virgin is spinning. A Knight girded for combat embracing his Lady Love. Several studies of Miss Herbert (Mrs Crabbe). A most beautiful pen-and-ink study of Topsy's 'stunner' at Oxford[160]... We went off at dusk and dined at the Cock, and afterwards adjourned to 24 Dean Street, Soho, to see 'Fanny'. Interesting face and jolly hair and engaging disposition.[161]

160 This was Jane Burden, who had modelled for the Oxford murals and became William 'Topsy' Morris's wife.

161 Fanny Cornforth (1824–1906). From now on a fixture in both Rossetti's and George's lives. She was much admired by the PRB artists for (among other things) her mass of corn-coloured hair.

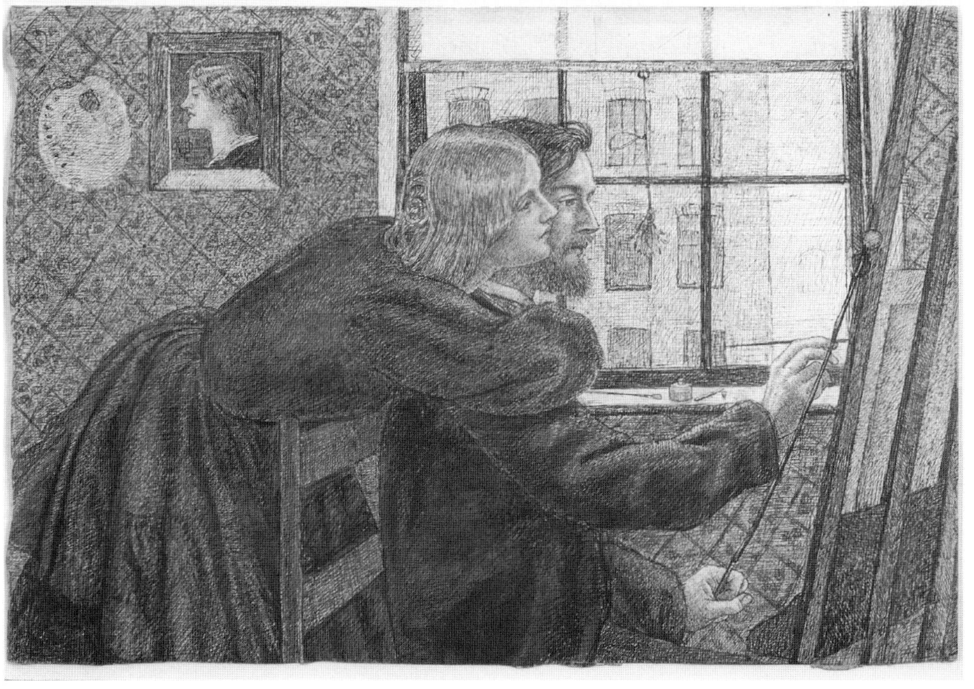

George and Fanny Cornforth at Chatham Place *D.G. Rosetti*

Fanny Cornforth first came to the attention of the Pre-Raphaelites when Ford Madox Brown saw her in Red Lion Square. She modelled for one of Rossetti's most famous pictures, 'Bocca Baciata' which was purchased by George. After Lizzie Siddal's death, she seems to have moved in with Rossetti, but she was certainly fond of George too, and this drawing is evidence of their three-way affection

According to Virginia Surtees, Fanny Cornforth first came to the attention of the PRB artists in early 1858 when Ford Madox Brown saw her in Red Lion Square. Though possibly at one time a prostitute, she was now well established as a model and, when George encountered her, was also sitting to Spencer Stanhope, who occupied the floor below Rossetti's, and was 'painting on his picture of a gay woman in her room by side of Thames at her toilet'.

On 26 December, George went to see Madox Brown and his 'Work' picture. 'Some fine stuff in it, but will scarcely be appreciated but by a few'.[162] On the 27th he reported that Rossetti had taken away his 'Caper nimbly' and

[162] 'Work' took Ford Madox Brown twelve years to complete and, with its heroic portrayal of the working classes at their labours, demonstrated a Pre-Raphaelite concern with social realism.

'Annunciation' pictures to work upon … He wants to convert the former into a Borgia subject. He said it was one of the best drawings he ever did.'

There is no doubt that George was smitten with Fanny. On 17 January 1859, he recorded meeting her at the Argyll Rooms:[163] 'Took her to supper at Quinns. She was in considerable trepidation lest Rossetti should come in – and lo! He did so.'

❖

George was abruptly diverted from such distractions by Joanna's early confinement. Sidney Boyce Wells was born at four in the morning on 19 January 1859. George wrote to Henry: 'I hail the good news with much delight. I had no idea the moment was so near at hand. I shall take it as a kindness if you will drop me but one line tomorrow to say how Joney and the youngster are going on.'

Henry was both anxious and joyful: 'At once I write you the "one line". Joney goes on well, but in these cases the patient is less bright and healthy looking on the second, third and fourth days than on the first. We have to be very careful with her, but the doctor assures me all is quite well and right. Annie saw her today. She is the only visitor allowed to enter the room. The boy is voted a very decent looking animal, – and Joney declares he has a good-shaped head – but "my eye" isn't he red!'

George swiftly replied: 'Couldn't you manage to appropriate some of the youngster's rubicundity, which seems to have filled you with such amazement, before it fades away? As I am curious to know the exact hue, I hope you'll match it carefully on your palette and keep for future use and reference. With love to Joney and glorying in my impudence.'

From Joanna's mother and brother Bob arrived two cards 'with kind enquiries'. Henry reported to George that he had returned 'a short, but for me sufficiently civil answer.' George himself first saw the new baby on 29 January, observing that 'the little kid rather a good-looking little animal – dark skinned, with no want of nose'.

George's note to his sister was full of droll affection. He bade her 'treasure up the sayings of the Nurse' and informed her that Henry had danced divinely at a gathering the night before. He was sorry she would be in no condition to join the 'Punch and Judy' entertainment on 5 February, which he later eloquently described in his diary:

[163] According to Virginia Surtees, a rather low supper and dancing house.

> At about ¼ to 3 our little friends with their attendants began to arrive to see our 'Punch and Judy' show. Clara, Ada and Edgar Mordan with Anne Kennedy, Bertie and Lilly, Harry and Clem Ridley with Lizzie Ridley, Burges's youngest sister, little Edmund Pugin, Arthur Meredith with his father,[164] May Poynter and her Mother, two little girl Aitchisons with their Mother, Nellie and Annie and little Sarah also witnessed the show, which went off very successfully – the Punch being an excellent one. We had bargained for the entire drama and so had the constable and the doctor, Joey the clown, Jack Ketch, Jim Crow, Shallaballa, the ghost and the coffin (a most humorous well-acted personage), who was constantly prefacing his remarks by Eh! Eh! and who objected to have that ugly thing, the gallows, erected in front of his house.
>
> The adults seemed to enjoy the affair as much as the children. After the 'Punch' all came up to partake of fruits, jams and ginger beer etc, in my room … On their leaving I presented Edgar, Arthur Meredith, Bertie and Harry and Clem with a 'Punch and Judy' book.

Reports on both mother and baby were reassuring. On 1 February Joanna was still 'on her back'. She was very weak, she told her aunt Mary, 'but as the doctor orders me lots of meat, wine *ad libitum*, and tonic medicine three times a day, I shall soon be as strong as a horse … On state occasions your quilt is spread over me to the admiration of every one. In fact I am quite jealous of it, for when that is to be seen no one looks at anything else in the room.'

To George she wrote: 'Baby and I are getting on capitally. I think he will be like all of us as children, a regular Turk, he keeps his lungs and muscles in splendid order, by fits of screaming and kicking and struggling, night and day.' The nurse was living up to expectations: '[She] makes some first-rate Malaprops. She calls baby "a beautiful little cubit" meaning Cupid, and others that are almost dangerous for a weak "hysterical female".'

George had bought her 'Elgiva' and on 4 February she wrote to thank him for it: 'I am very glad you do not regret the "Elgiva" bargain. I must confess that I by no means regard "the flimsy"[165] as flimsy nowadays. I and the little one are daily making away with too much for that. I wish I could sell more pictures and seriously (no) think of hitting off a few such things as old Leigh elegantly named "pot-boilers".' She added 'Next time you see Henry dancing divinely give his horizontal coat tails a sly tug and pull him down a peg.'

164 George Meredith, the novelist.
165 'Flimsy' was a slang term for a banknote.

That she was intensely happy as a wife and mother was clear from the lightness and affection of her correspondence – this, a note to her husband, sent after him to his studio on Valentine's Day:

> My darling boy,
> Just two lines to let you know that your three letters are stamped and posted – and to tell you I have been fidgeting ever since you left that I did not ask you if you had got rid of your headache and felt better this morning. I sent Nurse down after you, but you were gone. Before falling off to sleep I had been thinking about you, and during the few minutes you were in my room as usual I forgot the one thing I most wished to remember.
>
> Baby is sleeping like a top.
> Your own
> Joney
>
> Monday Feb. 14
>
> By the bye – this is your Valentine. You ought to have a 'Cubit' in it.

Devastatingly, her sister Anne's little boy died in the early hours of 25 February, on his first birthday. He had been a fragile baby. Joanna wrote from Corinth Villa to her aunt Mary: 'Poor Annie is in great grief and Mordan too. The sisters do not yet know of it. Such a splendid little fellow he was. Now thank God he is at rest, poor little sufferer.'

Henry, she told Matthias, was painting at his Stratford Place studio every night until 10 pm – 'poor deserted creature am I not?' – while she worked to finish two landscapes begun at Joldwynds. The Royal Academy exhibition loomed. She wrote to George hoping that he had got his pictures satisfactorily finished. Her own were in 'a hideous state'. In the event, 'Homestead on the Surrey Hills' was accepted by the Royal Academy, while her 'dark' painting of the woman and child toiling up a steep bank was rejected.

George, meanwhile, was almost certainly sharing Fanny's favours with his friend. Rossetti's love life was, in any case, a muddle. He once told William Allingham that he had given up a particular 'stunner' (she served tables at the Belle Sauvage Inn on Ludgate Hill) 'partly from a wish to narrow the circle of flirtations in which she had begun to figure a little'. On 11 February, George gave Fanny a sovereign to help her in the furnishing of her new house, and on

24 March he, Fanny and Rossetti went to the zoological gardens 'where D. G. R. wanted to draw a fawn for his Magdalen drawing. We stayed there for 3 or 4 hours, most amused by the brown bear, wombat and some owls'. On 11 April he 'gave Fanny a silver thimble I had promised her, and made a slight sketch of her'.

On 26 April, he left London for a prolonged stay at Streatley-on-Thames, an ancient town with the most ravishing river scenes to paint. He hoped that Joanna, Henry and the baby would come and visit him there, but Joanna decided against it for several reasons. Henry had 'the Marchioness of Stafford sitting to him for a head',[166] they had spent much more than they expected on the house, and the weather, lovely as it was, was too hot for her. Her boy, she told him, 'flourisheth extremely'. The news of their brother, however, was less positive: 'I am afraid there is trouble in store for us all about poor Bob. A kind of religious melancholy seems to be fastening upon him. Mamma seems to be desirous to be on friendly terms with us all again ... Do let me hear what you are painting. I am working at the baby picture, but it's slow work, especially as what I painted blue-green overnight, I found yellow-green in the morning – beware, oh beware of verdigris, it is the siren of colours ... Baby is jolly, and finds a new delight in tearing at his ears, believing them to be the rosettes of his hat which he hates.'

Bob's health began to deteriorate rapidly. On receiving a telegram from Ilfracombe to say that he was 'ill and in danger', Mrs Boyce at last sent for Joanna. She was in two minds how to respond and threw the burden of the decision on Henry, immediately despatching a note round to him at his studio and asking him to 'send word by bearer': 'Mamma is really not fit to travel alone; she has no servant who [she] can she take with her. Shall I go? ... If you think I ought not, or I had better not go – only say so.'

Of course she went. She wrote to him next from Ilfracombe, where George had joined them:

> Poor Bob is in the very greatest danger – still there is hope – the next twenty-four hours will decide. He seemed very glad to see me, but he can scarcely speak. George is with us. We got here by eight this morning, all three well. We have three medical men – a Dr Budd of Barnstaple, undoubtedly a first rate man, a Dr Stubbs of Ilfracombe, who is accustomed to act with him, and a Mr Wright from London, surgeon at Middlesex Hospital. Hoping to have good accounts of yourself and my dear baby.

[166] This miniature was shown at the Royal Academy Summer Exhibition of 1860.

Any hopes were ill-founded. Bob died on 14 July. 'A more gentle peaceful death than poor Bob's could not be,' Joanna told Henry:

> In the afternoon of Wednesday he appeared to be getting rapidly worse. We all stayed with him expecting he would be taken very quickly. The clergyman came and he received the sacrament. He sent his love to all of our family who were absent – to you twice over. He was still troubled with some doubt about the Roman and Protestant creeds. We tried to comfort him and I believe quite succeeded. He prayed silently and with intense earnestness for some minutes and then asked us to sing a hymn. We sang the evening hymn, he joining in with almost a loud voice, though it was a great effort to him to pronounce the words. We believed him to be sinking, but more than once he said he did not feel so very ill, and if he might get out of bed and stand on the floor he should get well again, and he asked if it were not his duty to try to live if he could. We of course encouraged and moved him, putting his legs over the side of the bed and supported him there. He said he was hungry. We told him he might have what he liked. Bread and cheese was what he seemed mostly to wish for. This he ate with relish, insisting on feeding himself exactly as though he were well and taking lunch with us; also he drank a good deal of wine and soda water and ate dry biscuit and sponge cake – afterwards a cup of coffee … The doctor declared him much better – that he might recover, but it would be little short of a miracle. I left awe struck and dared not hope … But he soon changed for the worse again. It was arranged that I should sit up with the London doctor until 5 o'clock in the morning, and then Mamma and George to get up and take our places. It was not long before his breathing became so oppressed and his pulse so low that the doctor agreed with me I must wake them. From this time he became gradually worse, rallying slightly occasionally until his death at ½ past 10 last night. An hour or two before, he became perfectly conscious for a few minutes, and kissed us each, recognising us individually …
>
> We leave tomorrow Saturday … dear Bob will be carried in a hearse from here to Barnstaple, and at the London station a hearse will be in waiting to carry him to Park Place from whence, as soon as arrangements can be made for the funeral, he will be carried to Kensal Green. I shall come straight home from the station (on Sunday morning) … I am quite well, though almost knocked up last night.

After Bob's death, George paid a brief visit to London on 23 July, where 'D. G. Rossetti persuaded me into giving him £40 commission for an oil portrait of Fanny, and asked me for £20 down which I could not refuse … He pleaded being very hard up, or I should hardly have let him have so much tin on account. I brought away my Borgia drawing.'

There was yet more trouble with Mrs Boyce. Joanna wrote to Matthias on 12 August, offering to pay the Ilfracombe expenses, and commiserating: 'I am deeply shocked (and ashamed) at Mamma's conduct just now. As for imputations against you, it makes me mad to think of her daring to cast them … Do not worry about it – we all know you and we all know her, and that means a great deal – all that you need care about.'

Mrs Boyce's complaints, as Joanna told George on 16 August, concerned Bob's money: 'She acknowledges she is not in want of [it], but nevertheless is not easy without it … Whether I will or no, this conduct destroys my belief in her suffering real grief for the loss of dear Bob, else, how could she be so grasping, so cruel and so unjust.'

She had heard from George on the 14th that he had once again hurt his hip getting out of an omnibus. That same day, she told him, Henry had attended Lady Waldegrave's fête at Strawberry Hill – 'Lady W.'s portrait gallery principally painted by Sant of luring beauties[167] … Bands, fruit, ices, dancing, games, Lady W. and some of the other ladies in grand style, the Duc and Duchesse d'Aumale etc being principal entertainments'. He had also attended the Royal Academy soirée – 'a much better meet than usual'. He was now installed at Littlecote near Hungerford, finishing the full-length portrait of Mrs Popham which he had begun in Rome. Joanna's letters to him were, understandably full of the baby. She had had a chance to compare her 'little tiny Puck' with Mrs Grainger's 'fair, fat, solid boy', and was concerned that all the work on the house – 'what with size, oil paint, and, I suppose soon, varnish' – would not be good for his health. 'I can't help thinking that instead of our going to the Lakes at once, we ought for the little man's sake to settle him in the country first.'

The main item of gossip concerned the author of *Adam Bede*, recently revealed to be 'a Miss Evans': 'I do not yet really believe it. It prove to be the truth, or the same thing, that the book is the joint production of Lewes and Miss Evans I should like to know what Carlyle would say to it.' Later she added: 'I

[167] James Sant (1820–1916). Fashionable genre and portrait painter.

suppose we must swallow the fact that Miss Evans is George Eliot. The mouthful is nauseous enough to me' – an intriguing reaction from a woman who did not in the least shrink from competing in a man's world.

Anne had invited Mrs Boyce to tea at Corinth Villa, telling her that Joanna and Sidney would be present: 'so we are in for it'.

Hennie had been to see the baby: 'His thinness no longer distresses her, but his large eyes, dear round little face, his briskness and his intelligence delight her. She still calls him a new sort of baby – my own peculiar and exquisite invention.' Joanna's painting of him, which she began later in the year, bears out his undeniable but singular charm.

10

THE GREATEST HAPPINESS ON EARTH

'Just when we're safest, there's a sunset touch ...'

'Bishop Blougram's Apology'

Towards the end of August 1859, Joanna and Henry set off for a 'flying trip to the Lakes', leaving Sidney behind. Henry's notes and journal, with added jottings from his wife, give an idea of the industrious nature of such holidays. Even though Joanna was not well for at least part of the trip, a great deal of sight-seeing was packed in – the waterfall at Rydal where Henry sketched a hut built against a huge piece of rock and Joanna sketched the old man who owned it, the Eagle Crag of Helvellyn, Patterdale church, Ullswater and Keswick where they joined Mrs Wade Browne and the Farwell girls. The following day they ascended to the David Stones. Joanna wrote: 'On our way caught in a heavy shower. Bertha and Henry being "waterproof" sat on a bank under a hedge, Emma on Bertha's lap, I on Henry's, and a queer group we must have made. Henry sketched the sisters. Arrived at the Druid Circle, the rain poured down. I made a scribble of H. squatting for shelter against a Druid Stone!!"

On the following day Joanna was confined to bed, probably as a result of the drenching she had received. While Emma and Mrs Wade Browne remained with her, the 'waterproof' Henry and Bertha went to visit 'Old Martin', who had known Southey, Coleridge and Wordsworth: 'The old man is 75 and quite blind,' wrote Henry; 'he has a good head and he is of marble paleness. I made a pencil sketch of his head, while I had my gossip. The old man told me before I left that he "was much uplifted with the clack with me".'

They postponed their return to Windermere so that Joanna could see the Falls of Lodore. Though still weak, she and Henry walked there and to the Bowder Stone, and, as Bertha was anxious to see Wastwater, they went, Joanna mounted on a pony, up the Sty Head Pass and down the side of Great Gable, sketching all the way.

Back in London and reunited with Sidney, they found that 'the almost fabulous accounts of his fattening, which we had received, seemed true'. Joanna was delighted. She wrote to Matthias on 8 September: 'He is so much fatter and bonnier that one would hardly have taken him for the same child. He sleeps well and has a tremendous appetite and is livelier than ever.' She and Henry attributed this improvement to the addition of Oswego corn-flour to his diet.[168]

Shortly after their return, the whole family, baby and nurse included, decamped to Stoatley Farm in Haslemere while work continued on the house in Upper Phillimore Gardens. George, meanwhile, was still at Streatley. His picture, 'Streatley Mill', would turn out to be one of his best paintings, though he was characteristically sardonic about his endeavours: 'I shouldn't wonder if some day I make as much as £20 – or say £30 – a year by my profession. I live, at least, in great hope thereof. One might almost be induced to get married on the splendour of such circumstances.'

Rossetti had written to him on 5 September, including a sketch for the portrait of Fanny that George had commissioned, 'which you will see has taken after all a rather Venetian aspect', and on the 14th Joanna also wrote in the hopes that he might pay them a visit at Haslemere. The idea of immortalising Sidney was taking shape: 'Baby does possess an exiguous beauty of form, too exiguous perhaps. I want sadly to paint him, but is it possible?' She had finished 'my little buttercup picture' – 'Do I Like Butter?' – which she intended for Ernest Gambart's Winter Exhibition, along with 'No Joy the Blowing Season Gives'. (*Plates XXXVIII and XXXIX*)

Henry, she told George, had brought down an immense ivory:

> on which he intends painting our two precious selves – as though taken on one of our mountain excursions in Italy – I on donkey-back.[169] He scarcely hopes to complete it for the Academy, as he has three full lengths to finish for the next exhibition, Lady Waldegrave, Mrs Popham, and Lady Stafford with a background chiefly composed of rhododendrons in bloom.[170] This background he painted last spring, – but the whole figure has to be done. I am very vexed you did not see a small miniature of Lady Stafford just finished. It is very lovely in

[168] Oswego corn-flour, derived from maize, was introduced in 1850 by the firm of T. Kingsford & Son of Oswego County, NY, in the United States. It was marketed as particularly pure, wholesome and nutritious, and was an instant success.

[169] This wonderful painting is reproduced as Plate I. The ivory has peeled away from its backing over the years and cracked, but by using an excellent black and white image taken by Alice's son, Philip Street, on 20 July 1925, and scanning the original to obtain the colouring, it has been possible – thanks to the skills of John Roberts – to recreate it with considerable accuracy.

[170] Their daughter Alice comments: 'This large miniature of Lady Stafford can never have been finished to my father's satisfaction, for it was found after his death wrapped up, lying in a drawer. The background of rhododendrons and the figure and dress are exquisitely painted, but the head is characterless and disappointing.' It was destroyed in 1942.

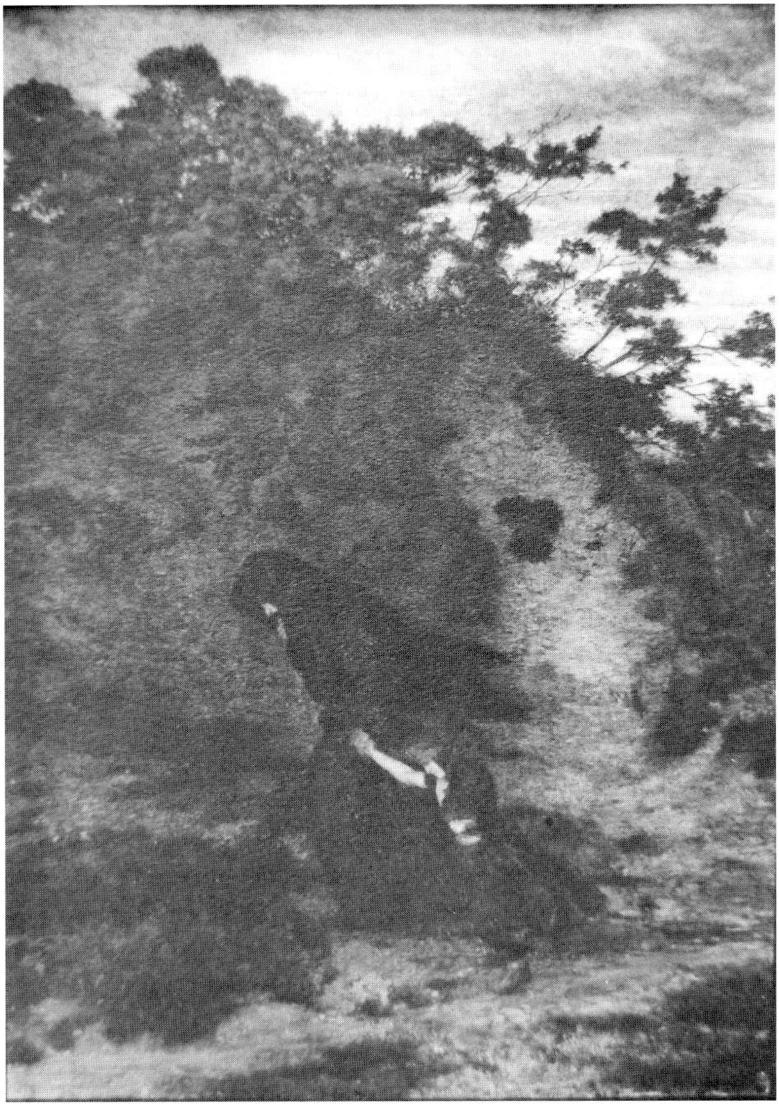

No Joy the Blowing Season Gives *Joanna Boyce*

'It is a very simple subject,' wrote Joanna on 10th October 1858 'merely a barren sandy bank, crowned with old nodding gorse, and a woman and child toiling up the path against the wind.' The painting was sold to Thomas Plint, 'owner of several Millais and Rossettis' at Gambart's Winter Exhibition in 1859. It was destroyed in 1942.

> colour, and a head, which, I think, is a good deal to your fancy – lovely to mine. She has had four photographs of it mounted with diamonds for four lady admirers ... 'Syd' is bonny, although he is suffering from an attack of the sniffles, which mingles harmoniously with an effusion of the slobbers.

George did not come. On 23 September Joanna was writing plaintively: 'Why have you not been to see us?' and though his own letter to her, written on the same day, indicated that he hoped to spend a few days with them before their return to London, his picture of the mill – 'its progress awfully impeded by violent wind and showers' – was of more immediate concern.

Money was an issue – Henry wrote to Matthias, also on the 23rd, to say that he was 'very low at my Bank' while 'good cash connected with my studio earnings remains still in other pockets, and cannot be brought into mine at this season without begging letters – which I abhor'. On the subject of Matthias's daughter Florence, who was not thriving as her parents wished, he recommended the Oswego corn-flour that had been so efficacious in Sidney's case.

No decisions had yet been made about Bob's tombstone and both Mrs Boyce's suggestions were disapproved of by George, the second being 'more objectionable than the first.' In his letter to Joanna, he suggested that it would be better 'to add instead a few words in testimony of his worth and character – such as "in Christian charity and resignation"'. With regard to their mother, he wrote: 'You are aware she is at present at Scarborough with Mr Hall and intends returning at the end of the month. She says the place and hotel routine suit her, but fears Mr Hall is sadly out of his element.' He added that Joanna had so taken to cracking up Henry's things that he was strongly inclined 'to commence a vigorous attack in the opposite direction', in order to keep him in a healthy state of mind.

Joanna ruefully confessed: 'Perhaps I do really admire his things more than is good for him. You men are so easily puffed up.' She was delighted, however, that 'folks are opening up their eyes and purses to the beauties of your drawings. You put too low a price on your things, I think.' She was still hopeful of a visit when she wrote to him on 7 October: 'If, after the above lively description of the way in which we mean to behave to you, you still can relish the idea, we shall be delighted at the sight of your emaciated person, and Henry promises to be more than usually charming and entertaining as soon as dusk sets in, to make up for the rest of the day.'

George was in London by 13 October, when he visited Rossetti's studio to admire the painting he had commissioned – 'a splendid portrait of Fanny ...

in late 16th century costume'.[171] On the 15th he visited Fanny bearing apples and walnuts, and was told that Rossetti was in the habit of sitting in her 'large chair o'nights reading Balzac's novels', but he soon returned to the country.

For Joanna, 'No Joy the Blowing Season Gives', shown at Ernest Gambart's Winter Exhibition, finally reaped its reward. According to George, in a letter dated 20 November, the following accolade appeared in the *Spectator*: 'A picture by Mrs Wells [of] a woman and child plodding home against the boring wind along a lane side under the close of evening, is striking for the effect of natural gloom; it is a painted thought, and very simply painted.'

In letters to George dated 6 and 13 December, Joanna expressed her pleasure at notices in both the *Spectator* and *The Times*, adding that Gambart had sold the painting to a 'Mr Plenth [sic][172] of Leeds, owner of several Millais and Rossettis … The little buttercup girl is still for sale. Your "Impending Catastrophe" looks capital and Henry's landscape also and your Venice Study. Millais has a lovely little picture, a study of the subject of my Millais. Hunt has a study of a little girl singing – universally disliked – and deservedly so, I think, flesh common in colour and painting.'

She also told him that Henry had joined the South Middlesex Rifle Corps on the first night that the Kensington division was formed and attended drill regularly. The outbreak of war earlier in the year between France, Piedmont and Austria had increased Britain's deep-seated fear of invasion from France, and there was a nationwide appeal for able-bodied volunteers who could be called up in such an event. Joanna commented: 'More than one Artists' Corps is afloat or trying to float.' She and Henry had received notice of at least two organised by their Pre-Raphaelite friends, but Henry remained with the Kensington division on the grounds that it made more sense 'to join the Corps of the neighbourhood in which you live and of which the drill and practising ground is nearest to you. One volunteers because one is an Englishman and not because one is an artist.'

She also alluded to her brother's complicated love-life: 'Burges and Smallfield dined here together the week before last. Burges always talks tenderly about you and did on this occasion, and wanted to know whether you were not in a very susceptible state about Lizzie Ridley – how could I answer him?'

George remained in Streatley until early December. As he told Joanna on 20 November, 'You may well wonder at my still being [here] … I stayed purposely to make a few colour-memoranda now in the time of the autumnal tints, which by the way are far from as bright and rich as they were last autumn.

171 'Boccas Baciata'

172 Thomas Plint was a Leeds stockbroker who built up one of the most impressive collections of Pre-Raphaelite art in the country.

But, as I am never long without being in some pickle or other, this time I have strained myself a little in rowing, and although not badly it has been sufficient to make a differing of at least three weeks in my work.'

From Streatley, he went straight to St Lawrence, in the Isle of Wight, where he worked on a water-colour entitled 'Undercliff' before the bad weather drove him back to London on 20 December. On the 22nd, he received a visit from Annie Miller, 'in an excited state' and seeking work as a model. 'All was broken off between her and Hunt. I pitied the poor girl very much, by reason of the distraction of her mind and heart.' He went straight away to Hunt to suggest that rather than sitting for a stranger, he, George should employ her and Hunt agreed. 'Finding that he could not get her to do what he wanted to make her a desirable wife for him, nor to wean herself from old objectionable habits, he had broken off the engagement; but the whole affair had preyed on his mind for years.' On 28 December, she came and sat for him and Rossetti: 'She looked more beautiful than ever.'

Mystery surrounds a powerful landscape, 'Shanklin, Isle of Wight', which was painted not by George but by Joanna. (*Plate XL*)The date of its composition is usually given as 1859 but it is highly unlikely that – heavily pregnant – Joanna would have visited George at that time and even more unlikely that this would have passed without comment. There is no reference to any visit to the Isle of Wight, with or without Henry, in any of their surviving diaries and correspondence: and yet the authorship of the painting is not in dispute. Perhaps she made the picture from sketches or photographs by George, to occupy herself during the late stages of her pregnancy. Perhaps it is a much earlier work undertaken on a family visit of which no record survives.[173] It demonstrates a close attention to the local geology which, thanks to Ruskin's preoccupation with 'strata', was a feature of early Pre-Raphaelitism, and though Joanna continued to paint landscapes throughout her career, her style became more impressionistic. It's an intriguing conundrum.

❈

On 4 January 1860 Joanna gave birth to their second child, Alice Joanna. The arrival, as with Sidney's, took her by surprise. She had been to hear Michael Faraday[174] lecture the previous afternoon, and their friend Wetton, who was staying

173 Some experts, including Pamela Gerrish Nunn in her exhibition catalogue for *Pre-Raphaelite Women Artists* (Manchester 1997), do not date the painting.

174 Michael Faraday (1791–1867). One of the most influential of all nineteenth-century scientists. His research into electromagnetism and electrochemistry led to electricity being transformed from a curiosity into a powerful technology. He instituted Friday evening discourses and the Christmas lectures at the Royal Institution, both of which continue to this day, and he himself gave the Christmas lectures a record nineteen times.

with them, was promptly co-opted as Alice's godfather. Henry was working at Stratford Place, and her notes to him are small windows into their family life: 'Your little girlie is flourishing. Sidney's interest in her increases. His "hoo-ees and oh dears" get louder, but he cannot make up his mind to kiss her. [Mat], Lilly and Bertie came in a fly today. Bertie looked very pretty. Mat, I fancied out of spirits.'

George, who had returned to the Isle of Wight in early January to finish his painting of the 'Undercliff' (it was later sold to Francis Astley for 36 guineas), came back to London and visited his sister and the new baby on 15 January: 'The little girl has pretty hands and feet.' He spent a great deal of time at the Hogarth Club, where, on 30 January, he met William Morris's wife, Jane, for the first time, and found himself 'surprised at the fine and beautiful character of her face'.

Rossetti was much in evidence. It seemed that whenever Annie Miller sat to him, Rossetti appeared and carried her off. On 20 February he noted: 'Rossetti came in towards dusk and touched on my oil portrait of her begun, and went away with her.' Rossetti was at the time working on a commission for Llandaff Cathedral, and on the same day George records him 'painting from a little naked child that was squalling awfully'. On the 27th he wrote: 'Miss Miller came to sit to me, but Rossetti coming in soon after, I did scarcely any work. D. G. R. put his initials to the Borgia and "Belle Dame sans Merci" drawings.'

Henry took his volunteering seriously; on 25 February he wrote to Matthias: 'Last Thursday my private squad had a few minutes of bayonet exercise. It was hard work and set every muscle in my body quivering … Last Wednesday my corps paraded in Hyde Park, 400 strong, making a goodly-looking battalion.' There was no sign, however, that George had any intention of joining him. Indeed, the damage to his hip would probably have ruled it out. His diary paints a picture of an artist's social and working life, including meetings with 'a Yankee painter of the name of Stillman[175] with whom I had an interesting chat and exchanged cards', and, at the National Gallery, 'a Gallicized Yankee, Whistler[176] by name, who was very amusing and with whom I walked part of the way home.'

On 12 March, the Hogarth Club had a model for the first time, and he, Prinsep, Brett,[177] Burne-Jones, W. M. Rossetti and Major Gillum – patron,

[175] William James Stillman (1828–1901). Journalist and painter, He fell under the spell of Ruskin, Millais and Rossetti and became known as the 'American Pre-Raphaelite'.

[176] James Abbott McNeill Whistler (1834–1903). He studied in Paris before settling in London in 1859. He became known for what one critic called his 'recklessly bold manner', and though he was associated with the Pre-Raphaelites, his style was more in tune with the Aesthetic movement. He and Ruskin famously came to blows over one of his 'Nocturnes'.

[177] John Brett (1830–1902). Pre-Raphaelite landscape painter with an interest in portraiture who was a disciple of Ruskin. His sister Rosa was also a painter.

amateur painter and founding member of the club – gathered to draw her. On 16 March: 'Met Millais at dinner at Joney's and Wells'. He spoke of my drawings at the Hogarth in very high terms. We had a fight about the Academy. He looked at Joney's Boys' Crusade picture and suggested some improvements.' (*Plate XLI*)

The Royal Academy was the subject of vigorous debate at that time, not least because Millais and Holman Hunt had begun to hanker after the respectability the Royal Academy could bestow, while George and Rossetti continued to regard it with dark suspicion: indeed, Rossetti never exhibited there. During 1859 a petition protesting against the all-male membership of the Royal Academy Schools was presented, and in 1860 the painter Laura Herford[178] submitted a picture signed A. L. Herford as an application for membership. She was accepted. After that, a small quota of female students was grudgingly admitted, but they were not allowed to attend the nude life classes. Yet women painters enjoyed some distinguished support: David Roberts[179] was overheard by George Eliot saying, 'If ever one sees a fine picture now it is by a woman.'

On 17 April George took Joanna and Henry to meet Ruskin for the first time: 'He was very courteous and kind, and showed us a lot of beautiful Turner drawings.'

By the end of the month George was off again – this time to Mapledurham, a small village on the north bank of the Thames in Oxfordshire, where he stayed at the King's Arms. Before he left, he delivered a peacock's feather to Burne-Jones, and presented Joanna with a copy of William Allingham's *Nightingale Valley*, bound in rough calf. This had already been sent back to Bumpus's once as being 'so badly bound and contrary to direction that I returned it'. George had exacting standards. No wonder Henry had been reluctant to take responsibility for the *Nineteenth-Century Poets*.

On 7 May George was back in London: 'To Academy early in the morning, imagining that as my Isle of Wight had been accepted, it would be hung. It was not hung, so I retired ignominiously.' 'Joney's picture of the Boys' Crusade', he added, 'most shamefully and unjustly hung.' 'My poor "Crusade",' wrote Joanna to George on 9 May. 'I only wish it had shared the fate of Sidney' – this, a reference to her portrait of her son, which had been rejected. (*Plate XXXVIII*)

178 The pioneering Anne Laura Herford (1831–70) was the aunt of Helen Paterson, also an artist, famous for her cottage paintings, who later married the poet William Allingham.

179 David Roberts (1796–1864). Revered Royal Academician, particularly famous for his series of detailed lithographs covering the Holy Land, Syria, Idumea, Arabia, Egypt and Nubia which were published 1842–49.

George replied immediately:

> In all sincerity I think it about the meanest and most unjust act I remember the Academy hangmen to have committed, for the rejection of the picture would have been one of comparative mercy and courtesy. I hope you will send the picture to Liverpool and exhibit little Syd on the first good opportunity. Without taking any trouble to enquire into the Academy's doings this year, except as regards my own two drawings, I perceive that they have rejected Arthur Hughes's picture, which I was told was excellent, two of Inchbold's – the one accepted being villainously placed … Fortunately Henry's miniatures, I found, were universally appreciated and admired.

The weather, he said, was very cold and windy, but he had begun a painting of an 'old red brick house, almost entirely hid by foliage'[180] of which he did not despair.

Joanna commiserated wholeheartedly over the Royal Academy's treatment of him. On 16 May she wrote:

> I think I may safely say, I feel more real satisfaction in the hearty sympathy I have had about the placing of my picture, than if I had been on the line at the RA, because, amongst other reasons, it is far more reliable proof that my work is good for something …
>
> But as for the treatment they have given you!! It is absolutely ludicrous that they should have turned out your Undercliff drawing, or in fact any that you could send. The only possible explanation is that they knew that they had been shown at the Hogarth and dared to turn yours out, when the cowards dared not turn out Holman Hunt's 'Study of a head' for the same reason.

She went on to tell him that she and Henry had dined with the Madox Browns and the Seddons[181]. Anne had given birth recently and her baby was getting on well. Her own baby had, she said, 'been christened and vaccinated'. Then, evidence of the depth of their regard for each other, she responded frankly to his account of his emotional entanglements:

[180] 'The Old Red House at Mapledurham'.
[181] Probably John Pollard Seddon and his wife

> According to your wish, I destroyed the last sheet of your letter and made no mention of it to Henry. I am sure you must be beginning to feel you were not meant for an old bachelor. If you will allow me to speak plainly, that which always makes me sorry in thinking of you is that you have not one deep, all absorbing affection for one girl. (I am certain that I could never have been happy in marriage if this had not been the case with Henry.) It is not only that a girl with really deep feeling and strong capabilities of loving requires this, but I do not see how a man is to be happy in marriage unless he feels that there is only one woman in the world for him ... Now if you wish to marry, I am sure you ought not to be indulging in the society – in the way you do – of one girl after another, whose presence give you certain pleasure.
>
> You ask me about Jeannie N., but really dear George, I seriously believe I should be doing a wrong to her (and to Lizzie Ridley, both of them my friends), by helping you to an opportunity of finding a passing pleasure again in her society. I know that you pooh, pooh at the mention of Lizzie Ridley's name – no doubt you say you feel nothing more than a brotherly liking for her and Charlotte too. But I am really afraid the time will come, if you do not take care, when Mr and Mrs Ridley may take a severe view of your conduct.

She apologised for her impertinence, but added: 'I believe that in true marriage lies the greatest happiness on earth, when it really consists, as it ought to do, in the exquisite companionship of two souls striving in emulous spirit of loving rivalry to become better, to become wiser, teaching each other to soar.'

There was no more touching accolade to her own marriage, achieved with such a struggle, that she could pay. Also she knew her brother. She returned to the subject on 31 May: 'Am I wrong in supposing that of late you have seen the R[idley]'s more frequently than any one section of your family? ... I do not look upon you as that odious thing "a man flirt". You have not a taint of the character that term implies, but carelessness of conduct may bring about the same results to others.'

She did not, she said, set her face against his renewing his acquaintance with Jeannie. Only, she said, 'I would not be the means of doing what seemed to be an injury to two girls, both beloved friends of mine.'

Having invited him to visit the following Sunday, 3 June, she then wrote on 1 June to say that Jeannie Naylor had proposed herself for the same day. A certain excitement (in spite of herself) infused her letter:

> You can come or no exactly as it pleases you ... Understand me, dear George, I am neither a match-maker nor match-marrer. I neither wish to bring about nor to prevent your marriage either with L.R. or J.N. I like both and respect both exceedingly, and if I have in any way interfered, it has been with the wish to save them pain and you from finding yourself in an embarrassing and painful position. If you told me you had made up your mind to pay your addresses to one or the other, I should then be in a very different position.

He did visit and so did Jeannie: 'I could detect', he wrote, 'no latent sign of her caring for me, other than as a mere acquaintance.' And in spite of his recurring interest in both Jeannie and Lizzie Ridley, he was probably more at home at this stage of his life in the easy-going and raffish environs of his Pre-Raphaelite friends. D. G. Rossetti had finally married Lizzie Siddal, whom he had first met ten years earlier and who was, by this time, in the words of his sister, Christina, 'wan with waiting'. For Fanny Cornforth, Rossetti's mistress, it was a dreadful blow. On 5 June, George, having heard from Burges that she was ill, called on her: 'Found her so in bed. It appears she frets constantly about R[ossetti], who is with his wife in Paris, the latter very ill and in a deep decline. Altogether a most melancholy state of things.'

He returned to Mapledurham on 6 June, and later in the month recorded a visit to Bradfield College to see Burne-Jones's stained glass, which 'though powerful and glowing, looked a little glaring and coarse. The subjects the "Fall of Man", "Tower of Babel", "Solomon and the Queen of Sheba" and another ... Saw a marvellous and beautiful phenomenon in the sky. The sun and mock sun and two rainbows, each with an opposing moon, the upper bow being very vivid in colour.'

It was July before Joanna wrote again, to tell her brother that she had only heard once from Jeannie Naylor since that Sunday evening, and assumed she had left town. Perhaps Jeannie had needed that meeting with George to persuade herself once and for all that he was not for her. The epitaph on Bob's tomb had at last been completed, and Joanna was planning a visit to Kensal Green to inspect it. Henry's commissions had dried up again: 'A lady did call one day and talked about two full-lengths. She came in a carriage fit only for a duchess with powdered flunkeys, and gave Henry the idea of an unmitigated parvenue, and seemed about as foolish and ignorant on art matters as the class she aspires to generally is.' She ended: 'Did you make off with my *Nightingale Valley*? I have never seen it since the night you were here – I am quite uneasy about it.'

Henry was doing chalk heads now, and planned to leave his Stratford Place chambers ('£130 a year') to make his studio at Upper Phillimore Gardens.[182] He had, in 1855, purchased a strip of land at Holmbury Hill from Mr Wetton. It had a wonderful view over the Sussex Weald and through the Shoreham Gap to the sea, and his plan was to build 'a country painting box' on it. He had taken George to see it in April, when work had already started on 'clearing the ground of trees and stumps'. By the beginning of July there had been little progress: 'The works at Joldwynds',[183] Joanna told George, 'are of course at a standstill from bad weather and want of cash'.

Now it was Matthias's turn to cause the family disquiet. Lilly had given birth to a second daughter, Jessie, at the beginning of July, and Matthias was also in the process of buying land on which to build a house. Henry went by train from London Bridge to visit the site, at Southborough in Kent, and heartily approved the situation – 'it seems to me to answer all your wants; it is well elevated in a pretty country – you are a good distance from London – on the most convenient railway.' But he had severe misgivings about the grandiose plans for the house, which, he told Mat, could potentially be 'a sad drag upon you'. He had hoped that Matthias's architect, Baxter, would 'give you a charming irregularity about your house', to distinguish it from the other houses in the area: 'They are mostly of the square box and portico order of architecture, and if I may use strong language, "detestably cocknified".' But the actual plans seemed to him to be hugely inflated. With his usual forthrightness, he detailed his objections at length in a letter dated 10 July, to which Joanna added her own misgivings: 'On Sunday I would not say a word. I felt how aggravating it must be to you to have all your relatives dissuading you from the very thing on which you had set your heart.' But she could not resist warning her brother against a Mr Micawber-like confidence that 'something will turn up'.

On 23 July she confided her unease to George: 'You know that he has bought ground and is going to build a house. He is going into it all on so large and expansive a scale, and with borrowed money, that I cannot help believing he will seriously embarrass himself for the years to come.' Both Mordan and Henry had advised him to modify his plans, 'but he has not yielded one inch'. She was delighted to report that she had found *Nightingale Valley*: 'I had fancied the binding dark brown instead of quite light as it is.'

George returned to Buckingham Street on 28 July and spent the evening with Anne and Mordan, chatting 'about Mat's imprudence'. The following

182 This plan did not materialise.

183 George was under the impression that the piece of land was a present from Mr Wetton (Diary, 11 April) but, according to the family, Henry had purchased it. It was close to Joldwynds, hence the rather confusing references to the different properties.

evening he dined with Joanna and Henry – 'Henry had had his miniature of the Marchioness of Stafford returned upon his hands, in spite of its beauty and excellence.' Afterwards he 'went on to see Rossetti for the first time since his marriage. He was painting on his "Adoration of Christ" picture for Llandaff and had an Italian (of Parmigiano) sitting to him. Morris and his wife, whom D.G.R. familiarly addresses as "Janey", came in.'

On 31 July he spent the evening with his mother playing cribbage: 'She is in a great way about Mat's building speculation and says he must, if he persists, indubitably ruin himself.' For his own part, George had fallen in love with a design by Burne-Jones for the panel of a piano: this he managed to acquire, and indeed later commissioned the piano (from his old landlord in Great Russell Street, William Eavestaff) to go with it. On 3 August he went to stay with William Morris at Red House, designed for him by the architect Philip Webb.[184] Of Jane, Morris's wife, he wrote, '[she] is a tall, dark woman of a fine and rare type of beauty … Her quietness contrasts strangely with his noisy restlessness.' The house, he loved: 'altogether the best designed and most interesting I know … He has a lot of beautiful things in it. Eastern and Mediaeval'.

In early August Henry got a commission at last. He was summoned to Tehidy Park, near Redruth in Cornwall, to paint the portraits of a Mr and Mrs Bassett. The saga of the Bassett miniature[185] is a sustained and fascinating insight into the world of the portrait painter at that time. Mr Bassett was one of the 'new rich', having made his fortune in tin-mining. He and his wife were both on their dignity, and neither was particularly prepossessing:

> The fact is [wrote Henry] I have been constantly changing my mind in respect to the view of Mrs Bassett's head. I find it quite hopeless trying to get any interest in it. The complexion is good, *voilà tout.* After turning the head all ways and designing groups accordingly, I have decided on a profile. Tomorrow I begin from them upon the ivory. I will scribble you a notion of the group when I get leisure … Last night Mr Bassett sought me in my room and tried to open afresh the question of price. He pretended he was under a mistake, thought that considering it was only a miniature really £200 would be sufficient, and of course alluded to large oil paintings.

184 Philip Webb (1831–1915). Dubbed the 'Father of Arts and Crafts Architecture'. With Morris, Burne-Jones, Madox Brown, Rossetti, P. P. Marshall and Charles Faulkner, a partner in the decorative design company that became known as Morris & Co. In 1854 Webb became a junior assistant to G. E. Street, whose son later married Alice, the daughter of Henry and Joanna.

185 'J. F. Bassett Esq & the Hon. Mrs Bassett' was exhibited at the Royal Academy in 1861.

> I can, as you know, stand a great deal, but this did put my 'monkey up'. I gave him a bit of my mind, and told him considering my prices were legibly written both in my own rooms and in the list given to Mrs Bassett ... if people did not like my prices they were not bound to ask me to paint ... This morning at breakfast Mrs Bassett told me that her husband and herself had both very much remarked that I had 'two kinds of touches'. After a while I discovered that this enigmatic statement meant that I dealt in two kinds of wares, and that the lady and her husband were too much on the alert to render it safe for me to palm upon them the 'inferior article'. Dickinson's are doing portraits of these worthies in 'another style' (her words); and she strongly objected to one of my projected arrangements, because they had done something similar. Another time she would not go into a pose I suggested, because it was so 'ungraceful'. Don't you think I must like these people? When one does leave one's dear wife it is a satisfaction to pass the time in such society!

Joanna sent him news of his babies: 'Sidney's one eye tooth is through, the other very nearly. He seems perfectly well and not suffering with them at all ... Sidney put his arm round Alice this morning and looking up into her face began telling her about you "oodly, goodly pa-pa" etc, etc. Maria [Henry's sister] brought him a drum, which is his great delight – your favourite plaything, so your sister says according to tradition.'

She was fascinated by his patrons and full of advice: 'Certainly you have not fallen amongst "paragons" ... Do not put up with too much. I can't help thinking it would be wise and quite safe to take the high hand with such poor creatures. I should ask for an exact description of the "two touches"! Don't let any of these ignorances slip – keep a notebook for my sake.'

Henry, meanwhile, was getting the measure of his sitters: 'Mr Bassett's head ought not to take much longer. Mrs Bassett has a temper, gives herself decidedly the airs of a Martyr, and has already declaimed against the inconvenience and loss of time at the sittings.' He held his own pretty well, but was reluctant to show them the miniature 'because I know from that moment such people have the game against the painter – even if he were a Velasquez'. In the room in which he painted were packing cases full of pictures, including two Van Dycks, which he was not allowed to see:

> My days are spent in this way. A cup of tea and I leave the house at 8.30 a.m. for a walk until breakfast. I never can begin work until 11

> o'clock, but, with the exception of 15 minutes for luncheon, I work until 6 o'clock. Mr and Mrs Bassett each give two sittings of 1½ hours – one before, one after luncheon – dinner about ½ past 7. (I take a short walk for an appetite.) Between 9 and ½ past 9 p.m. I come to my room, when I write and look at the miniature. Generally I am sleepy and my eyes tired. Last night I could not write or paint, so I got into bed soon after 10 o'clock.
>
> I have not yet told you that a walk of fifteen minutes takes me to the edge of the cliffs over the sea. It is the boldest rock-bound coast I have ever seen in England. The cliffs are so high and steep, that I have not yet gone down to the water, but tomorrow I will take a path, which I have caught sight of and will dabble my hands in the brine. ['Remember, oh reader of the "Idylls",' he had written to her earlier, 'this is the land of King Arthur and his Knights.']
>
> Enclosed is a sketch of the group. The heads are the only parts to which I am positively pledged. I wish I had you near to advise me in the matter. I feel in great difficulty about the background. I want drapery for colour, and I really believe I shall have to adopt a column and curtain. Mr Bassett's coat and waistcoat are black velveteen – with high wading boots. Mrs Bassett's dress is a light poplin wrought with gold tissue – (colour something like your famous piece of satin – cream) – trimmed with broad bands of blue velvet over which is white lace. The shawl she is holding is white lace.

He added: 'I make my deafness an excuse for not talking during the sittings, so my sitters have generally the most unlovely expressions on their countenances. No visitors ever make their appearance to enliven them with conversation.'

Joanna sent him family news and small nuggets of gossip in reply, but she kept from him the fact that, in his absence, the rumbling over Matthias's plans had exploded into a full-blown row. In a letter dated 10 August, Matthias wrote to his sister complaining that it was one thing to disapprove of his plans, and quite another to stir up disapproval on the part of other members of the family. He was furious that Henry had expressed his views so strongly to Mordan and told her that, far from changing his mind, their united 'pressure' had only made him the more determined to proceed.

Joanna fought back. She was 'hurt and annoyed' by his letter, and particularly by its singling out of her husband. She told Matthias that the more they thought about his schemes, 'the more dangerous do they appear to us'. She went on: 'I in particular begged Mordan to do what he could to persuade you

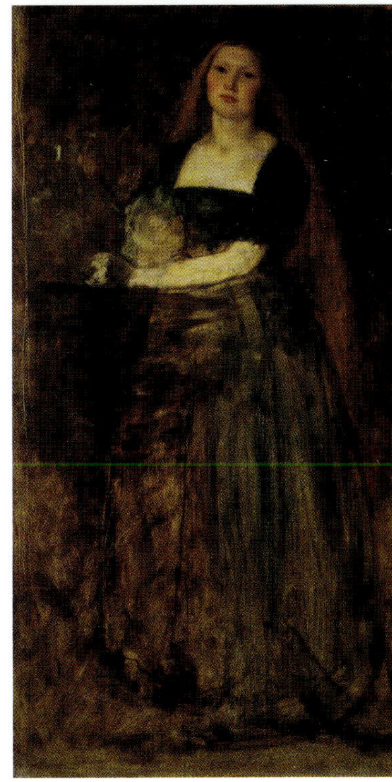

XLVIII *Gretchen*
Joanna Boyce Wells

George described Joanna's starting on this painting as 'the grand commencement' and although it was never finished, Rossetti later deemed it 'the finest thing she had done'. The critic Alexander Gilchrist said it was 'throughout almost Venetian in lyrical glow'. The woman with the long red-blonde hair, may have been inspired by Goethe's Faust, but it may simply have been a full length portrait of her children's nurse

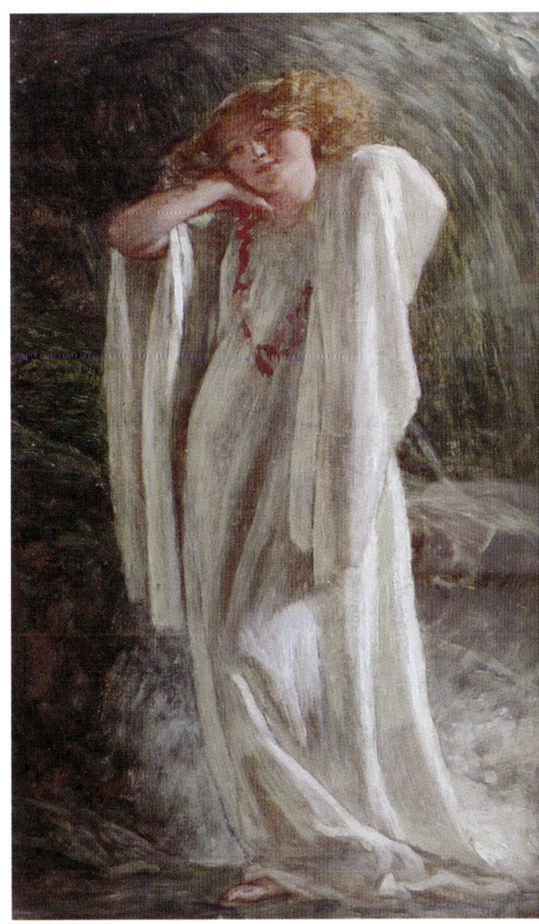

XLIX. *Undine*
Joanna Boyce and Henry T. Wells

Joanna died leaving only one morning's work on this picture, in a neutral tone. Henry wrote in his diary: 'I have long seen the picture in my own mind completed. I will now endeavour really to make it so... It will be to me a glorious privilege to fulfil her work after her death.' It proved an impossible task.

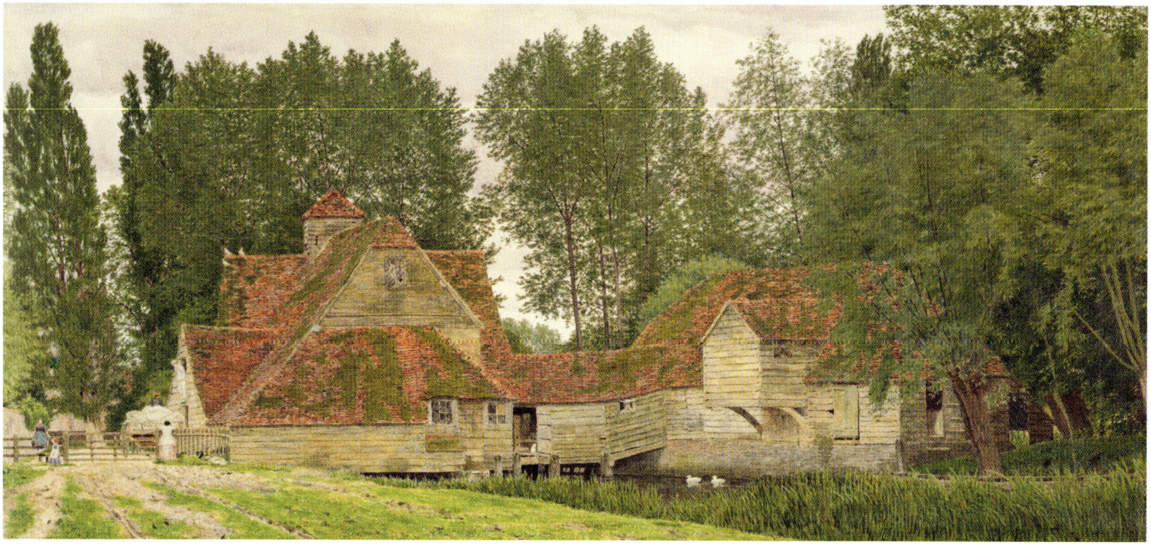

L. *The Mill on the Thames at Mapledurham* George Price Boyce

George went to Mapledurham, a small village on the north bank of the River Thames in April 1860 and remained there for several months indulging his passion for rural buildings and their settings. The following year, on 5 June, he sent the picture to Lord Carrington at his house in Whitehall, 'with a letter stating that with the £2 for the frame, the amount would be in all £27.'

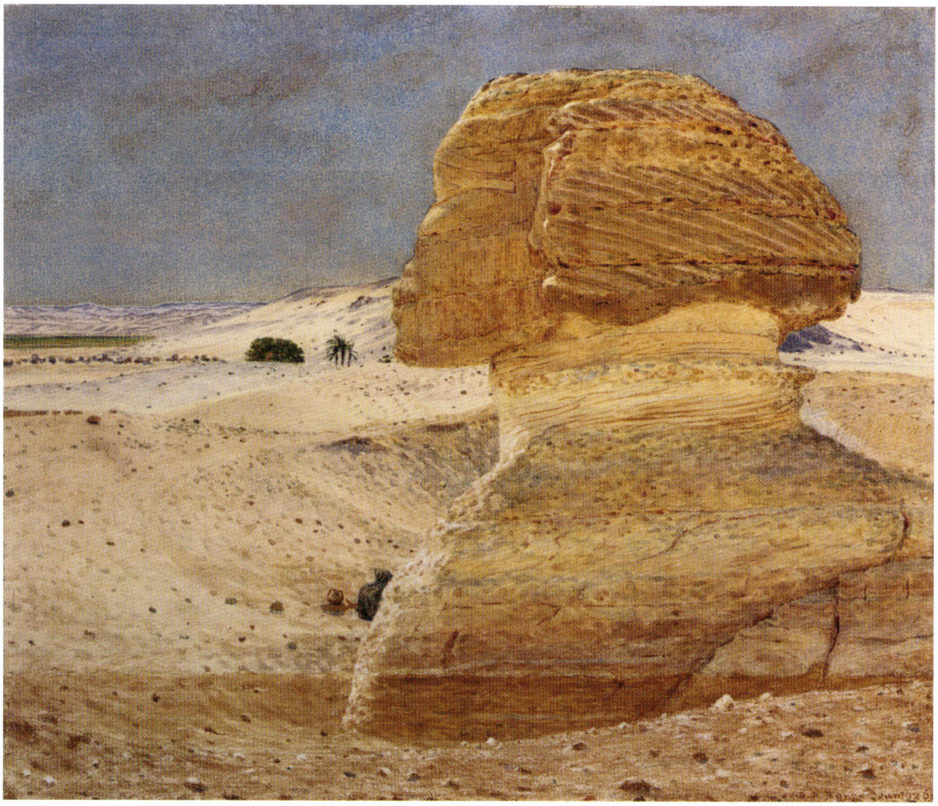

LI. *The Great Sphinx at Gizeh* George Price Boyce

After his sister's death, George went to Egypt. Following in the footsteps of several of his Pre-Raphaelite friends. Rossetti was dismissive of the work he had done there, saying that 'the things that artists brought from the East were always alike and equally uninteresting', but then Rossetti was averse to travel.

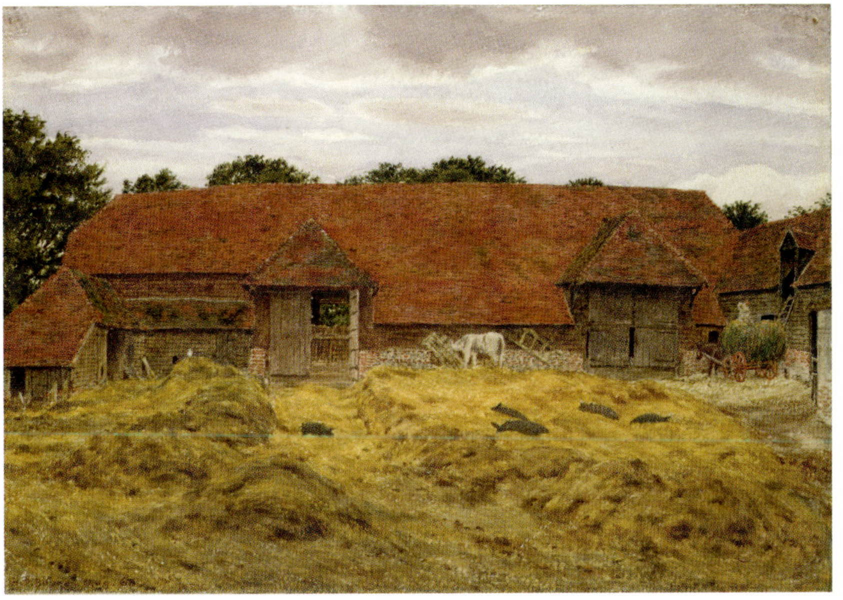

LII. *The Red Barn at Whitchurch* George Price Boyce

George loved the Thames valley. This finely detailed painting of an old barn, with a lot of black Berkshire pigs 'snoozing in the straw in the foreground' embraces two of his great passions – for vernacular architecture and for pigs. On 31 July 1849 he had lamented that Joanna was not there to paint some in for him: 'There are many of my favourites here – pigs – but they are never quiet a minute and consequently awkward subjects for sketching'. Painting them snoozing was one answer.

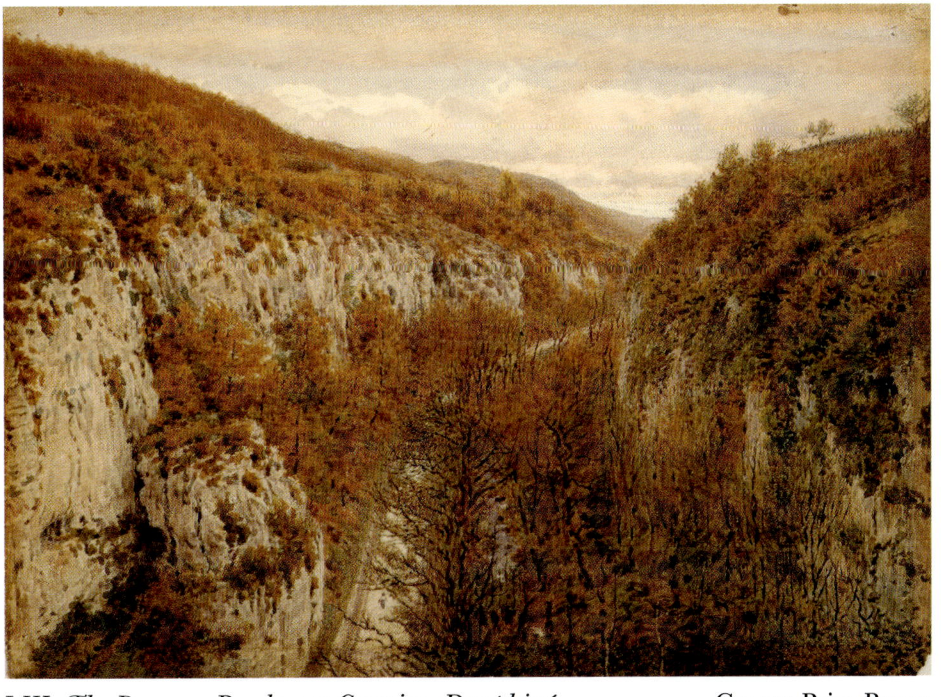

LIII. *The Bourgon Road near Cremieu, Dauphiné* George Price Boyce

This French landscape may well have been painted by George on a visit to Caroline Soubeiran's family. He first met her in 1860, though they were not married until 1875.

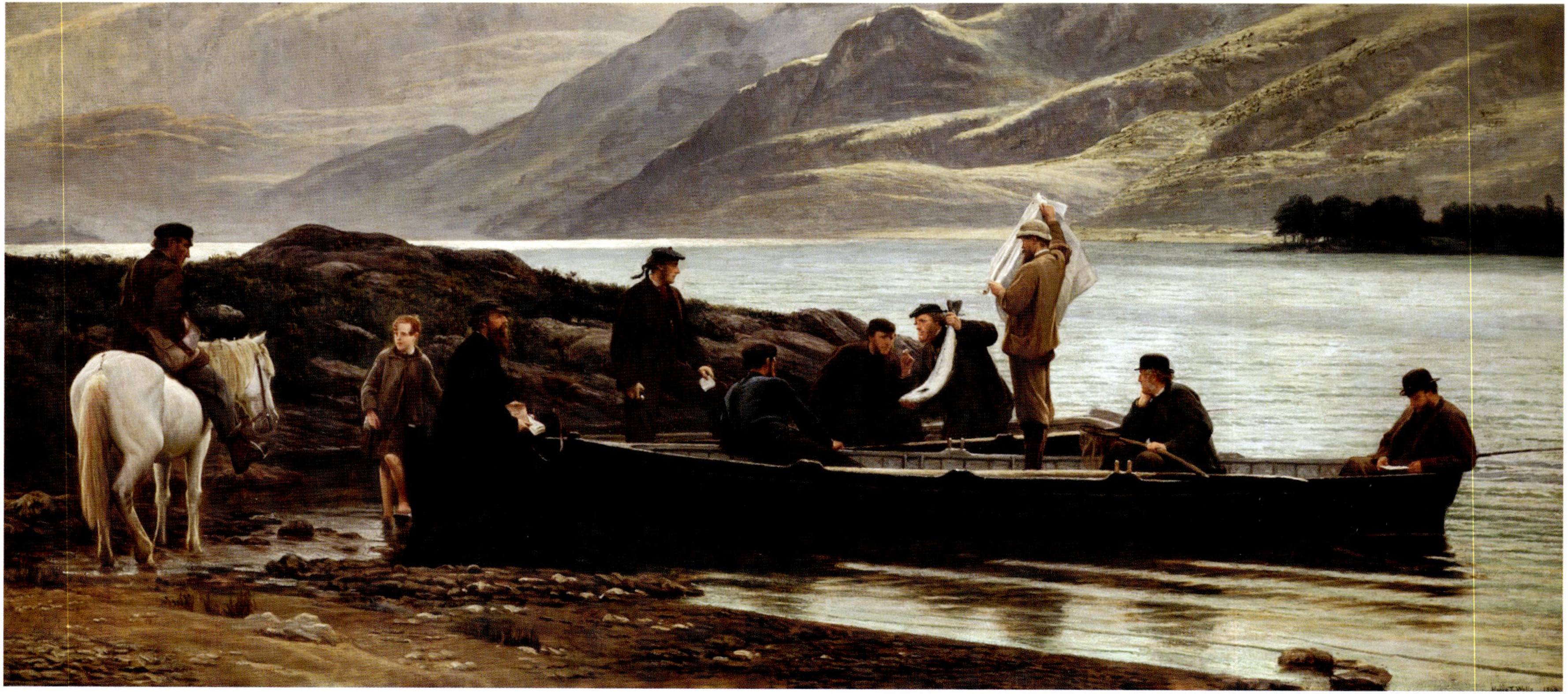

LIV. *Letters and News from the Lochside* Henry T. Wells

In 1862 Henry visited Arisaig, his friend Astley's Scottish retreat, in the company of Millais and his wife. This painting was done on a later visit, in 1868, when Millais was again of the party, and shows their host receiving the mail from a mounted postman on the shores of the loch. Henry submitted it as his diploma work after his election to the Royal Academy in 1870, but in 1883 two of Francis Astley's daughters asked Henry if they could have the lochside painting as a wedding present for their sister Beatrice. Henry wrote to the Royal Academy offering to substitute 'Volunteers at the Firing Point' as his diploma piece; this was agreed and the painting was sent to Arisaig House, where it still hangs. The figures in the painting are, from left to right: the postman, Donald Macdonald; Christopher Macrae (aged 11); Francis Astley, in the bows of the boat, owner of Arisaig; John Millais, standing; John MacDonald, crewman, and Donald MacDonald, captain of Astley's steam yacht; Duncan Macrae, holding a sea-trout; Angus MacDonald, the water-bailiff; and, in the stern, Henry Evans, a banker known for his expertise as a deerstalker and naturalist, who lived on Jura for many years. It is a vivid picture of the kind of gathering that Henry experienced at Arisaig.

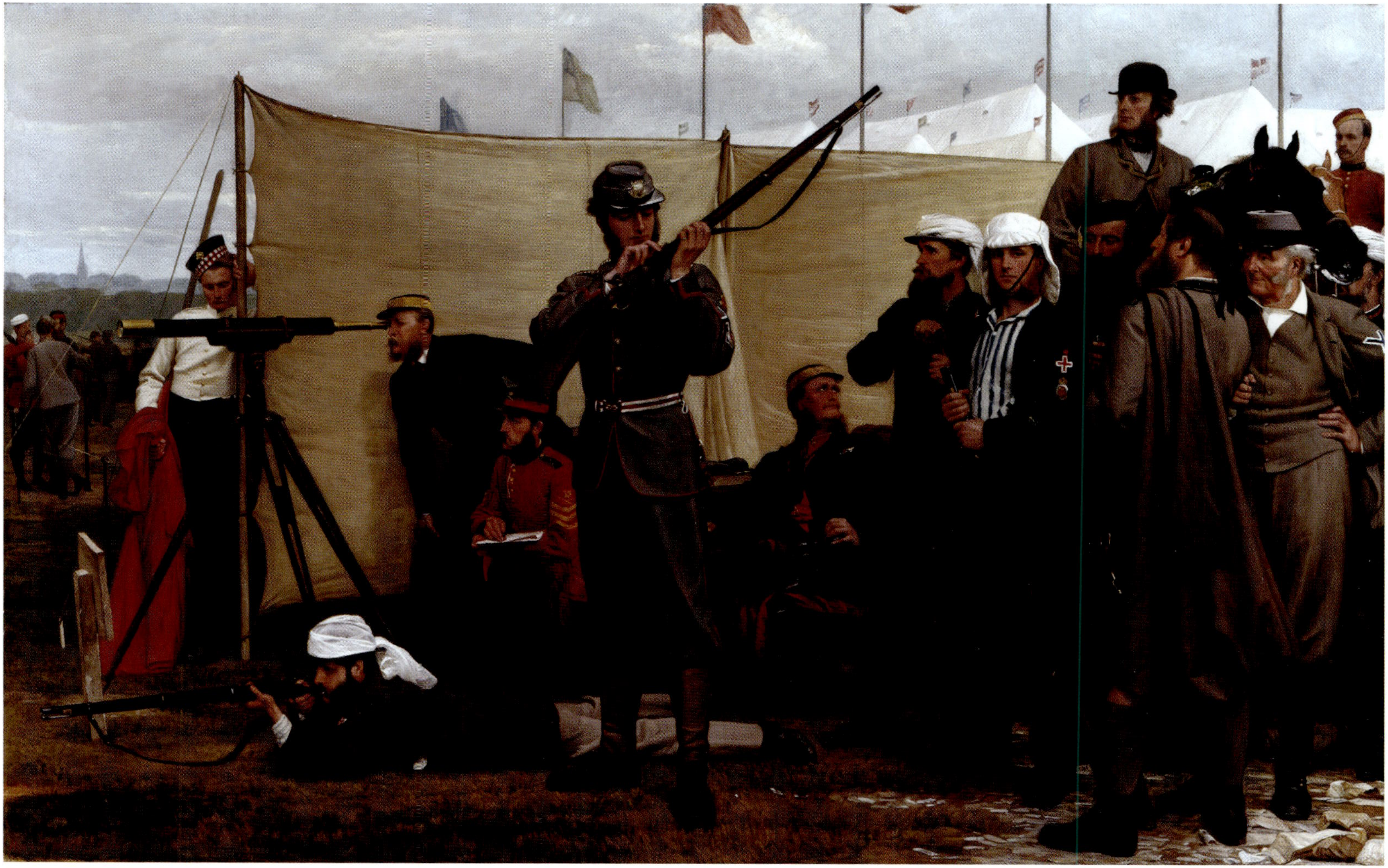

LV. Volunteers at the Firing Point Henry T. Wells

Henry was among the first to join the Volunteers – a citizen army of part-time rifle, artillery and engineer corps, established in 1859 in response to widespread unrest in Europe. He joined the South Middlesex Rifle Corps, attended drill assiduously and was a fine marksman until his eyesight failed him. This picture of 'Volunteers at the Firing Point' was substituted as his diploma picture at the Royal Academy in 1883.

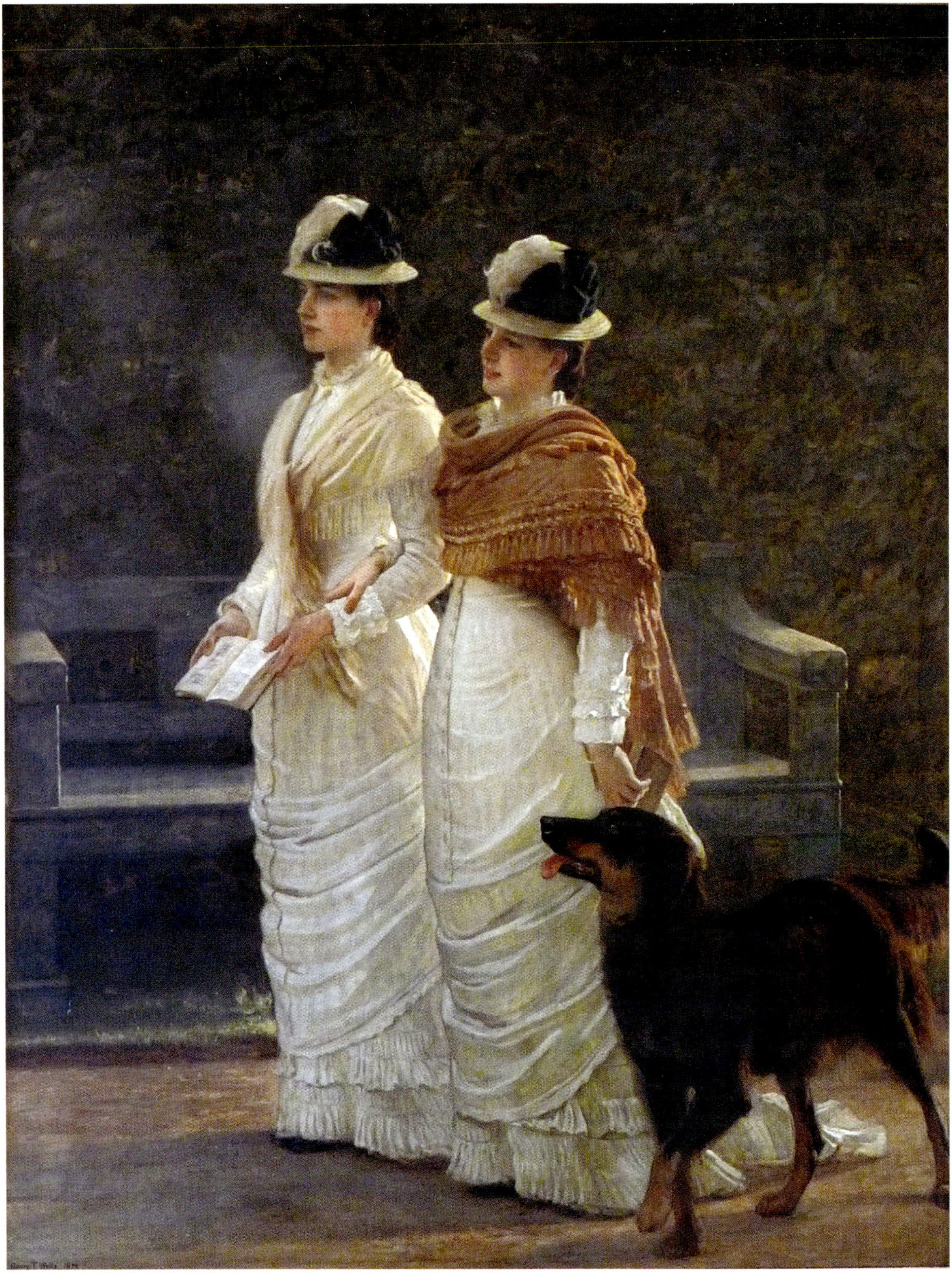

LVI. *Alice and Joanna Margaret* Henry T. Wells

This portrait of his daughters, painted when they were 19 and 17 respectively, is reminiscent in style of the French painter Tissot.

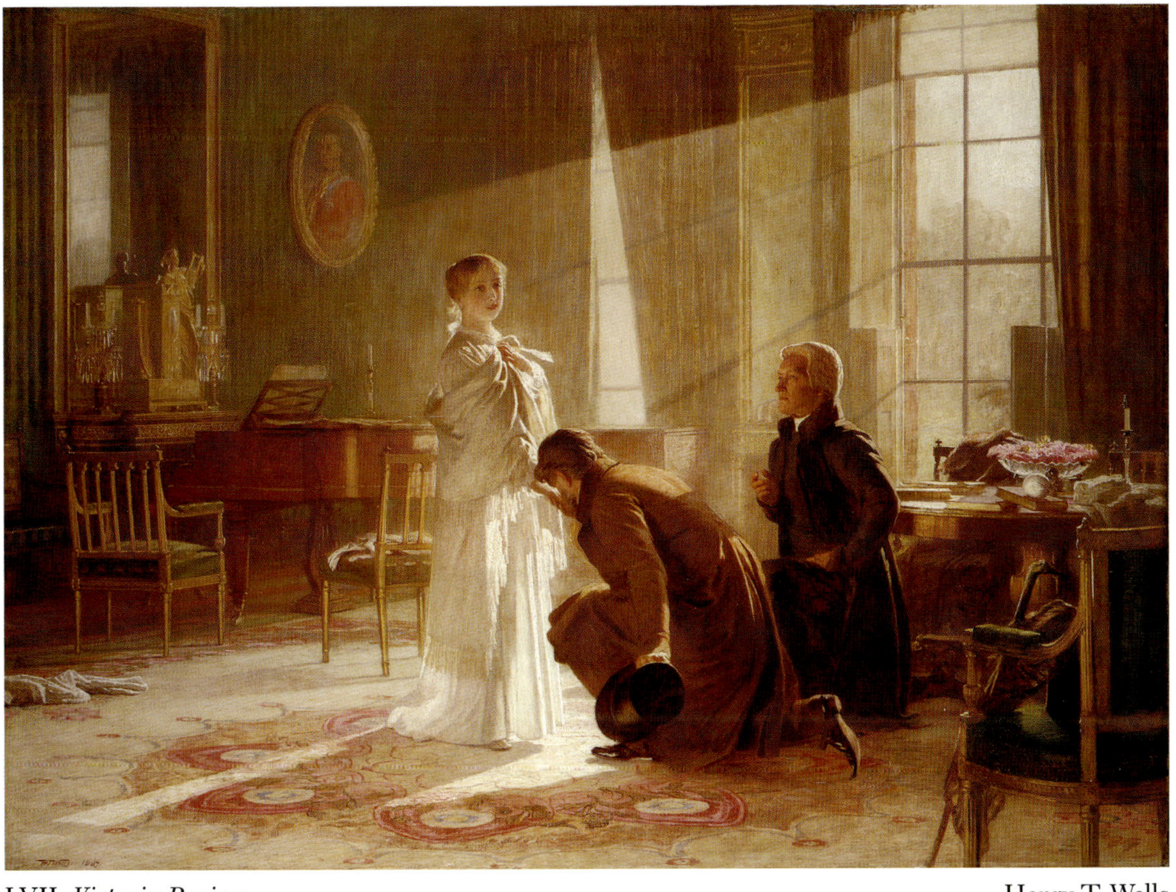

LVII. *Victoria Regina* Henry T. Wells

This painting depicts the moment in the early hours of the morning on Tuesday 20th June 1837 when Princess Victoria hears of her accession to the throne. Henry was inspired by the description of the incident he read in the diaries of Miss Frances Williams Wynn and first attempted a much larger version which he exhibited at the Royal Academy in 1880 (Tate Britain). This painting is a later version and the figures are grouped against a different background. Henry has included a portrait of Princess Victoria's father, the Duke of Kent and the still life objects on the table - a ball, book and flowers - allude to the childish pursuits the Princess will now have to abandon. It was presented to Edward VII by Alice Street after her father's death.

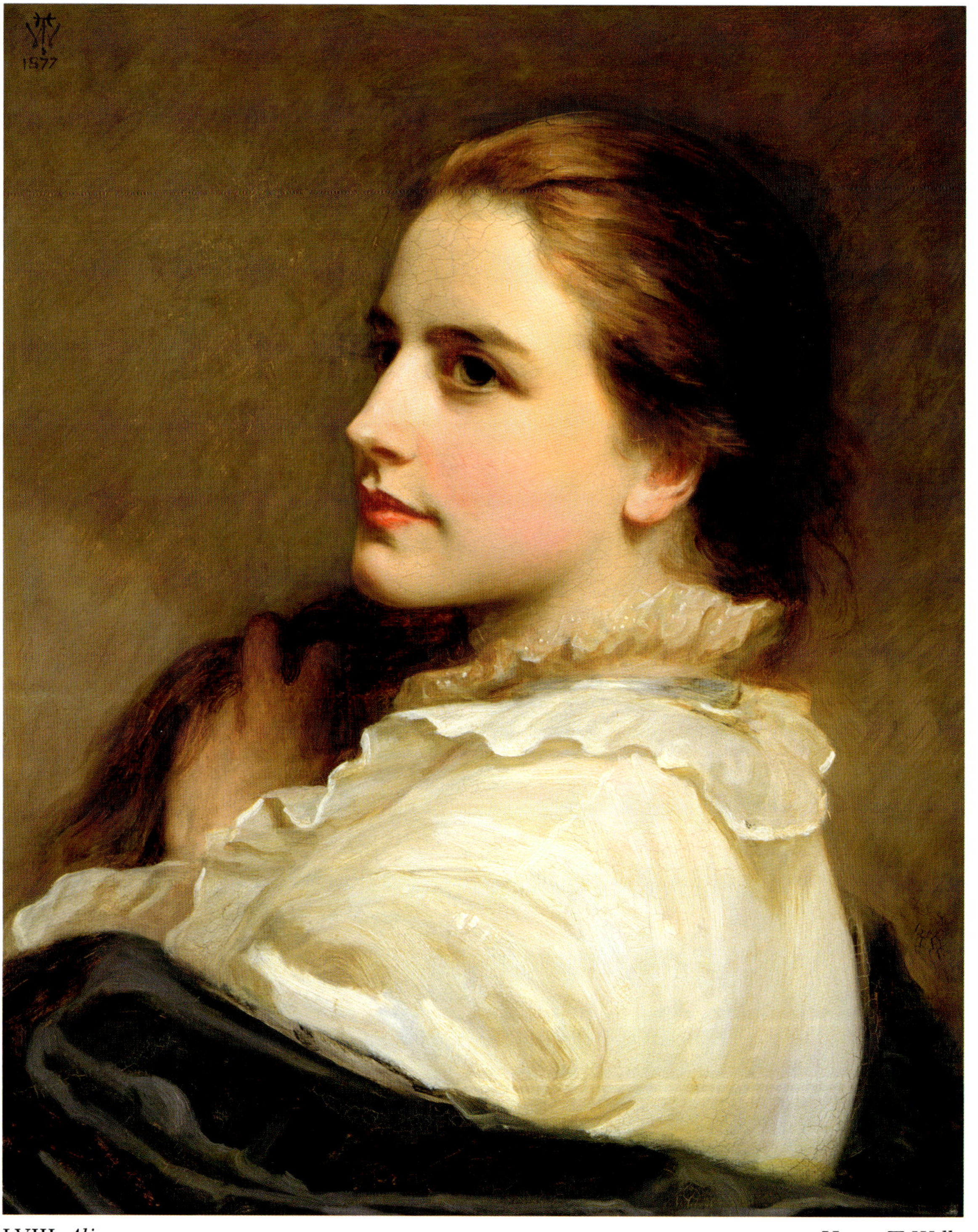

LVIII. *Alice* Henry T. Wells

An affectionate portrait of his elder daughter aged 17. Alice was responsible for the selection and editing of the diaries and letters in the typescript version, which is the only part of Henry's archive to survive.

to change your mind, thinking that he as a man of business would have great influence with you.' Never one to shirk plain-speaking, she ended: 'I should have hoped that the days of mere schoolboy and schoolgirl obstinacy were over for all of us.' They were, she reminded him, prompted only by interest in and affection for him.

Matthias's reply of 13 August was the epitome of the 'soft answer'. The burden of his complaint was that he had known that Henry was against the plans and had asked him not to express the full force of his opinion to Mordan. He had in fact already decided either to reduce the plan to bring it within the limits, or to give it up altogether. He ended: 'When will you come and spend an evening with us?'

It was a note which, as she immediately conceded, ended 'this little battle between us'. She knew what it was to be 'badgered' and had disliked being obliged to 'join the badgering company'.

Henry was kept in ignorance of this squall because Joanna knew how fond he was of her brother and did not wish to wish anything to undermine that affection. She wrote to him instead about his sketch:

> I like your picture very much. Mr Bassett's figure especially – there is a nice feeling of slight action about it and at the same time it is quiet. Mrs Bassett's is large in style and composes well with the other figure – but the arm that is holding out the shawl away from the body gives one an uncomfortable sense of fatigue. Is she supposed to be just about to wrap it round her, or is she making a signal to someone out of the picture? I like very much the way you have placed them at the top of some terrace steps, I suppose – and it gives a capital 'motif" (if I may use the word in such a sense) to the man's figure, making him stand a step below. His figure, I suppose, comes partly against sky and distance, and hers – not against 'column and curtain' if you can do without them; would cypresses or *arbor vitaes* and an old red brick parapet fall in with your notions and be useful as colour? – deep, gemmy, twilight yew green, behind that dress would come fine – would it not? I am fancying the velvet trimmings deep blue, not sky blue, of course.

She ended her letter: 'I wish that when I die I could take just two or three of your letters with me.' And, as always, with that wonderful marriage of heart and art that characterised her letters, added that she had been working on the sleeves of her Charlotte Ridley picture ('La Veneziana') and on different parts of 'Peep-bo', or, as she called it, her 'baby picture'. *(Plate XLIV)* About his miniature she added: 'Another suggestion for the background – fancy them standing close against a room opening to the terrace. Could not a deep window curtain be useful?' And with regard to the Van Dycks: 'I would get up at night and unscrew them, look, and screw them up again. It would serve the dogs in the manger right.'

Henry replied on 15 August: 'Mrs Bassett has sat SIX hours today and really with a steadiness equal to a paid model, so I must cease to call her hard names on this score. I finished painting the right arm and hand and have almost finished the left ditto, ditto … I have not shown the miniature yet, altho' I would now if they asked to look at it. I think I have not told you that I find myself here in the very midst of the mining works of this country. The presence of mines about here is in fact the explanation of Mrs Bassett's wealth.'

Always curious, he went down to one of the mines to glean information from its superintendent, and favoured his wife with a lengthy description of the process, which from first to last, appeared to the stranger to be 'nothing but elaborate manipulations of mud puddings. The shining ore [tin] is nowhere to be seen, and when at last he is shown the pure metal as it is shipped off to the smelters in South Wales, it is as a handful of fine black sand.'

On Thursday evening he added: 'I have all along felt strongly the danger of placing Mrs Bassett's left arm, as I have drawn it. I am not at all sure that one ought to paint an arrested action. ' He described that day's work:

> Today I have been sketching Mr Bassett's coat and boots, and I have nearly painted his left hand. From Mrs Bassett I have been painting throat etc, etc, and hand and arm, a bracelet and necklace. It is fortunate I require no dogs or background special to the place, as I should not have had time to paint them … I wish I had you here to overhaul the heads etc. There is not a soul to whom I could show them. Visitors do not make their appearance. In spite of all I get on pretty well. They are wholesomely afraid of me, and I have Mrs Bassett's word, that they have discovered I am 'obstinate' and have a will of my own.

Joanna's main concerns were Hennie, whose love-life was once again in a state of flux, and the War of Independence in Italy. The liberation army, commanded by Garibaldi, had conquered Sicily at the end of July, and she was following its progress closely: 'Of course you read the letter from Sicily. I should like to have caught sight of Garibaldi as he repeated Ugo Foscolo's lines. If ever there was a subject for an Epic – he is the man.'

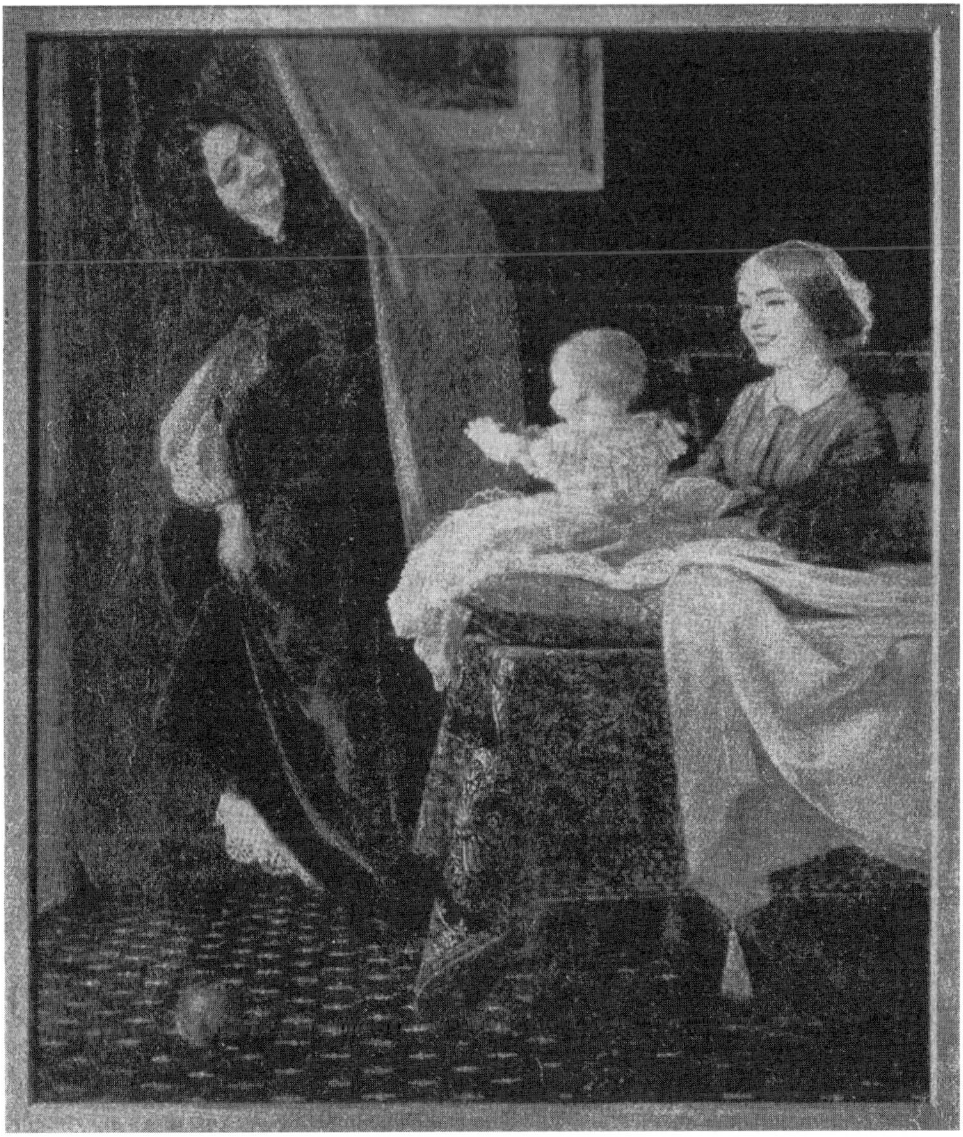

Peep-bo *Joanna Boyce*

Joanna's 'baby picture' was inspired by a visit from her sister Anne, her children and their nanny to Joldwynds. Joanna then failed to find a suitable model for the mother and turned it into a self-portrait in which she shares a domestic moment with her baby Alice and the nursemaid Susan. It was exhibited at the Royal Academy in 1861, the Saturday Review *(on 12 May) commented that its strength lay in the painter's 'womanly delight in her subject and a strong feeling for art'.*

By Friday 17 August, the miniature was almost finished. He was pleased with it and so, thankfully, were Mr and Mrs B.:

> But really they are such noodles in art matters that I receive only a negative satisfaction from their approval. I am quite sure, if the world and their friends form an opposite opinion the Bassetts will veer round and ignore their words of today. One of Mr Bassett's clergymen called this afternoon and sat with us some time while the sittings were going on. He was a smiling, cringing fellow and rather a goose … I had already finished Mr Bassett's head and was finishing Mrs B.'s, when he said looking at them 'It is difficult to form an opinion at so early a stage before the features are formed' – to which Mr B.: 'Ha-ha, Mr – you had better not continue to look at the miniature now, it would interfere with your appreciation of it, when it is quite finished.' You see I am yet suffering from want of a sensible or an honest opinion. I am quite sure my parson would have given the most fulsome applause, if he had known his patron had already applauded.

When he left Tehidy Park 'Mrs B. tried to make a pretty speech at parting to the effect that "when they had the miniature, they would always look back to this time of painting it with pleasure", but I would not have it at all, but joked it off.' He did not come straight home, but went to East Looe in Cornwall to stay for a few days at St Martin's, the home of the Farwells.

Joanna had been to Henry's studio to see his chalk drawing of Lady Alice Kerr, which charmed her:[186] 'It is lovely in colour and delightful in expression … it seems odd perhaps to notice the colour first in a chalk drawing, but that was really what struck me at first glance.' She had also found his portraits of Lady Waldegrave and Mrs Popham and had turned them round so that the light would not spoil them. The proposed move from Stratford Place had not materialised – perhaps Henry had had second thoughts about working at such close quarters with his children.

No such qualms affected Joanna, in spite of her original misgivings about combining art and motherhood. The Armsteads and Wilday were constant visitors and she was much amused by her children's effect on the latter: 'Alice is quite as great "a little rebel" as Sidney. I must not say so to Wilday, or he will get frightened about the awful character of our progeny' and 'Sidney only bellowed at the Armsteads and Wilday the other evening. It seemed to disturb

186 It was exhibited at the Royal Academy in 1861.

Wilday tremendously ... I'm sure he thinks Sidney an awful child.' Armstead, she said, had treated her to 'two of those remarks for which he is famous'. On looking at a neighbouring house from the Wells's garden he said: 'Well, really it is a treat to see architecture like that, and doesn't it make these (looking at ours) look like workhouses.' Then, after wolfing a second helping of macaroni, he had pushed away his plate saying: 'Oh, isn't that a stinking cheese!' Tact was never their brother-in-law's strong point.

She saved the most important news until last: 'Mat has relinquished his house building scheme *in toto* – the estimates having come to much more than he expected. Lilly is very disappointed, but quite nice about it, as of course she would be. Altogether it is a weight off my mind, but I can't help remembering that the frame of mind which led him to dream of doing what he intended is not one which will make him as careful as we would like to see him.'

While Joanna had encouraged Henry to stay in Cornwall for long enough to recover from his exertions at Tehidy Park, she would, she said, 'be glad enough to see your dear old face again'. She had worried overmuch about losing her former nurse, Susan, and, though she had finally found a German girl, Gretchen (who had wonderful long red hair) to replace her, had become depressed: 'This afternoon I have taken the strongest medicine for the cure of the mopes with me, viz. reading over some of your old letters, and it has done its work. It seems so foolish that I should feel so much parting with a servant, but the kindness and care she has given to the little ones and my anxiety at having a stranger in her place account for it in a great measure.'

She had also been much preoccupied with the controversy in Parliament over whether or not to establish a shady 'ride' along the north edge of Kensington Gardens. The proposal had given rise to an outcry among those (of whom Joanna was one) who wished to preserve the park as a safe haven for pedestrians, 'undisturbed', as *The Times* mockingly put it, 'by a gaudy crowd of chattering equestrians.'[187]

She wrote to Henry: 'That discussion on the subject of the horse ride was most aggravating. I feel inclined to cry out "that beastly *Times*". I wish *Punch* would equip the affair from our point of view ... If members are really Centaurs and cannot take enjoyment like the rest of us, then I think some few bipeds ought in justice to be allowed to vote on such a question with our four-hoofed governors.'

She was further enraged when an article appeared in the *Saturday Review*, also in support of the ride: 'I am aggravated beyond measure to read

[187] *The Times* leader, 10 August 1860.

an article in the SR quizzing … the opposers of the ride as much as any *Times* writer. I am afraid there is little or no chance of our side winning the day.'[188]

The *Saturday Review* also contained news of a new set of tales by Hans Andersen, which pleased her more. 'Some day we must get them and the Grimm's book for the little ones. Fancy Sidney listening in rapt attention to a fairytale! Alice seizes him by the hair and ill treats him with the delicious unconcern of an eight months baby. He bellows and then while his face is still red and the tears in his eyes, puts up his tiny mouth to hers and says "kish, kish".'

Henry wrote to her every day: 'St Martins looks very like what I left it – the garden not quite so trim seems to tell the tale of the family – the young ones all on the wing, the elder ones losing care of this kind in their home … Bertha's presence here is, as you know, very unusual.' He hoped their own children, 'if we have many', would be more attentive.

He returned to London on 23 August, and he and Joanna set off together almost immediately to stay at the Red Lion Inn at Ockley, 'an exquisite little village', according to Joanna, 'at the foot of Leith Hill and about 3½ miles from Joldwynds.' They had intended to stay only a week and had left Sidney behind, but the weather proving promising they sent for him and stayed a further week. 'The rain set in on his arrival and scarcely cleared up before we left.' They saw the Wettons frequently and Joanna had hoped that George, who had been at Sonning in Berkshire since 4 August, might have joined them, but by the time he replied to her invitation they were ready to return to London. Her letter to him on 23 September began with a scolding: 'What a bad fellow you were not to write before'. She told him about Henry's Bassett miniature – 'the finest thing he has done … not particularly good subjects, especially the lady, but the colour is perfect.' He intended sending 'the oil head of the little girl, which you saw' to the Winter Exhibition: 'I shall send the Crusade, Sidney's portrait, the gorse-woman and the Pigeon house.'

George returned briefly to London on 6 October and, after his flying visits to Henry, Burne-Jones and others, finished up at Rossetti's on the 8th: '[He] showed me some admirable new things … among which was one exquisite profile of his wife. He was also at work on a pen-and-ink drawing of "Hector and Cassandra" and one of two lovers meeting their doubles in a wood.[189] His wife was in the studio but he said she had been sleeping and was not in a state to see any visitor.'

[188] In fact the proposal was defeated.

[189] 'How They Met Themselves'. Rossetti referred to this strange picture as his 'bogie drawing'. It reflected his abiding fascination with the *Doppelgänger* legend and he produced at least three versions of it. This one was begun, specifically for George, while Rossetti was on his honeymoon in Paris.

He also dined with Henry and Joanna: 'Sydney, taking me for Val Prinsep, who frightened him a few days ago, was again greatly alarmed and I was obliged to retire.' But on 9 October he left again, for Shiplake, where he intended to concentrate on his work for the next month. 'Wrote to Gabriel Rossetti', he noted on the 10th, 'telling him I'd be glad if he would paint me a drawing for £30.' In Shiplake, apart from games of bagatelle at the 'George and Dragon' and the odd musical evening, George spent all his time painting: 'In the morning made an outline in a meadow between the Henley road and the backwater bounding Wargrave Marsh … At even fall took a stroll by way of Wargrave Hill to a farm most picturesque in itself and in situation, called Chamberlain's on the map, but now called another name – a beautiful group of old barns and buildings, backed by trees – orchards about.'

Back in London on 7 November, he called on Rossetti and Burne-Jones, and dined with Joanna and Henry, before visiting his aunts in Shropshire for a month. There, on an excursion to Knightsford Bridge on 22 November, he made a sketch from Ankerdine Hill and remarked on the 'lovely landscape subjects all about'.

His next visit to Rossetti took place on 14 December when he went to collect his picture: 'He is making his place very comfortable. Has painted a fine head of his wife as "Regina Cordium". I brought away the drawing he has just completed for me, "Bonifazio's Mistress". It is rather rough and incomplete in finish, but fine and touching in design, and beautiful in colour.'

Mindful, perhaps, of their spat over the house, Matthias had written to Joanna on 7 December to say that, though both now had new family responsibilities, 'as brother and sister we have ever so loved and had confidence in each other, that we may look forward with certainty to our future relationship.' Her response was warm: 'Your little note on my birthday gave me heartfelt pleasure and I thank you for it sincerely. I need not tell you how truly I reciprocate your long-tried affection, or what a solid satisfaction it is to me, that although we have both made closer ties, still we are truly a brother and sister to each other with a strong, faithful love in both our hearts.' She had not forgotten all he had done to further her happiness.

❁

The year 1861 began with an invitation. On 2 January Rossetti wrote to George: 'Wells and your sister are coming here to tea on Monday at 8 o'clock. I know not if you will then be in town, but, if you are, will you come too, and let me introduce you to my wife. No one else is coming except Miss Howitt that was –

now Mrs Watts – and her husband.[190] No sort of party. Don't tog, for I shall be in my painting coat.'

But Lizzie was not well enough to receive them. A further appointment was made for the 22nd, but this too was cancelled, Rossetti writing to Joanna on the 16th:

> My wife has been in such a very fluctuating state of health since I saw you, that it makes us quite afraid of failing at the last moment in our appointment with you for Tuesday – in which case Lizzie would never pardon herself after her first disappointment and vexation at being prevented from seeing you the other evening ... Nevertheless I hope you and Wells will not look on us as perfect outcasts meanwhile. If ever an opportunity offers for your calling here together I hope you will let me see you, and if fortunately it happens that my wife was pretty well, nothing would give me greater pleasure, or her either, that she should get known to you both, and I am sure you would all like each other ... I am especially disappointed in not seeing your faggot picture,[191] of which I have heard so much from Watts and others. Have you it? – and for how long? – and where? – and would you show it me if I came by myself some time? (*Plate XLVI*)

George saw Ruskin on the 3rd (when Ruskin 'deprecated my want of perspective knowledge') and on the 4th, when he dined with father and son at Denmark Hill: 'Old Ruskin gave us some sherry out of the same cask that Nelson drew his from before the battle of Trafalgar.[192] It was very strong. Principal topics of conversation – spirit rapping, immortality of the soul, Spurgeon,[193] modern Christianity, ridicule, joking, its use, harmfulness. Ruskin quoted the saying of an Arab, that he would rather perish than belong to a race capable of perpetrating a caricature.'

On the 10th, George was introduced by Ruskin to Mr and Mrs John Simon,[194] who had expressed interest in both his and Rossetti's pictures. The meeting was a great success. George dined with them on the 19th, Ruskin and 'a

[190] Anna Mary Howitt had destroyed her paintings again when criticism by Ruskin, the rejection of 'Boadicea' by the Royal Academy and the marriage of her great friend, Barbara Leigh Smith, precipitated breakdowns in 1856 and 1857. In 1859 she married a childhood friend, Alaric Alfred Watts.

[191] 'The Heather-Gatherer, Hind Head.'

[192] Ruskin's father was a wine-merchant.

[193] Charles Haddon Spurgeon (1834–92). A popular Baptist preacher.

[194] John Simon (1816–1904). Medical Officer of Health for the City of London and a prominent sanitary reformer.

Mr Hume'[195] present: 'A tremendous and learned and very interesting theological discussion took place after dessert. Mr H. wonderfully versed in Ancient and Eastern literature and philosophy – said the word "logos" wrongly translated in our testament, "word" ought to have been translated "reason". The philosophy and doctrine of the Old Testament founded on Buddhism … Mr Simon addressed Ruskin once as the "Great prophet of the imagination".'

Joanna upbraided George for 'being so lazy and cowardly about the Old Water Colour Society', but George now had a new enthusiasm – his piano. On 15 December he had been to collect the pen-and-ink designs for the panel which he had purchased from Burne-Jones some months before, and on 26 January he repaired to Eavestaff with his design – 'we talked it over at the tea-table. Afterwards to Jones, who was at work on a pen and ink of Childe Roland. He gave me a rough pencil sketch done then and there of my future playing on a piano with a Robin Redbreast singing under a rose spray on the top'. Burne-Jones told George that he, Morris, Rossetti and Webb 'were going to set up a sort of shop, where they would jointly produce and sell painted furniture.'[196]

The finished drawings were finally delivered to Eavestaff on 1 February. Rossetti called and 'seemed to like a good deal three little drawings I was preparing for the Hogarth, and said that had he the money to spend in pictures he would like to buy the "little red house at Mapledurham".'

On 3 February George recorded: 'From an omnibus saw Holman Hunt with nose high in the air.' It is a reminder that for some reason – possibly a coolness resulting from the Annie Miller episode – Hunt, unlike so many of the Pre-Raphaelites, was no longer a constant in George's life. George visited William Morris at Upton on 3 March and found Mrs Gabriel Rossetti visiting Mrs Morris: 'The latter as beautiful as ever – not at all altered by the bringing of the little girl into the world. Jones has painted 4 beautiful compartments in distemper on the walls of the drawing room – each of Rossetti's gorgeous Dante subjects on the bookcase panels … I gave Morris the little yellow Chinese spill pot with the tree and parrot, which he liked.' On 16 March he spent the evening with Burne-Jones and his wife: 'Made a rough sketch of Jones whilst he was at work on his pen and ink drawing of "Childe Roland to the Dark Tower came", and whilst his wife was singing old English ditties.'

George's diary is the principal source of news for the first few months of the year, but he, Joanna and Henry were so close that it is not hard to imagine

195 Daniel Douglas Home (1833–86). Spiritualist medium who had gained a large following after his arrival in London in 1855. Elizabeth Barrett Browning was a disciple, and he was probably the original for Robert Browning's satirical *tour de force*, 'Mr Sludge the Medium'.

196 The Morris firm had its first premises in Red Lion Square.

their lives as well as his. He was sitting to Henry – probably for the conversation piece, destroyed in the Bath air-raid,[197] which shows George, Joanna and Henry seated at a table with John Clayton standing behind, as they listen to Joanna reading aloud. Alice later described how the picture came about. Henry had left the room 'to fetch, I believe, a volume of Browning's poems. On re-entering he beheld the three others grouped round the dessert table forming such a happy composition and one so exactly suited to his purpose, that he bade them remain without stirring, while he hastily jotted down on an envelope the main lines and masses of the group he saw before him.'(*Plate XLVII, frontispiece*)

The three of them swapped – and bought – each other's pictures (there is a letter from Henry to George on 5 February indicating the businesslike nature of these transactions as well as their genuine appreciation of each other's talents), and shared their worry about Edgar, Anne and Mordan's eldest, who had fallen ten or twelve feet from the banisters, breaking his wrist and cutting his forehead badly.

On 27 March Henry wrote to George: 'It has quite lately struck me that Joney, yourself and myself might most years make up a little exhibition of average interest – and as we are so near kith and kin there would be a propriety in our clubbing together.' He suggested that they could exhibit at Stratford Place, but added: 'I would not advise you to join with us unless you are inclined to enter heartily into the scheme and send as important an exhibition as you can.'

By the end of the month, Edgar, apart from a bloodshot eye, had recovered, and Henry had departed for Brighton where he was to take part in a 'sham fight' – practice manoeuvres in the event of the volunteers being called up.

There was much discussion among members of the Hogarth Club about its proper function. Ruskin, George reported, had made himself extremely unpopular: 'Voted that in reply to Ruskin's letter of resignation, in which he talks about boys playing at billiards, his resignation should be accepted with a regret on the part of the Club that he should have couched his letters in terms offensive to the same.' (Virginia Surtees comments that Ruskin was 'apt to be prejudiced against the game of billiards, though here some reference may have been intended to blackballing which seems to have been endemic to the Hogarth Club'.)

By April, George's social and artistic round was frankly frenetic. In a typical entry in his diary, dated the 7th, he reported: 'To see Abraham, Simeon and Miss Rebecca Solomon's pictures … Miss Solomon's picture – a deserter captured, who has turned actor – made the best picture she has ever painted … Thence to Leighton's … With Joney and Henry (whom I met at Leighton's by

[197] The oil sketch Henry made survives, however, and is reproduced here as Plate XLVII. Philip Street's photograph of the original appears as the frontispiece.

appointment) to Dillon's, where we saw two beautiful little Eastern landscapes of his … Thence to G. F. Watts at Little Holland House. Mr and Mrs Dalrymple and Dicky Doyle there. Watts's finest work an unfinished head of Gladstone, also a portrait of Miss Prinsep, of Mrs Prinsep, chalk study of Henry Prinsep and a delicious little landscape study. Dined with Henry and Joney.'

The proximity of Henry and Joanna to the Holland House Circle was evidently beginning to rub off on George. He was selling his work too – among others, to William Debenham and Alfred Bell.[198] On 9 May there was a large gathering at Stratford Place to admire the works that Joanna, George and Henry intended to submit to the Royal Academy that year. George was delighted with Millais's particular praise for his and Joanna's work, and his singling out of one of Henry's portraits. On 11 May he recorded: 'Man from Royal Society came for pictures. Sent – Rossetti's "Bocca Baciata", Millais's portrait [of 'Sophie Gray'], Joney's Buttercup girl, five unframed drawings: (N side St Marks, Corner of Fenice, Edward Confessor's Chapel, Westminster, 2 Grand Canal Moonlights') and, from the Hogarth, "Mapledurham House", and 'Cle[e]ve Mill'.

On 29 May George and a large group of friends, including Woolner, John and William Millais, Mr and Mrs Abraham Solomon, Tom Taylor and a lady, had decided to go to the Derby and George had been much struck by the 'thunder and tramping rush' of the eighteen horses running in the Derby Stakes. Infused with this sublime moment, he adjourned to Cremorne pleasure gardens in the evening, 'which was densely thronged by men and women in all states of hilarity and inebriety'. Millais and George du Maurier – artist and author of *Trilby* – were also there. The next day George went down to Red House with Henry, whom he introduced to Mrs Morris. 'After we had strolled about the house – inside and out – for some time, Morris arrived and we had another prowl with him. He showed us some work Mrs Morris is doing for the shop – net-work, needlework on velvet, etc.' William Morris was now installed at 8 Red Lion Square, where ' "the firm" have already in their rooms some bits of furniture and wall paintings and screenwork and embroidery in hand'. Swinburne, whom George had earlier accused of lacking humanity, had become a friend. On 2 June he wrote: 'Swinburne breakfasted with me. We looked over Doré's *Voyages aux Pyrenées* together. He afterwards recited two of his own poems – both on Lucrezia Borgia.'

In early June, he and Henry paid a visit to the Wettons, lunching at Joldwynds and visiting the site of Henry and Joanna's new cottage. Dinners with 'Wells and Joney' were a frequent feature of his social calendar. He also makes

198 George's patrons may have been the fashionable photographer William Elliott Debenham (1839–1924) and Alfred Bell (1837–95) who, with John Clayton, ran a hugely successful stained glass workshop.

several references to the money he was earning from his pictures. On 4 June a Captain Moore had called and bought his 'little Mapledurham drawing, with peacock on the wall'. There is no indication of the price Captain Moore paid, but the following day George sent his 'Mapledurham Mill' picture to Lord Carrington at his house in Whitehall, 'with a letter stating that with the £2 for the frame, the amount would be in all £27'. (*Plate L*) Joanna's pictures were also selling, though at least some of them were selling to George. On 5 June he sat to Henry for three or four hours and handed him a cheque for £43 3s in Joanna's name. This was to pay for 'La Veneziana'[199] (£63) and a small Haslemere landscape in oils (five guineas), minus the money for his 'little Wargrave Church drawing' (ten guineas) and his 'little bridge near Wargrave and Shiplake' (twelve guineas).

From Joanna directly, little was heard. She was pregnant again – her baby expected in July – and had been unwell. On 14 June she wrote to her 'dearest Hennie': 'Come by all means on Saturday 22nd, but do not be surprised if I turn you out of your bed in the middle of the night. I am going to use that room for my confinement, as the heat would be unbearable in our own. The doctor says July 12th is about my time… I am just getting over a very sharp attack of influenza, which has quite done me up for some days. The chicks have escaped with a mild form of cold.'

Her 'Bird of God' was finished, or nearly so, 'but disappoints me sadly'. It was, with 'The Departure: An Episode of the Child's Crusade', one of only two religious paintings she made and was based on a poem by her beloved Robert Browning – 'The Guardian Angel':

> 'And suddenly my head is covered o'er
> With those wings, white above the child who prays
> Now on that tomb – and I shall feel thee guarding
> Me, out of all the world.'

It was, for her, a powerful image. In her article on Ruskin's *Harbours of England* she referred to the desire of poets and artists to possess 'the wings of a dove – the bird of God'.(*Plate LII*) Of her other work, 'Sybil', she told Hennie, was untouched and a large picture of 'Undine' projected but not as yet on the canvas. Henry, she said, was working, 'but no commissions' – though Millais had paid him the compliment of wishing him to paint his wife, for which Henry would be paid with 'a picture some day hence'. The cottage was progressing, 'but of course

199 The model for 'La Veneziana' was Charlotte Ridley. The picture was painted in 1859–60 and glowed with greens and gold – Joanna noted that she was aiming for Titian colour. George always displayed it as a companion piece to 'Elgiva', hanging them facing each other in his various abodes.

won't be habitable till next year'. She hoped that Hennie would be sure to come: 'If you don't mind, I should rather like turning you out and having you near me in my trouble.'

To Lilly, in late June, she wrote: 'Cannot carry out my promise of bringing the children – am so much driven with all sorts of disturbing engagements – done no painting – Henry is in a perfect rage ... I am quite unfit now to go about ... I am perfectly well in health – only the bearing of the child tries me much more than ever before.'

Her baby, a girl, was born on 3 July. On 12 July, George, in Whitby, received a telegraph message: 'Joanna is so seriously ill that you had better come at once to town.' He arrived in London in the early hours of the following morning, and later that day wrote: 'Her disorder is gastro-uterine fever... Opiates, calomel and applications of turpentine and linseed etc to deaden and keep under the pain have been the remedies used. The baby is now being brought up by hand. The doctor and nurse and Henry are the only persons who see her. Every cause of the least excitement, which instantly forces her pulse up, is avoided. She herself aware of this and, exerting an astonishing energy of will, will not even allow Henry to speak to her, except a word or two at a time.'

Sunday, 14 July, was the second anniversary of Bob's death. Joanna, according to Henry, was more cheerful and composed, and he opened the casement of her room and placed groups of roses about. 'These and the sky and distant trees and other combinations of colour seemed to delight her much.' It seemed that she wished to soothe him. George said: 'She must purposefully have avoided giving Henry any notion that she believed she was going to die, for it appears that on this very day she said to the nurse: "Nurse, I am going (or slipping) away, and it's the leaving of Henry and my children only that makes me sorry."'

By the following morning 'our poor, dear sister was sinking'. George and Mat were summoned at 8 in the morning. 'A collapse had occurred. Of course all went up to her. She was not so changed as I feared to find, but she was also none the less doomed. Once she partly woke up for an instant and said: "I am so ill", and once again also she recovered enough to open her eyes and give a most heavenly smile.' She died some time after half past twelve, 'gradually, peacefully and painlessly ceased, so that we knew not the exact moment of her passing away. Around the dear, loving soul's deathbed were Henry, self and Mat, Mother, Hennie Moore, Nurse, Mr Harper and Maria Wells.'

The nurse, Mrs Snelgrove, later told George that Joanna had, at an earlier stage, asked for a looking-glass. An artist to the end, she wanted to see herself 'with all the paraphernalia of a sick room about, and so be thoroughly impressed with the aspect of an invalid in a sick room. She was evidently thinking of turning it to account in her painting.'

❋

'At Henry's request', wrote George, 'I went to Gabriel Rossetti to ask him to come up to make a study of her head. He was very shocked at hearing of her death, and embraced and sympathised with me in a most touching manner, which I shall never forget.'

He was comforted to find that Henry had already made 'a most admirable oil study of her head'. That afternoon 'Rossetti made a most wonderful and beautiful study… and Henry made a slight sketch recalling much of her. I could do nothing, my eyes being blinded with tears and my whole self prostrated.'

Rossetti it was who bitterly summed up the conundrum that had exercised Joanna throughout her short life: 'A great artist sacrificed to bringing more kids into the world, as if there were not other women just fit for that.' Henry never forgave him.

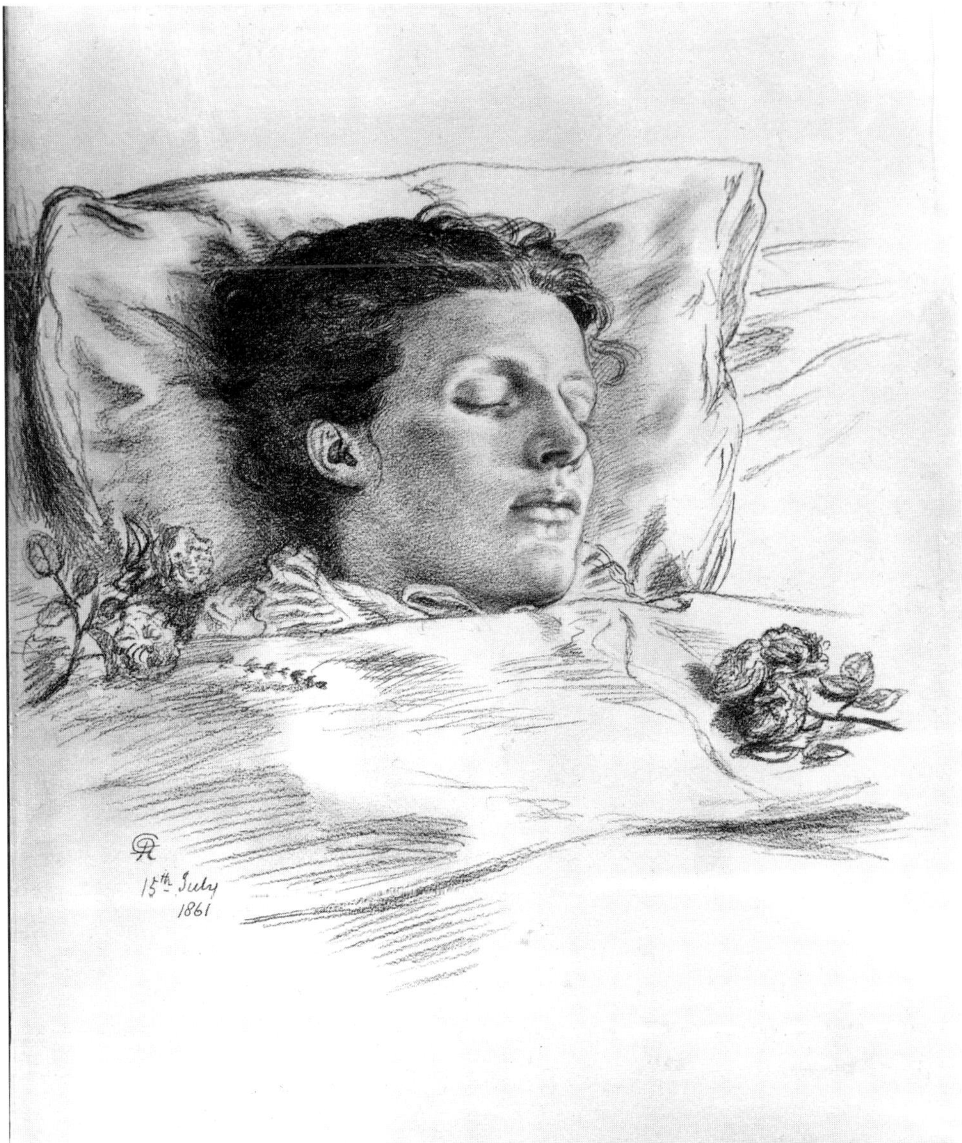

Joanna on her deathbed *Dante Gabriel Rossetti*

Immediately after Joanna's death George sought out Rossetti to draw her portrait. It was, he said, 'a most wonderful, beautiful study' and included the roses that Henry had placed on her bed. It remained a private family keepsake.

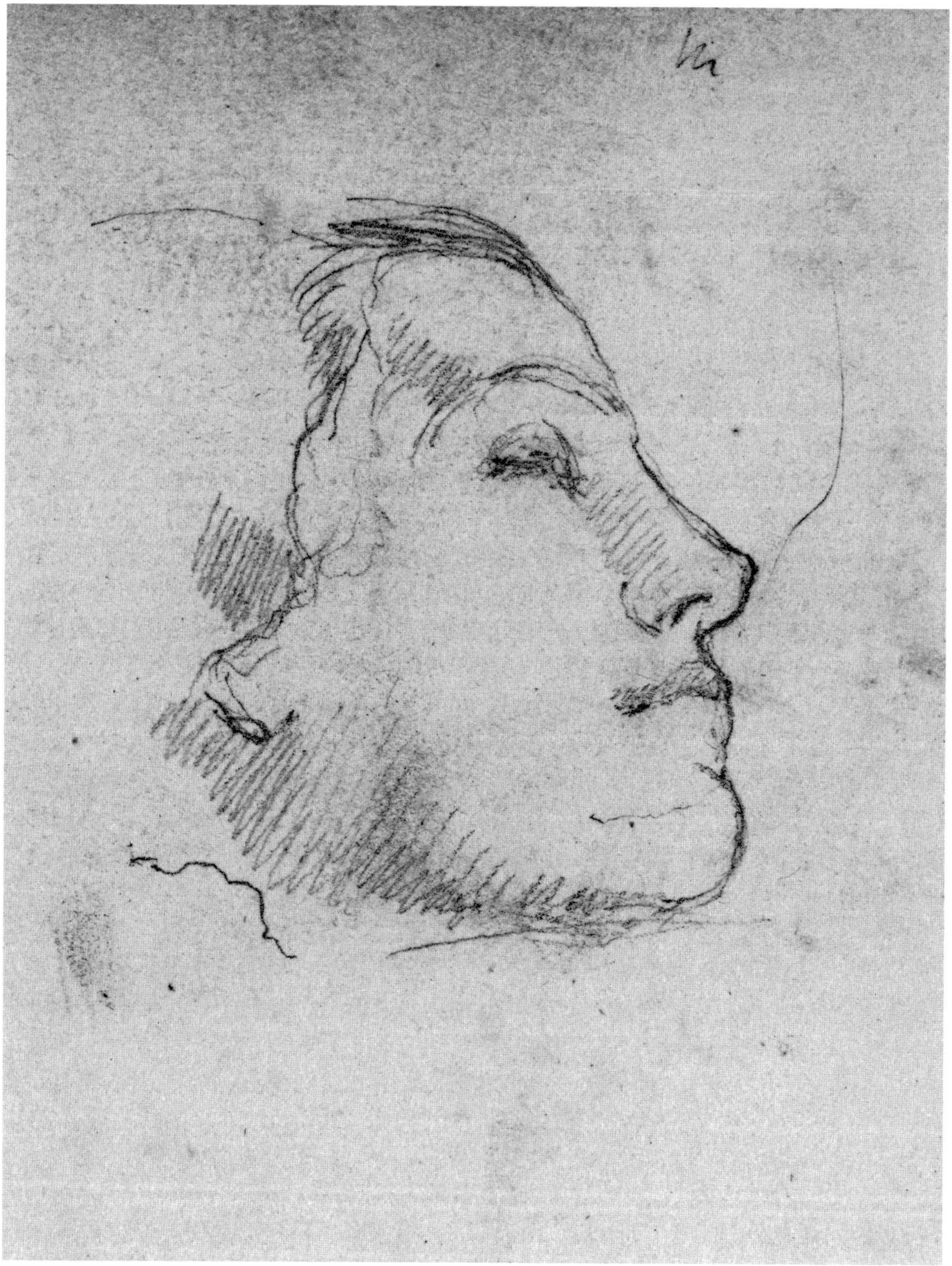

Drawing of Joanna — *Henry Wells*

'A slight sketch', wrote George, 'recalling much of her.'

AFTERWARDS

'Your ghost will walk…'

'De Gustibus'

The day after Joanna's death the sculptor John Foley[200] arrived to make a death mask. George wrote: 'Foley came with his man Lacchese and took with much difficulty, as the head had to be raised up, a cast of her entire head in 3 pieces. All the hair thickly oiled first, then the lower front of the head dropped in plaster of Paris up to the ears; when that was set another piece was laid on in spoonsful up to the crown and starting from the back of the ears. The last covered the face and ears and part of the neck.'

That evening he returned to the house and found John Clayton there, who, with Rossetti, was anxious that Joanna's artistic career should be properly recorded in the journals, and he and Henry 'drew roughly together some data, of which he took away a copy'.

On 17 July Rossetti wrote to George:

> Gilchrist[201]… was as sincerely grieved as all true lovers of Art must be, when he heard of your terrible loss; and he had seen your sister enough, though only casually, to perceive something of what she was personally also.
>
> He will be glad to write in his paper (the 'Critic') from the data you give. I fear no other source of publication is in any way open within my knowledge at present, except what my brother is sure to do. It was only the other day that Taylor was telling me – as regards Scott's pictures – what difficulty he was in getting any art matter inserted except obvious news of the day; and Ruskin is away …

200 John Henry Foley (1818–74): Born in Dublin and one of the most important sculptors of the day. He was particularly famous for his work on the Albert Memorial in Kensington Gardens.

201 Alexander Gilchrist (1828–61). Biographer of Etty and Blake, who had recently become friends with Rossetti. His obituary of Joanna appeared four months before his own death.

> I was trying yesterday evening to make a sketch of your sister from memory, meaning, if I succeeded at all, to beg your acceptance of it.
>
> Gilchrist was suggesting how much interest would attach to a collection at the Hogarth or elsewhere of all which your sister did. I think, if the idea met with Wells's and your approval, that he is right …
>
> Such a calamity relating to so truly glorious a woman can never fade from the minds of any, who have come within its more immediate influence.

Rossetti's sense of loss was heartfelt. He wrote to James Leathart (one of the Pre-Raphaelites' northern patrons) at about the same time, saying that there was 'no conjecturing to what this wonderfully gifted woman would not have reached in her Art, and in private life her greatness of goodness was no less rare'. His wife Lizzie's response was equally touching: she wrote to her husband on the day of Joanna's death: 'My dearest Gug, It is indeed a dreadful thing about poor Mrs Wells. All people who are at all happy or useful seem to be taken away. It will be a fearful blow to her husband for she must have been the head of the firm and most useful to him.'

In the days following Joanna's death, many artists came to her studio to see her work, Ford Madox Brown and Rossetti included. The latter, George noted on 18 July, was especially taken with the 'Bird of God' and with 'the grand commencement of "Gretchen", which he deemed the finest thing she had done'. *(Plate XLVIII)* The news also reached Ruskin in Boulogne, who wrote an agonised letter to George:

> I did not think that after Mrs Browning's[202] death, anything could have again very deeply troubled me, for I felt stunned by that, but at this moment I feel as if this death were almost worse. For Mrs Browning's work was done – your sister's beginning.
>
> I cannot write anything to comfort you. All my own mind is just now in darkness about these things – like birds the serpent draws. Every morning I see the risen sun with a deeper sense of the horror of all he sees – and worst of all that he ceases to see – as if all our work here were vanity, and there were none in the grave.
>
> To think of the useless – foolish – cruel – harmful – horrible people that keep living on, and these – these two, I can't help thinking of them together – gone in a month; one at half life – one young.

[202] Elizabeth Barrett Browning had died only two weeks earlier, on 29 June 1861.

'Received a kind but curious letter from John Ruskin,' wrote George in his diary on 20 July. It was the day of Joanna's funeral: 'Henry arranged pictures (her own) and flowers on and about dear Joney's coffin, and placed on the latter her old favourite Bible, given to her and Annie by Aunt Mary … Archdeacon Sinclair, who had previously called on Henry and volunteered to perform the burial service, did so with great simplicity and impressiveness.'

After the service Henry, Sidney, Alice and Gretchen, the nurse, left with Mr Wetton for Joldwynds. Henry's sister Sarah took charge of the baby, who was to be called Joanna Margaret, 'and for whose Godmother Henry is very much inclined to impress Miss Naylor'. Mother, wrote George, 'very much cut up'.

There was a long and discriminating notice in the *Spectator* that day: 'A few weeks before her death she finished a lovely work … the head and bust of an angel. Its execution seems to have called forth her utmost efforts. Full of the tenderest and most loving work.' It described her as 'no less a fervent Christian than a gifted painter' and expressed the hope that 'one of Mrs Wells's pictures may hereafter find a home in one of our national collections'. Spencer Hall drafted a short notice for the *Gentleman's Magazine*. George went to see Foley's cast and pronounced the 'brow and eyes very fine'. It was, however, 'faulty (owing of course to the moment at which it was taken) about the nose and mouth, one side of which is very painfully drawn down. Still,' wrote George, 'it has to be a very valuable record and in a particular light and viewed from the left side, recalls her very vividly.' The bust Foley made later shows a strong, handsome face, very arresting, with large eyes, a strong straight nose, full mouth and cleft chin – 'the upward pressure on her mouth making her look older than she was'. She was indeed 'the head of the firm'.

From Joldwynds, on 24 July, Henry wrote to their dear friend, Hennie, with whom they had both shared so much. He was already thinking in terms of Joanna's posthumous reputation. 'My little pets are very well indeed and happy in their companions – the baby I hear is going on rightly, so I trust the little thing will be reared. I have a sort of feeling that she may grow most like Joney – if so what a great thing it will be for me … I wish you would look over Joney's letters and be prepared to show me what would be useful to the purpose of a Memoir. Did I tell you I have found a diary of 1852, 53 and 54? You are mentioned in a way you will like to read … Dear noble girl lived long enough to get some recognition.'

Gilchrist's long and touching obituary appeared in the *Critic* on 27 July. 'In her', he wrote, 'English art has lost more than it knows.' He recognised her debt to the Pre-Raphaelites, 'which did much to form her taste, though in no slavish spirit … She was still a student – had hardly begun to reap what she

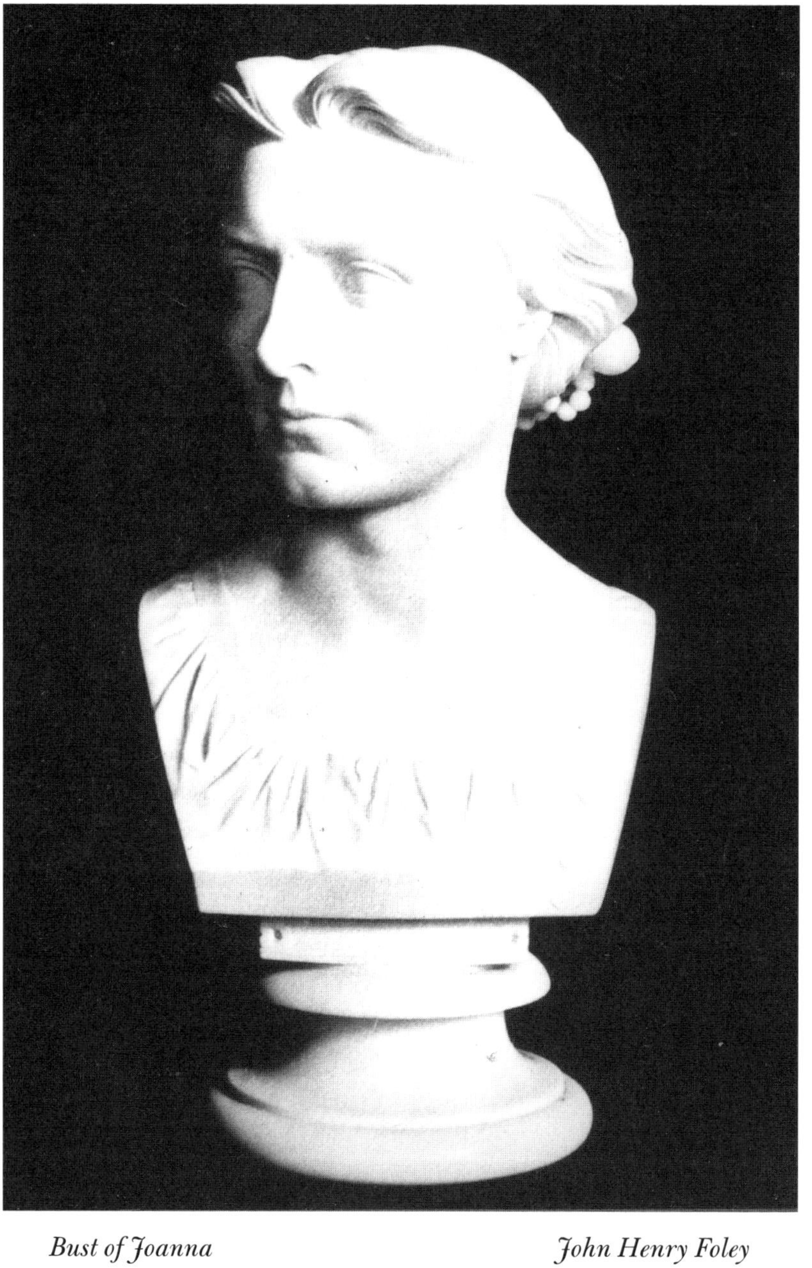

Bust of Joanna *John Henry Foley*

Foley's death mask of Joanna recalled her, according to George, 'very vividly'. It is a strong, handsome face. The finished marble bust was exhibited at the International Exhibition in 1862 as one of 'England's Worthies'. It was destroyed in 1942.

had sown. She was early attaining a thorough mastery of drawing and of colour, and had already attained to a bold, swift, decisive felicity of handling.' He also noted her 'unbounded devotion to her husband and children, which were never neglected for her art, but preferred to it', An anonymous obituary in the *London Review*, published on the same day, ended with the words: 'In the prime of life, when her genius, long pluming itself, was fitted to take flight and to cleave the air with steady wing, the power was withdrawn. "The beautiful is vanished and returns not".' The language smacks of Spencer Hall.

Henry stayed at Joldwynds until 30 July. He slept soundly – 'this power of sleeping has been a great boon to me at such a time. My dear little Sydney and Alice so healthy and happy and very delightful.' The diary he kept gives some idea of the way in which he spent the weeks and months after his wife's death. He too saw Foley's work in progress: 'It is a good cast but painful and giving no idea of her beauty. Putting the back of it to the light and looking at the profile in broad, reflected light, I got a glimpse of you, my Joney, but not so lovely or more vivid than I constantly see you in imagination.'

A visit to Augustus Egg increased his intimations of mortality: 'I was sad at sight of him. I fear he has not long to live.'[203] On 31 July, Edward Burne-Jones spent the evening with him: 'We remained in your study, Joney, until it was quite dark. Jones has a fervent admiration of my noble wife, and was full of sympathy, and did not seem to tire at my speech about her. Her death has made him think much about his own wife, who is now near her confinement. He seemed, I was grieved to notice, full of fears.'

On another visit to Joldwynds, he took Sidney and Alice to the top of Holmbury Hill, the scene of 'No Joy the Blowing Season Gives'. He had already written to Jeannie Naylor to ask her to be godmother to the baby, who had been crying a great deal. Finally, on 7 August he took up a large oil portrait of Joanna, left uncompleted two years before: 'I had not seen it until yesterday for a year and a half. I was agreeably surprised for although bad in many respects, it is certainly like. Everything that is the least like is now valuable to me; and I think I may make this rather better with a little work.'

Ever practical – and kind – he wrote to Hennie on 8 August, asking her if she would consent to take charge of his children and his house. 'This, Joney, is what you would most like, is it not? I have thought earnestly on the subject for three weeks. I believe I have thought rightly.' An attempt to make an etching of himself and Joanna in a 'sou-wester' on Holmbury Hill was 'v. disappointing. Altogether there is a rotten look about it. Joney's head an utter failure.'

[203] Egg went to live abroad shortly afterwards, dying in Algiers in March 1863.

The photographer Herbert Watkins had found three negatives which he gave to Henry: 'I am the most thankful for the full-face photograph. I have hunted, but have been unable to find a single impression of it. It is the only full-face photograph ever taken from my darling Joney. It will be not only most valuable for Foley's bust, but invaluable to me, since I am about to paint a large oil picture of my darling, full-face in her Holland painting dress.'

Anne called on him: 'She is quite pleased with my last portrait of Joney (the reading one)'.[204] She took away "The Heather-Gatherer". 'Peep-bo' had been bought by Mr and Mrs Calvert Toulmin, who possessed a large collection of 'flat and unprofitable' pictures: 'Oh Joney, if you could have crept to my side, as I looked at your "Peep-bo" in the midst of these works, how we should have pressed each other, and how your eyes would have glistened at what I should have said to you. You were indeed one of God's gifted ones – while these others!' (The Toulmins later sold the painting, and Henry negotiated its purchase on behalf of Joanna's mother.)

On 12 August, he and the children said 'a long goodbye' to Joldwynds – 'the scene of much happiness to me'. He was grateful that the six weeks they spent there in the year following their marriage had proved 'no happy island of the past' but proof of a happiness that did not fail them in their brief life together. Joldwynds was the symbol of that happiness, and the Wettons, 'who admired and loved my wife directly they knew her, and always treated her like a queen (as she was)', a loving reminder of his married bliss.

He saw his baby the following day – 'very thin and small' – but his sister Sarah thought her healthy and on the 14th the birth of Joanna Margaret was registered. He decided to have a proper christening and this took place at Kensington Church on 20 August. Neither of the godmothers – his sister Maria and Jeannie Naylor – could be present but Matthias, the godfather, was.

He was finding it hard to work, and he had heard from Hennie on 16 August refusing his offer: 'Her relations object to her coming here to take charge of the children and house. Out of spirits – absolutely no work at all.' On the 25th he wrote: 'Made a start upon the chalk study of my darling Joney's head – full-face. Oh Joney dearest, I always at other times seem to see you vividly before me, – but, as I worked at the drawing, you seemed more distant and indistinct. I pray I may succeed, if only to prove to myself, how you are branded in my memory.' Hennie wrote to him again on the 26th. She was suffering very much from the attitude her father was taking, and though he sympathised, Hennie's inability to stand up to her

[204] This is the portrait of Joanna in Henry's conversation piece. Her head and hands were painted directly on to the canvas only a month or so before she died. His study of George was virtually completed, but he still had to incorporate it into the main picture.

father depressed Henry further. 'This is in every way bad conduct on his part, and she seems passive in his hands. I wrote a careful and strong letter to her.'

❁

Re-reading some of his letters to Joanna, Henry could not help but be reminded of the 'madness and fullness' of his love. His diary after her death describes a desolation, briefly punctuated by small excitements like the march of the Coldstream Guards from Aldershot to London: 'The men hurrahed at sight of their comrades and band waiting at the Turnpike to head them. The men "fell out" for twenty minutes in Hyde Park and then marched into the Wellington barracks; I like a schoolboy followed all the way.'

On 26 August, he brought away the cast of Joanna's head from Foley's. 'Drawing all day on the chalk study for her portrait, the cast placed before me – a painful day's work – so far no success.' The following day was better: 'Began to paint the full face of my dear Joney on the canvas, worked in neutral tint, with great uncertainty. There is some little promise that I may reach a likeness.'

He was also concerned to complete his wife's unfinished work.[205] At the end of the month, he 'commenced painting on my Joney's picture of Undine'. (*Plate XLIX*) She had died leaving only one morning's work in neutral tint on the canvas: 'I have long seen the picture in my own mind completed. I will now endeavour really to make it so. It will be to me a glorious privilege to fulfil her work after her death.'

He had found some kind of rhythm at last, and some kind of solace. Disappointed of Hennie, he commented: 'I think, my darling Joney, this ought not to be the fruit of your one great friendship.' He decided to ask his sister Augusta instead. This he did on 30 August. On 9 September he received yet another letter from Hennie: 'Warton objects to her coming here. So the question is at an end.' As far as her father and suitor were concerned, Hennie had found herself between a rock and a hard place. [206] Days passed in painting Joanna – the likeness seemed to come and go – and working on 'Undine'. At the end of August he took the family to Lancing, where they joined Mrs Wetton's family and his own children were introduced, Alice screaming with fright, to the beach and the sea. They were to spend a fortnight there while Henry painted in his studio and undertook a small walking tour on his own.

205 This is not such an impertinence as it might appear. There are many recorded instances during this period of artists painting on each other's pictures, and there is an added dimension here in Henry's determination to conjure Joanna back to life in whatever way he could.

206 Hennie eventually married Henry Warton in Kensington on 28 December 1869.

On 23 September Augusta moved in, which must have somewhat assuaged his loneliness, in that she too had artistic talent and could share his passion. The running of the house was a constant distraction nonetheless: 'Until ½ p. 11p.m. investigating the charge against Conyard [the cook] of her having her brother-in-law to sleep in my bed during my absence from town. It appears to be a false charge.'

He did not see George again until 7 October, when he came home to find him with the children in the nursery. It was the first time they had met since the funeral. George, ever restless, was on the move again – this time to Cairo.

❁

On 14 October, Henry, in the company of Francis Astley, travelled to West Dean, where he was to paint Constance Astley's portrait. She had been ill for a year and most of the work was accomplished in her room. Henry recorded: 'She in her bed, the room very dimly lit, so much so that I could not define the exact outline of her face in some parts. Her face is greatly emaciated but of a very grand order. There could be no finer model for a *Mater Dolorosa*.' He worked steadily, and was home before the end of the month. 'Found all well.' He had evidently established a *modus vivendi* with Mrs Boyce, to the extent of letting her have 'the little Babbacombe girl painting, which my darling gave me as a present (her first) before we were engaged – but it is only a gift for life'. Being Henry, he was careful to get this in writing.

On 8 November he was back with his beloved: 'Painted on the mouth of Joney's portrait until 1 o'clock. I do not get on with this. I am almost desperate about it – yet I will carry it thro' at any cost of time and pain.'

He was also now painting his own head into his conversation piece, 'in grey and white'. Gretchen brought the children to the studio to see their mother's portrait, but Sidney did not recognise her. 'This is painful to me, for I would sooner he saw her thro' that than any other.' It was a little hard on a two-year-old.

With December came the anniversaries of Joanna's birthday and their marriage. Gretchen made evergreen wreaths for Joanna's portrait and photograph, and Sidney and Alice gave their mother's photograph a kiss. On the 9th, their wedding anniversary, Matthias, Lilly and Anne joined him for dinner: Mordan was in Germany on business, and his mother-in-law 'wished not to come this year'.

On 15 December, Queen Victoria's husband, Prince Albert, died. Henry wrote: 'I cannot help thinking of our good Queen. As a National loss it is, I think, greater than we have allowed ourselves to imagine.'

His family gathered at Stanhope Terrace on Christmas Day: 'Our party consisted of Father, Mother, Charlotte, James Symonds and two children, Matilda, myself and two children, Maria, Sarah, Armstead and two children, Emma, Augusta and Uncles Edward and Arthur.' He felt the absence of his wife profoundly: 'The year is now come to an end. The bells are ringing in the New one … I will try so to pass each day that I may be fit for communion with my beloved wife, if it is God's will that our souls may meet. May I never cease to feel her presence near and by imagination see her vividly as until now I have done. Oh Joney, Joney, most beloved and cherished by me … Oh God, may my little ones be preserved to me! and may I so act to them that when I die they may think of me as I do of their Mother.'

He began the New Year as he had finished the old – in attempting to assuage his grief through painting. He worked on his group portrait throughout the dark January days, 'injuring Clayton's head' because the light was so poor. Each detail was relentlessly recorded in his diary, as if the painting of a napkin or a tablecloth were proof of a life extinguished in every other way.

George was still attempting to get elected to the Old Water-Colour Society, and, in his absence, Henry did his best to advance his cause by writing letters to Ruskin and others on his behalf. A meeting with Ruskin at Stratford Place took place as a result on 2 February:

> He was quite crotchety in his criticisms – found fault with and admired George's drawings in a way that was unlooked for – always opposed if he detected a fixed opinion of one's own. He did not seem to care for my portrait group, not even for Joney's head; would poke his nose against it, and when I remonstrated that I had painted for a station point, where the entire picture could be seen, he said he always looked in like manner at the Titians. He looked much at our miniature group, seemed to like it much – thought evidently that I was losing all my delicacy and refinement. What would Joney have said to him, seeing him now find out beauties in my miniatures. She, who used to anger herself because he never, when he wrote his pamphlets, looked at my works (these very ones) or said a word about them. He lavished most of his love upon my chalk drawings. It was his perverse mood to think I was born for that work.

The following day, having changed his mind about which of George's drawings to present to the Old Water-Colour Society, he went to prepare 'Crypt of San Nicolo' and sent it off with the others he had chosen. He himself had been led to believe that he was the preferred artist for a large commission – 'The Meet on Ashdown' – and was cast down on 10 February to discover that he had not after all been chosen. Several members of the committee had expressed their doubts as to his ability to paint horses. He felt he had been made a fool of. The following day he learned that George had not been elected.

These setbacks were compounded when, on 12 February, he called on Burne-Jones and found the family in great distress. 'Mrs Rossetti died yesterday morning. She had taken an overdose of laudanum on Monday evening – became insensible and never rallied. Poor Rossetti. That fatal 10th February.' The inquest into Lizzie Siddal's death took place on 12 February and returned a verdict of accidental death. The reality was grimmer: by the time of her death she was a ghost of her former self, disturbed, erratic, and heavily addicted to opium. It is believed that she was also suffering from post-natal depression following the birth of her still-born child. Yet over the twelve years of her involvement with Rossetti, the unconventional beauty with the unlucky red hair had acquired a reputation of her own as an artist. During 1855, Ruskin had even offered her a retainer of £150 a year for everything she produced.

All this time Henry never ceased to work, on 'Undine', on his group portrait, on Constance Astley's picture. The focus, if not the reason, for all this industry was the International Exhibition of 1862. Inspired once again by Prince Albert, though he did not live to see it, the aim of the exhibition was summed up by Lord Tennyson in a Festival Ode: 'Gathering all the fruits of peace and crown'd with all her flowers.' The Queen was in mourning, so pomp and ceremony were absent, and in spite of attracting more than six million visitors, the enterprise was financially disastrous.

But it proved a wonderful showcase for the decorative arts. The *Illustrated London News* noted that 'Pre-Raphaelitism had descended from art to manufacture' and indeed the exhibition was the perfect platform for William Morris's 'firm' – Rossetti, Burne-Jones and Madox Brown combining to decorate a cabinet for it. By the end of February Henry was nailing 'waterproof' to the back of the miniatures he intended to submit and had been to George's studio to fetch Joanna's painting, 'Do I Like Butter?'. As the Royal Academy would only allow one submission from a deceased artist, he was determined to submit as many of Joanna's pictures to the International Exhibition as possible. In the event, five were sent, including 'La Veneziana' and 'The Heather-Gatherer', and on that day he noted in his diary: 'Ah my darling, darling – these are your last!' In addition Foley had cast his bust of Joanna, much to Henry's pleasure, and suggested sending it to the exhibition as one of 'England's Worthies'. It was accepted.

Henry went back to West Dean in the middle of March to complete his oil portrait of Constance Astley and to make a chalk drawing of Gertrude, the Astleys' daughter. When he told Astley that he intended charging sixty guineas, Astley insisted on paying him a hundred.

George returned from Cairo towards the end of March and had to be incorporated into Henry's conversation piece. Henry had already made some progress, with the help of the study he had made earlier, but the coat gave him particular trouble: 'Painted again on coat – got desperate and rubbed yellow into it and so painted it to a warmer tint – anything but pleasant in itself, but the picture is improved.'

On 14 April George celebrated his return with a visit to his old friend Rossetti: 'He read me one or two of his sister's poems. Did not like what I had done in the East. Said that all the things that artists brought from the East were always alike and equally uninteresting.' Rossetti did not appear to be unduly grief-stricken by the death of his wife. A week later he, his brother, William, and George went on an excursion to Greenwich Park, where 'Gabriel, catching sight of a girl with a paintable face, made up to her and got her address'. After dinner at the Trafalgar Hotel they returned to the park: 'Kiss in the ring and out of the ring and larking generally going on. Tea at my place.'

There was a private view for Exhibitors at the International Exhibition on 25 April, to which Henry went.

> Joney's 'Heather-Gatherer' and 'Peep-bo' beautifully placed ... Millais and the other good [artists] fully acknowledge her position in the first rank. All must do so now. Her 'Crusaders', 'Veneziana' and 'Do I Like Butter' are by no means ill-placed. My miniatures and chalk drawings are quite well placed, but my one oil picture is hoisted to the very top. This is a mistake, for it quite holds its own amongst the works of the men now painting. Treachery has been done to miniature art, for Ross is represented by only two of his works. My miniatures are, I think, as good or better than Thorburn's. The little heads of the Wetton girls and Edward Coke are about the best things amongst the miniatures.

George took Henry to the private view of the Old Water-Colour Society on 26 April and was generous about the exhibition – even buying a 'little moonlight drawing' by an artist called Francis Finch. 'Was more glad I had done so when Holland informed me that the painter had been for a second time struck by paralysis and that the money would be useful to him.' Four days later he went with Arthur Hughes to see Frith's picture 'The Railway Station': 'Not so good as Derby Day.'

On that same day Henry attended the Exhibitors' private view at the Royal Academy and found 'Joney's "Bird of God" against the door of South West Room on the line'. His own portrait group was hung in the East Room, also on the line, with 'Constance Astley' and 'Joseph Stansfield' in the West Room, the latter as a pendant to Millais's 'Silverpenny'. 'So, I am most excellently treated.' He was even more delighted by a notice in *The Times* praising his portrait group 'most tenderly'.

But he was at the mercy of his grief and a prey to nervous sickness. He went to the House of Commons on 3 June to hear a debate at which Palmerston, Disraeli and Bright were among the speakers, but in the middle 'I had to leave – sick as usual – only just out of Westminster Hall in time'. The children were in Lancing with his sister, but news of their coughs and colds (in Alice's case whooping cough) made him wretched. The baby's birthday, on 3 July, was a poignant reminder of what he had lost – 'Oh Joney, my beloved, may her life in some way prolong the splendour of yours, which was sacrificed for her.' He castigated himself for not having done more 'to preserve her memory and fame (altho' God knows how precious they are to me)', and, always hard on himself, worked on doggedly, beset with misgivings and feelings of failure. On the anniversary of her death, 'I pledged myself to my darling wife in writing on the margin of Rossetti's portrait of her. Shall now fasten it in the frame and hang it over the mantelpiece of her bedroom in the place she devoted to her father's portrait.'

In August, at the invitation of his friend Astley, and in the company of Millais, his wife, his wife's sister, Alice, and the Reverend Sidney Smith, he went to Arisaig, a journey commemorated in an etching entitled 'On board the "Victoria", 11 August 1862'. He returned in time to take Sidney and Alice to the International Exhibition, and was thrilled that 'with the least possible prompting Sidney, and even Alice, recognised Foley's bust of their blessed Mamma'.

Most of his diary entries are memories of Joanna, combined with a passionate longing to rejoin her. Visiting her grave in Kensal Green cemetery, he remembered standing with her while she wept over her father's grave as he now wept over hers. When, on 3 November, he heard news of Constance Astley's death, he wrote: 'For a long time past she had seemed like a purified spirit of the other world', and it was a comfort to him to visit his old friend at West Dean so they could share their memories: 'He likes to talk of her, as I do of Joney.' A meeting with Matthias on 7 December gave him all he needed for his peace of mind: probate of Joanna's will, all the documents relating to the Holmbury property[207] and the letter giving him the right to be buried, with Joanna and their three children, in the same vault.[208]

George and Henry saw each other regularly, but were no longer part of the same set. While Henry retreated to his studio and painted and repainted, George plunged into a life of Pre-Raphaelite comings and goings.

There was Swinburne's house-warming at 77 Newman Street ('Swinburne recited much from his own poems and compositions, to the frantic delight of his guests'), discussing Ruskin with Burne-Jones and Rossetti, calling on Whistler whose 'Joe' was present – 'a handsome girl with red hair and altogether fine colour'. Swinburne had acquired a copy of *Justine* by the Marquis de Sade, which George and Rossetti examined before all three went to the International Exhibition to have 'some ices at a stall near the Egyptian things, where there was a very lovely girl of whom Gabriel obtained a promise to sit for him'.

On 22 October 1862, Rossetti moved to Tudor House, at 16 Cheyne Walk, Chelsea. George called on him on 13 November and found it furnished 'most picturesquely, mostly with fine old Renaissance furniture'. Fanny Cornforth was there, and a few weeks later, on 7 December, he dined with them both. 'He gave me a pencil sketch of her as she lay on a couch, hair outspread, and her right hand under her head.'

He did not seem to mind too much that he had been worsted again by Rossetti in a contest of love. His eye for a pretty girl was satisfied, on this occasion, with a drawing.

And there were other models. To Agnes Manetti he 'gave a little Florentine Mosaic brooch', and to Lizzie Gresham his 'copy of Tennyson's poems and a little silk handkerchief.' Annie Miller, whom he had encountered at the International Exhibition 'looking as handsome as ever, walking with a young man, rather a swell', was back in the fold. In March 1863 Rossetti is recorded as 'going on with Annie Miller's head, which he has converted into Helen of Troy – ships burning in the background'.

George was finally elected to the Old Water-Colour Society, along with Burne-Jones, in 1864, and was disgusted to find all his works poorly displayed – 'on the floor, one against the ceiling and 4 below the line'. *The Times* reviewed the exhibition: 'My things well spoken of, but Jones's with so little judgment or appreciation that I don't feel at all honoured.' (*Plates LII and LIII*)

207 The house Henry built on the land bought from the Wettons had been completed.

208 Henry had a new vault built in 1890 for his family in the Kensal Green cemetery where the Boyce vault was. Joanna was reburied when the Wells vault was ready, with Sidney who had died in 1869.

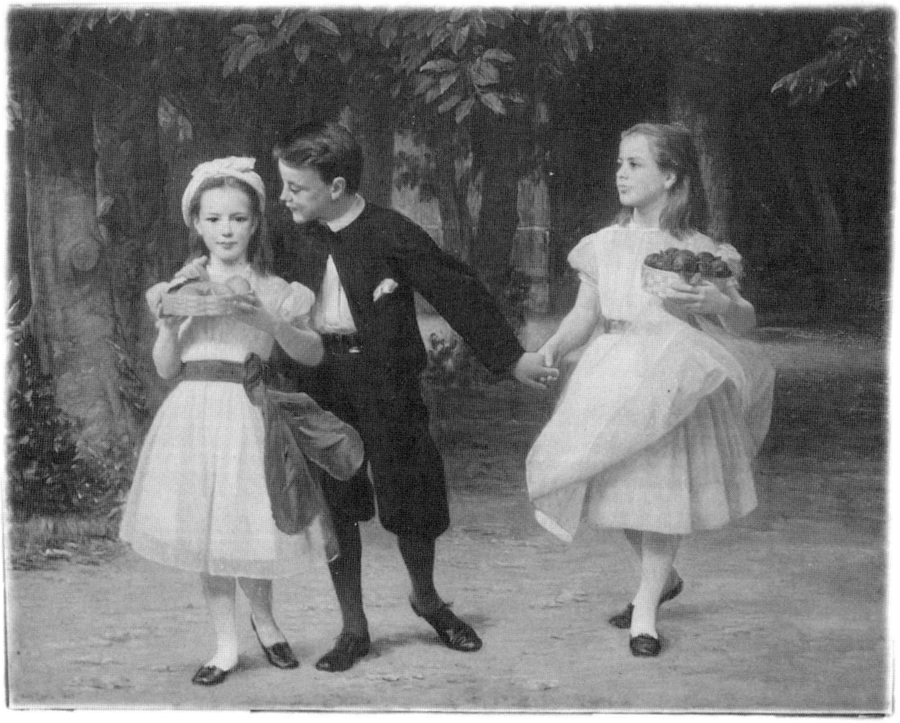

Joanna Margaret, Sidney and Alice *Henry T. Wells*

Sidney with his sisters, Alice and Joanna Margaret. The painting must have been completed not long before Sidney died, of scarlet fever, at the age of ten.

George spent the years that followed largely in the company of Rossetti and his coterie. On one occasion he joined Rossetti for an expedition to Ruskin's house in Denmark Hill to draw the white roses. Ruskin (according to Henry Treffry Dunn in his *Recollections*) had become very prejudiced and sarcastic, and took George to task over his painting of Blackfriars Bridge in the process of demolition, which depicted, among the ruins, an old brick wall with two or three black cats on in. 'These cats seemed to act upon Ruskin pretty much as a red rag does to a bull, for he chafed poor Boyce most unmercifully about their introduction: "Cats on a wall, cats on a wall! Whenever I see a drawing by you there are sure to be cats on a wall." Boyce declared that he wasn't aware he had ever painted such an incident before but his statement was of no use. Ruskin would have it so.'

And there was Rossetti's menagerie. George describes a quaint barn owl in the studio and two fierce foreign owls in the garden, 'besides peacocks, pigeons, hens, ravens etc', while Dunn remembered that 'among the indoor pets was a singularly morose parrot. Its sole delight seemed to be to get visitors to stroke its head and then, without any warning, suddenly fasten upon their fingers, finishing up with a sly, low chuckle.' There was also an escaping raccoon and two armadillos.

There are hardly any references to his family in George's later diaries, with the exception of the tragedy that struck on 13 October 1869, when Sidney, Joanna and Henry's 'starry paladin', died at the age of ten. George wrote to his mother to tell her the news. He had not been allowed to see his nephew: 'The poor little fellow was dreadfully altered in appearance by the disease[209] which was of the severest kind.' To Matthias, Henry wrote: 'Mat, my heart ought to break. I worshipped that boy.'

In 1871 George moved into a house in Cheyne Row he had commissioned from Philip Webb, the architect of Morris's 'Red House': 'Chelsea', wrote Rossetti, 'is gradually filling.' Here George was able to display his pictures and furnishings to advantage. His income following his father's death enabled him to indulge his love of Sheraton and Hepplewhite furniture and he was adept at hunting down exquisite bargains in the shadowy corners of old shops. He had an impressive collection of Rossettis, including 'How They Met Themselves', 'Dr Johnson at the Mitre', the transformed 'Borgia' picture, 'La Belle Dame Sans Merci', 'Bonifazio's Mistress', 'Girl at a Lattice', the recently-acquired 'Monna Pamona', and 'Bocca Baciata', which always hung on the left side of his mantelpiece. 'Bocca Baciata' was Fanny to the life: Arthur Hughes told Allingham that it 'was such a superb thing, so awfully lovely' that George might be tempted 'to kiss the dear thing's lips away.' Joanna's 'Elgiva' and 'La Veneziana' were hung facing one another: Lizzie Ridley might have escaped him in one way but he captured her in another. Moreover his excellent eye was not confined to the Pre-Raphaelites: he acquired one fine portrait, the pride and joy of his later years, which, experts agree, was almost certainly by Holbein.[210]

After Lizzie's death, Rossetti took refuge in chloral – a drug that was erroneously credited with all the virtues and none of the vices of other fashionable narcotics. In the middle of 1872 he suffered a serious breakdown, possibly as a result of the savage reaction of the critics to his first collection of poetry but also because he was already in an severely weakened state. He attempted suicide by drinking laudanum, and though he recovered, he was never well. 'In fact,'

209 Probably scarlet fever, as he had been vaccinated against smallpox.
210 It was exhibited as 'Portrait of an Englishman', no. 125, at the New Gallery in Regent Street in 1890.

wrote George on 12 June, 'he had for the time quite lost his head. The symptoms became obvious about a week ago, when he became possessed by the idea that people were lying in wait for him and wished to destroy him'. Following his breakdown, he spent a long convalescence at Kelmscott Manor – the Morrises' new country house – and George saw little of him throughout the following year. The news of Ruskin was also bad. Rossetti, who begged help for a friend from Ruskin, received a letter in April 1873 in which Ruskin told him that he had 'turned entirely sulky miserly and ill-natured, and never goes anywhere nor does anything for other people, but expects them to do everything for him'.

By the end of the year George, too, was depressed: 'No one comes to see me. Feel unhappy, hopeless and damned. Elizabeth [his servant] in the sulks, scarcely answering when I speak to her. Warren has sent me some Xmas lines with a kind message of affection. If it were not for him whom I rarely see and for Philip Webb, whom I greatly esteem and am much attached to, and for my brother Matthias, I seem to have no real friend.'

On 21 August 1875 he took the train to Cheltenham, and arriving at about six, took a cab to Prestbury. From thence he walked to Miss Hawkey's School, Yew Tree House, on the south side of the churchyard, and there, in the 'most strange and uncomfortable state of mind', he met 'poor Caroline Soubeiran'. The details about their relationship are sketchy. He appears to have met her first towards the end of 1860, but as several pages are missing from his diary for December of that year, there are no details of their acquaintance at that time. He met her again in the summer of 1871 through her aunt, Mrs Southern, who lived in Ludlow close to his own aunt and uncle, and was sufficiently attracted for he and Mrs Southern to compose a letter, at the end of July 1873, to Mrs Southern's brother, M. Soubeiran, in Paris 'referring to my penchant for his daughter'. By 6 August he was in Paris: 'The door was opened by sweet Caroline who seemed pleased to see me.'

As with the earlier 1860 diary entries, those for 14 August to 17 September of that year have been torn out, so we can only guess at what happened, but he had clearly asked for her hand, only to fly away, just as he had fled so many relationships. Now, in 1875, perhaps because he was getting older, perhaps (dare one say it?) because it provided a solution to his servant problem, perhaps because, after all, he had missed her, he screwed himself to the sticking point. On 22 August, he plighted his troth to her again and felt 'almost as by a miracle, happier and better'.

On 31 August 1875, George Price Boyce, born in London, married Augustine Aimée Caroline Soubeiran, born in Paris, and his diary comes to an end. William Michael Rossetti recorded the event thus: 'Rather late in life he married a prepossessing French lady.'

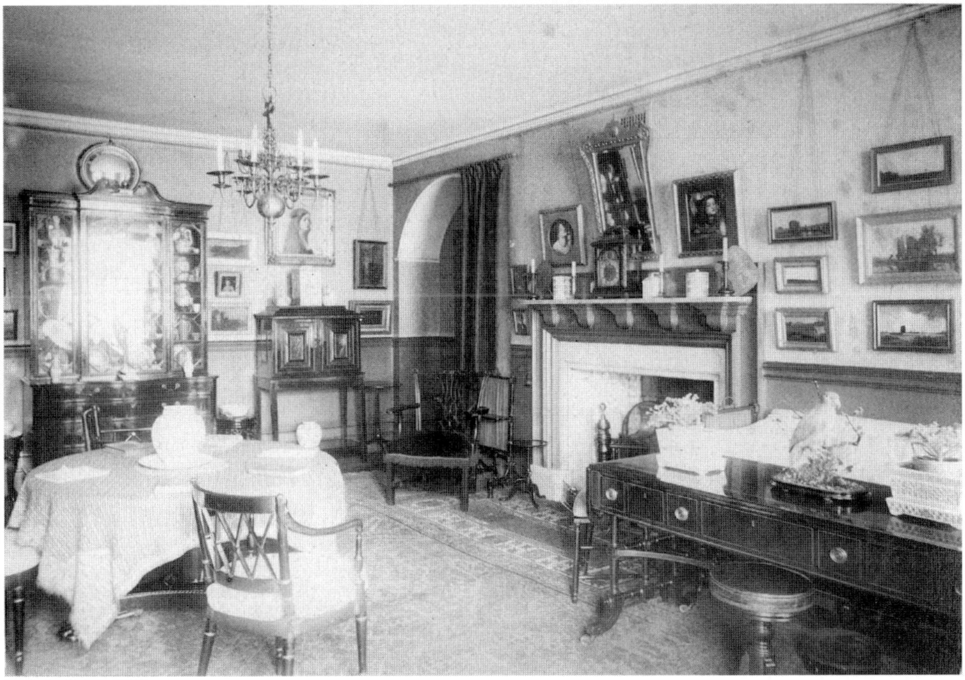

Dining Room at Glebe Place *George Price Boyce*

George moved to Glebe Place, a house in Cheyne Row designed for him by Philip Webb, in 1871. He had an impressive collection of Rossettis, including 'Bocca Baciata', which always hung on the left side of his mantelpiece. Joanna's 'Elgiva' and 'La Veneziana' were hung facing one another.

In some senses George and Joanna were more alike than might at first appear. Both valued their independence fiercely; both felt themselves unequal to the demands of love; both ran for the hills when under pressure.

For Joanna, the marriage and motherhood she had so feared became her subject, a touching reflection of loving, unashamed and even defiant domesticity. Her paintings tended to be small scale, and even when she was in a position to paint larger subjects (for example, when she had her own studio at the 'North Star') she did not usually choose to do so. Her rejection of Rosa Bonheur's teaching in favour of the *tête d'expression* was indicative of a life-long preference, as was, in a different way, her manifold joy in her son Sidney's 'Lilliputian' attributes. The size of most of her pictures, added to the fact that some of her best works were brought by George and other family members, may have contributed to her gifts being underrated during her lifetime.

Motherhood had a profound effect on her, personally and artistically, and as 'domesticity' was always a dangerous subject – even Millais was regarded as having 'sold out' after his marriage to Effie – this probably added to a general failure to give her work sufficient appreciation. Not that she minded. One of her more endearing qualities was her independence from the views of the wider art world. If it satisfied her (and it rarely did) that was all that mattered.

For George, the sympathetic milieu provided by his artist friends had, for many years, accommodated his gregarious impulses while leaving him free to indulge his craving for travel and solitude. Once that particular Round Table was dissolved, he, perforce, moved on. In a letter to William Allingham in 1878 he confessed that he had not seen Rossetti 'for a long while, not since his illness last autumn, neither in his house, nor elsewhere. It seems strange and unnatural and I regret it, but there appears no prospect of a change.' He never saw Rossetti alive again, though after his death in 1882, he travelled to Birchington to stand by the grave of his friend.

William Michael tells us that George's mind was not strong in later life and that when he died of a stroke on 9 February 1897, at the age of seventy, he left no will: 'I fancy that his property of various kinds went away in directions he had not forecast.'

For Henry, his Joney – so intensely wooed, so hardly won, so passionately loved – remained forever the focus of his life. Before she died, his career as a miniaturist had already begun to peter out and he had turned to paintingportraits in oils– partly because photography had usurped the place of miniatures in the artistic firmament, and partly because his eyesight had begun to suffer. Some of his first full-scale oil portraits were of Joanna and his children, and he quickly established himself as a leading practitioner; there are over a hundred portraits by him in the National Portrait Gallery alone, and a large number in public and private collections. His style in commissioned works is often rather formal, though the character of the sitter is usually well caught. His was appointed as an Associate of the Royal Academy in 1866, and as a full Academician in 1870, and as his diploma work following his election had submitted a painting made on a visit to his beloved Arisaig, entitled 'Letters and News from the Lochside'. (*Plate LIV*) In 1883, however, two of Francis Astley's daughters asked Henry if they might have it as a wedding present for their sister Beatrice, and Henry accordingly wrote to the Academy offering his painting 'Volunteers at the Firing Point' (*Plate LV*) as a substitute. This was agreed and 'Letters and News from the Lochside' was sent to Arisaig House where it still hangs.

'Volunteers at the Firing Point' reflected a lasting loyalty. Henry was a keen marksman and remained a volunteer until his eyesight failed. The picture is in the style of a number of others, including works showing quarries at Portland and the brickmakers at Holmbury Hill, in which he made use of bright light and sharply defined colours. He seems to have painted deliberately in a variety of styles when not working on commission: "Letters and News from the Lochside' has elements of Landseer, while a delightful picture of his daughters is in the manner of Tissot. (*Plate LVI*) During the 1880s he painted several large royal canvases, including 'The Queen Receiving News of her Accession' – known as 'Victoria Regina' . (*Plate LVII*). The Queen did not commission the painting: Henry was inspired by a description he had read in the diaries of Miss Frances Williams Wynn of the moment when the princess hears that she is to be queen and painted more than one version of the scene. The version reproduced in this book was presented to Edward VII by Henry's daughter Alice, after her father's death.

Perhaps predictably – Henry was essentially a conservative soul – he played an active part in defending the existing order at the R. A. in the face of agitation for reform initiated in *The Times* in 1886 by Holman Hunt. On the more positive side, he acted as deputy president in 1895 during Frederic Leighton's absence, and was active in the cause of artistic copyright when legislation was passed in 1900. He was a familiar figure among the Kensington coterie: the son of the illustrator Luke Fildes remembered how every year he supported the amateur dramatics at their children's Christmas party.

For the rest of his long life, Henry's failure to recreate Joanna's image to his satisfaction haunted him. Let his daughter Alice, who began this story, give her account of what she believed she saw at the very end, on 16 January 1903:

> He had lain for many hours half-conscious, his eyes closed ... I was leaning over the foot of his bed intently watching him, when his eyes opened – a look of joy overspread his face, and with a whispered 'Joney', he tried to raise himself in bed. As the nurse propped him up with pillows he slowly raised his right hand as though holding his paint brush. With a look of wonderful happiness he went through the action of painting in the air between us, as though giving strokes of drawing and touches of colour on an imaginary canvas.

He worked on and on, until his strength gave way and he went, at last, to meet her.

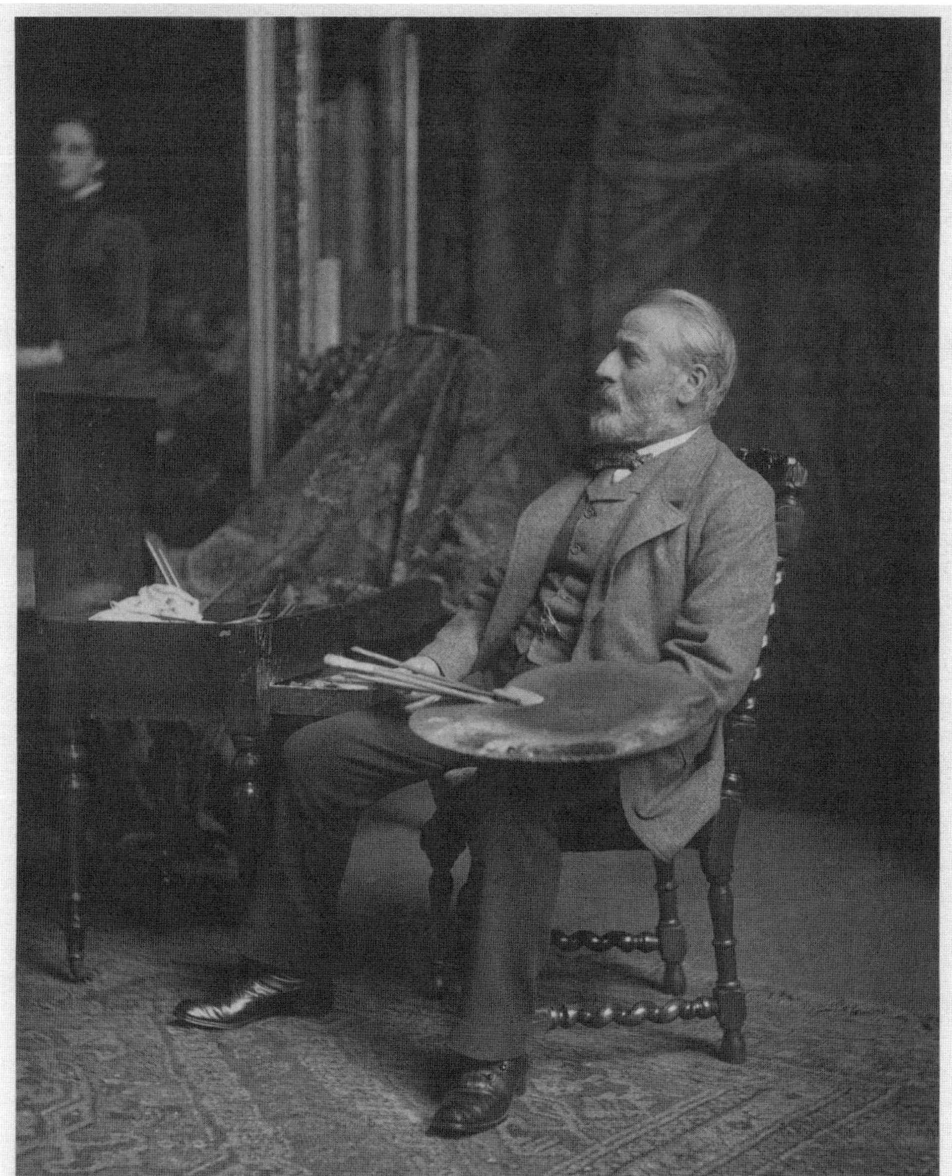

The painter in his studio *Ralph W. Robinson*

This photograph was taken in the studio which Henry built at Thorpe Lodge, Campden Hill.

Select Bibliography

Allingham, William. *The Diaries* ed. H. Allingham and D. Radford (London 1990)

Barnes, Martin. 'Photography and the Pre-Raphaelites', in *The Pre-Raphaelites*, National Museum exhibition catalogue, ed. Mikael Ahlund (Stockholm 2009)

Bevington, Merle Mowbray. *The Saturday Review 1855-1868: Representative Educated Opinion in Victorian England* (New York 1941)

Browning, Elizabeth Barrett. *Aurora Leigh* (London 1856)

Browning, Robert. *Men and Women* (London 1855)

———.*Poems of Robert Browning* (Oxford 1963)

Casteras, Susan and Peterson, Linda H. *A Struggle for Fame* (New Haven 1994)

Cherry, Deborah. *Painting Women: Victorian Women Artists* (Routledge 1993)

———. *Beyond the Frame: Feminism and Visual Culture, Britain 1850-1900* (London 2000)

Cooper, Suzanne Fagence. *Pre-Raphaelite Art in the Victoria & Albert Museum* (London 2003)

Dakers, Caroline. *The Holland Park Circle: Artists and Victorian Society* (New Haven 1999)

Davis, John. *The Great Exhibition: Mystery, Magic and Awe* (Frome 1999)

Gaunt, William. *The Pre-Raphaelite Tragedy* (London 1942)

Dunn, Henry Treffry. *Recollections of Dante Gabriel Rossetti and His Circle*, ed. Pedrick Gale, London 1904

———. *The English Miniature (*Exhibition Catalogue) (New Haven 1981)

Eyler, John Marvin *Victorian Social Medicine: The Ideas and Methods of William Farr* (Baltimore 1979)

Forrest, Derek, Anthony Storr *The Evolution of Hypnotism: A Survey of Theory and Practice from Mesmer to the Present Day* (London 1999)

Hall, The Reverend Robert. *Fifty Sermons from Notes Taken at the Time of Their Delivery by the Revd Thomas Grinfield MA* (London 1843)

Hawksley, Lucinda. *Lizzie Siddal: The Tragedy of a Pre-Raphaelite Supermodel* (UK) *Face of the Pre-Raphaelites* (US) (London and New York 2004)

Ironside, Robin *Pre-Raphaelite Painters* (Oxford 1948)

Lanigan, Dennis T. *Dream of the Past: Pre-Raphaelite and Aesthetic Movement Painting, Watercolours and Drawings from the Lanigan Collection* (Toronto 2000)

E. D. Lardner, Dr, and others. *The Great Exhibition and London in 1851* (London 1852)

Mainardi, Patricia. *Art and Politics of the Second Empire: The Universal Exhibitions of 1855 and 1867* (New Haven 1987)

Marsh, Jan. *The Pre-Raphaelite Sisterhood* (London 1985)

———. *Pre-Raphaelite Women: Images of Femininity in Pre-Raphaelite Art* (London 1987)

Marsh, Jan and Nunn, Pamela Gerrish. *Pre-Raphaelite Women Artists* (Catalogue for the exhibition at the Manchester City Art Gallery) (London 1998)

Marshall, John. *Anatomy for Artists* (London 1878)

Martineau, Harriet. *Life in the Sickroom: Essays by an Invalid* 1844 edition, ed. Maria H Frawley (London 2004)

———. *Letters on Mesmerism* (London 1845)
Moyle, Franny. *Desperate Romantics: the Private Lives of the Pre-Raphaelites* (London 2009)
Nahum, Peter. *Pre-Raphaelite, Symbolist, Visionary* (Exhibition catalogue) (London 2001)
Newall, Christopher and Judy Egerton. *George Price Boyce* (Exhibition catalogue) (London 1987)
Nunn, Pamela Gerrish. 'Artist and Model: JMB's Mulatto', *Journal of Pre-Raphaelite Studies* 1993) 'A Centre on the Margins' (September 1994)
Peterson, M. J. *The Medical Profession in Mid-Victorian London* (Berkeley, 1978)
Pre-Raphaelite and Other Masters: The Andrew Lloyd-Webber Collection (London 2003)
Prettejean, Elizabeth. *The Art of the Pre-Raphaelites* (London 2000)
Rose, Andrea. *The Pre-Raphaelites* (London 1981)
Rossetti, William Michael *Some Reminiscences* (London 1906)
Ruskin, John. *Modern Painters* 5 vols. (London 1843-60)
Ruskin, John and J. M. W. Turner. *Harbours of England* (London 1856)
Smith, Alison 'The Enfranchised Eye' in *The Pre-Raphaelites: Truth To Nature* (London 2004)
Staley, Alan and Newell, Christopher. 'A Pre-Raphaelite Vision' in *The Pre-Raphaelites: Truth to Nature* (London 2004)
Surtees, Virginia *The Diaries of George Price Boyce* (Newmarket 1980)
Thackeray, William Makepeace. *The Newcomes* (London 1855)
Wilcox, Scott. *Sun Wind and Rain: The Art of David Cox* (New Haven 2008)
Winter, Alison. *Mesmerized: Powers of Mind in Victorian Britain* (Chicago 1998)
Wood, Christopher. *Burne-Jones: The Life and Works of Sir Edward Burne-Jones, 1833-1898* (London 1998)

Index

Numerals in roman indicate colour plates.